TRANSCONTINENTAL DIALOGUES

Critical Issues in Indigenous Studies

Jeffrey P. Shepherd and Myla Vicenti Carpio
SERIES EDITORS

ADVISORY BOARD
Hōkūlani Aikau
Jennifer Nez Denetdale
Eva Marie Garroutte
John Maynard
Alejandra Navarro-Smith
Gladys Tzul Tzul
Keith Camacho
Margaret Elizabeth Kovach
Vicente Diaz

TRANSCONTINENTAL DIALOGUES

ACTIVIST ALLIANCES WITH INDIGENOUS PEOPLES OF CANADA, MEXICO, AND AUSTRALIA

EDITED BY
R. AÍDA HERNÁNDEZ CASTILLO,
SUZI HUTCHINGS, AND BRIAN NOBLE

THE UNIVERSITY OF
ARIZONA PRESS
TUCSON

The University of Arizona Press
www.uapress.arizona.edu

© 2019 by The Arizona Board of Regents
All rights reserved. Published 2019

ISBN-13: 978-0-8165-3857-7 (cloth)

Cover design by Carrie House, HOUSEdesign llc
Cover artwork: Mi'kmaq basket "compass design" by unknown quill-worker, mid-19th century, from collections and with permission of Nova Scotia Natural History Museum [top]; Tsotsil textile made by Margarita López Hernández, photograph by Irene Heras [center]; Western Macdonald Ranges in central Australia, view from an Aboriginal community, photo by Sarah Holcombe [bottom]

Library of Congress Cataloging-in-Publication Data
Names: Hernández Castillo, Rosalva Aída, editor. | Hutchings, Suzi, editor. | Noble, Brian, editor.
Title: Transcontinental dialogues : activist alliances with indigenous peoples of Canada, Mexico, and Australia / edited by R. Aída Hernández Castillo, Suzi Hutchings, and Brian Noble.
Other titles: Critical issues in indigenous studies.
Description: Tucson : The University of Arizona Press, 2019. | Series: Critical issues in indigenous studies | Includes bibliographical references and index.
Identifiers: LCCN 2018039124 | ISBN 9780816538577 (cloth : alk. paper)
Subjects: LCSH: Anthropology—Research. | Indigenous peoples—Research—Canada. | Indigenous peoples—Research—Australia. | Indians of Mexico—Research. | Communication in anthropology.
Classification: LCC GN42 .T73 2019 | DDC 301.072—dc23 LC record available at https://lccn.loc.gov/2018039124

Printed in the United States of America
♾ This paper meets the requirements of ANSI/NISO Z39.48-1992 (Permanence of Paper).

CONTENTS

Acknowledgments — vii

Introduction — 3
R. AÍDA HERNÁNDEZ CASTILLO AND SUZI HUTCHINGS

PART I. CANADA

Map 1. Indigenous Regions Mentioned in the Chapters about Canada — 36

1. What Is Decolonization? Mi'kmaw Ancestral Relational Understandings and Anthropological Perspectives on Treaty Relations — 37
SHERRY M. PICTOU

2. Committing Anthropology in the Muddy Middle Ground — 65
L. JANE MCMILLAN

3. Research Partnerships and Collaborative Life Projects — 93
COLIN SCOTT

PART II. MEXICO

Map 2. Indigenous Regions Mentioned in the Chapters about Mexico — 112

4. Legal Activism and Prison Workshops: The Paradoxes of Feminist Legal Anthropology and Cultural Work in Penitentiary Spaces — 113
R. AÍDA HERNÁNDEZ CASTILLO

5. Decolonizing Anthropologists from Below and to the Left 143
XOCHITL LEYVA SOLANO

6. Maya Knowledges, Intercultural Dialogues, and
Being a *Chan Laak'* in the Yucatán Peninsula 166
GENNER LLANES-ORTIZ

PART III. AUSTRALIA

Map 3. Indigenous Regions Mentioned in the Chapters about Australia 192

7. Indigenous Anthropologists Caught in the Middle:
The Fragmentation of Indigenous Knowledge in
Native Title Anthropology, Law, and Policy in Urban
and Rural Australia 193
SUZI HUTCHINGS

8. Eclipsing Rights: Property Rights as Indigenous Human
Rights in Australia 220
SARAH HOLCOMBE

Epilogue. Grounded Allies: Acting-With,
Regenerating Together 241
BRIAN NOBLE

Contributors *263*
Index *267*

ACKNOWLEDGMENTS

This book is the result of a collective effort among three editors and six authors who participated in this project. Creating bridges between Canada, Mexico, and Australia, considering the different time-zones and university schedules, was a big challenge.

We want to give special thanks to the Committee on World Anthropologies (CWA) of the American Anthropological Association (AAA) who created a space of encounter among the editors and many of the authors by inviting us to organize a panel that gathered voices and experiences of Indigenous and non-Indigenous anthropologists from Canada, Mexico, and Australia, regarding the challenges of building alliances and producing truly transformative knowledge together with Indigenous organizations and peoples. A special recognition to Dr. Susana Elena Narotzky, Molleda Chair of the Transnational Relations and Collaborations, Sub-Committee of the CWA, who encouraged us to organize the panel in the AAA Congress of 2014 and supported our project to work on an edited volume. To Alexandre Duchêne, chair of the CWA and Carla Fernández, managing officer for the CWA, for providing the funding that made possible the translation of some of the chapters from Spanish to English, and to Alejandro Reyes for his work as a translator.

We further extend our gratitude . . .

To all of our contributing authors, for their deep humility and their commitment to the freedom and self-determination of the extraordinarily resilient

Indigenous peoples with whom they engage and undertake emancipatory action research.

To AntropoSig, the Geographic Laboratory of the Center for Advanced Studies in Social Anthropology (CIESAS), and especially to Bulmaro Sánchez Sandoval, for his patience in the elaboration of the maps that illustrate our book. The geographic representation of Indigenous territories was a challenge: considering the colonial legacies that exist in map making, it was necessary to work through multiple different versions in dialogue with the authors. The outcome was as effective and historically contingent as any such outcome may be.

To our institutions, Dalhousie University's Department of Sociology and Social Anthropology in Canada, CIESAS in Mexico, the School of Global, Urban and Social Studies at RMIT University in Australia, all of which supported the research and fieldwork that made possible our academic work.

To the editors of the Critical Issues in Indigenous Studies series at University of Arizona Press, Jeffrey P. Shepherd and Myla Vicenti Carpio, for believing and supporting our book proposal. To Amanda Krause, Allyson Carter, Leigh McDonald at the University of Arizona Press, and copyeditor Melanie Mallon, for their careful support and work at different stages of the book.

To Mercedes Pisoni and Nina Hoeschele, for their support in the elaboration of the index and other editorial support at different moments of the book process. To the Tsotsil artist and weaver, Margarita López and the unknown nineteenth-century Mi'kmaw crafters for their textile and basketry art that graces the cover of our book. Also, our thanks to Sarah Holcombe for allowing us to reproduce her photo as part of the cover art, and to the Nova Scotia Museum of Natural History, and their curator of ethnology, Roger Lewis, for permitting use of the Mi'kmaw basketry for the cover.

This book is dedicated to the Indigenous peoples and organizations in Canada, Mexico, and Australia who continue to confront colonial violence and to struggle in the defense and resurgence of their sovereignty and territories, and of all their relations. We are honored.

—*Aída Hernandez-Castillo, Suzi Hutchings, Brian Noble*

TRANSCONTINENTAL DIALOGUES

Introduction

R. AÍDA HERNÁNDEZ CASTILLO AND SUZI HUTCHINGS

This book is the product of a dialogue that began in December 2014, in the context of the annual meeting of the American Anthropological Association. At the initiative of the Committee on World Anthropologies (CWA), R. Aída Hernández Castillo and Brian Noble, two coeditors of this volume, were invited to organize a panel that gathered voices and experiences of Indigenous and non-Indigenous anthropologists from Canada, Mexico, and Australia, regarding the challenges of building alliances and producing knowledge together with Indigenous organizations and peoples. As a result, a panel was held with the complex title "Alliances of, with, as Indigenous Peoples: The Obligations and Actions of Anthropologies and Anthropologists in the Middle," which aimed at encompassing several political and epistemological experiences. The CWA was founded in 2010 for the purpose of broadening the dialogues of the American Anthropological Association with other theoretical traditions, building transcontinental academic bridges. Among the committee's objectives was to "engage a diversity of international voices and perspectives and involve both academic and applied anthropology in this endeavor."[1]

Although on its website, the CWA does not raise the issue of decolonization of anthropology and the geopolitics of knowledge, these types of initiatives enable encounters and the construction of new alliances that to a certain extent contribute to the processes of epistemic decolonization (to confront the colonial legacies in the way we produce knowledge), which are an integral part of the political projects with which several of the authors of this book collaborate. The hegemony of U.S., British, and French anthropological traditions in academic programs around the world makes it urgent to include other theoretical traditions. Indeed, the imperative to decolonize the academy has been a central focus of Indigenous scholarship coming out of Latin America, New Zealand, Australia, the Pacific, and Canada since the 1990s. Since 1971 in the Declaration of Barbados, Indigenous representatives denounced the colonial role that anthropologists have played in the nation-building projects of Latin America, and they made a call for the decolonization of the social sciences.[2] Other Indigenous intellectuals from the Abya Yala have written about the need to reject the colonial legacies that are being reproduced through Western knowledges in academic institutions (see Rivera Cusicanqui 2010; García Leyva 2012; Quidel Lincoleo 2015; Itzamná 2016).[3]

Epistemic colonialism has also been denounced by organized Indigenous women, since the beginning of the 1990s, who have rejected liberal feminisms and reasserted the need to recognize their collective rights as members of their communities, as a condition for the full exercise of their rights as women.[4] They have also written about the principles of *communality* (*comunalidad*) and *good living* (*buen vivir*) as fundamental perspectives in the questioning of the civilizing project of the West. Activists and intellectuals of a new generation have theorized from what they call their *sentipensar* (feeling and thought) as women and Indigenous people. In their theorizations and through their political struggles, these young intellectuals strive for the principle of *harmony and respect*, central to *communality*, to become fundamental values in the struggle against gender violence.[5]

These works echo the groundbreaking writing of Linda Tuhiwai Smith (2012), whose work over the past two decades influenced a generation of Indigenous academics across the globe to reject colonial research paradigms, which insist the Indigenous other is the subject of research at the hands of non-Indigenous academics (Johnson and Larsen 2013). Rather, Indigenous knowledges theory (Smith 2012; Moreton-Robinson 2004, 2015; Watson 2015; Hutchings and Morrison 2017); Indigenous critical and plural thinking; Indigenist theory (Rigney 2017; Martin and Mirraboopa 2003); feeling-thinking (*senti-pensar*) Indigenous theory (Méndez Torres 2013; López Itzin 2013); and Indigenous standpoint theory (Nakata 2007; Tur, Blanch, and Wilson 2010; Ardill 2014), in providing methods to decolonize academic inquiry, all call for the Indigenous researched to be respected as the Indigenous researcher, at the center.⁶ This combines with the emergence of reflective accounts by Indigenous researchers about their journeys as academics. Many of these authors comment on their struggles and successes in producing work that honors their Indigenous cultural traditions, while meeting the standards expected of them as students and teachers in the academy (e.g., Bainbridge 2016; Thomas 2013).

Johnson and Larsen (2013, 8) point out how difficult it is for Indigenous researchers as insiders to "negotiate the tricky ground" of the liminal space they occupy between researcher and researched. Nevertheless, the rewards of this position are immense in working toward community-determined outcomes. The position of insider is all the more taxing for those of us who are Indigenous anthropologists, as the Indigenous authors in this volume attest (Hutchings, Llanes-Ortiz, Pictou). The position of the inside researcher as connected to community is explored throughout all the chapters in this volume. As the authors illustrate, it has become essential to engage with Indigenous-centered knowledge, if the Indigenous peoples we work with as anthropologists are to be part of alliances and dialogues that ensure effective liberation strategies in Indigenous peoples' everyday worlds, as well as in the academy.

This volume is therefore timely and innovative, in taking the disparate anthropological traditions of three regions, Canada, Mexico, and Australia, to explore how the interactions between anthropologists and Indigenous peoples, in supporting Indigenous activism, have the potential to transform the production of knowledge within the historical colonial traditions of anthropology.

What is presented in this book is, however, much more than this. In general, comparative studies on the struggles of Indigenous peoples under modern colonialism have been with those countries that have similar colonial invasion histories, such as Canada, Australia, and New Zealand, which are all part of the Commonwealth of Nations (formally the British Commonwealth) (e.g., Archer 2003; Scholtz 2006; Green 2007; Simpson 2010; Moreton-Robinson 2016). Or, the attention has been from those anthropologists working across the global north-south divide who work with Indigenous peoples within the same region such as Latin America (Assies, van der Haar, and Hoekema 2000; Brysk 2000; Hernández Castillo and Canessa 2012; Leyva, Speed, and Burguete 2008; Sánchez Néstor 2005; Sieder 2017) and Africa (ACHPR 2006; Laher and Sing'Oei 2014). A few books also compare the political struggles of Indigenous peoples in Canada and Mexico in relation to specific issues, such as women and the environmental problems they face (Altamirano-Jiménez 2016) and their demands for self-government (Cook and Lindau 2000).

This volume presents pieces that do not take the usual political or geographic paradigms as their starting point. The particular dialogues from the margins that we present in this book arise from a rejection of the geographic hierarchization of knowledge, notably one in which the global south continues to be the space for fieldwork, while the global north is the place for its systematization and theorization. The linguistic borders that separate Latin American academies from Australian, African, or Canadian academies further hinder knowledge dialogues. We recognize the geopolitical hierarchies among our three countries, and that producing academic knowledge in the English language allows Australian and Canadian anthropologists to engage more deeply with the hegemonic academias of the global north (for example with U.S. and northern European academic production). On the other hand, this positioning of the English language as a reflection of the broader heirarchies of British colonial regimes at the expense of an understanding of the dynamics of Indigenous/non-Indigenous relationships in other parts of the world raises the specter of even deeper political and epistemic logics of neocolonial workings, particularly the marginalization and erasure of Indigenous languages themselves by both English and Spanish anthropologies in the field and within academic circuits.

Indigenous and non-Indigenous intellectuals who do not publish in English are barely quoted, or taken into consideration, in the theoretical debates of the North American and northern European academies. For these reasons, the efforts of the CWA to promote spaces of encounter and academic dialogues with other anthropological traditions is important for the decolonization of our discipline. In this case, English became the lingua franca that allowed us to share experiences and methodological and political pursuits, but we hope to be able to translate to Spanish our academic dialogues, for a broader audience in Latin America.

The interaction between anthropologists and the people they work with in Canada, Australia, and Mexico is the bases on which the authors in this volume explore the often unintended, but sometimes devastating repercussions of government policies (such as land rights legislation or justice initiatives for women) on Indigenous people's lives. We hope that by contrasting experiences of colonial domination and anticolonial struggles in different national contexts, we can contribute to the development of a comparative analysis in anthropology that is so needed in a context of globalized structures of domination. We further envisage that by juxtaposing these divergent analyses in this volume, we present new understandings for how Indigenous activism and academic inquiry can be combined to combat the insidious effects of modern colonialism on Indigenous peoples across the globe. This is timely because, as Indigenous scholar Glen Sean Coulthard (2014) warns, the new politics of recognition, whereby the state acknowledges the unique cultural presence of its Indigenous citizens, merely hides its coloniality, while it cements ongoing relations of power and domination by the state over its Indigenous subjects. New understandings of resistance, refusal, and resurgence, as presented by the authors in this volume, may offer the genesis of alternative ways forward and also ways to understand how these play out every day.

When drafting this introduction, we were able to corroborate the great scarcity of comparative studies between Canada, Mexico, and Australia; they are theoretical traditions that have developed in isolation from one another.[7] Throughout the chapters of this book, however, we see that the challenges faced by anthropologists who bet on the coproduction of knowledge with Indigenous peoples and vindicate the ethical and methodological importance of activist research are similar in the three geographic spaces.

Despite the shared challenges, it is important to consider the differences in the relations between Indigenous peoples (Aboriginal, Indigenous, or First Nations, or named in their own languages, depending on their own self-denomination) with colonial and postcolonial nation-states. The different genealogies and specific forms of domination and dispossession in Canada, Mexico, and Australia have influenced Indigenous peoples' strategies of resistance and the actions of the anthropologists who work with them as allies.

Different Colonial Genealogies

The lives of the Indigenous peoples of the three geographic regions covered in this book were deeply affected by colonial violence, territorial dispossession, and forced displacement imposed by colonial governments. The characteristics of the different colonial ventures, however, have had an influence on the forms of the struggles for rights, the types of political demands developed, and how the indigeneity discourse is articulated.

We do not intend here to engage in a deep historical reconstruction of the various colonial genealogies, but we would like to point out some of the differences we found among the three regions. The various denominations used in Canada, Mexico, and Australia to refer to Indigenous peoples are themselves a product of these different colonial histories.

In the Canadian milieu, First Nations became a term of recognition most notably in the 1970s, with the formation of the Canada-wide chiefs organization, the Assembly of First Nations, though only after a long history of state oppression and territorial dispossession. These realities still persist, while made to look accommodating via a liberal modality, in the context of the current neocolonial state. Historically, notably in the eighteenth and nineteenth centuries, autonomous Indigenous political societies were, de facto, acknowledged and engaged with as such by British colonial authorities via established military and trade alliances, and eventually via land-sharing compacts affirmed through various treaties. These treaties were subsequently and preponderantly ignored by the state, or subverted beneath imposed Crown legislation after the 1867 Confederation of Canada. Much of the subsequent state institutional controls were brutally assimilative, even genocidal, as has been discussed in regard to Indian residential schools and bureaucratically controlled oppressive reserve conditions.

Many Indigenous peoples who did not arrive at historical treaties nonetheless persisted in understanding the integrity of their political, territorial, and cultural societies, even while challenged by state practices that worked persistently to trivialize them through policies of withering cultural, political, and economic subordination, land dispossession, and enfranchisement into the settler polity and its imposed sovereign legal frameworks. Only in the period since the 1950s, with some slackening of state controls in relation to a developing post–World War II internationalist human rights ethos, have Indigenous nations been able to organize and begin to self-name as such, eventually arriving at the First Nations pluralist terminology. That said, in their own lands and communities, most Indigenous territorial collectives identify themselves variously in their own languages (e.g., Piikani Nation, Kwakwaka'wak'w, Secwepemc, Anishinaabeg, Mi'kmaq), each of these identifying a people organized in their own distinct political society.

In Australia, the British treated the Indigenous populations differently than how it negotiated the settlement of its other colonies, including in Canada. Approximately 250 Aboriginal language groups were living on the continent at the time of the arrival of the first fleet of British ships at Botany Bay in 1788. Yet, Britain declared the country uninhabited, or terra nullius, and this established the legal relationship between Britain and the Indigenous population for the next two hundred years. Under the guise of such legal title to land, Britain was not obliged to negotiate treaties with the Indigenous populations or take land by conquest. The legal position of Aboriginal Australians was reinforced by subsequent legislation enacted by the federal government and the separate states of Australia on the Federation of Australia in 1901. In 1967 a referendum saw significant changes to the legislative treatment of Indigenous people, because the majority of Australians voted to mandate the federal government to implement policies to benefit Aboriginal people. One of the most significant changes leading from this was the implementation of land rights legislation in the Northern Territory in 1976 and native title legislation almost twenty years later. Regardless, Aboriginal Australians continue to suffer significant discrimination, lower health outcomes, and an ongoing struggle for recognition of Aboriginal title to land. With the implementation of land rights, however, has also come an acknowledgment of equal status of Aboriginal Australians among an increasing number of the dominant population, culminating most recently with three elected Aboriginal members to federal Parliament in the most recent election of July 2016.

On the other hand, the wrongly termed "Indian peoples" of Mexico were integrated in colonial administrations since the sixteenth century, through a legal and geographic separation that created the so-called Republic of Indians and Republic of Spaniards. This implied the maintenance of the local power structures of the Republic of Indians, with a legal regime that was separate from, but inferior to, that of the Republic of Spaniards. In many regions, Indigenous people who were dispersed were concentrated in Indian pueblos, which became the main social and organizational space during and after colonial times. A sense of communal belonging was thus created, which is still important in contemporary political struggles. The policy of evangelization, witnessed in different ways in Canada and Australia, was partly responsible for this social and linguistic segregation but also for the maintenance of Indigenous languages, since in theory the Spanish Crown, unlike the British Crown, required evangelists to preach in Indigenous languages.

In the case of Australia, the legal fiction of the common-law rule of terra nullius was the ideological and moral justification for occupation and dispossession of Aboriginal lands, without treaty or payment. The fact that treaties were not negotiated with Indigenous peoples and that limited colonial political institutions were created for them, has set the subsequent history of treatment of Aboriginal Australians apart from all other colonized countries, including those we discuss in this volume, Canada and Latin America.[8] The arrival of Captain Arthur Phillip and his crew to Botany Bay in 1788 marked the beginning of the historically recognized European invasion of Australia.[9] Before Phillip, Captain James Cook had already claimed eastern Australia for Great Britain, declaring the sovereignty of the British Crown over land that was considered "wasted and unoccupied." These were the bases for the establishment of the first colonies, denying the existence of the Aboriginal population and, therefore, any right over the colonized lands. This position was legally ratified as recently as 1971 with the Gove land rights case (*Milirrpum v. Nabalco Pty. Ltd.*), in which Justice Richard Blackburn rejected the doctrine of Aboriginal title because it was overridden by the land being claimed by right of occupancy under conquered or ceded colonies.

On encountering peoples assumed to be nomadic and who apparently did not till or fence off their lands, the British colonizers imposed a right to take possession of those territories, which they considered "unoccupied." It has, of course, been well documented that many Indigenous Australian language groups living in coastal regions of the country, such as southeastern South Australia and southwestern Western Australia, have complex land-holding systems based on long-term seasonal occupation of defined regions that defy a nomadic labeling (e.g., Bates [1938] 1966; Jenkin 1979; Berndt and Berndt 1993). For those peoples who may be categorized more stereotypically as nomadic, including Western desert peoples, the term is also a misnomer that belies the highly complex land-owning systems that dictate their community and religious practices (see, for example, Berndt 1959; Meggitt 1962; Munn 1970; Myers 1986; Bell 1993; and Holcombe, this volume, to name just a few).

The High Court decision in *Mabo v. Queensland* (No. 2) of 1992 saw the doctrine of terra nullius overturned. This watershed in Australian legal and political history, after more than two hundred years of European occupation, led to important changes in the national recognition of Aboriginal Australians as the original occupiers of the nation, culminating with the Native Title Act (1993) (Hutchings, this volume). Two decades prior, the battle by Indigenous peoples and their supporters for recognition of traditional Aboriginal occupation of Australia had been hard fought in the Northern Territory. In the 1970s, among the broader Australian population the political climate was ripe to support change to the conditions under which Aboriginal Australians lived and worked. After the Gurindji people walked off the Wave Hill pastoral property in the mid-1960s in protest over substandard wages and with the adverse decision in the Gove land rights case, a populist land rights movement emerged. Eventually, as a result of the 1967 referendum to include Aboriginal people in federal government decisions, grassroots protests and general political pressure influenced the federal Labor government to introduce land rights legislation for the Northern Territory, over which it had jurisdiction. The Aboriginal Land Rights Act was implemented under the subsequent conservative Liberal-Country coalition government, led by Malcolm Fraser, in 1976, and influenced some state governments to introduce land rights in other regions under their specific jurisdiction.[10]

Despite these legislative milestones affecting the treatment of Aboriginal Australians by the dominant population, government and church control over Aboriginal Australians has historically been uneven across the country. Regardless, the establishment of missions throughout Australia from the mid-1800s saw large-scale removal of Aboriginal children from their communities and the forced migration of Aboriginal people onto government reserves over many generations. A majority of these people have since become known as the Stolen Generation.[11] Their experiences of removal have led to devastating disruptions to cultural knowledge and practice, which many Aboriginal Australians attempt to rectify with varying degrees of success, via their participation in litigated and negotiated outcomes under native title legislation (see Hutchings, this volume).

Canadian colonial hegemonies of dispossession echo certain elements of those met in Australia, but they have also diverged in crucial ways. For Canada's Indigenous peoples, those in political societies now referred to as First Nations, a long, if uneven, tradition of alliance making is still central to their political and land struggles, begun as early as the seventeenth century. Indeed, the treaties at first signed with English colonial authorities in the eighteenth century, and then later around the time of Canadian Confederation in the nineteenth and early twentieth centuries, continued this tradition. The Peace and Friendship Treaties, discussed by L. Jane McMillan and Sherry M. Pictou in this book, emerged in the earlier period, without the encumbrance of territorial cession or land relation rights, though clearly indicating the mutual acknowledgment of a compact between "nations," Indigenous ones and the British Crown. The later confederation treaties (see Asch 2014) were prompted by the 1763 Royal Proclamation, understood as Canada's first constitutional instrument, facilitating later confederation, which required the Crown to enter into treaties with extant, de facto Indigenous nations. These treaties did involve land negotiations, but Indigenous nations consistently held that lands were shared, with only a cession to allow access for the purpose of sharing worked out through continual relations. Regardless of such Indigenous understandings, the Crown inevitably made instrumentalist legal arguments that lands were absolutely ceded and surrendered.

By the latter part of the twentieth century, however, the Government of Canada had introduced a new tack, with land cession and modification of rights to assure this as a practically nonnegotiable aspect of what it referred to as "modern day treaties" or "comprehensive claims," which many observers view instead as contracts, but ones that open up innovative cogovernance arrangements, if ultimately under Crown authority. The James Bay Cree, with whom Colin Scott (a contributor to this book) has collaborated, negotiated such comprehensive cogovernance agreements.

In the latter half of the nineteenth century, in what may be seen as the "high colonial" moment with its imposed civilizing imperative, Canada also put in place new strategies of population control, in the form of the oppressive 1876 Indian Act, which developed alongside, yet forcefully undermined, the treaty-making tradition between peoples. The act was undergirded by the 1867 British North American Act, the initiating constitutional instrument at the time of Canadian Confederation, which in sections 91 and 92 divided state, or Crown, jurisdictional powers between the federal and provincial governments, and then in section 91(24) presumptively subordinated "Indians" (Indigenous peoples) *under* Crown jurisdiction, as if the nation-to-nation dimension of treaties was artifactual and illusory.

This move superseded treaties, thereby giving all the more force to the Indian Act in its several iterations, all in a moment when the presumed superiority of European-based knowledge, so-called civilizational orders, and the expansive assertion of state sovereignty and possessiveness was taken for granted in the imperial colonial ethos of the time (Chakrabarty 2000). It was believed that it was the responsibility of the British Crown and its representatives to bestow agriculture, the gospel, civil education, property, and a European work ethic on Indigenous peoples, who were offensively seen as inferior to Europeans and to the immigrating settler polities through the visor of then-prevalent discourses of evolutionary scientific racism. The act set in place myriad colonizing practices, including state-controlled reserve land systems, state-dictated blood status and band membership rules, strict cultural and ceremonial prohibitions, and acculturating, ethnocentric schooling practices in the form of the oft-brutal Indian residential schooling system, all of which worked together to underwrite dispossession and effective ethnocide—some argue genocide—in the name of a civilizing superiority of the settler polity.

The act displaced the sociopolitical authority sustained by First Nations in their lands, through the unilateral passing of statutory jurisdiction to the federal Department of Indian Affairs. Through this new department, the Crown became responsible for "caring for and civilizing" Indigenous peoples, thus giving rise to a tutelage policy that continues to this day. This history has made the demands for "self-determination and sovereignty" so important in the Canadian context, explaining why the treaties signed since the 1700s continue to be advanced both for their legal weight internationally and as tools for political struggle today, vexing as the Crown response typically turns out to be. The fact of the legal force of these treaties and of ongoing unceded land rights known as Aboriginal title, especially in the many Indigenous territories where no treaties were established, have been braced in the last thirty years by the inclusion of section 35 in the Canadian Constitution Act, 1982, which states, "The existing aboriginal and treaty rights of the aboriginal peoples of Canada are hereby recognized and affirmed." Many Supreme Court decisions have followed, so shaping and authorizing such rights, but subordinating them to Canadian law, rather than in terms of the autonomous laws of Indigenous nations themselves (see McNeil 2018).[12] Taken together, these conditions set out the coordinates for the decolonial projects and the forms of alliance making and positioning of anthropologists with Indigenous peoples, as discussed in this volume by Sherry Pictou, Jane McMillan, and Colin Scott.

The underlying Indigenous responses to the relentless control and brutality of colonization in countries like Canada have only relatively recently been seriously embraced in Australia by an increasing number of Indigenous academics and activists, influenced by the writings of Indigenous scholars from Canada and New Zealand in particular (e.g., Smith 2012; Andersen 2014; Coulthard 2014; Simpson 2014, 2017), which discuss sovereignty and decolonization as standpoints to address the ongoing effects of the colonial project (see Hutchings in this volume; also Moreton-Robinson 2015; Watson 2015).

In Mexico, the political and social life of Indigenous communities has been characterized by the coexistence of parallel spaces of government and Indigenous justice established since colonial times, when the Indian Laws recognized Indigenous jurisdictions subordinated to the Spanish Crown.[13] The so-called Indigenous legal systems and today's Indigenous municipalities have gone through several processes of reconstitution in permanent dialogue with the legal systems of postcolonial nation-states. The political demands of today's Indigenous movements have focused on the recognition of community or municipal autonomy, which implies control over the land and territory, but also recognition of their own forms of self-government and justice. More than ancestral political and legal systems, they are historical products that incorporate both Indigenous people's own principles and epistemologies and Catholic moral and religious principles, which are the product of five hundred years of colonial occupation, as well as legal procedures incorporated from state justice. Although the liberal reforms of the nineteenth century imposed legal monism in most Latin American countries, these parallel systems continued to function in practice and were tolerated in many contexts, given the state's inability to respond to the legal needs of Indigenous regions. These independent spaces are vindicated by autonomous Indigenous movements in Mexico.

A watershed in the history of Indigenous resistance in Mexico was the Zapatista uprising on January 1, 1994. Armed and unarmed troops of Tseltal, Tsotsil, Tojolabal, Chol, and Mam peasants from the central highlands of Chiapas and the Lacandon jungle, formed the Zapatista National Liberation Army (EZLN). The group's name, method, and message invoked the spirit of the Mexican Revolution of 1910, as it put forward a platform of work, land, housing, food, health, education, independence, liberty, democracy, justice, and peace. Twelve days into an armed confrontation between the very poorly equipped EZLN and the Mexican Army, the government came to the negotiating table.

Shortly after the public emergence of the EZLN in January 1994, demands for Indigenous rights and self-determination began to take center stage in the Zapatista's negotiations with the government and later grew to include a wide range of Indigenous communities, nations, and movements, which eventually consolidated into a national network. The Zapatista rebellion of 1994 initiated a nationwide process of reassessing the relationship between the Mexican state and Indigenous peoples.

For the last twenty-five years, the Zapatista movement has created its own autonomous regions and has centered the demands of Indigenous peoples in the national political debate. After the government failed to implement the peace accords with the EZLN, signed in 1996, Indigenous autonomy became the heart of the Zapatista project (see Mora 2018). Communities in Chiapas and in other regions of Mexico, such as Cheran in Michoacan, declared themselves autonomous regions and began implementing parallel governments and setting up their own systems of education, healthcare, agriculture, and more. The declarations and living experiments in autonomy at the local level in Chiapas connected to a larger national movement for Indigenous self-determination and rights that has denounced the continuity of the colonial project in contemporary Mexico.

These three colonial histories allow us to understand why the demands for sovereignty, autonomy, and the recognition of land rights and native title are so important for the Indigenous peoples of the three regions. Simultaneously, at a global level, we are witnessing the emergence of a new political identity involving the Indigenous, which has traveled through rural roads of five continents, reaching the most isolated villages through workshops, marches, or encounters. The global struggles for recognition of so-called Indigenous rights have started to articulate these various political and cultural identities to denounce the effects of colonialism in their lives and territories. Thus, in addition to the local terms for self-definition—Maya, Mi'kmaq, or Arrernte—a new sense of identity has been incorporated: being Indigenous, which has led to the development of an encompassing *community* with other oppressed peoples from around the world. This has come especially in the wake of the political fallout generated by Indigenous delegates from across the globe over their disappointment with the United Nations *Declaration of the Rights of Indigenous Peoples* (*UNDRIP*), 2007, to seriously account for Indigenous concerns. It has been repeated with further disappointment over the failure of the UN to listen to subsequent attempts by Indigenous representatives for the UN to embrace change by challenging colonial governments to a point of true decolonization for world Indigenous peoples (e.g., Pictou, this volume; Holcombe, this volume; Watson 2017; Venne 2017, 163). Multiple analysts point out that the movement for Indigenous rights was born as a transnational movement (Brysk 2000; Niezen 2003; Tilley 2002) because since its inception, it transcended local struggles and self-definitions. These experiences of Indigenous activism have challenged the perspectives of national anthropological traditions, forcing us to establish transcontinental dialogues and question our owns methodological nationalisms. Several chapters of this book are framed in this global context of struggles for the rights of Indigenous peoples, locating the debates in the national contexts of Canada, Mexico, and Australia, but in permanent dialogue with transnational Indigenous movements.

Knowledge Coproduction and Epistemic Dialogues

A common pursuit of all the authors in this book is the need to look for different ways to produce knowledge in dialogue or collaboration with Indigenous peoples of Canada, Mexico, and Australia. The challenge to the *extractivist perspectives* of social research, which are based solely on the researcher's theoretical or academic curiosity or the needs of the financing states or foundations, is reflected in the authors' defense of knowledge coproduction.

Our discomfort with the role of "experts" that has been assigned, especially to those of us who participate in legal struggles, is problematized in several chapters. We analyze from several perspectives the challenge of *destabilizing* knowledge hierarchies through epistemic dialogues that recognize other ways of "being in the world," while we use our anthropological knowledges as "expert knowledge" in the struggles for rights.

In one way or another, all the authors in this book confront positivist academies that defend a "neutral" and distant knowledge, disqualifying any research undertaken in alliance with movements for social justice by characterizing it as "ideological." This book's chapters refute this stance, defending the epistemic wealth implied in doing research in alliance or collaboration with Indigenous peoples, simultaneously asserting that social research can contribute to developing critical thought and to destabilizing the discourses of power, thus contributing to the struggles of movements that work toward social justice.

The three Indigenous anthropologists who participate in this collection—Sherry Pictou (Mi'kmaq from L'sɨtkuk, Canada), Genner Llanes-Ortiz (Yucatec Maya from Mexico), and Suzi Hutchings (Central Arrernte from Australia)—and those who, without being Indigenous, work in alliance and collaboration with Indigenous peoples or movements, have set for ourselves the challenge, which has been inspired by an unceded Indigenous presence, of producing a type of knowledge that transcends the limited spaces of the academy. We believe, however, that critical thought is not at odds with scholarly rigor, and that building a research agenda in dialogue with the social actors with whom we work, rather than devaluing anthropological knowledge, bolsters it and allows us to transcend the limited borders of the academic world. It is also a space with which to include the dialogues with the Indigenous activists with whom we work and their own perspectives on justice and rights. Whether this be through showing how Indigenous native title applicants reinscribe a community Indigenous knowledge by combining archival material with knowledge handed down from ancestors to prove claims to territory (e.g., Hutchings, this volume); through the possibilities of the *UNDRIP* to provide a mechanism for Australian Aboriginal woman living in desert communities to assert a human rights agenda in combating family violence (Holcombe, this volume); through the use of creative writing to denounce state patriarchal violence and institutional racism against Indigenous women (Hernández Castillo); or even through Mi'kmaw worldviews merging with anthropological perspectives to confront new forms of colonialism as experienced by Native fishing families (Pictou, this volume).

But the "political alliances" and the "coproduction of knowledge" we undertake here have another sui generis characteristic: that we all work with fellow citizens with whom we relate, not only in solidarity with their struggles for justice, but through the common need to build fairer, more inclusive, and more sustainable national projects. In this regard, Colin Scott speaks to us not only of collaborative research projects, but also of collective life projects, whereby knowledge dialogues allow us to build shared futures that are more respectful of both nature and humans. Building those shared projects requires, as a first step, making our knowledge intelligible, opening ourselves to other ontologies or ways of being in the world, and allowing ourselves to destabilize our certainties. In this respect, Scott says,

> The first challenge for academic researchers is to nurture relations of knowledge coproduction that are intelligible from the perspective of Indigenous relationalities and life projects. Reciprocally, the life projects of researchers come to intersect with, if not be transformed by, those of Indigenous partners. Intersecting and allied projects lend endurance to knowledge co-production capable of building shared views and community in ways that might possibly collapse the usual hegemonies.

Along the same lines, in Xochitl Leyva Solano's chapter, she invites us to produce insurrectionary knowledges and practices through joint work with Indigenous movements, allowing us to destabilize what she characterizes as "academic capitalism." The Mexican anthropologist denounces the commodification of knowledge as part of a production chain that reproduces the academy's own machinery for the benefit of several industries, including the book industry. Her call to seek more creative, inclusive, and "insurrectionary" ways of producing knowledge is the result of an awareness of the global process of commodification: "It is important to locate the other knowledge practices mentioned here, in contrast with those that emerged from the changes that have taken place since the 1980s, which have displaced public universities and inserted them in the market (Slaughter and Leslie 1999). The patterns of professional academic and scientific work have undoubtedly changed over the last hundred years, but we should place special emphasis on the drastic (not to say dramatic) changes resulting from the emergence of neoliberal global markets."

This same influence of the political ideals of the Zapatista movement can be seen in the chapter by Genner Llanes-Ortiz, who vindicates Yucatec Maya pedagogies as ways of producing knowledge based on collective practice and through various textual strategies, including literature and art. As Colin Scott does, both Leyva Solano and Llanes-Ortiz set forth the need to work toward the construction of a collective life project that, as the Zapatista slogan says, may allow us to build "a world where many worlds may fit."

Understanding academic knowledge as a space to contribute toward social justice, not only for Indigenous peoples, but for the broader society to which we belong, shifts the location of anthropology's enunciation in these peripheral traditions. Almost two decades ago, Brazilian anthropologist Roberto Cardoso de Oliveira (1998) pointed out that anthropology in Latin America had created a new cognoscitive subject, which was no longer a stranger constituted from the outside but a member of the society it studied, having implications regarding the place of the *other* being studied. This proposal has been revisited by Colombian anthropologist Myriam Jimeno Santoyo (2011) to write about the "citizen researcher," noting that the work done by many of us who research our own national contexts revolves around a permanent interest in our own society and the way it is constituted, the social conditions of those being studied, and the repercussions of our own concepts. This place of enunciation, as citizens and researchers in our own national society, entails different ethical responsibilities than those involved in researching remote societies with little or no political ties. This is what Sherry Pictou calls "relational responsibility."

It is important to recognize, however, that this citizen research does not necessarily imply a challenge to the structures of domination in the context of which we produce our knowledge. In Australia, as Suzi Hutchings writes in this volume, for instance, "The number of qualified Indigenous anthropologists working in native title . . . can be counted on one hand," and this, it could be argued, contributes to an inability to contest the status quo, particularly from the citizen researcher who is also the Indigenous subject of anthropological investigation. Sarah Holcombe, also in this book, points out that their position as "conationals" is precisely what has kept many Australian anthropologists from delving into the issue of human rights violations against Aboriginal peoples. Holcombe points out,

> Perhaps yet another reason that Australianist anthropologists have been tardy or dismissive of applying this rights discourse within the Australian context is

because of the "co-nationals" status of our "subjects," as Jeremy Beckett (2010) has referred to the settler colony politic. For my purposes, this national anthropology identified by Beckett has had the instrumental effect of eliding the value of this rights discourse. Regardless of our ideological perspectives on the values of neoliberalism and formal rights *or* the welfare state and substantive rights, Indigenous Australians as cocitizens surely do not require the same recourse to human rights instruments as, say, those in war-torn or corrupt states in Africa or South America. As part of a stated multicultural Australia, the policy rhetoric of equality in Indigenous-focused policies such as "Closing the Gap" surely does not require recourse to human rights by activist anthropologists.

Resisting the temptation of self-complacency, this book's authors recognize the limitations of a socially committed anthropology that remains marked by the hierarchies of knowledge characterizing the nation-states where we exercise our discipline. A permanent self-criticism and self-reflection regarding our own practice is the point of departure for the knowledge dialogues that we propose here.

Legal Activism and Rights Struggles

Another issue that traverses several of this book's chapters is the tension between a critical standpoint regarding the legal apparatus as a neocolonial strategy of control and domination, on one hand, and the political possibilities that many Indigenous movements find in the appropriation of rights discourses and in strategic litigation for their defense, on the other. This paradox is described by Sherry M. Pictou in her chapter, when she notes, "Therefore, it is a tragic irony that Indigenous people would have to turn to the very legal system that all but destroyed them as a people in their struggle for Aboriginal and treaty rights." Although most of the authors recognize this tension in what Boaventura de Sousa Santos (2002) calls the regulatory or emancipatory possibilities of the law, not all of them share the same standpoint regarding the dilemma. At least five of the book's authors have participated in the elaboration of anthropological expert witness reports for the recognition of land rights (Holcombe and Hutchings), of Indigenous rights to livelihood fishing (Pictou and McMillan), and for the legal defense of Indigenous prisoners (Hernández Castillo). Yet, our assessment of anthropologists' role as "experts" and of expert witness reports as political tools are very different.

In Australia, Suzi Hutchings and Sarah Holcombe document how the recognition of Aboriginal land rights since 1976 hegemonized the Native population's human rights struggles, creating new political challenges and renewing neocolonial strategies. The so-called Justice Blackburn decision led to a debate regarding the Aboriginal population's territorial rights, setting the bases for the enactment of the Aboriginal Land Rights Act in the Northern Territory in 1976. It was the struggle of the Yolngu people against the establishment of a bauxite mine in the Gove peninsula by the Nabalco Mining Company that revealed the absence of a legal framework to defend the common-law rights of the Aboriginal population. It was the first time that a Native population took a lawsuit to the Supreme Court, and unfortunately Justice Blackburn rejected their action, noting that Yolngu customary law included norms regarding land property, but that those norms had no legal standing nor were they recognized by the Australian government. As noted above, this case sparked the beginning of a struggle for recognition of Aboriginal land rights. It also led Meriam activist Eddie Mabo and his legal team to contest the colonial position established by the British that the common-law rights of Aboriginal people to hunt, fish, and observe traditional practices on the Gove peninsula had been extinguished with settlement. In 1992 a majority of High Court judges upheld the claim that the lands of Australia were not terra nullius. In *Mabo v. Queensland* (No. 2), the High Court acknowledged the existence of Aboriginal native title, finally leading to the establishment of native title rights in Australian law after more than two hundred years of British invasion and settlement of the continent.

This new legal framework, which could be interpreted as advancement in Indigenous peoples' access to justice, implied a process of juridization of politics that, according to these authors, has been limited. The struggle for land rights and recognition of prior ownership has become central in Aboriginal peoples' struggles, legitimizing essentialist discourses regarding "Indigenous authenticity" and excluding other rights discourses. It could be said that the Northern Territory Aboriginal Land Rights Act (1976) and the Native Title Act (1993) established the language on which resistance was based. Resorting to William Roseberry's definition of hegemony, we could say that, in Australia, the land rights discourse developed "a common language or way of talking about social relationships that sets out the central terms around which and in terms of which contestation and struggle can occur" (Roseberry 1994, 360–61).

Many Australian anthropologists have focused their political efforts on the struggle for Indigenous property, contributing to the development of a legal framework that legitimizes those rights and accompanying the demands for native titles with expert witness reports. Based on their experiences as experts in support of those struggles, Suzi Hutchings and Sarah Holcombe point out two main challenges set forth by this new hegemony of rights discourses. As an Aboriginal anthropologist who questions essentialist perspectives of identity, Hutchings maintains that the struggle for native titles revictimizes the population that has most suffered the impact of colonialism through dispossession and displacement. This Stolen Generation peoples, who were cast out of their lands, dispossessed of their language, and severed from their communal structures, face the most difficult challenges in order to "prove their indigeneity" and obtain their right to the land. The burden of proof is imposed on them based on authenticity criteria defined by the neocolonial state itself. Hutchings, with her double identity as an Indigenous woman and anthropologist, describes her situation as a "double-edged sword" and as "being stuck in the middle," since she rejects the imposition of limited definitions of "tradition" to demand rights, yet, as an expert, she is obliged to follow the rules established by a system that she continues to recognize as colonial. Meanwhile, Sarah Holcombe reflects on how, by reducing the struggle for Indigenous peoples' rights to land rights, many other aspects have been left out, such as a life free of violence for women or social rights, which are rarely considered in lawsuits that Australian anthropologists have supported. Both authors point out that while the recognition of land rights has implied what Peterson and Langton (1983, 3) describe as "regaining some fraction of the personal and group autonomy which existed prior to colonisation," this autonomy has been marked by new forms of violence and exclusion.

Forty-two years have passed since the enactment of the Aboriginal Land Rights Act in the Northern Territory and twenty-five years since the passing of the Native Title Act. Yet, remarkably few native title claims are unreservedly successful throughout Australia, and land rights generally remains the success of Indigenous groups legally identified as more authentically Aboriginal because they live in locations where it is easier to continue traditional cultural practices. Thus, most land rights are recognized for those people living in remote or rural areas of the Northern Territory, Western Australia, Queensland, and South Australia, where such recognition in general does not affect the interests of white Australians. Significantly, most of these regions remain characterized by social exclusion, extreme poverty, and violence.

In Canada, Jane McMillan and Sherry Pictou take as their starting point a decision by Canada's Supreme Court known as *R. v. Marshall*, which recognizes

Indigenous peoples' fishing rights. Based on the case of Mi'kmaw fisherman Donald Marshall Jr., who appealed the prohibition of commercial eel fishing, the Supreme Court recognized the validity of the treaties established in 1760 and 1761 between Mi'kmaw authorities and the British Crown, stating that fishing regulations, the establishment of prohibitions, and the requirement of special licenses violated such treaties, recognized by current-day governments.

Both authors write from a privileged position of deep immersion in the political milieus of Indigenous struggle in the settler-colonial state. Sherry Pictou is a Mi'kmaw woman and an Indigenous activist who has defended her people's rights and, simultaneously, an Indigenous feminist anthropologist who aims at reflecting and theorizing on the political struggles in which she has participated. Jane McMillan was part of the legal team that worked on the *R. v. Marshall* case, as well as being an eel fisherwoman and now a legal anthropologist who knows the First Nations treaties and rights. Both authors defend activist research and the appropriation or mobilization of rights discourses, and they demonstrate the epistemic possibilities of doing research in collaboration with the social actors with whom we work. Rather than a limitation of the development of a "distant and objective" perspective, their participation in the struggles of the Mi'kmaq have allowed them to understand the internal challenges faced by the appropriation and use of rights discourses.

From different perspectives, both authors manage to maintain the tension as they "analyze the complex processes through which laws and policies shape social lives, and how legal disputes shape and alter cultural rights and governance practices" (McMillan, this volume), while they use these same legal strategies analyzed to advance in the struggle for access to justice.

In the Mexican context, R. Aída Hernández Castillo responds to those who claim that the choice is between two incompatible options: either you opt for a critical analysis of state legality, or you reproduce hegemonic standpoints regarding the law and rights by supporting legal activism. From this perspective, any legal activism reproduces hegemonic definitions of culture and Indigenous peoples, restricting the political imaginaries regarding justice (Brown and Halley 2002). Hutchings and Holcombe seem to share this reflection in their collaborations in this book, identifying the difficulties in challenging the social structures in Australia from within the discipline of anthropology, which has a significant history as a handmaiden to the colonial enterprise of the nation-state in relation to its Indigenous citizens. Differing from this standpoint, Hernández Castillo claims that it is possible to maintain a permanent critical reflection on the law and rights, while supporting struggles for justice for Indigenous peoples and organizations, by appropriating and resignifying national and international legislations. Using as an example her experience in elaborating anthropological expert witness reports to support the defense of Indigenous women in national and international legal actions, the author demonstrates how the collective dialogues that have nurtured these expert reports have also contributed to a critical reflection on Mexico's state justice.

The historical and geographic context, the organizational and political genealogies of Indigenous peoples, and the social fabric of the places where the struggles for rights take place determine the various forms and emancipatory or regulatory possibilities of legal activism and the potential effectiveness of anthropologists' participation in those struggles. The different experiences analyzed here allow us to break away from generalizing perspectives of the law and rights as either simple tools of neocolonial states or as mere strategies of Indigenous resistance. The various aspects of hegemonic and counter-hegemonic, colonial and decolonial, processes are reconstructed in detail by each of the authors of this book.

The Book's Chapters

The case studies analyzed in this volume do not attempt to be representative of the experiences of Indigenous peoples in each country, but they are examples of the efforts and challenges that anthropologists, Indigenous and non-Indigenous, confront when producing knowledge in alliances with Indigenous peoples. We were not able to address all the intraregional diversity in each country, because the complexity of each national context is beyond the scope of a single volume, but we hope that this first effort to build bridges between Mexico, Canada, and Australia will be the beginning of future political and academic dialogues.

We divided this collective book into three sections that correspond to the three geographic regions covered by the studies. Traveling from north to south, we start with the three case studies in Canada (See Map 1).

We begin our journey in Southwest Nova Scotia Mi'kmaq lands and waters, where the Bear River First Nation has been struggling for recognition of their territorial rights to fishing, hunting, and control over their natural resources. In this first chapter, entitled "What Is Decolonization? Mi'kmaw Ancestral Relational Understandings and Anthropological Perspectives on Treaty Relations,"

Mi'kmaw anthropologist Sherry M. Pictou analyzes the limitations of her people's legal struggles and the new challenges they face with the arrival of private capital in the region's fishing industry. As an activist researcher who has accompanied her people's struggles for fifteen years as an adviser, educator, and representative of the Coordinating Committee of the World Forum of Fisher Peoples, the author turns her own experience as an activist/anthropologist into a window to reflect on the limits of academic decolonization.

Continuing in the same region of the world, in L. Jane McMillan's chapter, "Committing Anthropology in the Muddy Middle Ground," she takes as her point of departure the same legal case regarding fishing rights to reflect on what she calls the ontological and political responsibilities implied in the struggle for Indigenous rights to their natural resources. Based on the *R. v. Marshall* case, the author analyzes the repercussions that the suitors' cultural and political practices have on legal disputes. Through the processual perspective of legal anthropology, she analyzes the everyday struggles of Indigenous peoples to build their sovereignty and break away from current forms of neocolonial dependence.

Finally, we conclude our journey through Canadian territory with the work by Colin Scott entitled "Research Partnerships and Collaborative Life Projects." In this chapter, the author explores the conditions and outcomes of knowledge coproduction involved in the partnership between anthropologists and First Nation people. In pursuing this concern, the chapter builds on the notion of collaborative "life projects" as part and parcel of research partnerships—underwritten by a sharing of values and agendas that have certain "ontological" preconditions and consequences. What do these life projects entail for the coproduction of knowledge about the world? How are they positioned within the larger community of life transcending the human? How is coproduced knowledge shaped by the relational ontology of reciprocity through which Cree hunters see—and potentially researchers and other citizens of the mainstream might come to understand—our relations within a larger community of life? These themes and perspectives are pursued in light of the author's engagements with the James Bay Crees of Eeyou Istchee on themes of land rights, conservation, and alternative models of development over four decades.

Continuing our journey through the American continent, we move on to the cases in Mexico (see Map 2), beginning with R. Aída Hernández Castillo's chapter "Legal Activism and Prison Workshops: The Paradoxes of Feminist Legal Anthropology and Cultural Work in Penitentiary Spaces," in which the author explores the possibilities and limitations of legal activism from the perspective of feminist anthropology. Based on two activist research experiences with incarcerated Indigenous women, the author reflects on the new ethical and political challenges posed by the elaboration of anthropological expert witness reports for the defense of Indigenous prisoners. She describes the experience of the Sisters of the Shadow Editorial Collective of Women in Prison (Colectiva Editorial de Mujeres en Prisión Hermanas de la Sombra), where she accompanied the elaboration process of life histories of imprisoned Indigenous women, through writing workshops that have served as spaces for collective reflection on the multiple exclusions experienced by imprisoned Indigenous and peasant women. She also describes her experiences as anthropological expert witness in defense of imprisoned Indigenous women, in particular in the case of Commander Nestora Salgado García, a member of the Regional Coordination of Communal Authorities (CRAC) of Guerrero, unjustly imprisoned for her participation in an Indigenous justice system.

Continuing with reflections on the epistemological and political possibilities of knowledge coproduction, Xochitl Leyva Solano, in her chapter "Decolonizing Anthropologists from Below and to the Left," analyzes a sui generis experience of collective knowledge production and the elaboration of multilingual texts and audiobooks. Based on an analysis of the political and epistemic challenges posed by the Zapatista movement for Mexico's academy, the author shares the experience of the Chiapas Network of Artists, Community Communicators, and Anthropologists (RACCACH), a collective of scholars, artists, and communicators who have worked together to create multimedia materials encompassing the written word, photography, and painting, in three Mayan languages and in Spanish. The pedagogies of self-reflection and collective production using various textual strategies are approached by the author as strategies to decolonize anthropology, seeking to confront what she calls "academic capitalism."

We conclude the section on Mexico with the chapter entitled "Maya Knowledges, Intercultural Dialogues, and Being a *Chan Laak'* in the Yucatán Peninsula," by Yucatec Maya anthropologist Genner Llanes-Ortiz. In this chapter the author explores the current situation of Pan-Yucatec Maya social movements from the vantage point of the author's collaborative work with and for activist networks and communities. This work offers an anthropological interpretation of the difficulties faced by Pan-Yucatec Maya individual and collective actors in defending their territorial, linguistic, and political rights. On being a *chan láak'* (little brother) for these activists, the author contends that a body of Indigenous collaborative scholarship can be developed to fight discrimination and disempowerment, as well as to open up fruitful conversations with and for Indigenous rights demands in this context.

We begin the third section, devoted to Australia (see Map 3), with the work by Suzi Hutchings, "Indigenous Anthropologists Caught in the Middle: The Fragmentation of Indigenous Knowledge in Native Title Anthropology, Law, and Policy in Urban and Rural Australia." In this chapter, the author discusses three issues related to native title from the position of an Indigenous anthropologist: the imposition of the burden of proof in native title for Aboriginal communities who have historically suffered removals from land and tradition as a result of colonization; how native title has become an illusory means to reempower disenfranchised urban and regional Aboriginal communities by providing a conduit to reinstate and redefine cultural tradition; and the invidious position of Indigenous anthropologists who work on native title claims involving rural and urban Aboriginal communities.

We continue our reflections on Australia with Sarah Holcombe's chapter, "Eclipsing Rights: Property Rights as Indigenous Human Rights in Australia." In this chapter the author takes as a point of departure the 1971 Justice Blackburn decision that culminated in the Aboriginal Land Rights Act to analyze the consequences of anthropological involvement in land struggles. She argues that anthropologists were strong advocates for the recognition of Indigenous property rights and were instrumental in developing the categories of law that now define Indigenous Australian land tenure in these legally discursive contexts. Since 1992, with the recognition of native title following the Mabo decision, even more anthropologists are involved in writing claims for recognition of native title or assisting with heritage clearances to facilitate land-use agreements. The comfort of this historical fit, however, has since been called into question, principally from within the discipline. An outcome of this abiding disciplinary focus on land rights is the eclipsing of other aspects of Indigenous human rights. The chapter analyzes how this focus on such a narrow form of cultural rights has uncoupled the anthropological project from the broader set of human rights concerns, and while this has created a legacy that is difficult to shift, it is also reflective of the broader Australian political milieu.

We conclude our book with the epilogue, written by Canadian anthropologist Brian Noble, our editorial partner, who was also one of the organizers of the panel that gave rise to this book. Based on his own experience as an activist anthropologist, he reflects on both the cross-cutting and the locally divergent praxes and conditions of the multiple colonialisms and the emergent counter-practices and antidotes posed by the authors gathered in this book. Drawing these together, he then suggests how the linked concerns and practices operate on two registers of decolonial action and alliance: one addressed to the disruptive promise of resurgent relations between Indigenous and non-Indigenous experts in their collaborations; the second addressed to the potential interruptive remaking and decolonizing of interpolitical relations between Indigenous peoples and the states in which their struggles have so vexingly played out up to the present. In this, he points to some of the parameters for alternative and plural praxes in modes of anthropological engagement discernible in this three-country consideration of the conditions of possibility for Indigenous practices of freedom.

Notes

1. See "Participate and Advocate," America Anthropological Association, accessed September 13, 2018, http://www.americananthro.org/ParticipateAndAdvocate/CommitteeDetail.aspx?ItemNumber=2227.
2. The Declaration of Barbados can be found at "Primera Declaración de Barbados: Por la Liberación del Indígena," Servindi, accessed September 13, 2018, http://servindi.org/pdf/Dec_Barbados_1.pdf.
3. Abya Yala means "land in its full maturity" or "land of vital blood" in the Kuna language and is the name used to refer to the American continent since before the arrival of Columbus. The continental Indigenous movement has decided to appropriate this term to refer to the Americas instead of the colonial terms of North America and Latin America.
4. There is an extensive bibliography written by Indigenous women intellectuals discussing their conceptions of gender justice and criticizing Western feminism (Summit of Indigenous Women of the Americas 2003; FIMI 2006; Méndez et al. 2013; Sánchez Néstor 2005). An analysis of these perspectives can be found in Hernández Castillo (2016).
5. The concept of communality was theorized at the end of the 1980s by the Ayuuk intellectual Floriberto Díaz (2007) to refer to the importance of internalized communal values and of how these values were converted into internalized cultural structures or habitus, which prioritized the "common good." The values of collective solidarity, respect for Mother Earth, and promotion and defense of communitarian democracy were promoted by Floriberto Díaz in diverse spaces of political struggle, from the community level to the level of national and international forums. While Floriberto Díaz did not theorize in his writings about the specific rights of Indigenous women, his proposals have been taken up by a new generation

of Indigenous feminists who theorize about gender justice from a communitarian perspective (Méndez Torres 2013; Vargas Vásquez 2012; Vázquez García 2012, 2015; Osorio Hernández 2015; Robles 2015).
6. For indigenous critical and plural thinking, see, for example, Comunidad de estudios mayas (Maya studies community), last updated July 19, 2016, http://commaya2012.blogspot.mx/. For feeling-thinking (*senti-pensar*) indigenous theory, see Comunidad de historia mapuche (Mapuche history community), accessed September 13, 2018, https://www.comunidadhistoriamapuche.cl/quienes-somos/.
7. Among the exceptions are the comparative studies between Mexico and Canada by Isabel Altamirano-Jiménez (2013) and Cristina Oehmichen Bazan (2005), and between Mexico and Australia by Barry Carr and John Minns (2014) and Gabriela Coronado Suzán (2007).
8. For example, in 1990 the federal Labor government, under Prime Minister Bob Hawke, established the Aboriginal and Torres Strait Islander Commission (ATSIC). This body, while always subject to government oversight, nevertheless consisted of elected Indigenous representatives whose goal was to overview government initiatives for Indigenous Australians by commentary and recommendations. ATSIC was dissolved under the federal Liberal government under Prime Minister John Howard in 2005.
9. Aboriginal Australians had many early encounters with traders, explorers, sealers, and whalers from Indonesia, Europe, and the Americas before a sustained period of British occupation of the country. For example, the French made landfall and named the town of Esperance in Western Australia in 1792, and this region had been consistently visited by American and French whalers and sealers since the early 1800s; Aboriginal people living in tropical Arnhem Land in northern Australia have traded with Makassan trepangers from Indonesia from the early 1700s (McIntosh 2000).
10. For instance, the South Australian state government enacted the Anangu Pitjantjatjara Yankunytjatjara Land Rights Act in 1981. The New South Wales government introduced the Aboriginal Land Rights Act for that state in 1983.
11. The first use of this term has been attributed to historian Peter Read in 1981 (Read 2006; Thomas 2010). It has now become synonymous with all those Aboriginal people who were removed from their communities and families as a result of government assimilation policies, as well as those people in succeeding generations who suffer intergenerational trauma because members of their families had been removed.
12. Kent McNeil (2018) discusses how by no means can Canada's sovereignty be construed as legitimate unless it first acknowledges it is conferred by the acts of treaty making with Indigenous peoples, who have been acknowledged as sovereign peoples prior to colonial settlement in decisions of the Supreme Court of Canada.
13. In the so-called Laws of Indians (Leyes de Indios), book 5 legislates several aspects of public law, jurisdiction, functions, competency, and attributions of mayors, chief magistrates (*corregidores*), and other Indigenous lower civil servants.

References

African Commission on Human and Peoples' Rights (ACHPR). 2006. *Indigenous Peoples in Africa: The Forgotten Peoples?* Copenhagen: IWGIA.

Altamirano-Jiménez, Isabel. 2013. *Indigenous Encounters with Neoliberalism: Place, Women, and the Environment in Canada and Mexico*. Vancouver: UBC Press.

Andersen, Chris. 2014. *"Métis": Race, Recognition, and the Struggle for Indigenous Peoplehood*. Vancouver: UBC Press.

Archer, Keith. 2003. "Representing Aboriginal Interest: Experience of New Zealand and Australia." *Electoral Insight* 5 (3): 39–55.

Ardill, Allan. 2014. "Australian Sovereignty, Indigenous Standpoint Theory and Feminist Standpoint Theory: First Peoples' Sovereignties Matter." *Griffith Law Review* 22 (2): 315–43.

Asch, Michael. 2014. *On Being Here to Stay: Treaties and Aboriginal Rights in Canada*. Toronto: University of Toronto Press.

Assies, Willem, Gemma van der Haar, and André J. Hoekema, eds. 2000. *The Challenge of Diversity: Indigenous Peoples and Reform of the State in Latin America*. Amsterdam: Thela Thesis.

Bainbridge, R. 2016. "Mapping the Journey of an Aboriginal Research Academic: An Autoethnographic Study." *International Journal of Critical Indigenous Studies* 9 (2): 1–10.

Bates, Daisy. (1938) 1966. *The Passing of the Aborigines: A Lifetime Spent Among the Natives of Australia*. London: John Murray.

Bell, Diane. 1993. *Daughters of the Dreaming*. Minneapolis: University of Minnesota Press.

Berndt, Ronald M. 1959. "The Concept of 'The Tribe' in the Western Desert of Australia." *Oceania* 3 (2): 81–107.

Berndt, Ronald Murray, and Catherine Helen Berndt. 1993. *A World that Was: The Yaraldi of the Murray River and the Lakes, South Australia*. With John E. Stanton. Vancouver: UBC Press.

Brown, Wendy, and Janet Halley, eds. 2002. *Left Legalism/Left Critique*. Durham, NC: Duke University Press.

Brysk, Alison. 2000. *From Tribal Village to Global Village: Indian Rights and International Relations in Latin America*. Stanford, CA: Stanford University Press.

Cardoso de Oliveira, Roberto. 1998. *O trabalho do antropólogo*. São Paulo: UNESP.

Carr, Barry, and John Minns. 2014. *Australia and Latin America Challenges and Opportunities in the New Millennium*. Canberra: ANU Press.

Chakrabarty, Dipesh. 2000. *Provincializing Europe*. Princeton, NJ: Princeton University Press.

Cook, Curtis, and Juan David Lindau. 2000. *Aboriginal Rights and Self-Government: The Canadian and Mexican Experience in North American Perspective*. McGill-Queen's University Press.

Coronado Suzán, Gabriela. 2007. "Fuzzy Identities for an Inclusive Anglohispanic Dialogue." *World Futures* 63 (3–4): 237–49.

Coulthard, Glen Sean. 2014. *Red Skin, White Masks: Rejecting the Colonial Politics of Recognition*. Minneapolis: University of Minnesota Press.

de Sousa Santos, Boaventura. 2002. *Toward a New Legal Common Sense*. 2nd ed. London: Butterworths LexisNexis.

Díaz, Floriberto. 2007. *Comunalidad, energía viva del pensamiento*. Mexico City: UNAM.

Fermantez, Kali. 2013. "Rocking the Boat: Indigenous Geography at Home in Hawai'i." In *A Deeper Sense of Place: Stories and Journeys of Indigenous-Academic Collaboration*, edited by Jay T. Johnson and Soren C. Larsen, 103–24. Corvallis: Oregon State University Press.

Foro Internacional de Mujeres Indígenas (FIMI). 2006. *Mairin Iwanka Raya: Indigenous Women Stand Against Violence*. A Companion Report to the United Nations Secretary-General's Study on Violence Against Women. New York: International Indigenous Women's Forum.

García Leyva, Jaime. 2012. "Oralidad, historia y educación de Na Savi." In *De la oralidad a la palabra escrita: Estudios sobre el rescate de las voces originarias en el sur de México*, edited by Floriberto González González, Humberto Santos Bautista, Jaime García Leyva, Fernando Mena Angelito, and David Cienfuegos Salgado, 115–38. Chilpancingo: El Colegio de Guerrero.

Green, Joyce A., ed. 2007. *Making Space for Indigenous Feminism*. London: Zed Books.

Hernández Castillo, Rosalva Aída. 2016. *Multiple Injustices: Indigenous Women, Law, and Political Struggle in Latin America*. Tucson: University of Arizona Press.

Hernández Castillo, Rosalva Aída, and Andrew Canessa, eds. 2012. *Género, complementariedades y exclusiones en Mesoamérica y los Andes*. Quito, Ecuador: Abya Yala Press and IWGIA.

Hutchings, Suzi, and Anne Morrison, eds. 2017. *Indigenous Knowledges Proceedings of the Water Sustainability and Wild Fire Mitigation Symposia 2012 and 2013*. Underdale: University of South Australia.

Irabinna-Rigney, Lester. 2017. "Indigenist Research and Aboriginal Australia." In *Indigenous Peoples' Wisdom and Power*, edited by Julian E. Kunnie and Nomalungelo I. Goduka, chap. 3. London: Routledge.

Itzamná, Ollantay. 2016. "¿Es posible descolonizar la academia?" *América Latina en movimiento*, October 4, 2016. https://www.alainet.org/es/articulo/180701.

Jenkin, Graham. 1979. *Conquest of the Ngarrindjeri*. Adelaide: Rigby.

Jimeno Santoyo, Myriam. 2011. "El lugar de la diferencia cultural: Cambios en la definición de nación." *Innovación y ciencia* 18 (4): 36–43.

Johnson, Jay T., and Soren C. Larsen. 2013. *A Deeper Sense of Place: Stories and Journeys of Indigenous-Academic Collaboration*. Corvallis: Oregon State University Press.

Laher, Ridwan, and Korir Sing'Oei. 2014. *Indigenous Peoples in Africa: Contestations, Empowerment and Group Rights*. Pretoria: Institute for Global Dialogue.

Leyva, Xochitl, Shannon Speed, and Araceli Burguete, eds. 2008. *Gobernar (en) la diversidad: Experiencias indígenas desde América Latina—Hacia la investigación de co-labor*. Mexico City: CIESAS.

López Itzin, Juan. 2013. "Ich'el ta muk': la trama en la construcción del Lekil kuxlejal (vida plena-digna-justa)." In *Senti-pensar el género: Perspectivas desde los pueblos origi-*

narios, edited by Georgina Méndez Torres, Juan López Itzín, Sylvia Marcos, and Carmen Osorio Hernández, 73–107. Mexico City: Red de Feminismos Descoloniales.

Martin, Karen, and Booran Mirraboopa. 2003. "Ways of Knowing, Being and Doing: A Theoretical Framework and Methods for Indigenous and Indigenist Re-search." *Journal of Australian Studies* 27 (76): 203–14.

McIntosh, Ian S. 2000. *Aboriginal Reconciliation and the Dreaming*. Boston: Allyn and Bacon.

McNeil, Kent. 2018. "Indigenous and Crown Sovereignty in Canada." In *Resurgence and Reconciliation: Indigenous-Settler Relations and Earth Teachings*, edited by Michael Asch, John Borrows, and James Tully, 293–314. Toronto: University of Toronto Press.

Meggitt, Mervyn J. 1962. *Desert People: A Study of the Walbiri Aborigines of Central Australia*. Sydney: Angus and Robertson.

Méndez Torres, Georgina. 2013. "Mujeres Mayas-Kichwas en la apuesta por la descolonización de los pensamientos y corazones." In *Senti-pensar el género: Perspectivas desde los pueblos originarios*, edited by Georgina Méndez Torres, Juan López Itzín, Sylvia Marcos, and Carmen Osorio Hernández, 27–63. Mexico City: Red de Feminismos Descoloniales.

Méndez Torres, Georgina, Juan López Itzín, Sylvia Marcos, and Carmen Osorio Hernández, eds. 2013. *Senti-pensar el género: Perspectivas desde los pueblos originarios*. Mexico City: Red de Feminismos Descoloniales.

Mora, Mariana. 2018. *Kuxlejal Politics: Indigenous Autonomy, Race, and Decolonizing Research in Zapatista Communities*. Austin: University of Texas Press.

Moreton-Robinson, Aileen. 2004. "Whiteness, Epistemology and Indigenous Representation." In *Whitening Race: Essays in Social and Cultural Criticism*. Edited by Aileen Moreton-Robinson, 75–88. Canberra: Australian Studies Press.

Moreton-Robinson, Aileen. 2015. *The White Possessive: Property, Power, and Indigenous Sovereignty*. Minneapolis: University of Minnesota Press.

Moreton-Robinson, Aileen, ed. 2016. *Critical Indigenous Studies: Engagements in First World Locations*. Tucson: University of Arizona Press.

Munn, Nancy D. 1970. "The Transformation of Subjects into Objects in Walbiri and Pitjantjatjara Myth." In *Australian Aboriginal Anthropology: Modern Studies in the Social Anthropology of the Australian Aborigines*, edited by Ronald M. Berndt, 141–63. Nedlands: University of Western Australia Press.

Myers, Fred R. 1986. *Pintupi Country, Pintupi Self: Sentiment, Place, and Politics Among Western Desert Aborigines*. Canberra: Australian Institute of Aboriginal Studies.

Nakata, Martin. 2007. "The Cultural Interface." Supplement, *Australian Journal of Indigenous Education* 36:7–14.

Niezen, Ronald. 2003. *The Origins of Indigenism: Human Rights and the Politics of Identity*. Berkeley: University of California Press.

Oehmichen Bazan, Cristina. 2005. "Report of the Project 'Ethnic and Gender Relationship in Mexico and Canada.'" Latin American and Caribbean Studies, International Council for Canadian Studies, Ottawa.

Osorio Hernández, Carmen. 2015. "Obra y pensamiento de las mujeres Ñuu Savi en su proceso organizativo: Una expresión de la comunalidad." Paper presented at Primer

Congreso Internacional de Comunalidad Luchas y estrategias comunitarias: Horizontes más allá del capital, Puebla, Mexico, October 26–29.

Peterson Nicolas, and Marcia Langton, eds. 1983. *Aborigines, Land and Land Rights.* Canberra: Australian Institute of Aboriginal Studies.

Quidel Lincoleo, José. 2015. "Del por qué y cómo fueron violentados y sobrepasados los mapuche en su pensamiento y espiritualidad." In *Violencias coloniales en el Wajmapu,* edited by Enrique Antileo Baeza, Luis E. Cárcamo-Huechante, Margarita Calfío Montalva, and Herson Huinca-Piutrin, 21–57. Temuco: Ediciones Comunidad de Historia Mapuche.

Read, Peter. 2006. *The Stolen Generations: The Removal of Aboriginal Children in New South Wales, 1883 to 1969.* Surry Hills: New South Wales Department of Aboriginal Affairs.

Rivera Cusicanqui, Silvia. 2010. *Ch'ixinakax utxiwa: Una reflexión sobre prácticas y discursos descolonizadores.* Buenos Aires: Tinta Limón.

Robles, Sofía. 2015. "Semblanza sobre la vida y obra de Floriberto Díaz: Sus aportes a la comprensión de la comunalidad." Paper presented in Primer Congreso Internacional de Comunalidad Luchas y estrategias comunitarias: Horizontes más allá del capital, Puebla, Mexico, October 26–29.

Roseberry, William. 1994. "Hegemony and the Language of Contention." In *Every Day Forms of State Formation: Revolution and the Negotiation of Rule in Modern Mexico,* edited by Gilbert M. Joseph and Daniel Nugent, 355–66. Durham, NC: Duke University Press.

Sánchez Néstor, Martha, ed. 2005. *La doble mirada: Voces e historias de mujeres indígenas latinoamericanas.* Mexico City: UNIFEM/ILSB.

Scholtz, Christa. 2006. *Negotiating Claims: The Emergence of Indigenous Land Claim Negotiation Policies in Australia, Canada, New Zealand, and the United States.* London: Routledge.

Sieder, Rachel, ed. 2017. *Demanding Justice and Security: Indigenous Women and Legal Pluralities in Latin America.* Newark, NJ: Rutgers University Press.

Simpson, Audra. 2010. "Under the Sign of Sovereignty: Certainty, Ambivalence and Law in Native North America and Indigenous Australia." *Wicazo Sa Review* 25 (2): 107–24.

Simpson, Audra. 2014. *Mohawk Interruptus: Political Life Across the Borders of Settler States.* Durham, NC: Duke University Press.

Simpson, Audra. 2017. "The Ruse of Consent and the Anatomy of 'Refusal': Cases from Indigenous North America and Australia." *Postcolonial Studies* 20:1–16.

Slaughter, Sheila, and Larry L. Leslie. 1999. *Academic Capitalism: Politics, Policies, and the Entrepreneurial University.* Baltimore: Johns Hopkins University Press.

Smith, Linda Tuhiwai. 2012. *Decolonizing Methodologies: Research and Indigenous Peoples.* 2nd ed. London: Zed Books.

Summit of Indigenous Women of the Americas. 2003. *Memoria de la Primera Cumbre de Mujeres Indígenas de América.* Mexico City: Rigoberta Menchú Tum Foundation.

Thomas, Andrina Komala Lini. 2013. "The Process that Led Me to Become an Indigenous Researcher." In *Indigenous Pathways into Social Research: Voices of a New Genera-*

tion, edited by Donna M. Mertens, Fiona Cram, and Bagele Chilisa, 41–58. Walnut Creek, CA: Left Coast Press.

Thomas, Tony. 2010. "Peter Read Invents the 'Stolen Generations.'" *Quadrant Online*, May 12, 2010. https://quadrant.org.au/opinion/history-wars/2010/05/peter-read-invents-the-stolen-generations/.

Tilley, Virginia. 2002. "New Help or New Hegemony? The Transnational Indigenous Peoples' Movement and 'Being Indian' in El Salvador." *Journal of Latin American Studies* 34 (3): 525–54.

Tur, Simone Ulalka, Faye Rosas Blanch, and Christopher Wilson. 2010. "Developing a Collaborative Approach to Standpoint in Indigenous Australian Research." In "Indigenous Studies, Indigenous Knowledge: Dialogue or Conflict in the Academy?" Supplement, *Australian Journal of Indigenous Education* 39S:58–67.

Vargas Vásquez, Liliana Vianey. 2011. *Las mujeres de Tlahuitoltepec Mixe, Oaxaca, frente a la impartición de la justicia local y el uso del derecho internacional (2000–2008)*. Mexico City: Instituto Nacional de las Mujeres.

Vargas Vásquez, Liliana Vianey. 2012. "Las mujeres de Tlahuitoltepec Mixe: Frente a la impartición de la justicia local y el uso del derecho internacional (2000–2008)." In *Género, complementariedades y exclusiones en Mesoamérica y los Andes*, edited by R. Aída Hernández Castillo and Andrew Canessa, 302–18. Quito, Ecuador: Abya Yala Press and IWGIA.

Vásquez García, Carolina María. 2012. "Miradas de las mujeres ayuujk: Nuestra experiencia de vida comunitaria en la construcción del género." In *Género, complementariedades y exclusiones en Mesoamérica y los Andes*, edited by R. Aída Hernández Castillo and Andrew Canessa, 331–46. Quito, Ecuador: Abya Yala Press and IWGIA.

Vásquez García, Carolina María. 2015. "Los espacios comunitarios en las experiencias de las mujeres Ayuujk." Paper presented at Primer Congreso Internacional de Comunalidad Luchas y estrategias comunitarias: Horizontes más allá del capital, Puebla, Mexico, October 26–29.

Venne, Sharon. 2017. "How Governments Manufacture Consent and Use It Against Indigenous Peoples." In *Indigenous Peoples as Subjects of International Law*, edited by Irene Watson, 141–70. London: Routledge.

Watson, Irene. 2015. *Aboriginal Peoples, Colonialism and International Law: Raw Law*. London: Routledge.

Watson, Irene, ed. 2017. *Indigenous Peoples as Subjects of International Law*. London: Routledge.

PART I
CANADA

ONE

What Is Decolonization?

Mi'kmaw Ancestral Relational Understandings and
Anthropological Perspectives on Treaty Relations

SHERRY M. PICTOU

As an Indigenous activist and an interdisciplinary doctoral student returning to university in 2012, I initially grappled with situating my experience in the academy. Since graduating with a master of arts, I had more than fifteen years of experience working for several Indigenous organizations, including my own Mi'kmaw community, L'sitkuk (meaning "water cutting through high rocks"), in a struggle for food and livelihood in fisheries and through other natural resources.[1] This struggle was marked by a Supreme Court of Canada decision in 1999, known as the Marshall decision, upholding a Mi'kmaw treaty right to a moderate livelihood in the fishery based on the 1760 and 1761 Peace and Friendship Treaties (*R. v. Marshall* [1999] 3 SCR 456 [No. 1] and *R. v. Marshall* [1999] 3 SCR 533 [No. 2]). The Marshall decision refers to the court case of the late Donald Marshall Jr., a Mi'kmaw from the Membertou community in Unama'ki (Land of the Fog), or Cape Breton, for fishing and selling eels without a license. The federal government responded with communal commercial fishing agreements based on Canada's mainstream commercial fishery. These agreements set the parameters for the only way Mi'kmaw communities in Nova Scotia could enter the commercial fishery. In other words, what a treaty right to a livelihood could mean or how it could be perceived from a Mi'kmaw viewpoint was preempted by the existing regulatory regime. Therefore, L'sitkuk, (along with Paq'tnkek, meaning "by the bay," and for a long time Sipekne'katik, meaning "area of wild potato or turnip") rejected these fishing agreements. L'sitkuk has instead continued striving to determine what and how a livelihood fishery (and other natural resource livelihoods) can be realized for the community as a treaty right (Pictou 2017; Stiegman and Pictou 2007, 2010, 2016a; also see Prosper et al. 2011).

For almost two decades, much political and economic attention has been given to the communities that have entered the commercial fishery through these agreements with the Department Fisheries and Oceans (DFO). Meanwhile the Mi'kmaq chiefs entered "treaty" negotiations with the federal and Nova Scotia provincial governments in what is known as the Made-in-Nova Scotia Process. But what about those who did not enter the commercial fishery this way, and why have they not? And if they are struggling to realize a livelihood fishery, how are they going about it? As an Indigenous researcher/activist participating in this process, I set out to answer these questions through my doctoral research by centering the learning experiences of L'sitkuk and our local and international allies in their pursuit of livelihood as a treaty right. But the question remained: If I was finding it difficult to situate my experience with L'sitkuk and our allies in the academy, how was I going to undertake research that proposed to do the same?

This chapter in part represents an autoethnographic research journey to address these questions and is based on a revised, condensed version of some central arguments I present in my doctoral thesis, "Decolonizing Mi'kmaw Memory of Treaty: L'sitkuk's Learning with Allies in Struggle for Food and Lifeways" (Pictou 2017). To inform decolonizing approaches to research, I begin by discussing how, from an Indigenous perspective, neoliberalism and capitalism are interrelated processes that form an extension of colonialism. To illustrate this point, I situate L'sitkuk's struggle within the political context of the Marshall decision, followed by my own position as an Indigenous activist/researcher aiming to center our experience within the academy. Then I explore the concept of allied theories as a way to frame the potential of Indigenous/Mi'kmaw relational worldviews alongside emerging anthropological perspectives on treaty making and obligations to work against extensions and new forms of colonialism. This is followed by a brief discussion (based on my doctoral research) about how centering the voices of L'sitkuk and allies in their pursuit of livelihoods in the fishery and through other natural resources constitutes a broader concept of treaty relations beyond formal political frameworks. In conclusion, I discuss how this broader concept is more aligned with Indigenous and anthropological understandings of treaties as renewing relations and responsibilities for ensuring reciprocal obligations among all people living in the northern part of Turtle Island (known today as Canada).

Why Indigenous Peoples Struggle for Decolonization Against Neoliberal Colonial Capitalism

One of the greatest challenges to understanding decolonization and decolonizing approaches to research and activist work is the misconception that colonialism, neoliberalism, and capitalism operate in isolation from one another and from state governments (Alfred and Corntassel 2005; Mack 2011; Stengers and Pignarre 2011). Further, colonialism is predominantly understood in the context of historical modes of settler colonialism—of expanding territories and exerting power over Indigenous peoples—and capitalism as the accumulation of capital and wealth by dispossessing others from wealth or land and by exploiting labor in a free market system. Neoliberalism initially referred to state social policy interventions intended to provide societal well-being, through better wages, healthcare, and education, in response to the global financial crisis of the Great Depression in the 1930s. Since the 1970s and 1980s, however, neoliberalism has increasingly promoted market deregulation and divestment in social programs in response to underemployment and inflation caused by the overaccumulation of capital in advanced capitalist countries. Yet, rich countries continue to tout economic development as contributing to social well-being. This dominant narrative drives ongoing economic restructuring on a global scale—globalization—in efforts to regain profitability in the market system.

Neoliberalism is further complicated in how the concept plays out in decolonization because of the postcolonial view that "developing" countries acquire independent statehood by becoming "developed." Defining statehood in this way distorts how neoliberalism, colonialism, and capitalism are interrelated and continue to influence globalization, not only internationally but domestically as well (Altamirano-Jiménez 2013; Gordon 2010; Tuck and Yang 2012). Boaventura de Sousa Santos (2009, 228) writes, "Knowing to what extent we live in postcolonial societies is problematical. Moreover, the constitutive nature of colonialism in western modernity underscores its importance for understanding not only the nonwestern societies that were victimized by colonialism, but also the western societies themselves, especially as regards to the patterns of social discrimination that prevail inside them." How is it possible, then, for marginalized peoples within "developed" countries to strategize for social justice (locally and globally) when those very countries are driving globalization and the marginalization of other countries? Harvey (2005, 2) defines neoliberalism as an "institutional framework characterized by strong private property rights, free markets, and free trade." Property rights enable the privatization of natural resources and the separation of commodity from social relations (Atamirano-Jiménez 2013; Bargh 2007; Choudry 2015; Gordon 2010; Mackey 2016; Schmidt 2018; Tuck and McKenzie 2015).

Domestically, natural resource privatization has become the hallmark of formal state-Indigenous negotiations and what Glen Sean Coulthard (2014) argues is an ongoing process of dispossession of Indigenous peoples' ancestral lands and their land and water practices for securing food and sustaining lifeways. Indigenous contestations against tar sands, oil and gas pipelines, mega dams, and fracking in recent years demonstrate just how intensive the neoliberal processes of dispossession have become (Choudry 2015; Coulthard 2014; Lindroth 2014; MacDonald 2011; Mackey 2016; Preston 2013). In this context, it is impossible for Indigenous peoples living in Turtle Island (North America) to separate neoliberal practices from those of colonialism and capitalism because they are all interrelated and have transcended generations of Indigenous peoples and their struggles—for Indigenous (and human) rights, including treaty rights, and against what I term *neoliberal colonial capitalism*.

Indigenous scholars and anthropologists among others also have analyzed how Aboriginal and treaty rights are driven by economic agendas and how this raises issues about what constitutes sovereignty, self-government, and self-determination (Alfred 2009; Altamirano-Jiménez 2013; Asch 2014; Blaser, Fiet, and McRae 2004; Deloria and Wildcat 2001; Gordon 2010; Hale 2006; Noble 2007, 2008; Tully 2009). Wotherspoon and Hansen (2013, 23) further point out, "There is extensive evidence to demonstrate that these [economic] benefits have not been experienced or shared equitably with Indigenous people and their communities." This is why Taiaiake Alfred (2009, 44) argues that little "empirical evidence" supports the claim that increased wealth and economic development contribute to the well-being of Indigenous people.

Indeed, comparing the findings in the *Report of the Special Rapporteur on the Rights of Indigenous Peoples: The Situation in Canada* (Anaya 2014) with those of

People to People, Nation to Nation: Highlights from the Report of the Commission on Aboriginal Peoples, released eighteen years earlier (RCAP 1996), reveals that the well-being of Indigenous peoples and their communities is in constant decline, which is further marked by the disproportionate number of missing and murdered Indigenous women (Amnesty International 2014) and high rates of suicide epidemics among Indigenous youth (Puxley 2016; Picard 2016). Yet, while these reports, along with the recent *Truth and Reconciliation Commission of Canada: Calls to Action* (TRC 2015), have highlighted the impact of residential schools, colonialism, and abject poverty, they continue to tout neoliberal economic development frameworks for political and economic equality as a way to improve well-being.[2]

Further, even though the central principle of "free, prior and informed consent" underlying the *United Nations Declaration on the Rights of Indigenous Peoples* (*UNDRIP*; United Nations General Assembly 2008, 6) has the potential to disrupt current treaty and other negotiations, as with treaties, the question of how *UNDRIP* will be implemented remains unresolved. Canada's recent introduction of a new legislative framework on Indigenous rights indicates that *UNDRIP* will remain subject to state interpretations of the law. On a closer examination, Indigenous policy analyst Russell Diabo (2018, 31) argues that this new framework is being imposed without the consent of Indigenous peoples and concludes that the "Trudeau government is developing a 'Canadian Definition' of UNDRIP to recolonize Indigenous Peoples with racist, colonial laws and termination policies." Jeremy J. Schmidt (2018, 902), in his analyses of the First Nations Property Ownership Initiative, describes this practice of recolonizing by reinterpreting as a "transliteration into a series of regulatory gaps" consistent with Western legal perspectives on land as property for commodification.

These contradictions present challenges for seeking decolonization within the process that instituted colonialism to begin with (Bargh 2007; Connell 2007; Coulthard 2014; Mackey 2016; Schmidt 2018; Tuck and McKenzie 2015; Tuck and Yang 2012). Within Canada this becomes particularly complex because treaty agreements initially made with the British Crown are now constitutionally the responsibility of the federal government. In light of this, how do we strategize for decolonization while our treaty rights are contingent on agreements with our "colonizers," so to speak? To illustrate the complexity of this issue, next I situate L'sitkuk's story within the political context of the Marshall decision and the Made-in-Nova Scotia Process.

L'sɨtkuk, the Marshall Decision, and the Made-in-Nova Scotia Process

L'sɨtkuk is situated in my ancestral homelands, broad hunting and fishing ecosystems in Kespukwitk (meaning "end of the flow"), a region geographically similar to what is now known as southwest Nova Scotia. Our community today is referred to as Bear River First Nation (BRFN), representing only a fraction of our ancestral homelands. Nearby, Fort Anne (British succession in the early 1700s) and Port Royal (the place of contact with Samuel de Champlain in 1605) heritage sites are historic reminders of the longest history with colonialism in the northeastern part of Turtle Island, known today as Nova Scotia.

Traditionally Mi'kmaw food and lifeway practices were inherently guided by an understanding and performance of reciprocal relations among humans and with the natural worlds in which they lived: "Personal and reciprocal relationships extended to the animals and other objects considered inanimate in Western world view, such as rocks, mountains, certain stages of the production of wood products, winds, weather, and so forth" (Sable and Francis 2012, 24). The lifeways of the Mi'kmaq, and other Indigenous peoples across northern Turtle Island, were severely disrupted by the imposition of horrendous and contradictory colonial, provincial, and federal policies, including formal education systems (including day schools on the reserve, residential schools, and public schools); control of reserve life by colonial governments and later by the Indian Act enacted in 1876; and more recently, as Indigenous scholars argue, treaty and land claim negotiations and consultations (Alfred 1999, 2009; Coulthard 2014; Corntassel 2012; Diabo 2012). Such policies resulted in land dispossession, denial of political and economic rights, and the criminalization of those speaking Indigenous languages and practicing ceremonies. Most severely affected were (and continue to be) Indigenous women, children, and two-spirit people (Indigenous people who identify as a third gender or gay, lesbian, bisexual, transgender, or queer) as these legislative polices were institutionalized within Western heteropatriarchy coupled with racism (Driskill 2010; Coulthard 2014; Monture-Angus 1995; Pictou 1996; also see Belcourt 2016). Therefore, it is a tragic irony that Indigenous people would have to turn to the very legal system that all but destroyed them as a people in their struggle for Aboriginal and treaty rights.

For the Mi'kmaq, treaty rights are founded on the chain of five Peace and Friendship Treaties negotiated between the Mi'kmaq and the British Empire throughout the eighteenth century, before confederation (Grand Council, UNSI, and NCNS 1987; Metallic and Cavanaugh 2002; Reid 2012; Wicken 2002, 2012). The intergenerational experience with settler colonialism, including treaty obligations being outright ignored by colonial, provincial and federal governments, informed the Mi'kmaw conception of treaties as rights and the bases for Mi'kmaw legal agency in Canada's judicial system (Wicken 2002, 2012). Thus when the Supreme Court of Canada upheld a treaty right to fish for livelihood in the Marshall case, there was a sense of vindication after generations of resistance against colonial oppression throughout Mi'kmaki (ancestral homelands). Any sense of justice, however, became quickly overshadowed by a public backlash (including from government and industry), unveiling deeply rooted, colonial racism and corporate greed (Borrows 2016; Pictou and Bull 2009; Stiegman and Pictou 2010, 2016a).

Immediately following Marshall, violent clashes took place between DFO officers and Mi'kmaw harvesters, and between Mi'kmaw harvesters and commercial fishermen throughout Mi'kmaki. Racist media coverage further fueled public antagonism and disagreement with the Marshall decision. Within two short months, the Supreme Court justices qualified their own unprecedented decision by clarifying the treaty right to fish as a "communal" treaty right to "participate in the large regulated commercial fishery" (as a means of conservation) for a moderate livelihood, not to "accumulate wealth" (Wicken 2002, 232). Undoubtedly the "Supreme Court's recontextualization of Mi'kmaq rights largely favored non-Mi'kmaq interests and changed the balance of power following the decision" (Borrows 2016, 81).

The federal government responded with communal commercial fishing agreements based on the Aboriginal food strategy agreements that had been contrived in response to an earlier Supreme Court decision upholding the right to fish for food—the 1990 Sparrow case (see *Acadia First Nation v. Canada (Attorney General)*, 2013 NSSC 284; *R. v. Sparrow* [1990] 1 SCR 1075). This time, however, the commercial agreements involved much more money, and therefore the government quickly appointed envoys to negotiate individual communal commercial fishing agreements on a community-by-community basis (Stiegman and Pictou 2010). Given the socioeconomic challenges faced by many Indigenous communities, most in Atlantic Canada signed on to what were supposed to be interim fishing agreements, while in Nova Scotia, the chiefs and the federal and provincial governments entered the Made-In-Nova Scotia Process to negotiate how to implement a treaty right to fish for livelihood.

Yet, only after the Assembly of Nova Scotia Mi'kmaq Chiefs initiated a court application in 2013 in the Nova Scotia Supreme Court, challenging the government's failure to implement a treaty-based fishery, did the federal government finally obtain a "mandate" to negotiate treaty rights to a livelihood fishery (Mi'kmaq Rights Initiative 2013; *Acadia First Nation v. Canada (Attorney General)*, 2013 NSSC 284). There is still no definitive process for implementing treaty rights. In the meantime, communal commercial fishing agreements based on a corporation-driven fishery have become the only way for Mi'kmaw communities in Nova Scotia to enter the commercial fishery. As L'sitkuk learned from other commercial fishers, the fishery industry was already undergoing corporate privatization, resulting in a concentration of the industry in the hands of a few companies (Pictou and Bull 2009; Stiegman and Pictou 2010, 2016a; Wiber et al. 2010). In this sense, these agreements go against the legal notion of not accumulating wealth as a treaty right. For example, the imposition in the early 1990s of the individual transferable quota (ITQ) policy, through which companies could accumulate and stack licensed quotas, made it difficult for independent fishers to compete. Even though the ITQ system contravened the federal government's own fleet separation and owner-operator regulations, requiring quotas to be fished by vessel owners, quotas could now be accumulated and shared without having to fish them. Subsequently, independent fishers either transferred their quotas of fish or, if they had no quotas, were driven out of the fishery altogether. In other words, the fish became privatized and corporately owned (Pictou and Bull 2009; Stiegman and Pictou 2010, 2016a; Wiber et al. 2010). Meanwhile, L'sitkuk continues to seek a way to fish for livelihood without compromising our treaties.

The Made-in-Nova Scotia Process and "Modern" Treaty Making

Current treaty negotiations are often confused as processes to produce modern-day treaties because they encompass negotiating new treaties with Indigenous peoples who had never entered a treaty (British Columbia and Northern Canada), as well as negotiating the implementation of historical treaties reaffirmed in Canada's legal system. The treaties with the Mi'kmaq are considered preconfederation historical treaties (Asch 2014; Barsh 2002; Tully 2009; Wicken 2002, 2012). Much debate centers on how the comprehensive land claims (CLC) policy is driving current treaty negotiations (Diabo 2012; McIvor 2014; Pasternak, Collis, and Dafnos 2013). Modern treaties and CLC are financed by loans against any final agreed compensation. The Idle No More (INM) movement (in response to Bill C-45, the Jobs and Growth Act, which eased environmental laws and privatized reserve lands for development) triggered such a debate about the Made-in-Nova Scotia Process in 2013 (Council of Canadians 2013). Though the Mi'kmaq Rights Initiative (the administrative body for the Made-in-Nova Scotia Process) insists that no loans finance the negotiations (Gorman 2013), the question remains if indirect funding already received for related programs (such as fishery programs) will be considered as partial treaty compensation. Further, the CLC process requires "extinguishment" of title to ancestral lands, an old policy now under the guise of "rights and benefits" in settlement agreements—that is, in exchange for rights and benefits, an Indigenous community can make no further claims outside the agreement (Coulthard 2014, 122–23; also see Cameron and Levitan 2014). Therefore, some Mi'kmaw leaders and their communities view any agreement that includes rights and benefits principles to negotiate or implement a treaty (historical or modern) to be in fact terminating our treaty rights. For example, Sipekne'katik (formerly Indian Brook) withdrew from the Made-in-Nova Scotia Process in 2013 and from the Assembly of Nova Scotia Mi'kmaq Chiefs in 2016 to oversee their own negotiations—because the community feared that their treaty rights were being compromised and because the process would not facilitate broader consultation with community members on a natural gas storage project that put at risk a river system used by the community (Gorman 2013; Sipekne'katik 2016). The Millbrook First Nation raised similar concerns on May 18, 2016 (MFN 2016). Indeed, the Made-in-Nova Scotia Process and modern-day treaty negotiations follow a similar process to that of CLC, which progresses through a series of agreements to a "final" agreement. The Nova Scotia Mi'kmaq Chiefs are negotiating with the federal and provincial governments, however, to position the Made-in-Nova Scotia Process outside the CLC/modern-day treaty framework, with the possibility of several time-limited agreements as opposed to one final agreement (Chief Carol Dee Potter, BRFN, pers. comm., May 18, 2016). In the meantime, the policy of requiring legal and economic "certainty," established by the former Conservative government and applying to all negotiations with Indigenous peoples, remains a challenge (Diabo 2012; Mackey 2016; Schertow 2012; Schmidt 2018; also see Lindroth 2014). For example, treaties are directly referenced in *Renewing the Comprehensive Land Claims Policy* as a means to "achieve certainty over unresolved Aboriginal rights claims, in relation to land and resources and other rights addressed in the treaty by negotiating agreements that provide for a respectful reconciliation of the rights of the Aboriginal people with the rights of other Canadians" (AANDC 2014, 11). Further, the Nova Scotia Office of Aboriginal Affairs (NSOAA) *Statement of Mandate* since 2014 references the Made-in-Nova Scotia Process as a "modern treaty" or "modern treaty making process" (NSOAA 2014, 2015). More recently, in a Nova Scotia Provincial Court case involving two Mi'kmaw food harvesters charged for fishing salmon outside their Aboriginal Fishing Strategy agreement, Judge A. Peter Ross references current negotiations as "modern-day agreements" and a "modern-day treaty" throughout his final judgment (*R. v. Martin*, 2016 CanLII 14 [NSPC]). This case clearly sets the pretext of political and legal jurisprudence for confining "rights and benefits" to modern agreements. These political and legal perceptions of the Made-in-Nova Scotia Process are congruent with other modern treaty and land claims processes that require "certainty."

Note that in addition to our treaties, the 1982 Canadian Constitution Act protects Aboriginal title based on precontact usage of the land but through a postcontact legal framework (Borrows 2016; Slattery 2000). In a legal sense, title appears to be a strong precedent to treaty. Yet title can be significantly altered by treaty negotiations through the use of the federal government's *certainty technique*, meaning a "legal model used in a treaty to ensure that any pre-existing Aboriginal rights related to the subject matters addressed in the treaty, such as lands and resources, do not continue, from the effective date forward, to have independent legal effect outside of the terms of the treaty" (Schertow 2012, 2). Thus, despite constitutional protection, Aboriginal title and treaty negotiation and implementation processes demand a certainty of title that equates to the older CLC principle of extinguishment. In other words, the certainty technique incorporates title (and treaty) into neoliberal colonial capitalist processes under the guise of modern treaties while precluding any "alternative socioeconomic visions" (Coulthard 2014, 66; also see Corntassel 2012).

Thus L'sɨtkuk's choice not to sign a food or commercial fishery agreement because there was (and still is) a great mistrust that those initial agreements would prejudice our treaty rights was rooted in fears that proved to be well founded. The unsigned communities in the fishery quickly became economically and politically sidelined by the very political organizations representing them, as the fiscal and policy priorities shifted to engage government-funded programs for incorporating the "signed" communities into the existing commercial fishery.

Indigenous Research/Activism and Allied Theories

Formal negotiations aside, L'sitkuk has managed to maintain a small food lobster fishery despite being intimidated by DFO's constant surveillance as well as by the threat of other fishers sabotaging our traps. L'sitkuk has also managed to reassert a moose-hunting tradition and initiate several learning projects, such as reconnecting to ancestral knowledges and waterways, building relationships and alliances with non-Indigenous fish harvesters, and pursuing advocacy work on the international level through the World Forum of Fisher Peoples (WFFP) (Pictou 2015, 2017; Stiegman and Pictou 2007, 2010, 2016a). This incredible resilience and resurgence of L'sitkuk food and lifeways encouraged me to explore what we have learned and how we view treaties since the Marshall decision.

As an Indigenous researcher/activist from L'sitkuk, I continue to play a small role in some L'sitkuk endeavors as an advisor, an educator, and, until recently, a representative of the WFFP coordinating committee. To tell this story, I use the terms *Mi'kmaw*, *Mi'kmaq*, *Indigenous*, *Indian*, *Aboriginal*, *Native*, and *First Nations* interchangeably, because portrayals of Indigenous peoples have evolved from those of Indian savages in Canadian history books to identities that range from Indigenous to Aboriginal to First Nations (Pictou 1996). *Mi'kmaq* marks my experience at home, and the term *Indigenous* adheres to a broader international political agency in asserting Indigenous worldviews and experiences against knowledge-production practices (rooted in neoliberal colonial capitalism) that aim to sever our relationships with other humans and with natural ecologies, including the land (also see Kenrick and Lewis 2004; Lowman and Barker 2015). Though the Liberal government had changed the name of Aboriginal Affairs and Northern Development (formerly known as Indian Affairs) to Indigenous and Northern Affairs to signify a new approach to building relationships, more recently the department was dissolved and replaced with two entities: Crown-Indigenous Relations and Northern Affairs Canada and Indigenous Services Canada. Therefore, it appears that the potential for international political agency associated with the term *Indigenous* has been domesticated and confined to state interpretations or double meanings. This has been the case with other terms, such as self-government, self-determination, development, sustainability, traditional ecological knowledge, reconciliation, recognition, and now negotiation and consultation. These terms are often co-opted in meaning and transformed into state- and corporation-driven interpretations that set the pretext for state-Indigenous relations.

Therefore, as an Indigenous researcher/activist, I am by no means objective, nor would I force myself to be, because, like other Indigenous scholars, I have an ongoing responsibility—what Shawn Wilson (2008, 97) describes as a "relational responsibility" (also see Kovach 2009, 2010; Mackey 2016; Smith 1999)—to my community. I also have a commitment to the academic institution under which authority I conduct research as part of an academic degree. This raises a challenge in how to balance the two commitments. Since I wrote my MA thesis in the mid-1990s, centering Indigenous worldviews within research has been advanced as a decolonizing approach by a broad range of Indigenous scholarship (Absolon 2011; Alfred 1999, 2009; Bargh 2007; Battiste 2013; Blaser, Feit, and McRae 2004; Coulthard 2014; Henderson 1997; Jacobs 2008; Kovach 2009, 2010; Little Bear 2000; Mack 2011; Prosper et al. 2011; Smith 1999; Stiegman and Pictou 2010, 2016a; Tuck and McKenzie 2015; Wilson 2008). Further, centering Indigenous worldviews is a decolonizing approach against the erasure of Indigenous presence and relationship to the natural world by dominating narratives about land and water as resources only for commodities. In this context, I agree with anthropologists Justin Kenrick and Jerome Lewis (2004, 7) in their assertion that the term *Indigenous* requires a relational understanding that "emphasizes both the negative experiences of colonization (in its broader sense) . . . and the positive resilience . . . through which [I]ndigenous peoples experience their relationships with their land, resources, and other peoples."

In this sense, I find it useful to borrow Indigenous scholar Kathy Absolon's (2011, 148) concept of "allied theories" to support "Indigenous methodologies in Indigenous knowledge production" as a way to engage other theoretical understandings that speak to this broader experience. Here I turn to an exploration of an alliance between Mi'kmaw/Indigenous worldviews and anthropological perspectives of treaties that go against formal or state-driven frameworks of neoliberal colonial capitalism.

Mi'kmaw Relational Understandings and Anthropological Perspectives on Treaties

My master's thesis, "The Life Long Learning Experiences and Personal Transformations of Mi'kmaq Women" (Pictou 1996), revealed deep, complex reciprocal relationships with others and with natural worlds such as land that are entrenched in the past, present, and Indigenous hopes for the future. Alfred

Metallic and Robin Cavanaugh (2002, 10) describe this relational worldview as a "complex and representative of a comprehensive holistic knowledge system. It is a timeless process of interrelationships through which Mi'kmaq people understand and relate to the rest of creation." Indigenous scholarship increasingly supports and elaborates on this concept of relationality grounded in Indigenous knowledge and experience. Mi'kmaw/Indigenous worldviews are also composites of more than five hundred years of experience with colonialism and its evolution into neoliberal forms of colonial capitalism (globalization). Within this context, complementary, or allied, theories critical of globalization, alongside ancestral and anthropological perspectives on treaties, deepen our understanding of the tensions between Indigenous worldviews—especially in struggles to implement treaty obligations—and processes of neoliberal colonial capitalism.

Critical Indigenous scholarship argues that only the resurgence of Indigenous land-based practices can disrupt land claims and treaty negotiation processes that are informed by ongoing colonial capitalism through which land and other resources become property for extracting commodities. (Alfred and Corntassel 2005; Coulthard 2014; Simpson 2014; Tuck and McKenzie 2015). Emerging anthropological perspectives on treaty relations also help identify strategies in struggles for social justice and social change in how treaty obligations are currently being interpreted and negotiated. The critical contributions of anthropologists Michael Asch (2014), Charles Hale (2006), Harvey Feit (2004), Justin Kenrick (2009), and Brian Noble (2007, 2008, 2013, 2015), to mention a few, have opened up opportunities for mobilizing the field of anthropology for social, economic, and political justice by transdisciplinary Indigenous scholarship and research, and by Indigenous communities themselves (also see Frisby 2013). These interventions have further helped to bridge alliances and create affinities between anthropologists and Indigenous scholars and communities around the world (see Blaser, Feit, and McRae 2004; Khasnabish 2008; Biolsi and Zimmerman [1997] 2004). Here in Mi'kmaki, the work by anthropologist L. Jane McMillan and Elder Kerry Prosper (McMillan 2012; Prosper et al. 2011), foregrounding Mi'kmaw perspectives and knowledge practices in Mi'kmaw food and lifeways, has contributed significantly to the analysis of Mi'kmaw efforts to implement treaty rights for subsistence and livelihood. The work of anthropologist Trudy Sable and Mi'kmaw linguist Bernie Francis (2012) transcends geopolitical impositions by reclaiming Mi'kmaw linguistic interpretations of the Mi'kmaki landscape. From an interdisciplinary perspective, scholar/filmmaker Martha Stiegman undertakes a participatory approach as a form of decolonizing research practice, in producing films and casting local voices in collaboration with L'sitkuk and Paq'tnkek communities, to delineate Mi'kmaw worldviews against neoliberal interpretations of treaty rights relating to the fisheries (Stiegman and Pictou 2007, 2010, 2016b; Stiegman and Prosper 2013). These allied forms of interdisciplinary scholarship inform how anthropological investigations of treaty understanding can strengthen Mi'kmaw/Indigenous understandings.

Mi'kmaw Ancestral Understandings

Located in what is now known as Bedford, Nova Scotia (just outside Halifax), a Mi'kmaw petroglyph depicting an eight-pointed star, dated as more than five hundred years old, has become an important symbol representing the Mi'kmaq (Lenik 2002). There have been several interpretations of what the star represents, ranging from the sun, which played a significant role in Mi'kmaw ceremonies (Wicken 2002; Lenik 2002), to the seven ancestral fishing and hunting districts of the Grand Council (Mi'kmaw traditional governance structure) and the addition of Ktaqmkuk (across the waves/water)—Newfoundland (Sable and Francis 2012; Migmawei Mawiomi Secretariat, n.d.). Elder Joe B. Marshall (2015) explains that the Mi'kmaw artistic use of the eight-pointed star in basketry and porcupine quillwork started to emerge with the making of the Peace and Friendship Treaties. This history has evolved into an interpretation of the eight-pointed star as a representing the treaty relationship between Mi'kmaq and the British Crown: "By entering into the treaty, Britain joined our circle of brother nations, the Wabanaki Confederacy [Mi'kmaq, Maliseet, Passamaquoddy, Abenaki, and Penobscot alliance], and we joined its circle of nations later known as the Britain Commonwealth. The Mi'kmaq symbolized this important relationship by adding an eighth point—Great Britain—to the seven pointed star representing the seven districts of our nation" (Grand Council, UNSI, and NCNS 1987, i). The Mi'kmaq had practiced treaty making long before the arrival of the Europeans. In the Mi'kmaw language, concepts of Ankukamkewe (making relations) and Ankukamkewel (more than one) form a relational understanding as a basis for treaty making and treaty relations (Battiste 2016, 143). Further, the Mi'kmaq enacted relational agreements with other Indigenous peoples in economic trade, political, and social contexts, such as joining the Wabanaki Confederacy (Leavitt and Francis 1990; Henderson 1997; Prins, n.d.; Speck 1915; Wicken 2002). This alliance would serve as a unified resistance against common enemies (other Indigenous and postcontact non-Indigenous) and later as a political alliance in treaty negotiations with the Crown. Underscoring these alliances was a deep respect for each other's autonomy and sovereignty and, just as important, for the autonomy of natural ecosystems.

Mi'kmaw scholar Tuma Young (2016, 86) explores how many of our stories are about finding allies for securing "ecological health and even survival" in human and nonhuman worlds of family, community, animals, and beings of the spirit world. This form of alliance building was viewed as negotiating "mutual empowerment" in a "world in constant change and flux" (86). Young's analysis of allies can also be applied within the context of making relations through treaty. The relational basis for establishing alliances was informed by principles of mutual responsibility, obligation, and interdependence, described by Metallic and Cavanaugh (2002, 30) as an "extended family system ideology whereby we enter into sacred agreement for the purpose of extending our interconnectedness and interdependency with each other." These principles were extended to sharing resources among families and with other Indigenous peoples (Henderson 1997; Metallic and Cavanaugh 2002; Wicken 2002, 2012), and some were expressed in the form of woven wampum agreements—belts that mark the reciprocal responsibility of the relationship—which would later include treaty relationships with non-Indigenous peoples (Asch 2014; Henderson 1997; Whitehead 1991; Wicken 2002, 2012). Wampum belts were entrusted to a designated story or treaty keeper referred to as the Putus, who used the belts as a reference to orate the details of the obligations between the treaty partners (Henderson 1997). William C. Wicken's (2012) study of Mi'kmaw treaties further demonstrates how the Mi'kmaw relational concept of treaties comprised a renewal of the relationship by tracing how the 1726 treaty is reaffirmed in the 1760 and 1761 treaties (Grand Council, UNSI, and NCNS 1987; also see Sark 2000). Another central tenet of treaty making and renewing relationships is the protection of land and resources by practicing netukulimk—providing for families by taking only what you need (McMillan 2012; Prosper et al. 2011; Pictou 2017; also see Young 2016, 90). Netukulimk is a fundamental principle for sharing the land and resources in a sustainable way.

Anthropological Perspectives

Political anthropologist Michael Asch (2014), in his examination of the history of making the numbered treaties (postconfederation), takes up how mutual understandings formed a reciprocal obligation for honoring the treaties as a way to share the land between Indigenous peoples and the Crown. Though there is evidence that Indigenous treaties were informed by a shared concept of *nation to nation*, or a respect between treaty partners as autonomous peoples, the promises of mutual consent to share the lands were never honored by the settler state (Asch 2014; Pulla 2012). Instead, the Western political concept of sovereignty was and continues to be imposed over Indigenous peoples' own perceptions of sovereignty (Alfred 2009; Blaser, Feit, and McRae 2004; Mack 2011). Today, for example, as part of the land and treaty negotiation process, Indigenous leaders are offered interim economic development agreements that focus on resource extraction and exploitation propositions, which often threaten the land-based relational practices the treaties were founded on (Alfred 2009; Coulthard 2015; Hale 2006; Tully 2010). Social anthropologist Brian Noble (2015, 429) refers to this intersection of intercultural and interpolitical dynamics as the "double bind" of coloniality. Most definitely, formal negotiation processes undermine any regard for relational understandings of sustainability and broader processes for consent within Indigenous communities as treaty partners. L'sitkuk's struggles with the fisheries, the INM movement, and Sipekne'katik's resistance to the recent natural gas storage project certainly expose these shortcomings.

Thus Asch (2014, 186) argues, "In order to implement these treaties, then, we need first to conceptualize how to form a relationship that falls outside the range of possibilities offered to us in contemporary political thought." In other words, Asch does not restrict his analysis to just written treaties but also considers the "spirit and intent," or the relational basis, of the treaties (and wampum). Asch, along with others (Alfred and Corntassel 2005; Hill and McCall 2015; Lowman and Barker 2015; Gordon 2010), argues that we need a retelling of history to illustrate that all Canadians are part of the treaties.

In this sense, anthropological perspectives complement and strengthen Indigenous worldviews in treaty making and relations by extending the treaty "relationship" to include all Indigenous peoples and settler Canadians. Thus, the principle of relationality in treaty understandings offers a way forward out of current legal and political deadlocks, or the "double bind," that prevent treaties from being implemented outside neoliberal contexts. Instead, as Asch (2014) and John Borrows (2005, 2016) argue, restoring relational understandings, or the spirit and intent, of the treaties in turn restores the treaty relationship with all settler Canada. The need for this approach is a point taken up by Lynne Davis, Vivian O'Donnell, and Heather Shpuniarsky (2007, 97): "In reality, many non-Aboriginal people in Canada know little about how Aboriginal and non-Aboriginal relationships have evolved historically, or even the name and provisions of the treaty that makes it possible for them to occupy the community they call 'home.'" Just as significant, the relational implication of the treaties extends the responsibility for their implementation to the wider Indigenous and settler populations as having a responsibility to fulfill their obligations to the treaties as treaty peoples or treaty partners (also see Lowman and Barker 2015). This is not to suggest that we create a dual process for negotiating and implementing treaties. Instead, informal relations present an opportunity to inform that process by rebuilding mutual relational understandings and practices between broader Indigenous and settler societies and, just as important, with the land itself. Elsewhere I have borrowed James Tully's (2010, 251) concept of "small 't' treaty partnerships" to investigate opportunities for social change in small *t* treaty relations between L'sitkuk and local and international alliances in the struggle for livelihood in the fisheries (Pictou 2015). This Indigenous and anthropological scholarly move, or "treaty turn" (Noble 2015, 429), toward relational understandings is critical because it offers the most hope for moving forward. This is because the current processes of treaty negotiations, like the Made-in-Nova Scotia Process, have not yet fully realized mutual treaty re/implementation and obligations, which for many Indigenous communities also include obligations to the land.

L'sitkuk and Allies: Understandings of Treaty

Since the Marshall decision, most of the political and economic mandates of Indigenous organizations in the Atlantic region have focused on integrating Indigenous/Mi'kmaw fisheries into the mainstream commercial fishery. L'sitkuk chose instead to explore other ways to realize a livelihood, which include a fishery and other natural resources. This exploration has evolved into building local and international alliances in community research, advocacy work, and learning projects associated with the Bay of Fundy Marine Resource Centre and a Coastal Community-University Research Alliance project, which led to establishing a community food fishery and annual moose hunt, community food harvester gatherings, and projects for revitalizing stream and ancient canoe routes in our ancestral homelands (Pictou 2015, 2017; Stiegman and Pictou 2016b). This approach invoked the research questions about what L'sitkuk and their allies have learned and how they view treaties since Marshall.

Together, these voices generate an intergenerational concept of treaties through remembered ancestral teachings and the presence of the spirit world in current land and water practices for procuring food and sustaining lifeways. Not unlike our ancestral understandings, central to these practices is the ability to learn how to harvest and share food with others throughout hunting and fishing seasons and community events. Harvesting and sharing food involves an element of relational mobility, or freedom to move beyond reserve boundaries, to harvest fish from inland and marine aquatic systems and to hunt moose in Unama'ki (Cape Breton). The community also continues to engage in learning how to restore ancestral canoe routes as a way to restore our relationship to the land.

> It is good to be able to step into them foot prints that were there before us. Like for me, myself, it was like being able to travel the routes my uncle took, my grandfather took. Both of my grandfathers were guides. They guided Americans for years. There was no limit. It wasn't just living on the reserve. Everything around us was used. The land, hunting, and fishing, berry picking, anything. It wasn't just on reserve. We can move past our boundary. It's our woods, our land, we grew up on it, and we should be able to share it. (Freddy Robar Harlow in Stiegman and Pictou 2016b)

Our allies provided further insights, through various shared learning opportunities, into how these relational practices mark a departure from the unsustainable commodification of natural resources since Marshall. These opportunities include local and international cross-cultural learning with other fishers and participation in the WFFP at the international level in developing the *Voluntary Guidelines for Securing Sustainable Small-Scale Fisheries in the Context of Food Security and Poverty Eradication* (FAO 2015).

As a way to inform strategies for learning and practicing treaty relations in the future, these reflections with our allies also include some of the challenges we face, such as gaining access to ancestral homelands for food and livelihoods (our lifeways), how to address the tension between relational understandings and economic development as a treaty concept, and how to address the effects of overexploitation, pollution, and climate change on sources of food and other natural resources. An integral principle underlying any strategy expressed by L'sɨtkuk and allies is the increasing need for collective responsibility (Indigenous and settler Canadian) for ensuring that sustainable food and livelihoods continue for future generations. Thus, L'sɨtkuk and allies also emphasized the need to enhance our relational understandings of treaties by enacting and maintaining communication strategies within the community and with our allies as a whole. L'sɨtkuk relational understandings—like our ancestral understandings of netukulimk—inform a different spirit and intent of the treaties than what is being currently negotiated in formal state-driven treaty and other negotiation processes. With the voices of L'sɨtkuk and our allies, we build on Mi'kmaw and anthropological contributions to treaty making that privilege Indigenous worldviews as a way to deepen and strengthen our relational concept of treaties.

Conclusion

"Treaty is not a noun—it is a verb!" (Frank Meuse quoted in Pictou 2017).

Much of our knowledge about treaties, particularly the Peace and Friendship Treaties, has been framed by settler-Canadian legal and political systems. Thus, even when treaties are upheld or reaffirmed in the Canadian legal system, as the 1760 and 1761 treaties were in the Marshall decision, implementation processes are confined to neoliberal interpretations with little regard for Mi'kmaw/Indigenous perspectives. This political-legal framework also intersects with academic knowledge-production practices that have largely dismissed or ignored Indigenous worldviews and treaty understandings as constituting legitimate knowledge. Intersections bound by neoliberal colonial capitalism raise a challenge for Indigenous researchers in evoking decolonizing approaches to research while maintaining a relational responsibility to our communities and to the academic institutions under which research is being pursued.

The "Education for Reconciliation" recommendations in the TRC *Calls to Action* (2015) has ignited debates about what constitutes legitimate approaches for decolonizing the academy and research practice. Yet, Mackey (2016, 128) warns,

> One key problem here is that so often it is Indigenous people who are seen as the "problem," not the settler ideologies and practices. Other, equally well-meaning

non-Indigenous people—deeply concerned and wanting to avoid participating in the reproduction of colonial relations—may decide that they should stay out of the way of Indigenous people's autonomy and self-government. Are these really the only two choices? Who will take care of the difficult and necessary work of decolonizing relationships? Who will deal with the "settler problem?"

Indigenous scholar Vine Deloria Jr. ([1969] 1998) challenged the colonial practice of anthropology as early as 1969 (also see Biolsi and Zimmerman [1997] 2004). Decolonization as a conceptual practice was emphasized in the field of anthropology in the early 1990s (Frisby 2013; Harrison 1991; also see Smith 1999). This led to questioning the role anthropology plays within and between cultures and countries that continues to this day. Is the field actively contributing to social change or is it in fact perpetuating (neoliberal extensions) of colonialism? And what constitutes legitimate knowledge? Whose stories are told and whose stories are excluded? Important critical Indigenous analyses have fueled further debate about the concept and practice of decolonization by centering Indigenous knowledge as a way to expose extensions of colonialism, especially within neoliberal states like Canada. In this regard, the alliance of Indigenous and anthropological considerations has greatly exhilarated a reexamination of treaty making from Indigenous perspectives.

||||||||||||||||||||||||||||||||||||

This overview of my own experience conducting doctoral research about the experiences of L'sitkuk and allies in learning about treaties relies on the concept of allied theories as a decolonizing practice, to center Mi'kmaw/Indigenous voices on and experiences of treaty understandings, supported by anthropological perspectives, against neoliberal interpretations. Mi'kmaw concepts of ankukamkewe (making relations) and ankukamkewel (more than one) underscore practices of alliance building and treaty relations before and after the arrival of Europeans. Relational understandings of treaty practice, however, were not restricted to humans. Just as significant is the principle of taking only what you need, or netukulimk, to share the land with others in a sustainable way. In choosing to refrain from entering into DFO agreements, L'sitkuk instead focused on building local and international alliances in advocacy work for treaty and Indigenous rights, restoring streams and ancestral canoe routes, and establishing a food fishery and community moose hunt—all of which reinforces ancestral relational understandings of treaties. Central to these understandings is a practice of maintaining a balance between food and livelihood, which includes fish and other natural resources.

Thus the alliance of Indigenous and anthropological perspectives as a decolonizing practice further addresses our Mi'kmaw/Indigenous experience, rooted in Indigenous knowledge and land-based practices for food and lifeways, as a concept of treaty that is against extended forms of colonialism (neoliberal colonial capitalism), which seek to undermine the very knowledges and practices the treaties were founded on. Allied knowledges have the potential to restore the relational obligations that demand a collaborative approach between all Indigenous peoples and settler Canada for sharing the natural environments in which we live. Restoring the relational obligations of treaties also has the potential to shift neoliberal interpretations to this broader treaty responsibility to all living beings for future generations to come.

Notes

1. Though I am not a fluent Mi'kmaw speaker, I attempt to use the spellings Mi'kmaq (plural form) and Mi'kmaw (singular form) (Smith and Francis orthography, 1974) or Mi'gmaq (Listuguj orthography, Quebec) interchangeably with Indigenous.
2. In 2008, the Canadian federal government established the Truth and Reconciliation Commission to investigate Indigenous experiences and the effects of residential schools. *Calls to Action* is a summary of the TRC recommendations (TRC 2015).

References

Aboriginal Affairs and Northern Development Canada (AANDC). 2014. *Renewing the Comprehensive Land Claims Policy: Towards a Framework for Addressing Section 35 Aboriginal Rights*. Gatineau, QC: ANAC. http://publications.gc.ca/collections/collection_2014/aadnc-aandc/R3-217-2014-eng.pdf.

Absolon, Kathleen E. 2011. *Kaandossiwin: How We Come to Know*. Halifax, NS: Fernwood.

Alfred, Taiaiake. 1999. *Peace, Power, Righteousness: An Indigenous Manifesto*. Don Mills, ON: Oxford University Press.

Alfred, Taiaiake. 2009. "Colonialism and State Dependency." *Journal of Aboriginal Health* 5 (2): 42–60.

Alfred, Taiaiake, and Jeff Corntassel. 2005. "Being Indigenous: Resurgences Against Contemporary Colonialism." *Government and Opposition* 40 (4): 597–614.

Altamirano-Jiménez, Isabel. 2013. *Indigenous Encounters with Neoliberalism: Place, Women, and the Environment in Canada and Mexico*. Vancouver: UBC Press.

Amnesty International. 2014. *Violence Against Indigenous Women and Girls in Canada: A Summary of Amnesty International's Concerns and Call to Action*. Ottawa: Amnesty International Canada. https://www.amnesty.ca/sites/amnesty/files/iwfa_submission_amnesty_international_february_2014_-_final.pdf.

Anaya, James. 2014. *Report of the Special Rapporteur on the Rights of Indigenous Peoples: The Situation in Canada.* New York: United Nations. http://unsr.jamesanaya.org/docs/countries/2014-report-canada-a-hrc-27-52-add-2-en.pdf.

Asch, Michael. 2014. *On Being Here to Stay: Treaties and Aboriginal Rights in Canada.* Toronto: University of Toronto Press.

Bargh, Maria, ed. 2007. *Resistance: An Indigenous Response to Neoliberalism.* Wellington: Huia.

Barsh, Russel L. 2002. "Netukulimk Past and Present: Mikmaw Ethics and the Atlantic Fishery." *Journal of Canadian Studies,* 37 (1): 15–42.

Battiste, Jaime. 2016. "Treaty Advocacy and Treaty Imperative through Mi'kmaw Leadership: Remembering with Joe B. Marshall." In *Living Treaties: Narrating Mi'kmaw Treaty Relations,* edited by Marie Battiste, 138–65. Sydney, NS: University of Cape Breton Press.

Battiste, Marie. 2013. *Decolonizing Education: Nourishing the Learning Spirit.* Saskatoon: Purich.

Belcourt, Billy-Ray. 2016. "Can the Other of Native Studies Speak?" *Decolonization: Indigeneity, Education and Society,* February 1, 2016. http://decolonization.wordpress.com/2016/02/01/can-the-other-of-native-studies-speak/.

Biolsi, Thomas, and Larry J. Zimmerman, eds. (1997) 2004. *Indians and Anthropologists: Vine Deloria Jr. and the Critique of Anthropology.* Tucson: University of Arizona Press.

Blaser, Mario, Harvey A. Feit, and Glenn McRae, eds. 2004. *In the Way of Development Indigenous Peoples, Life Projects, and Globalization.* London: Zed Books.

Borrows, John. 2005. "Creating an Indigenous Legal Community." Fifth Annual John Tait Memorial Lecture. *McGill Law Journal* 50:157–72.

Borrows, John. 2016. *Freedom and Indigenous Constitutionalism.* Toronto: University of Toronto Press.

Cameron, Emilie, and Tyler Levitan. 2014. "Impact and Benefit Agreements and the Neoliberalization of Resource Governance and Indigenous-State Relations in Canada." *Studies in Political Economy* 93:25–52

Choudry, Aziz. 2015. *Learning in Activism: The Intellectual Life of Contemporary Social Movements.* Toronto: University of Toronto Press.

Connell, Raewyn. 2007. *Southern Theory: The Global Dynamics of Knowledge in Social Science.* Cambridge: Polity Press.

Corntassel, Jeff. 2012. "Re-envisioning Resurgence: Indigenous Pathways to Decolonization and Sustainable Self-Determination." *Decolonization: Indigeneity, Education and Society* 1 (1): 86–101. https://jps.library.utoronto.ca/index.php/des/article/view/18627.

Coulthard, Glen Sean. 2014. *Red Skin, White Masks: Rejecting the Colonial Politics of Recognition.* Minneapolis: University of Minnesota Press.

Council of Canadians. 2013. "Update: INM Fasters Achieve Goal!" Council of Canadians, March 7, 2013. Previously published as "INM Activists Fasting for Treaty Rights in Mi'kma'ki." http://canadians.org/node/3802.

Davis, Lynne, Vivian O'Donnell, and Heather Shpuniarsky. 2007. "Aboriginal Social Justice Alliances: Understanding the Landscape of Relationships Through the Coalition for a Public Inquiry into Ipperwash." *International Journal of Canadian Studies* 36 (Fall): 95–119.

Deloria, Vine Jr. (1969) 1998. *Custer Died for Your Sins: An Indian Manifesto.* Norman: University of Oklahoma Press.

Deloria, Vine, Jr., and Daniel R. Wildcat. 2001. *Power and Place: Indian Education in America.* New York: Fulcrum.

de Sousa Santos, Boaventura. 2010. "From the Postmodern to the Postcolonial—and Beyond Both." In *Decolonizing European Sociology: Transdisciplinary Approaches,* edited by Encarnación Gutiérrez Rodríguez, Manuela Boatcă, Sérgio Costa, 225–42. Burlington, VT: Ashgate.

Diabo, Russell. 2012. "Harper Launches Major First Nations Termination Plan: As Negotiating Tables Legitimize Canada's Colonialism." *First Nations Strategic Bulletin* 10 (7–10): 1–9.

Diabo, Russell. 2018. "*UNDRIP*: Lands, Territories and Resources and the Indigenous Forests in Canada." Presentation for the National Aboriginal Forestry Association, Stolen Algonquin Territory, Gatineau, Quebec, March 8, 2018. http://www.media coop.ca/story/undrip-lands-territories-resources-and-indigenous/36692.

Driskill, Qwo-Li. 2010. "Doubleweaving Two-Spirit Critiques: Building Alliances between Native and Queer Studies." *GLQ: A Journal of Lesbian and Gay Studies* 16 (1–2): 69–92. https://doi.org/10.1215/10642684-2009-013.

Feit, Harvey A. 2004. "James Bay Crees' Life Projects and Politics: Histories of Place, Animal Partners, and Enduring Relationships." In *In the Way of Development Indigenous Peoples, Life Projects, and Globalization,* edited by Mario Blaser, Harvey A. Feit, and Glenn McRae, 92–110. London: Zed Books.

Food and Agriculture Organization of the United Nations (FAO). 2015. *Voluntary Guidelines for Securing Sustainable Small-Scale Fisheries in the Context of Food Security and Poverty Eradication.* Rome: FAO.

Frisby, Kelly. 2013. "Decolonizing Anthropology, Version I." Political Anthropology. https://politicalanthro.wordpress.com/decolonizing-anthropology/.

Gordon, Todd. 2010. *Imperialist Canada.* Winnipeg: Arbeiter Ring.

Gorman, Michael. 2013. "Mi'kmaq Fast Continues." *Chronicle Herald* (Halifax, NS), March 8, 2013. Reprinted at Mi'kmaq Rights Initiative website. http://mikmaqrights.com/mikmaq-fast-continues/.

Grand Council of Micmacs, Union of Nova Scotia Indians (UNSI), and Native Council of Nova Scotia (NCNS). 1987. *The Mi'kmaq Treaty Handbook.* Sydney: Native Communications Society of Nova Scotia.

Hale, Charles R. 2006. "Activist Research v. Cultural Critique: Indigenous Land Rights and the Contradictions of Politically Engaged Anthropology." *Cultural Anthropology* 21 (1): 96–120.

Harrison, Faye V., ed. 1991. *Decolonizing Anthropology: Moving Further Toward an Anthropology for Liberation.* Washington, DC: Association of Black Anthropologists.

Harvey, David. 2005. *A Brief History of Neoliberalism.* New York: Oxford University Press.

Henderson, James Youngblood (Sekej). 1997. *The Mi'kmaw Concordat.* Halifax, NS: Fernwood.

Hill, Gabrielle L., and Sophie McCall, eds. 2015. *The Land We Are: Artists and Writers Unsettle the Politics of Reconciliation.* Winnipeg: Arbeiter Ring.

Jacobs, Donald T. 2008. *The Authentic Dissertation: Alternative Ways of Knowing, Research, and Representation*. London: Routledge.

Kenrick, Justin. 2009. "The Paradox of Indigenous Peoples' Rights." *World Anthropologies Journal* 4:11–55.

Kenrick, Justin, and Jerome Lewis. 2004. "Indigenous Peoples' Rights and the Politics of the Term 'Indigenous.'" *Anthropology Today* 20 (2): 4–9.

Khasnabish, Alex. 2008. *Zapatismo Beyond Borders: New Imaginations of Political Possibility*. Toronto: University of Toronto Press.

Kovach, Margaret. 2009. *Indigenous Methodologies: Characteristics, Conversations and Contexts*. Toronto: University of Toronto Press.

Kovach, Margaret. 2010. "Conversational Method in Indigenous Research." *First Peoples Child and Family Review* 5 (1): 40–48.

Leavitt, Robert M., and David A. Francis, eds. 1990. *Wapapi akonutomakonol—The Wampum Records: Wabanaki Traditional Laws*. Fredericton: Micmac-Maliseet Institute, University of New Brunswick.

Lenik, Edward J. 2002. *Picture Rocks: American Indian Rock Art in the Northeast Woodlands*. Hanover, NH: University Press of New England.

Lindroth, Marjo. 2014. "Indigenous Rights as Tactics of Neoliberal Governance: Practices of Expertise in the United Nation." *Social and Legal Studies* 23 (3): 341–60.

Little Bear, Leroy. 2000. "Jagged World Views Colliding." In *Reclaiming Indigenous Voice and Vision*, edited by Marie Battiste, 77–85. Vancouver: UBC Press.

Lowman, Emma B., and Adam J. Barker. 2015. *Settler: Identity and Colonialism in 21st Century Canada*. Halifax, NS: Fernwood.

MacDonald, Fiona. 2011. "Indigenous Peoples and Neoliberal 'Privatization' in Canada: Opportunities, Cautions and Constraints." *Canadian Journal of Political Science* 44 (2): 257–73.

Mack, Johnny. 2011. "Hoquotist: Reorienting Through Storied Practice." In *Storied Communities: Narratives of Contact and Arrival in Constituting Political Community*, edited by Hester Lessard, Rebecca Johnson, and Jeremy Webber, 287–307. Vancouver: UBC Press.

Mackey, Eva. 2016. *Unsettled Expectations: Uncertainty, Land and Settler Decolonization*. Halifax, NS: Fernwood.

Marshall, Joe B. 2015. "Mi'kmaw Resistance and the Formation of UNSI Lecture." Mi'kmaw Kina'matnewey Treaty Education Summit, Membertou, May 2015. Uploaded by Jaime Battiste, September 29, 2015. Video, 19:27 min. https://www.youtube.com/watch?v=xboHcj2iwzY.

McIvor, Bruce. 2014. "Canada's Misguided Land Claims Policy." *First Peoples Law*, November 24, 2014. http://www.firstpeopleslaw.com/index/articles/170.php.

McMillan, L. Jane. 2012. "'Mu kisimaqumawkik pasik kataq—We Can't Only Eat Eels': Mi'kmaq Contested Histories and Uncontested Silences." *Canadian Journal of Native Studies* 32 (1): 119–42.

Metallic, Alfred, and Robin Cavanaugh. 2002. "Mi'gmewey 'Politics': Mi'gmaq Political Traditions." Prepared for Mi'gmawei Mawiomi, May 1, 2002. http://www.about

ourland.ca/sites/default/files/files/resources/Mi'gmewey%20Politics%20Mi'gmaq%20Political%20Traditions_final.pdf.

Migmawei Mawiomi Secretariat. 2000. "Treaty Relationship." Speaking About Our Land Nm'tginen. http://www.aboutourland.ca/sites/default/files/files/resources/treaty%20relationship_0.pdf.

Migmawei Mawiomi Secretariat. n.d. "The Migmaq Star." Speaking About Our Land Nm'tginen. Accessed March 18, 2018, http://www.aboutourland.ca/resources/migmaq-stories/migmaq-star-0.

Mi'kmaq Rights Initiative. 2013. "Nova Scotia Mi'kmaq Leaders Meet to Discuss Fisheries Mandate." Press release, October 3, 2013. http://mikmaqrights.com/uploads/fisheriesreleaseoct3.pdf.

Millbrook First Nation (MFN). 2016. "Millbrook First Nation Takes the Road Less Travelled, Walks Away from the Kwilmu'kw Maw-Klusuaqn (KMK)/Made in Nova Scotia Process." Press Release, May 18, 2016. http://millbrookfirstnation.net/images/uploads/Press_Release_-_Millbrook_First_Nation_withdraws_from_KMKNO.pdf.

Monture-Angus, Patricia. 1995. *Thunder in My Soul: A Mohawk Woman Speaks*. Halifax, NS: Fernwood.

Noble, Brian. 2007. "Justice, Transaction, Translation: Blackfoot Tipi Transfers and WIPO's Search for the Facts of Traditional Knowledge Exchange." *American Anthropologist* 109 (2): 338–49.

Noble, Brian. 2008. "Owning as Belonging/Owning as Property: The Crisis of Power and Respect in First Nations Heritage Transactions with Canada." In *First Nations Cultural Heritage and Law*, vol. 1, *Case Studies, Voices, Perspectives*, edited by C. Bell and V. Napoleon, 465–88. Vancouver: UBC Press.

Noble, Brian. 2013. "Starting from Secwepemc Territorial Authority: Responding to Ancestors, Berries, Mining, and the Recognition of Aboriginal Rights in the Canadian Constitution." Paper presented in the Canadian Indigenous Symposium, Faculty of Law, University of Otago, Dunedin Aotearoa / New Zealand, May 7, 2013.

Noble, Brian. 2015. "Tripped up by Coloniality: Anthropologists as Instruments or Agents in Indigenous-Settler Political Relations?" *Anthropologica* 57 (2): 427–43.

Nova Scotia Office of Aboriginal Affairs (NSOAA). 2014. *Statement of Mandate, 2013–2014*. Halifax: NSOAA. http://novascotia.ca/abor/office/what-we-do/business-plan/.

Nova Scotia Office of Aboriginal Affairs (NSOAA). 2015. *Statement of Mandate, 2014–2015*. Halifax: NSOAA. http://novascotia.ca/abor/office/what-we-do/business-plan/.

Pasternak, Shiri, Sue Collis, and Tia Dafnos. 2013. "Criminalization at Tyendinaga: Securing Canada's Colonial Property Regime through Specific Land Claims." *Canadian Journal of Law and Society* 28 (1): 65–81. https://doi.org/10.1017/cls.2013.4.

Picard, André. 2016. "Putting Indigenous Communities under Suicide Watch Is No Answer." *Globe and Mail* (Toronto), November 1, 2016. http://www.theglobeandmail.com/opinion/putting-indigenous-communities-under-suicide-watch-is-no-answer/article32605055/.

Pictou, Sherry M. 1996. "The Life Long Learning Experiences and Personal Transformations of Mi'kmaq Women." Master's thesis, Dalhousie University, Halifax.

Pictou, Sherry M. 2015. "Small 't' Treaty Relationships Without Borders." *Anthropologica* 57 (2): 457–67.

Pictou, Sherry M. 2017. "Decolonizing Mi'kmaw Memory of Treaty: L'sitkuk's Learning with Allies in Struggle for Food and Lifeways." PhD diss., Dalhousie University, Halifax.

Pictou, Sherry M., and Arthur Bull. 2009. "Resource Extraction in the Maritimes: Historic Links with Racism." *New Socialist* 1:38–39.

Preston, Jen. 2013. "Neoliberal Settler Colonialism, Canada and The Tar Sands." *Race and Class* 55 (2): 42–59.

Prins, Harald A. L. n.d. "Storm Clouds Over Wabanakiak." GenealogyFirst.ca. Accessed September 10, 2018, http://genealogyfirst.ca/first-nations/Wabanakiak-Confederacy.

Prosper, Kerry, L. Jane McMillan, Anthony A. Davis, and Morgan Moffit. 2011. "Returning to Netukulimk: Mi'kmaq Cultural and Spiritual Connections with Resource Stewardship and Self-Governance." *International Indigenous Policy Journal* 2 (4): 1–17.

Pulla, Siomonn. 2012. "Resisting Regulation: Conservation, Control, and Controversy over Aboriginal Land and Resource Rights in Eastern Canada, 1880–1930." *International Journal of Canadian Studies*, nos. 45–46, 467–94.

Puxley, Chinta. 2016. "Manitoba First Nation Declares State of Emergency over Suicide Epidemic." *Globe and Mail* (Toronto), March 10, 2016. http://www.theglobeandmail.com/news/national/manitoba-first-nation-declares-state-of-emergency-over-suicide-epidemic/article29113402/.

Reid, John. 2012. "Imperial-Aboriginal Friendship in Eighteenth-Century Mi'kmaki/Wulstutkwik." In *The Loyal Atlantic: Remaking the British Atlantic in the Revolutionary Era*, edited by Jerry Bannister and Liam Riordan, 75–102. Toronto: University of Toronto Press.

Royal Commission on Aboriginal Peoples (RCAP). 1996. *People to People, Nation to Nation: Highlights from the Report of the Royal Commission on Aboriginal Peoples*. Ottawa: Minister of Supply and Services Canada.

Sable, Trudy, and Bernard Francis. 2012. *The Language of This Land, Mi'kma'ki*. Sydney: University of Cape Breton Press.

Sark, John J., ed. 2000. *Mi'kmaq and the Crown: Understanding Treaties in Maritime Canadian History*. Johnston's River, PE: Sark.

Satzewich, Vic and Wotherspoon, Terry (1993). *First Nations: Race, Class and Gender Relations*. Scarborough, ON: Nelson Canada.

Schertow, John Ahni. 2012. "Read It and Weep, Fill It Out and Say Good Bye: The Harper Government's 'Results Based' Questionnaire." *Intercontinental Cry*, November 27, 2012, 1–33. https://intercontinentalcry.org/read-it-and-weep-fill-it-out-and-say-good-bye-the-harper-governments-results-based-questionaire/.

Schmidt, Jeremy J. 2018. "Bureaucratic Territory: First Nations, Private Property, and 'Turn-Key' Colonialism in Canada." *Annals of the American Association of Geographers* 108 (4): 901–16. https://doi.org/10.1080/24694452.2017.1403878.

Simpson, Leanne B. 2014. "Land as Pedagogy: Nishnaabeg Intelligence and Rebellious Transformation." *Decolonization: Indigeneity, Education and Society* 3 (3): 1–25.

Sipekne'katik. 2016. "Response to the Assembly of Nova Scotia Mi'kmaq Chiefs." Press release, January 25, 2016. http://sipeknekatik.ca/727-2/.

Slattery, Brian. 2000. "Making Sense of Aboriginal and Treaty Rights." *Canadian Bar Review* 79 (2): 196.

Smith, Linda Tuhiwai. 1999. *Decolonizing Methodologies: Research and Indigenous Peoples.* London: Zed Books.

Speck, Frank G. 1915. "The Eastern Algonkian Wabanaki Confederacy." *American Anthropologist* 17 (3): 492–508. https://doi.org/10.1525/aa.1915.17.3.02a00040.

Stengers, Isabelle, and Philippe Pignarre. 2011. *Capitalist Sorcery: Breaking the Spell.* Translated and edited by Andrew Goffey. New York: Palgrave Macmillan.

Stiegman, Martha, and Sherry M. Pictou, dirs. 2007. "In Defence of our Treaties." Part 2 of *In the Same Boat?* Toronto: V Tape. DVD. 38 min. http://www.cinemapolitica.org/film/same-boat.

Stiegman, Martha, and Sherry M. Pictou. 2010. "How Do You Say *Netukulimk* in English? Using Documentary Video to Capture Bear River First Nation's Learning Through Action." In *Learning from the Ground Up: Global Perspectives on Social Movements and Knowledge Production*, edited by Aziz Choudry and Dip Kapoor, 227–42. New York: Palgrave Macmillan.

Stiegman, Martha, and Sherry M. Pictou. 2016a. "Recognition by Assimilation : Mi'kmaq Treaty Rights, Fisheries Privatization, and Community Resistance in Nova Scotia." In *Aboriginal History: A Reader*, 2nd ed., edited by Kristin Burnett and Geoff Read, chapter 14, sec. 5. Don Mills, ON: Oxford University Press.

Stiegman, Martha, and Sherry M. Pictou. 2016b. *We Story the Land.* Toronto: V Tape. DVD. 27:10 min. http://www.vtape.org/video?vi=8595.

Stiegman, Martha, and Kerry Prosper. 2013. "Seeking Netukulimk." Uploaded by Martha Stiegman, March 19, 2014. Video, 22:12 min. http://www.youtube.com/watch?v=jrk3ZI_2Dd0.

Truth and Reconciliation Commission of Canada (TRC). 2015. *Truth and Reconciliation Commission of Canada: Calls to Action.* Winnipeg: TRC. http://www.trc.ca/websites/trcinstitution/File/2015/Findings/Calls_to_Action_English2.pdf.

Tuck, Eve, and K. Wayne Yang. 2012. "Decolonization Is Not a Metaphor." *Decolonization* 1 (1). https://jps.library.utoronto.ca/index.php/des/article/view/18630.

Tuck, Eve, and Marcia McKenzie. 2015. *Place in Research: Theory, Methodology, and Methods.* New York: Routledge.

Tully, James. 2009. "Indigenous Peoples: Part 3." In *Public Philosophy in a New Key*, vol. 1, *Democracy and Civic Freedom*, 221–88. Cambridge: Cambridge University Press.

Tully, James. 2010. "Consent, Hegemony, and Dissent in Treaty Negotiations." In *Between Consenting Peoples: Political Community and the Meaning of Consent*, edited by Jeremy Webber and Colin MacLeod, 233–56. Vancouver: UBC Press.

United Nations General Assembly. 2008. *United Nations Declaration on the Rights of Indigenous Peoples.* New York: United Nations. http://www.un.org/esa/socdev/unpfii/documents/DRIPS_en.pdf.

Whitehead, Ruth. 1991. *The Old Man Told Us.* Halifax, NS: Nimbus.

Wiber, Melanie G., Murray A. Rudd, Evelyn Pinkerton, Anthony T. Charles, and Arthur Bull. 2010. "Coastal Management Challenges from a Community Perspective: The Problem of 'Stealth Privatization' in a Canadian Fishery." *Marine Policy* 34 (3): 598–605.

Wicken, William C. 2002. *Mi'kmaq Treaties on Trial: History, Land, and Donald Marshall Junior*. Toronto: University of Toronto Press.

Wicken, William C. 2012. *The Colonization of Mi'kmaq Memory and History 1794–1928: The King v. Gabriel Sylliboy*. Toronto: University of Toronto Press.

Wilson, Shawn. 2008. *Research Is Ceremony: Indigenous Research Methods*. Halifax, NS: Fernwood.

Wotherspoon, Terry, and John G. Hansen. 2013. "The 'Idle No More' Movement: Paradoxes of First Nations Inclusion in the Canadian Context." *Social Inclusion* 1 (1): 21–36.

Young, Tuma W. 2016. "L'nuwita'simk: A Foundational Worldview for a L'nuwey Justice System." *Indigenous Law Journal* 13 (1): 75–102.

Cases Cited

Acadia First Nation v. Canada (Attorney General), 2013 NSSC 284

R. v. Marshall, [1999] 3 SCR 456 (No. 1)

R. v. Marshall, [1999] 3 SCR 533 (No. 2)

R. v. Martin, 2016 CanLII 14 (NSPC)

TWO

Committing Anthropology in the Muddy Middle Ground

L. JANE MCMILLAN

In the courses of colonization, accumulating federal and provincial powers resulted in an increasingly complex bureaucratization that furthered the erosion of Indigenous people's control over their lives, leading to the destabilization of customary governance, survival strategies, and law ways that had enabled sustained community survival for thousands of years. In short order, paternalistic policies of containment, surveillance, and the criminalization of Indigenous activities undermined the values, principles, and positions constitutive of Indigenous identities, laws, and livelihoods. In Canada ongoing assimilation strategies and policies contribute in varying degrees to current economic, political, and social conditions, such as disrupted kinship, gender, and generational roles; severe class stratification; poverty; poor health; the normalization of violence tolerance; and community erosion. Much of the chaos stems from the failure of governments and settler society to honor treaty obligations and recognize the implementation of treaty rights, even in light of Supreme Court of Canada (SCC) decisions upholding those rights. The primary commitments of our engaged anthropological research are to document and expedite Indigenous responses to the disruption of collective cultural, economic, and social values and to work to foster reconciliation through self-determining capacity building. This is in aid of producing and translating community-driven ethical, moral, and practical strategies to meaningfully apply and sustainably exercise

Indigenous sovereignty within and against the often muddy spaces of the cultural imperatives of Western neoliberal accommodation. From my experiences as an anthropologist, activist, and eel fisher working with the Mi'kmaq Nation, I discuss the ontological and political responsibilities and frustrations at play in the assertion of Indigenous rights to livelihood fishing in Atlantic Canada. This essay presents an analysis of the effects and conflicts emerging from the SCC decision in *R. v. Marshall* ([1999] 3 SCR 456), which affirmed Indigenous treaty rights, including commercial rights, within the meaning of section 35 of the Constitution Act, 1982. I analyze the complex processes through which laws and policies shape social lives, and how legal disputes shape and alter cultural rights and governance practices. I explore the invocation of concepts of law and justice in the daily struggles of Indigenous peoples as they fight to rupture patterns of dependency, challenge inequality, and invest in or resist alliances and autonomy.

Stepping in the Mud

Two critical events shaped my decision to pursue legal anthropology and Indigenous studies. The Kanesatake Resistance, known commonly as the Oka Crisis, was a seventy-eight-day armed standoff in Quebec in the summer of 1990. Mohawk warriors were defending their traditional and sacred lands against the expansion of a settler-owned golf course. It was a shock to witness the escalation of extreme assertions of state power through the actions of the Sûreté du Québec, the Royal Canadian Mounted Police, and the Canadian armed forces. The acts of settler violence and overt prejudice, the explicit oppression of Indigenous peoples' sovereignty and their rights to their territories, triggered vivid visceral feelings of outrage, shame, and confusion as I followed the news coverage over the two and half months of conflict. This crisis revealed many problems in the formal and informal relationships between Indigenous peoples and settlers in this country. The protest ultimately played a significant role in the formation of the Royal Commission on Aboriginal Peoples (RCAP), an extensive research and community consultation process to examine the historical and contemporary relations of Indigenous and non-Indigenous peoples across the country. The RCAP report released in five volumes in 1996, called for significant changes to settler-Indigenous relations through 440 recommendations.

Around the same time as the Kanesatake Resistance, a second pivotal situation of systemic discrimination was getting national attention after the Royal

Commission on the Donald Marshall, Jr., Prosecution released its report. Donald Marshall Jr., a Mi'kmaw man from Nova Scotia, had been wrongfully convicted of murder when he was seventeen years old and had spent eleven years in prison until he could prove his innocence. He was the eldest son of the grand chief of the Mi'kmaw Nation, a nation whose territory had spanned the Atlantic coast, estuaries, and rivers for thousands of years. This was one of the first wrongful convictions to gain notoriety in Canada. It is a story so horrifying in its revelations of blatant and systemic racism, in policing specifically and more broadly in the justice system, that it shook the foundations of the courts and exposed the extensive unequal treatment of Indigenous peoples before the law. Donald Marshall's wrongful conviction resulted in a royal commission of inquiry to find out what went wrong in his prosecution, leading to eighty-two recommendations to address systemic faults in the administration of justice.

The commission found that

> The criminal justice system failed Donald Marshall, Jr. at virtually every turn, from his arrest and wrongful conviction for murder in 1971 up to and even beyond his acquittal by the Court of Appeal in 1983. The tragedy of the failure is compounded by evidence that this miscarriage of justice could—and should—have been prevented, or at least corrected quickly, if those involved in the system had carried out their duties in a professional and/or competent manner. That they did not is due in part at least to the fact that Donald Marshall, Jr. is a native. (Royal Commission on the Donald Marshall, Jr., Prosecution 1989, 1)

Donald Marshall's wrongful conviction epitomized how the structural effects of colonialism concretized the systemic discrimination and racism experienced by Indigenous peoples during the twentieth century (and now the twenty-first). Colonial processes and policies have disrupted and interfered with Indigenous lives and laws for hundreds of years. The release of the royal commission's findings in 1989 was an empowering turning point for the Mi'kmaq to regain authority over many aspects of their lives, to counter colonization, and to govern themselves. The seven volumes of the Marshall inquiry report made real the racism many Mi'kmaq experienced in the Canadian justice system. The commission dissected the legal processes leading to Marshall's wrongful conviction and challenged all facets of the provincial justice system. The case brought to light fundamental problems in policing and the judiciary in Nova Scotia, as well as raising important questions regarding the legitimacy, authenticity, and efficacy of the Canadian criminal justice system, particularly its treatment of Aboriginal peoples.

Together these events led me to look at the Canadian legal system critically, with concerns about social justice, equality, and human rights, and to examine the hegemonic intersections rejecting or incorporating Indigenous legal principles within, against, or alongside the criminal justice system. In 1991, I met Donald Marshall Jr. when I moved to Nova Scotia, shortly after the release of the Marshall inquiry report. We became partners, and I was his fishing wife. Through him I became immersed in Mi'kmaw cultural experiences and kinship networks and was introduced to the realities of Indigenous resistance, resilience, and revitalization. Between 1991 and 1997, as I was training to become an anthropologist, Donald Marshall and I fished eels together to make a living. On August 24, 1993, we fished eels using fyke nets in Pomquet Harbour, Nova Scotia, and sold the eels. We did not hold a license to fish or to sell eels; we understood our activities as a cultural practice recognized and protected by Mi'kmaw Peace and Friendship treaty rights and reaffirmed by the SCC in the *R. v. Simon* decision ([1985] 2 SCR 387), which upheld the validity of the Peace and Friendship Treaty of 1752, asserting the Mi'kmaq right "to have free liberty of Hunting & Fishing."[1] This was the shared legal consciousness of our eel-fishing community. Licenses were for settlers, not Mi'kmaw people. The Department of Fisheries and Oceans (DFO) charged us with three counts under the Fisheries Act.[2] This case got a great deal of attention in part because it followed on the heels of the infamy of Donald Marshall's wrongful conviction and the release of the royal commission inquiry report, but also because it became a significant treaty test case for the Mi'kmaw Nation that would recognize Indigenous treaty-protected livelihood rights (McMillan 2012; McMillan et al. 2016).

Modern interpretations of the Mi'kmaw Peace and Friendship Treaties, first signed in the 1700s, between the Indigenous peoples of present-day Atlantic Canada and the British Crown, allow for the restructuring of social relationships between Indigenous peoples and maritime settler societies. In September 1999, the SCC, in *R. v. Marshall*, affirmed that Indigenous nations in Atlantic Canada possessed a treaty-based right to derive a modest livelihood from commercial fisheries. A key question in the Marshall case was the contemporary interpretation of the 1760 treaty (Wicken 2002). According to the SCC, the treaty gave the Mi'kmaq the right to trade products of their hunting, fishing, and gathering for necessaries. The court interpreted this to mean the right to trade fish and wildlife resources for a moderate livelihood. The SCC decision stated that it was recognizing a treaty trading right. The court ruled that existing fishing regulations were unconstitutional, as they restricted Indigenous rights without justification.

This ruling altered permanently the political, economic, and social environment of Atlantic Canadian fisheries. In so doing, it has positioned the Mi'kmaq and other Canadian First Nations to assume a leadership role in reshaping natural resource management policies and priorities. Mi'kmaw responses to the decision reflect an increase in cultural productivity, as they figure out strategies to best articulate and assert the exercise of their rights. The decision bolstered the demands of the Mi'kmaq to govern their access and use of the fisheries on their own terms, a position they have held since the 1700s and certainly in response to the unilateral imposition of confederacy and DFO regulations.

As an original defendant in the fishing rights case *R. v. Marshall*, I have a unique and privileged position: eel fisher, litigant, and social scientific observer. By the time the case concluded, I was immersed in PhD studies. Since then, as a community-based anthropologist, I have worked in partnerships with the Mi'kmaw Nation, following a program of research that employs anthropologically informed decolonizing methodologies to develop and demonstrate results-rich approaches to organizing and conducting community-needs-driven social research, which builds on and respects Indigenous-determined consultative and inclusive processes (Kovach 2009; Smith 2012; Strega and Brown 2015). The strength of our research relationships fosters trust and helps navigate highly sensitive justice matters, ranging from treaty rights mobilization and fisheries governance to implementing Indigenous legal traditions, building policies to address family violence and offender reintegration, and reframing social assistance policy.

Committing Anthropology

Over the past two decades, much of my research has focused on the resurgence of Mi'kmaw legal principles, measuring the effects of the Marshall inquiry, and advocating for justice reforms and rights reconciliation, including the assertion of fisheries governance and substantive treaty implementation. Collaborative, engaged, community-initiated research, ethically situated and action oriented, that foregrounds Indigenous knowledge and ways of being are the principles on which I commit anthropology (Castellano 2014; Kovach 2009). As a legal anthropologist, I focus on colonial legal structures, processes, and ongoing consequences for Indigenous and settler relationships as the basis of social justice research design. Engaged and applied research methodologies work to counter the denial of the consequences of colonialism, cultural disruption, and oppression and focus on stemming the erosion of gender and generational logic through community-capacity rebuilding in customary legal enactments and in institution building (Borrows 2016; Hedican 2008; Jorgensen 2007). Methodologically, our research teams work to challenge the structures of inequality and to promote social justice through decolonizing agendas and praxis.

Working with members of the Mi'kmaw Nation—fishers and hunters, elders, lawyers, band councils, Grand Council keptins, knowledge keepers, and community members—who generate the research questions and design, we focus on why Indigenous people were and are treated differently and too frequently unfairly as well as on how best to redress systemic discrimination and inequality. As a legal anthropologist, I study the intersection of cultures and laws. Mi'kmaw partners question the premise of justice as one law for all, and together we investigate the potentials of legal pluralism and the practice of Indigenous legal traditions. In our collective research, we explore cultural production through the diverse lens of legal ontologies within and between the communities and institutions in which we work. We are concerned with how laws are constructed and shaped and how they are enacted and contested through social practice, customs, symbols, rituals, and beliefs. Our approach is holistic, considering the relationships between culture and law through which legality circulates and how laws are lived in Indigenous worldviews (Borrows 2016; Geertz 1983; Miller 2011; Mills 2016; Pavlich 2011; Rosen 2006).

Our studies examine the social constructions of wrongdoing and remedies, enforcement and compliance, and how these processes are legitimated, or not, within geopolitical, economic, and spiritual spheres. In this work we pay particular attention to structures of power, social fields of dominance and subjugation, resistance and accommodation. We consider legality as a socially constructed phenomenon that is both a precondition for and a product of social action. Using techniques of legal ethnography and concepts such as legal consciousness and legal pluralism, our team conducts fieldwork examining the practices of formal and informal rules, cases, and disputes to understand how people experience law and how they work with and fight against various legal regimes within particular historical and cultural contexts (Darian-Smith 2013; Ewick and Silbey 1998; Niezen 2009; Starr and Goodale 2002).

We compare legal orders, discourses, and encounters, and we analyze social change with the understanding that law is historically situated and that legal contests, conflict, and their competing, and at times contradictory, interests are constitutive of culture (Merry 2000; Miller 2011; Proulx 2003). In explorations of the intersections of lived law and the reach of law, whether considering the colonization of customary practices, the hegemony of the Canadian justice system, the effects of international declarations, or, more recently, the Truth and Reconciliation Commission (TRC) of Canada, we assess how legal transformations and their consequences change lives. From ethnographic participant observation in courtrooms and sentencing circles, to focus groups and surveys, life histories, case and policy analyses, I have had the great privilege of engaging with many people as they share their legal experiences and ideologies through their hunting and fishing and other justice stories.

The complex processes through which laws and policies shape social lives, and how power structures shape and alter cultures, rights, and governance practices, are expressed as people invoke law, justice, and rights in their daily struggles to resist oppressive cultural, gender, racial, ethnic, religious, and class-based inequalities. How legal systems achieve and maintain legitimacy as they embrace or resist accommodation of alternative or non-Western legal norms and cultural values is an increasingly important area of inquiry to track legal and institutional responses to the heterogeneity of society and the varying responses to reconciliation.

The work I do with Indigenous peoples is grounded in the direct and indirect legal exchanges between colonizers and colonized as well as the legal pluralism that develops or gets suppressed as a consequence of those exchanges. Viewing situations as legally plural leads to an examination of the cultural and ideological nature of law and systems of normative ordering. Through this perspective, we examine how social groups conceive of ordering, social relationships, and ways to determine truth and justice.

Law is not simply a set of rules exercising coercive power but a system of thought by which certain forms of relations come to seem natural and taken for granted, modes of thinking inscribed in institutions that exercise some coercion in support of their categories and theories of explanation. In terms of customary law, Indigenous peoples have multiple sources (Borrows 2010; Milward 2012; Napoleon 2012; Monture 1999). We investigate sources of Indigenous legal principles on the premise that people rely on culturally available narratives of justice to interpret their lives and their relationships. These narratives are not fixed; they shift with respect to audiences and purposes, as well as with people's changing biographies and circumstances (Conley and O'Barr 1998; Cruikshank 1998).

Legal consciousness is a conceptual and analytical tool used here to portray how people come to think, talk about, and understand the formal and informal laws that define social relations in everyday life (Ewick and Silbey 1998; Merry 1990). Legal consciousness reflects the ideas and concerns, the contests and contradictions, produced within and between Indigenous communities and mainstream society. As a conceptual tool, it provides a framework to interpret various narratives of crisis, conflict, solidarity, and resistance, which are part of the necessary struggles inherent in cultural production. Investigating the valued components of Indigenous legal traditions reveals various strategies of nation building, as communities adjust to internal and external pressures that shape and transform their articulations of indigeneity by re-creating legitimate alternatives to settler justice against ongoing forces of assimilation rooted in colonization (McMillan 2011).

Prior to colonization, Indigenous communities had governments, religions, economies, territories, laws, and comprehensive, complex geopolitical systems. Communities had ways of getting along and ways of managing problems when they occurred. Such organization enabled peoples to survive, create, and prosper for millennia. Indigenous peoples are rarely seen as legal innovators, but indeed they are and have been for thousands of years (McMillan 2018; Young 2016).

Colonialism did not simply reduce Indigenous forms of power to a theatrical shell of what had gone before. It redefined society, forcing people to attach new meanings and practices to old identities. Distinctive cultural structures inherited from the past leave traces in the present, but colonial processes also produced strong discontinuities in developments of institutions, practices, and beliefs. For example, the Mi'kmaw peoples of Atlantic Canada have ancient concepts of justice embedded in their language and daily lives, which hold teachings about managing right relationships with one another that are vital today, but not all Mi'kmaq are fluent speakers of their ancestral language, and many have converted to Christianity as devout Catholics (Young 2016). Our research examines, in part, the imposition of state infrastructure on Indigenous governance systems in various fields to assess and counter the obstacles that challenge collective treaty rights implementation, natural resource management, and self-determination (Metallic 2008).

When we think about Indigenous legal experiences, both colonial and contemporary injustices come to mind as grievous reference points, marking the foundations of complexly layered legal consciousness. Colonial policies wrought undue hardships, and the negative effects of forced assimilation, coerced settlement, and racism produced the foundations of legal ideology and consciousness characterized by resistance to these contradictory processes (Sider 2014). Accumulating federal and provincial powers resulted in an increasingly complex bureaucratization and furthered the erosion of Indigenous control over their lives, leading to destabilization of traditional authority and of normative survival patterns and customary laws. Paternalistic courses of containment, surveillance, and the criminalization of Indigenous activities undermined the values, principles, and positions constituting Indigenous laws. Colonization strategies and policies contribute in varying degrees to current economic, political, and social problems, such as family breakdown, disrupted gender and generational roles, severe class stratification, poverty, poor health, addictions, violence, and community erosion (Cannon and Sunseri 2018; Warry 2007).

In essence we look at customary legal practices, the effects of colonization on those practices, and contemporary challenges and successes in building community capacity for just and equal relations between Indigenous communities and settler societies. In Canada the concept of one law for all is pervasive in our legal consciousness, and yet even the dominant colonial legal orders failed to penetrate fully, as Mi'kmaw legal principles persist. In this context, we can consider Indigenous rights, treaty rights, and Indigenous legal traditions not as some historical artifacts, but as part of the social legal fabric today (McMillan 2018).

Collectively, we are challenging the settler states to be accountable in moving forward toward substantively reconciling Indigenous rights amid and against the increasing oppression of legislative dominance, which is suffocating Indigenous communities, and attempts to erode customary laws through new forms of coercive assimilation. Contemporary injustices flow out of historical injustices and are manifested in systemic institutional and social discrimination: police brutality, racial profiling, denying human rights and due process, placing the onus of proof of Aboriginal title and land claims on continuous use and occupancy, avoiding the duty to consult, and failing to see Indigenous peoples as vital, dynamic, diverse contemporary groups with the capacity to create, manage, and maintain sovereignty through self-governance and the operation of legal traditions in contemporary contexts. Access to justice is problematic under such fiscal and cultural restraint. Mi'kmaw people are forced to engage in adversarial justice processes, which have little to offer in terms of cultural relevance or remedy, because they are denied choice.

Our community-driven research examines the cultural mobilization of Mi'kmaw treaty rights and strategies for natural resource use against historical inequalities in resource access management and utilization in the post–Marshall decision era (Davis and Jentoft 2001; Hutchings 2014). While significant opportunities for employment, local empowerment, cultural protection, and cultural revitalization are transforming the local landscape, autonomous governance over Indigenous resource management and regulation has yet to be reconciled within the commercial fishery, and Mi'kmaq are still required to follow DFO regulatory schemes at the expense of autonomous fisheries governance. In our position, this is unjust and reflects a failure to fully implement treaty rights.

The Muddy Middle Ground

In Richard White's classic work *The Middle Ground: Indians, Empires, and Republics*, he suggests that the middle ground "was both the product of everyday life and a product of formal diplomatic relations between distinct peoples. Peoples from widely different social class and status had, for a variety of reasons, to rely on each other in order to achieve quite specific ends. It was these people who created a common ground—the middle ground—on which to proceed" (1991, 51). In his historical analysis of Indigenous-settler relations, White says, "The middle ground depended on the inability of both sides to gain their ends through force" (52). Indeed in the first years, after the *R. v. Marshall* decision, conflict, violence, and destruction were the order of the day, as Indigenous fishers had to legally and physically fight with settler society to access their treaty-protected and Supreme Court–affirmed rights (Coates 2000; King 2014). Many settler fishers felt their livelihoods were threatened by Indigenous access to the fisheries, and the DFO mandate of the day was strictly and marginally limited to accommodation of Indigenous peoples into government regulatory schemes.

White notes, "To succeed, those who operated on the middle ground had, of necessity, to attempt to understand the world and the reasoning of others and to assimilate enough of that reasoning to put it to their own purposes. Particularly in diplomatic councils, the middle ground was a realm of constant invention, which was just as constantly presented as convention. Under new conventions, new purposes arose, and so the cycle continued" (1991, 52). Following the Marshall decision, the Mi'kmaw Nation created the Made-in-Nova

Scotia Process to draft a framework agreement to pursue negotiations with federal and provincial governments. This led to the formation of the Assembly of Nova Scotia Mi'kmaq Chiefs, a unification to counter the divisive "one band at a time" approach the federal government was taking to accommodate Mi'kmaw participation in the commercial fishery. The Assembly of Nova Scotia Mi'kmaq Chiefs created the Kwilmu'kw Maw-klusuaqn Negotiation Office (KMKNO) to concentrate negotiation and research on treaty rights implementation in one body. *Kwilmu'kw maw-klusuaqn* means "we are seeking consensus."

Indigenous peoples seek the "power" that comes from knocking the order off balance, from asserting the personal, collective, and human exception, while the state and settler society relies on the imposition of hard and fast rules (White 1991). The Marshall decision instigated a redistribution of access to natural resources, allowing for increased opportunities for economic development and autonomy. The potential to remedy patterns of dependency and subjugation for Mi'kmaw communities and other Indigenous peoples across the country, in favor of sustainable community advancement, through the affirmation of treaty and Aboriginal rights, and through the substantiation of traditional knowledge, marks an unprecedented turn in colonial relations (McMillan 2018). Not everyone was happy about that.

In the years since the Marshall decision, the plethora of policies, rules, and regulations imposed on Indigenous fishers in order to include them in the commercial fishery have instigated diverse responses from Mi'kmaw communities. The analyses of the decision's repercussions fully reveal the problems of recognition highlighted recently by Glen Sean Coulthard (2014a). Coulthard notes that the "colonial architecture that frames Indigenous and state relations began to shift from a structure primarily reinforced by policies, techniques and ideologies to explicitly oriented around the exclusion and assimilation of Indigenous peoples to a structure that is now reproduced through seemingly more conciliatory set of language and practices that emphasize recognition and accommodation" (Coulthard 2014a, 56).

After the Marshall decision, Mi'kmaw access to the commercial fishery was obtained by selective participation in programs for the transfer of licenses, the purchase of used equipment from settler society, and training in provincial and federal regulatory compliance, the provisions of which change frequently and are all controlled by the DFO. All the post-Marshall fishery initiatives are framed as voluntary. Either Mi'kmaw fishers played by the rules of the state or they were excluded from the commercial fishery. These policies illustrated hierarchical social relations facilitating the ongoing dispossession of Indigenous peoples of their self-determining authority. The post-Marshall responses were individualized and divisive and did not treat with the Mi'kmaq as a nation; rather, separate contribution agreements were put in place with twenty-seven of the thirty-four Indigenous communities falling under the Marshall decision in Atlantic Canada (see Sherry Pictou's work, this volume).

If Mi'kmaq wanted to exercise their rights independently, they were still required to comply with DFO regulations—in other words, livelihood rights were constrained by the state and not reconciled with Mi'kmaw treaty interpretations. All this was done to maintain order and to ensure a peaceful and orderly future in the fishery according to settler laws and standards. While anxious to participate in commercial activities, many people complained that Indigenous knowledge and traditional ecological knowledge were absent within the regulatory schemes, and that elders had not been consulted in their design, implementation, and enforcement.

This structured dispossession, in the name of treaty rights recognition, demonstrates the state's commitment to maintaining ongoing access to resources that contradictorily provide the material and spiritual sustenance of Indigenous societies as well as the foundation of state, settlement, and capitalist expansion (Coulthard 2014a). These programs of accommodation and integration reflect what Kiera Ladner (2005) calls negotiated inferiority, rather than the equal partnerships envisioned by the signatories of the Peace and Friendship Treaties (McMillan and Prosper 2016).

In exercising their treaty rights, people were living in fear and getting hurt. In the years following the Supreme Court's decision, there were numerous accounts of gear conflicts in which boats and fish traps were damaged or destroyed. These conflicts persist today, and Mi'kmaw fishers report fearing for their family's safety when confronting the overt racism of non-Indigenous fishers who accuse Indigenous peoples of abusing their right to catch lobster for food and ceremonial purposes.[3] These acts proved very expensive and ruinous to Indigenous livelihood rights.

Committing to Indigenous Anthropology

To confront the systemic discrimination experienced by Indigenous commercial fishers, we focused our practice on Indigenous knowledge mobilization.

Seeking hope for the future of Indigenous rights implementation, we examined Mi'kmaw concepts and practices of ecosystem sustainability and stewardship, which are culturally rooted ways of being, informed by the respect and responsibility inherent in ancestral and treaty relations to reconcile resource harvesting with livelihood sustainability (McMillan and Davis 2010). Our research on seeking and mobilizing netukulimk was designed to consider Mi'kmaw governing strategies and to understand how people engaged in their relations with their territories and resources.

We found the concept of netukulimk indicative of a framework of laws recognizing the interconnection of every animate life form and inanimate object according to Mi'kmaw local knowledge (McMillan et al. 2016). Netukulimk is a cultural concept that encompasses Mi'kmaw legal principles and guides individual and collective beliefs and behaviors in resource protection, procurement, and management to ensure and honor sustainability and prosperity for ancestral, present, and future generations. According to Mi'kmaw elders, netukulimk is about respect, reverence, responsibility, and reciprocity. Its practice and philosophy embrace coexistence, interdependence, and community spirit. The teachings of netukulimk provide guidance for uniquely Mi'kmaw approaches to resource provisioning, use, and regulation that have the potential to frame sustainable natural resource management and to inform culturally aligned governance strategies against those imposed on Indigenous people by the state and its agents (Prosper et al. 2011; McMillan and Prosper 2016).

Respected Mi'kmaw elder Albert Marshall has instructed us:

> We need to embark on a co-learning journey of Two-Eyed Seeing in which our two paradigms will be put on the table to be scrutinized. We need to honestly be able to say that the essence, the spirit of our two ways, has been respected as we work to balance the energies of those ways. We need to put the two together, such that we have something so profound that we can sustain ourselves and at same time be very cognizant that our actions of today do not jeopardize the ecological integrity of area. Our actions have to be seen to be beneficial for people of the next generation. (Bartlett, Marshall, and Marshall 2012, 335)[4]

The goal is to generate an integrated sustainable fisheries management program informed by Indigenous ecological knowledge, using two-eyed seeing as a guide to engagement with fisheries scientists and the government bodies currently managing the resources. The idea is to bring together the strengths of Indigenous and Western science and ways of knowing (Martin 2012). Two-eyed seeing is both an ethos and a pedagogical approach to honoring traditional knowledge, a guiding principle for collaborative, cross-cultural, and transdisciplinary critical engagement. It is the best of both worlds, scrutinized and balanced for a better vision of tomorrow, resulting in two central recommendations: one is that traditional knowledge should be woven into all aspects of community life, including economic development, fisheries, health, social issues, law, environment, and education. The other recommendation is for each Indigenous community to encourage using traditional knowledge to inspire younger generations and to learn about and respect customary practices and laws, spiritual performances, and the languages related to hunting, fishing, and food gathering; medicine, ecology, and other sciences; the arts; and so on.

Our work developed from trying to understand and address these tensions, to work on capacity-building strategies for decolonizing Indigenous resource management by considering the potential of concepts like netukulimk to frame regulatory strategies and to inform dispute management processes resulting from their enforcement. Mi'kmaw customary law processes incorporate principles of netukulimk and apiksituaguan (a concept framing how to restore relations after a breach) in justice circles, which provide meaningful and culturally appropriate forums to hold an individual accountable for their actions and to enforce communal resource management plans.

Fishing in Circles

After the Marshall inquiry report, dealing with Donald's wrongful conviction, was released in 1989, significant changes in policy and political organization took place outside Indigenous communities, and the alternative justice movement gained momentum in Nova Scotia (McMillan 2011). Opposition to the adversarial justice system, which features the state as the victim and punishment as the cure in a relatively narrow adjudication process separated from community, precipitated the development of strategies supporting the philosophy of restorative justice. Restorative justice is commonly conceptualized in two ways: one, as a process that brings together all stakeholders affected by some harm done to discuss the harm and come to an agreement about how to right the wrongs; and two, as a set of values distinct from traditional punitive state justice—as a process of healing relations rather than punishing offenders (Braithwaite and Strang 2001).

Restorative justice derives from ancient concepts defining crime as a violation of relationships, similar to Mi'kmaw traditional juridical concepts, and employs practices to heal, compensate, and restore peace within the group. A central premise is the notion that violations disrupt relations for all community members, regardless of their direct involvement in the precipitating incident.

Restorative justice has its critics, and some suggest there is a danger in the quest for consensual and informal community controls. The fundamental problems emerge from idealized restorative justice processes, in which the community is imagined as a space free from coercion and overwhelming authority, and where individuals participate through freely chosen, agreed to, and peaceful solutions. This idealism helps promote restorative justice as the perfect alternative to the adversarial system and suggests that community control over sanctions is empowering. Others see problems in the state off-loading institutional reform onto communities. This is particularly challenging for Indigenous communities, where resources are extremely limited and where mechanisms for criticizing internal leadership and governance practices are not clearly delineated because of the absence of sovereignty, a sovereignty diminished through years of colonization and relationships of dependency (Miller 2001).

Negotiating Mi'kmaw justice identity is a challenge for Mi'kmaw justice workers, a small contingent of people who carry out community-based justice practices for the entire province. What is now known as the Mi'kmaw Legal Support Network was the first restorative justice program, handling repeat offenders and facilitating groundbreaking cases as Mi'kmaq in Nova Scotia moved into new areas of dispute management. These steps are evidence that Mi'kmaq are constructing contemporary justice narratives that look inward toward managing internal relations and focus on real community control over assets and resources, using concepts of forgiveness, healing, restitution, and symbols of Mi'kmaw identity to reinvigorate and legitimate community-based justice practices in the management of treaty-protected resource mobilization, like fisheries (McMillan 2018).

Mi'kmaw Legal Support Network processes emphasize restoring relationships through justice circles. Circles provide a forum for parties to deal directly with one another to discuss the harmful consequences of the wrongdoer's actions and to problem solve to find ways to make amends to the victim and to the community. The program has facilitated hundreds of circles. Mi'kmaw circles seek remedies for root causes of wrongdoing rather than simply addressing an offense. Circles are not forums for determining guilt or innocence; wrongdoers come to the circle when they willingly acknowledge their actions and desire to make amends. Each process is unique, and dispositions are flexible according to circumstance. The process involves talking out the problem with a group of community members relevant to the individuals involved and the facts of the case.

Through community-driven processes, the community, families of those directly involved, wrongdoers, and victims are empowered because responsibility for managing the dispute remains within the community rather than with the state, and the process and outcomes of dispute management are optimally most visible. Mi'kmaw justice circles are timely alternatives that permit participants to speak for themselves in a setting that is less adversarial and intimidating than the Canadian justice system, because it is local and culturally familiar. Dispositions appear to be fair because they are case specific and negotiated more than unilaterally imposed. Disputes are better mediated through shared knowledge of an individual's family background, the contributing circumstances of the event, and wider understanding of communal legal and historical consciousness. This approach helps to create meaningful resolutions and manageable healing plans and fits well with resource management concepts like netukulimk.

Justice circles are accountability-building mechanisms. Based on Mi'kmaw traditional legal perspectives, a forum of community members is convened and a person who is willing to accept responsibility for the offense voluntarily participates in a discussion with significant parties about the offense and its consequences. The justice circle process moves beyond formulating a sentence. The process is designed to produce outcomes that improve the working relationship among participants; to create better understanding and respect for the different circumstances and values of the participants; and to combine a broad range of interests in decisions that reflect the collective efforts of all participants (McMillan 2016). Reaching a consensus is not the primary objective; striving together to understand one another, rebuild relationships, and generate healthy connections are the objectives. Dispositions made are culturally relevant and reinforce culturally sanctioned laws, which are critical in the responsible exercise of collective treaty rights. The justice workers strive to gain legitimacy in their own communities rather than solely relying on the courts to divert their authority to the state.

Mi'kmaw people want to control their own justice processes as well as their resource management regulations and enforcement in self-determining ways. Our research delineates the characteristics of Mi'kmaw legal consciousness in opposition to those of the settler system players. Despite these differences, or perhaps because of them, the Mi'kmaw Legal Support Network Customary Law Program continues to be an organization of ongoing cultural production, which uses Mi'kmaw legal consciousness as a way to appropriate the legitimacy attached to authorize unconventional processes that separate it from settler justice. When resource management processes are entirely removed from the community, colonialism continues, and once again settler systems oppress Indigenous ontologies, and settler treaty responsibilities are denied (Asch 2014).

The Marshall inquiry and the Marshall decision produced a great deal of excitement about the potential for customary law to lead the way in community control of regulatory offenses and to expand the compass of Mi'kmaw treaty-based resource management. When communal fishing agreements were breached, Mi'kmaq identified the community of harm in ways that fit with their legal consciousness and the concepts of apiksituaguan (mutual acknowledgment of harm and forgiveness) and netukulimk, by addressing the resource, for example, lobster, as the victim and establishing meaningful mechanisms, elder reprimands, shaming, and reparations related to the ethos of sharing, for example, to repair the harms. Justice circles provide excellent opportunities for communicating the cultural principles desired for management strategies and demonstrating community accountability in terms of resource extraction. They allow for the expansion of Mi'kmaw legal infrastructure by building capacity and responsibility through experiential learning for the participants.

Contrary to commonly held fears that any cases dealing with fishing rights and treaty rights may somehow infringe on the enjoyment of those rights, treaty-rights exercise cases have the potential to entrench Mi'kmaw ownership over the implementation and management of those rights. Importantly, circles also have the potential for the Mi'kmaq to confront their historical adversaries, the government of Canada and its agents, the DFO, face to face in a venue that is Mi'kmaq constructed and controlled. These are beyond acts of reconciliation; these processes are necessary for resurgence. Circles create vital opportunities for Mi'kmaq to have their voices heard rather than silenced, as happened so many times before when exercising treaty rights. If only the state agents would show up.

The DFO has not participated in many customary law processes involving fisheries charges. There is a pervasive sense that DFO officials, as agents of the

Crown, in response to losing the Marshall case are aggressively asserting their regulatory power and control. Their stance, while reflecting the attitudes of their non-Indigenous constituents, is puzzling in light of the federal government's declaration that the most important relationship is the one with Indigenous peoples. Prime Minister Justin Trudeau, in his 2016 Mandate Letter to the Minister of Fisheries, Oceans, and the Canadian Coast Guard, stated that, "No relationship is more important to me and to Canada than the one with Indigenous Peoples. It is time for a renewed, nation-to-nation relationship with Indigenous Peoples, based on recognition of rights, respect, co-operation, and partnership."[5] In 2017 a federal DFO official said, "We've [DFO] been tested by the courts many, many times on issues relating to fisheries by Indigenous peoples in Canada and I'll put it bluntly to you, in most cases we come out on the losing side of those issues. And we need to be careful moving forward that we don't create another situation that results in another precedent, and that is a possibility. We didn't think we were going to lose the Marshall case, but we did" (Comeau 2017, A4). The DFO position rejecting Indigenous control over regulatory mechanisms demonstrates the federal government's inability to respect or embrace treaty rights implementation, Indigenous sovereignty, cultural differences, and self-determination. The government's position undermines the Mi'kmaw concept of netukulimk, which demands that people perform respectful and responsible resource procurement in ways that honor ancestors and treaty principles to ensure provisioning for future generations.

Mi'kmaw restorative approaches have the benefit of remedies that are permeated with cultural significance as well as community accountability, the building blocks of sovereignty (Alfred 2005; Simpson 2008). As external forces challenge Mi'kmaw rights, internally the Mi'kmaq resist the co-opting of their beliefs and laws by constructing valued components of Mi'kmaw legal culture and restoring respectful balance with the resource through responsible utilization.

Committing Anthropology—Forging the New Middle Ground

In our research on Mi'kmaq perceptions of the justice system and their treaty rights, criticisms pointed to systemic discrimination, widespread lack of awareness of Indigenous rights, and a general failure of settler society to appreciate and respect Indigenous value systems, practices, historical legacies, and rights to land, resources, and sovereignty.

Justice for many requires full recognition of Mi'kmaw rights and title, meaningful consultation, and fulfillment of the fiduciary obligations of the Crown. Without rights education and the implementation of Mi'kmaw treaties, systemic discrimination and poverty will continue to contribute to intergenerational repercussions, generate conflicts with the law, and limit opportunities for reconciliation. The authority of Indigenous customary justice knowledge and practice needs to be recognized and supported, and these systems need to be decolonized through incorporation and use of Indigenous ways of being through ceremony, knowledge translation, collaboration, and respect.

We held community forums across the Mi'kmaw Nation between 2013 and 2015 to talk about perceptions and experiences of justice. The Mi'kmaw participants articulated a wider situation of ongoing inequality, disempowerment, and systemic discrimination. There was a great deal of frustration in communities regarding the inadequacy of treaty implementation outcomes related to the SSC decision in *R. v. Marshall*. Many people who came to the community forums wanted to discuss their fishing rights and the problems they were experiencing in exercising their treaty rights. Indigenous rights cannot be compartmentalized into a category separate from justice. These dialogues are relevant to Mi'kmaq perceptions of colonial relations, their experiences of justice, and their ideas regarding the criminalization of their identities and the realities of poverty and systemic discrimination that they face daily. Collectively, these experiences inform the nature of the holistic justice priorities identified by community members.

In one community, a fisherman was charged with breaching a communal fishing agreement during a food and ceremonial fishery by hauling four traps (three over the permissible limit), one that was his own and three others he was fishing for elders, who needed to eat but could not manage to go out on a boat on their own. He caught a total of sixteen lobsters. The allowable catch for one trap is twenty, so at issue was not the number of lobsters but the number of traps. He was performing a significant and culturally relevant practice of providing for his elders. He had to go to court to protect his rights to perform his customary duties aligned with netukulimk, a heartbreaking battle that has cost him thousands of dollars, lost time, and the ability to provide for elders. A band councilor described the situation:

The band has a communal license imposed. We don't have an agreement. The problem with waiting at the council for someone to take action is everybody wants to have a *Marshall* decision and be the guy who won, but no one wants to be the band who took on a case that may lose and set a negative precedent for treaty rights. But what ends up happening here where the council is idle on any fishery issue, it comes down to it, you are on your own here and we do not want to incur any of the cost of managing our own fishery, which means buying your own tags, developing our management plan and making that available to everybody else. We say we have an imposed license and we do, but we take the license and tags too and we fish under protest and that is how we do things here. What that causes is, it is not here in the community, but in the justice system, part of the punishment is being charged in the first place and now you have to defend it [the treaty right]. If you are put out in the first court and that is half the battle and people just cannot afford to go, anyway they [the state] win a lot of cases they probably shouldn't, just because people cannot afford to fight them. We don't have the resources financially or the background with rights, and even if they did, fisheries is still going to rule the way they do. And that is why bands won't fight back because they get their funding from the government. You know what I mean? That's how it works. [Three-quarters] of the lawyers here in Yarmouth they don't want any thing to do with natives because they all have the non-native clients [nonnative fishers]. It creates a tension. They won't take a native case because the non-natives will say we will not take a case with you because you are working with the natives. Because in Yarmouth it is the fishermen that run the town. (Acadia Mi'kmaw Community Forum, transcript in the author's possession, 2013)

Meanwhile, elders go without their lobster. Under the regulatory framework of the federal government, kinship sharing and customary resource distribution patterns are halted. Intergenerational knowledge translation is interrupted, and cultural genocide persists. Whose treaty rights are at stake here? Settlers do everything in their considerable power to protect themselves first, ignoring the temporal priority of Indigenous peoples and both the SCC decisions and the constitutional affirmation of treaty rights. Settler society and its institutions must rethink their entire approach to reconciling treaty rights and relinquish totalitarian control over resource management. Educating people on treaty relations is essential to drive the needed systemic changes.

Similar situations of settler hostilities are occurring worldwide as Indigenous peoples assert their rights and try to survive. The Cucapá people of Baja

Mexico had their subsistence fish confiscated by armed Mexican marines and federal police because non-Indigenous fishers alleged that Cucapá fishers were violating a seasonal ban. Alejandra Navarro Smith, Alberto Tapia Landeros, and Everardo Garduño (2010) reveal that these fishing conflicts occur when Cucapá fishers are incorporated into the national productive regulatory schemes without taking into account the rights, like consultation, that all Indigenous peoples have. R. Aída Hernández Castillo's work *Multiple Injustices* examines the possibilities and limitations of legal pluralism in customary, national, and international law for Indigenous peoples, particularly women (Hernández Castillo 2016). In Nova Scotia the displacement and repossession of women's roles in the commercial fisheries is a key area for future inquiry.

Despite the rising discourse of reconciliation in the post-TRC era in Canada, some settler fishers are outwardly racist and hostile toward Indigenous fishers. Recent accounts tell us that fishers from Mi'kmaw communities had their gear vandalized. One fisherman from Potlotek Mi'kmaw Community, in his first foray into fishing, lost all his traps after someone cut the lines. He set more traps and said he was met with a nonnative protest, which led to more vandalism over the next two years. Last year things were relatively quiet because he stayed on his boat and slept there. He doesn't want to interfere in the nonnative fishery; he simply wants recognition for his rights and a share of resources under the treaty the Mi'kmaq signed affirming Aboriginal peoples' rights to fish for livelihoods.

> "I would ask every non-native fisher to think about what you are saying when you prevent me from fishing," he said. "You are saying my children do not have a right to eat. You are saying that my community does not have a right to their traditional gatherings. You are saying that I do not have a right to practice my faith. You are saying that I do not have a right to the same resources, which were shared so generously with you. . . . What I wish for is peace . . . between our people at long last, regard and respect for the resources that feed us all and the spirit of brotherhood that was intended by my ancestors." (*Chronicle Herald* [Cape Breton], November 24, 2014)

Community health and well-being come from reducing cultural distance perpetrated by colonial policies and assimilation. Creating programs and remedies that are meaningful to those who participate in them can minimize cultural distance. The Mi'kmaw communities in Nova Scotia have told us they want customary law programs to prevent abuses of treaty rights and to intervene to help families and individuals live in a good way. They want access to Mi'kmaw language, justice, and healing programs that are rooted in Mi'kmaw ways of being and framed by Mi'kmaw rights. Most importantly, they want meaningful, flexible, and culturally relevant mechanisms to help people work through their crises, enhance Mi'kmaw values for living right, and celebrate Mi'kmaw knowledge and identity (McMillan 2014).

Reconciling Injustices Through Two-Eyed Seeing Consultation and Negotiation

The Mi'kmaw Legal Support Network, with the support of the Assembly of Nova Scotia Mi'kmaq Chiefs and the Mi'kmaw Rights Initiative negotiation table, undertook the development of a customary law process for managing regulatory offenses related to fishing and hunting. Mi'kmaq wanted to address the disproportionate response of federal and provincial prosecutions on people exercising their treaty rights by creating an accessible and culturally proportionate dispute management protocol. It took years of bureaucratic wrangling, but finally, in 2011, a customary law pilot project was announced. Taking a two-eyed seeing approach, an advisory team comprising the KMKNO Mi'kmaw Rights Initiative (a significant outcome of the Marshall decision) negotiation team, the Unama'ki Institute of Natural Resources, the Nova Scotia Department of Natural Resources, Parks Canada, and the Mi'kmaw Legal Support Network oversaw the implementation of the collaborative protocol, including justice circles. To date, several cases of hunting regulation breaches have been successfully managed in this customary format. Nonetheless, Mi'kmaw fishers exercising their treaty rights are still being fined or forced to engage in expensive court battles to protect those rights affirmed by the Supreme Court and recognized in the Constitution (McMillan et al. 2016).

In a recent decision, *R. v. Martin* ([2016] CanLII 14 [NSPC]), two Mi'kmaw fishers who breached a communal fishing license under the Aboriginal Fisheries Strategy by catching and keeping salmon from a river that was catch and release only had their charges stayed. In a case that took five years to hear, it was found that the DFO had failed to consult with the Aboriginal authority holding the license prior to taking enforcement action, a consulting requirement found in the DFO's own 1993 policy statement. "While DFO was not precluded from laying charges it was honour-bound to engage in bona fide consultation before doing so" (*R. v. Martin*, 3). This finding should provide the DFO with the directive to engage with Mi'kmaw customary law processes as a comanagement strategy. Diverting such cases would be a step forward in reconciliation by enhancing Mi'kmaw legal authority, respecting customary protocols, and actualizing responsible treaty rights implementation by holding resource users accountable to their communities and to the resource.

Despite the many challenges, be they fiscal, legal, political, or jurisdictional, the necessity for Mi'kmaw control and facilitation of treaty processes, locally and nationally, remains paramount. For years we have witnessed the signs of enduring Mi'kmaw laws, which are the foundation of the nation, its survival, and its prosperity. Mobilizing Indigenous legal traditions and resource management institutions, which confront the adversarial justice system and provide for community-based self-determining practice, better reflects Indigenous treaties, rights, values, and unique circumstances and is foundational to journeying forward to reconciliation and the recognition that we are all treaty people (Asch 2014; Borrows 2016; Coulthard 2014b; Milward 2012; Monture 1999). The ninety-four calls to action in the final report of the TRC include the full adoption and implementation of the *United Nations Declaration on the Rights of Indigenous Peoples* and a commitment by "the federal, provincial, and territorial governments to . . . the recognition and implementation of Aboriginal justice systems in a manner consistent with the Treaty and Aboriginal rights of Aboriginal peoples [and] the Constitution Act, 1982" as a framework for reconciliation (TRC 2015, 228). In Canada the federal government has committed to pursuing a nation-to-nation relationship based on recognition, rights, respect, cooperation, and partnership with Indigenous peoples and has fully endorsed the UN declaration. What remains is the establishment of mechanisms and processes to ensure the full and meaningful enforcement and implementation of treaty rights. As anthropologists allied with Indigenous peoples, we must jointly review, reform, and develop federal laws, regulations, procedures, policies, and practices that respect Indigenous rights and self-government. Currently in Nova Scotia, the legacy of Donald Marshall lives on as we work collectively to prepare a treaty education curricula for all civil servants. It is my hope that treaty education will help shift the consciousness of settler society from seeing Supreme Court and constitutional affirmations of Indigenous treaty rights not as a loss, but as a set of rights to respect, honor, and recognize as a welcome duty, with the goal of ending systemic discrimination. As allied anthropologists we have an obligation to commit to getting Indigenous rights free from the muddy middle ground.

Notes

I am very grateful to Donald Marshall and all the people who participated in this research program, particularly the members of the Mi'kmaw Nation who generously shared their ideas, beliefs, and visions. This research was funded in part by the SSHRC Indigenous Research Program, the Mi'kmaw / Nova Scotia / Canada Tripartite Forum, and the Canada Research Chairs Program.

1. Article 4 of the 1752 Peace and Friendship Treaty Between His Majesty the King and the Jean Baptiste Cope, last modified July 3, 2016, https://www.aadnc-aandc.gc.ca/eng/1100100029040/1100100029041.
2. The Nova Scotia Provincial Court, which first heard the case, determined it to be a treaty test case and focused the matter on Aboriginal and treaty rights. As I am a settler, charges against me were dropped, but Donald Marshall was convicted. Eventually he was granted leave to appeal to the Supreme Court of Canada.
3. On Christmas Day 2017, the lobster pound of a Sipekne'katik band councilor was burned to the ground. In October, his boat was taken from the wharf and set on fire. These acts of violence are evidence of the tensions between Indigenous and non-Indigenous commercial fishers.
4. The Atlantic Policy Congress of First Nations Chiefs Secretariat, a regional Indigenous policy analysis team, is working with the DFO, specifically with the Aboriginal Aquatic Resource and Oceans Management Program, to embark on this colearning journey with fisheries scientists to generate sustainable interface with Indigenous fishers and to foster reciprocal relations and create a management plan that will reflect the values important to the Mi'kmaw Nation.
5. Mandate Letter from Justin Trudeau, Prime Minister of Canada, to Minister of Fisheries, Oceans and the Canadian Coast Guard, August 19, 2016, https://pm.gc.ca/eng/minister-fisheries-oceans-and-canadian-coast-guard-mandate-letter. Transcript on file with the author.

References

Alfred, Taiaiake. 2005. *Wasáse: Indigenous Pathways of Action and Freedom*. Peterborough, ON: Broadview Press.

Asch, Michael. 2014. *On Being Here to Stay: Treaty and Aboriginal Rights in Canada*. Toronto: University of Toronto Press.

Bartlett, Cheryl, Murdena Marshall, and Albert Marshall. 2012. "Two-Eyed Seeing and Other Lessons Learned Within a Co-learning Journey of Bringing Together Indigenous and Mainstream Knowledges and Ways of Knowing." *Journal of Environmental Studies and Sciences* 2 (4): 331–40.

Borrows, John. 2010. *Canada's Indigenous Constitution*. Toronto: University of Toronto Press.

Borrows, John. 2016. *Freedom and Indigenous Constitutionalism*. Toronto: University of Toronto Press.

Braithwaite, John, and Heather Strang, eds. 2001. *Restorative Justice and Civil Society*. Cambridge: Cambridge University Press.

Cannon, Martin J. and Lina Sunseri, eds. 2018. *Racism, Colonialism, and Indigeneity in Canada*. Don Mills, ON: Oxford University Press.

Castellano, Marlene Brant. 2014. "Ethics of Aboriginal Research." In *Global Bioethics and Human Rights: Contemporary*, edited by Wanda Teays, John-Stewart Gordon, and Alison Dundes Renteln, 273–88. Lanham, MD: Rowman and Littlefield.

Chronicle Herald. 2014. "Cape Breton Aboriginal Man Blames Boat Damage on Non-native Fisherman." *Chronicle Herald* (Cape Breton), November 24, 2014. Republished on *NationTalk*, November 25, 2014. http://nationtalk.ca/story/cape-breton-aboriginal-man-blames-boat-damage-on-non-native-fisherman-chronicle-herald.

Coates, Kenneth. 2000. *The Marshall Decision and Native Rights*. Montreal: McGill-Queen's University Press.

Comeau, T. 2017. "DFO Vows to Enforce Lobster Regulations in Southwestern N.S." *Chronicle Herald* (Halifax, NS), September 21, 2017, A4.

Conley, John M., and William M. O'Barr. 1998. *Just Words: Law, Language, and Power*. Chicago: University of Chicago Press.

Coulthard, Glen Sean. 2014a. "From Wards of the State to Subjects of Recognition? Marx, Indigenous Peoples, and the Politics of Dispossession in Denendeh." In *Theorizing Native Studies*, edited by Audra Simpson and Andrea Smith, 56–98. Durham, NC: Duke University Press.

Coulthard, Glen Sean. 2014b. "Place Against Empire: The Dene Nation, Land Claims, and the Politics of Recognition in the North." In *Recognition versus Self-Determination*, edited by A. Eisenberg, J. Webber, G. Coulthard, and A. Boisselle, 147–73. Vancouver: UBC Press.

Cruikshank, Julie. 1998. *The Social Life of Stories: Narratives and Knowledge in the Yukon Territory*. Lincoln: University of Nebraska Press.

Darian-Smith, Eve. 2013. *Law and Societies in Global Contexts*. Cambridge: Cambridge University Press.

Davis, Anthony, and Svein Jentoft. 2001. "The Challenge and the Promise of Indigenous Peoples' Fishing Rights—From Dependency to Agency." *Marine Policy* 25 (3): 223–37.

Ewick, Patricia, and Susan S. Silbey. 1998. *The Common Place of Law*. Chicago: University of Chicago Press.

Geertz, Clifford. 1983. *Local Knowledge*. New York: Basic Books.

Hedican, Edward. 2008. *Applied Anthropology in Canada: Understanding Aboriginal Issues*. 2nd ed. Toronto: University of Toronto Press.

Hernández Castillo, Rosalva Aída. 2016. *Multiple Injustices: Indigenous Women, Law, and Political Struggle in Latin America*. Tucson: University of Arizona Press.

Hutchings, Suzi. 2014. "Indigenous Knowledges Impacting the Environment." *AlterNative: An International Journal of Indigenous Peoples* 10 (5): 445–49.

Jorgensen, Miriam, ed. 2007. *Rebuilding Native Nations*. Tucson: University of Arizona Press.

King, Sarah J. 2014. *Fishing in Contested Waters*. Toronto: University of Toronto Press.

Kovach, Margaret. 2009. *Indigenous Methodologies: Characteristics, Conversations and Contexts*. Toronto: University of Toronto Press.

Ladner, Kiera. 2005. "Up the Creek: Fishing for a New Constitutional Order." *Canadian Journal of Political Science* 38 (4): 923–53.

Martin, D. H. 2012. "Two-Eyed Seeing: A Framework for Understanding Indigenous and Non-Indigenous Approaches to Indigenous Health Research." *Canadian Journal of Nursing Research* 44 (2): 20–42.

McMillan, L. Jane. 2011. "Colonial Traditions, Co-optations, and Mi'kmaq Legal Consciousness." *Law and Social Inquiry* 36 (1): 171–200.

McMillan, L. Jane. 2012. "'Mu Kisimaqumawkik Pasik Kataq—We Can't Only Eat Eels': Mi'kmaq Contested Histories and Uncontested Silences." *Canadian Journal of Native Studies* 32 (1): 119–42.

McMillan, L. Jane. 2014. "Still Seeking Justice: The Marshall Inquiry Narratives." *UBC Law Review* 47 (3): 927–90.

McMillan, L. Jane. 2016. "Living Legal Traditions: Mi'kmaw Justice in Nova Scotia." *University of New Brunswick Journal of Law* 67:187–210.

McMillan, L. Jane. 2018. *Truth and Conviction: Donald Marshall Jr. and the Mi'kmaw Quest for Justice*. Vancouver: University of British Columbia Press.

McMillan, L. Jane, and Anthony Davis. 2010. "'What Does This Tell Us About Us?' Social Research and Indigenous Peoples: The Case of the Paq'tnkek Mi'kmaq." *SPC Traditional Marine Resource Management and Knowledge Information Bulletin*, edited by Ken Ruddle, no. 27, 3–16.

McMillan, L. Jane, and Kerry Prosper. 2016. "Remobilizing *Netukulimk*: Indigenous Cultural and Spiritual Connections with Resource Stewardship and Fisheries Management in Atlantic Canada." *Reviews in Fish Biology and Fisheries* 26 (4): 629–47.

McMillan, L. Jane, Kerry Prosper, Morgan E. Moffitt, and Anthony Davis. 2016. "Netukulimk Narratives: Pathways to Rebuilding Sustainable Indigenous Nations." In *Sustainability Planning and Collaboration in Rural Canada: Taking the Next Steps*, edited by Lars K. Hallström, Mary A. Beckie, Glen T. Hvenegaard, and Karsten Mündel, 241–68. Edmonton: University of Alberta Press.

Merry, Sally Engle. 1990. *Getting Justice and Getting Even: Legal Consciousness Among Working-Class Americans*. Chicago: University of Chicago Press.

Merry, Sally Engle. 2000. *Colonizing Hawai'i: The Cultural Power of Law*. Princeton, NJ: Princeton University Press.

Metallic, Fred. 2008. "Strengthening Our Relations in Gespe'gewa'gi, the Seventh District of Migma'gi." In *Lighting the Eighth Fire*, edited by Leanne Simpson, 59–72. Winnipeg: Arbeiter Ring.

Miller, Bruce Granville. 2001. *The Problem of Justice: Tradition and Law in the Coast Salish World*. Lincoln: University of Nebraska Press.

Miller, Bruce Granville. 2011. *Oral Histories on Trial: Recognizing Aboriginal Narratives in the Courts*. Vancouver: University of British Columbia Press.

Mills, Aaron. 2016. "The Lifeworlds of Law: On Revitalizing Indigenous Legal Orders Today." *McGill Law Journal* 61 (4): 847.

Milward, David. 2012. *Aboriginal Justice and the Charter*. Vancouver: University of British Columbia Press.

Monture, Patricia. 1999. *Journeying Forward: Dreaming First Nations' Independence*. Halifax, NS: Fernwood.

Napoleon, Val. 2012. "Thinking About Indigenous Legal Orders." In *Dialogues on Human Rights and Legal Pluralism*, edited by René Provost and Colleen Sheppard, 229–45. Netherlands: Springer.

Navarro Smith, Alejandra, Alberto Tapia Landeros, and Everardo Garduño. 2010. "Sailing Against the Current: The Cucapás and Environmental Legislation." *Cultural* 6 (12): 43–74.

Niezen, Ronald. 2009. *Public Justice and the Anthropology of Law*. Cambridge: Cambridge University Press.

Pavlich, George. 2011. *Law and Society Redefined*. Don Mills, ON: Oxford University Press.

Prosper, Kerry, L. Jane McMillan, Anthony A. Davis, and Morgan Moffit. 2011. "Returning to Netukulimk: Mi'kmaq Cultural and Spiritual Connections with Resource Stewardship and Self-Governance." *International Indigenous Policy Journal* 2 (4): 1–17.

Proulx, Craig. 2003. *Reclaiming Aboriginal Justice, Identity, and Community*. Saskatoon: Purich Press.

Rosen, Lawrence. 2006. *Law as Culture*. Princeton, NJ: Princeton University Press.

Royal Commission on Aboriginal Peoples (RCAP). 1996. *Report of the Royal Commission on Aboriginal Peoples*. 5 vols. Ottawa: RCAP.

Royal Commission on the Donald Marshall, Jr., Prosecution. 1989. *Digest of Findings and Recommendations*. Halifax, NS: Royal Commission on the Donald Marshall, Jr., Prosecution.

Sider, Gerald M. 2014. *Skin for Skin: Death and Life for Inuit and Innu*. Durham, NC: Duke University Press.

Simpson, Leanne, ed. 2008. *Lighting the Eighth Fire*. Winnipeg: Arbeiter Ring.

Smith, Linda Tuhiwai. 2012. *Decolonizing Methodologies: Research and Indigenous Peoples*. 2nd ed. London: Zed Books.

Starr, June, and Mark Goodale. 2002. *Practicing Ethnography in Law*. New York: Palgrave MacMillan.

Strega, Susan, and Leslie Brown, eds. 2015. *Research as Resistance: Revisiting Critical, Indigenous, and Anti-Oppressive Approaches*. Toronto: Canadian Scholars' Press.

Truth and Reconciliation Commission of Canada (TRC). 2015. *Final Report of the Truth and Reconciliation Commission of Canada*. Vol. 1, *Summary: Honouring the Truth, Reconciling for the Future*. Toronto: James Lorimer.

United Nations General Assembly. 2007. *United Nations Declaration on the Rights of Indigenous Peoples*. New York: United Nations. http://www.un.org/esa/socdev/unpfii/documents/DRIPS_en.pdf.

Warry, Wayne. 2007. *Ending Denial: Understanding Aboriginal Issues*. Toronto: University of Toronto Press.

White, Richard. 1991. *The Middle Ground: Indians, Empires, and Republics in the Great Lakes Region, 1650–1815*. Cambridge: Cambridge University Press.

Wicken, William C. 2002. *Mi'kmaq Treaties on Trial: History, Land, and Donald Marshall Junior*. Toronto: University of Toronto Press.

Young, Tuma. 2016. "L'nuwita'simk: A Foundational Worldview for a L'nuwey Justice System." *Indigenous Law Journal* 13 (1): 75–102.

Cases Cited

R. v. Marshall, [1999] 3 SCR 456

R. v. Martin, [2016] CanLII 14 (NSPC)

R. v. Simon, [1985] 2 SCR 387

THREE

Research Partnerships and Collaborative Life Projects

COLIN SCOTT

Anthropology in Canada since the 1960s has been shaped increasingly by research partnerships with Indigenous communities and organizations, as well as other social agents in our fields of engagement. Such partnerships bring simultaneously into play four interconnected dimensions of research paradigms, identified by Opaskwayak Cree scholar Shawn Wilson (2008): ontological, epistemological, methodological, and axiological. In my own past work (Scott 1996, 2013), I have paid particular attention to how ontological assumptions shape Cree hunters' models of/for reality in experiential arenas of hunting, and I have also noted the normative implications for human and human-animal relations and land stewardship that are inherent in such a paradigm. Wilson (2008, 77) brings these explicitly to bear on research relationships: "From an epistemology and ontology based upon relationships, an Indigenous methodology and axiology emerge. An Indigenous axiology is built upon the concept of relational accountability. . . . Following this axiology, an Indigenous methodology must be a process that adheres to relational accountability. Respect, reciprocity and responsibility are key features of any healthy relationship and must be included in an Indigenous methodology." Hence, the conceptual, empirical, and normative aspects of research that engages territorial rights, conservation, and development alternatives are *relationally* embedded. Research partnerships involve knowledge coproduction toward goals and agendas that must, in some way and to some extent, be shared and mutually valued to be viable. This sharing is a conversation of several parts, joining and juxtaposing Indigenous knowledge and transdisciplinary academic, legal, and policy discourses that are "relationally accountable" to one another. Elsewhere Monica Mulrennan, Rodney Mark, and I have argued that such accountability depends on community-defined research agendas, collaboration throughout the research process, and research outcomes that are important to the community (Mulrennan, Mark, and Scott 2012).

In this chapter I explore, centrally, the qualities and conditions of knowledge coproduction in partnership, in practical arenas of engagement shaped by the relational ontologies and "life projects" of Indigenous collectivities (Blaser, Feit, and McRae 2004; Feit 2004). Necessarily and reciprocally, the life projects of researchers are in dialogue and negotiation with those of Indigenous partners, some of them academic researchers in their own right. My premise is that shared and allied purposes lend endurance to knowledge coproduction as a social process that may generate terms for relationship and community that escape ordinary hegemonies and hierarchies—in other words, a decolonizing knowledge process and methodology (Smith 2012; Kovach 2009).

My reflections on these phenomena are influenced by four decades working with Crees of Eeyou Istchee and with academic colleagues, both practically and theoretically, on a constellation of related topics: Cree hunters' knowledge (Scott 1996, 2006; Scott and Humphries, forthcoming); conditions for the continuity of hunting livelihoods and lifeways (Scott 1984; Scott and Feit 1992; Scott and Webber 2001); Cree tenure and struggles for legal recognition of Aboriginal title and rights (Scott 1988; Mulrennan and Scott 2001; Scott 2018); and protecting the ecological condition of the lands, waters, and biota of Cree territory in the face of resource-extractive industrial development (Scott 2005; Nasr and Scott, forthcoming; Scott and Mark, under review).[1] In a few pages, I obviously cannot go into all these matters. Yet the practical fulcrum for my thoughts in this chapter is an agenda that with several Cree and academic colleagues, occupying various institutional roles and from several disciplines, I have pursued over the past fifteen years—the establishment of a comprehensive regime of land and sea conservation for Eeyou Istchee, anchored in the customary tenure system and in a network of protected terrestrial and marine areas (for which state recognition is sought on terms acceptable to Cree people).

What does such an agenda, such a life project, entail for the coproduction of knowledge about the world and vice versa? How does it embrace a larger community of life transcending the human? How is it embedded in the relational ontology of reciprocity through which Cree hunters see—and potentially researchers and other citizens of the societal mainstream might come to understand—our relations within the larger community of life? "Living well" (Walsh 2010; Mejido Costoya 2013) in such community is at once a Cree preoccupation and a global problem, as we face proliferating capitalist growth-oriented resource-extractive development.

Life Projects, Partnerships, and Knowledge Coproduction

From the cultural perspective of Cree hunting, protecting a way of life and land-based livelihoods is inseparable from goals of conservation and environmental protection. *Relationship* and *respect* are anchoring premises of ontology, epistemology, ethics, and practical knowledge for land use and environmental responsibility. Further, the Cree way of doing politics assumes and advocates the primacy of respectful relationship—of community building—as a standard for interaction with agents of the state, corporate industry, and other members of Quebec/Canadian/global society (Feit 2004; Scott 2017), including researchers, of course. This is not to say that respectful relationships are always attainable in relations with others or among Crees; oppositional and antagonistic intervals, positions, and strategies occur. But there is a persistent dynamic of attempts to convert these moments of negative reciprocity into new relationships of positive reciprocity (see, for example, Scott 1989; GCC-EI and Québec 2002; GCC-EI and Canada 2008).

The relationship of Eeyou Istchee Crees with anthropologists and other researchers is long standing. More often than not, anthropologists have been regarded as allies in the politics of community building, from the engagement in the 1920s and '30s of such ethnographers as John Cooper and Frank Speck, who urged government intervention to protect Indigenous customary tenure against invasion and resource depletion by Euro-Canadian commercial trappers (Feit 1991; Morantz 2002; Scott and Morrison 2004, 2005); the applied anthropology of the McGill Cree Project in the 1960s (Chance 1968, 1970); and the research and testimony of Richard Salisbury (1986) and Harvey Feit (1986), among others, in the negotiation and implementation of the James Bay and Northern Quebec Agreement (JBNQA; GCC and Québec 1976), triggered by hydroelectric megaprojects (Diamond 1985); to continuous subsequent work that has contributed in diverse ways to the project of constructing the Cree Nation of Eeyou Istchee. Post-JBNQA history has involved a series of episodes in this project: the challenges of implementing a complex multijurisdictional agreement, where pressure had to be exerted on both Quebec and Canada to respect the letter and spirit of the treaty (Craik 2004); the orchestration of self-determined education and health and social services with agencies of state (Adelson 2000; Niezen [1998] 2009); the reestablishment and renewal of community sites (Preston 1982; Bosum 2001; Jacobs 2001); opposition to the Great Whale hydroelectric project (Tanner 1999; Patrick and Armitage 2001); understanding Cree sovereignty in the context of the Quebec independence referendum of the mid-1990s (Coon Come 1994; GCC 1995; Niezen [1998] 2009); efforts to put an end to industrial clear-cutting forestry practices (Feit and Beaulieu 2001); and the more or less continual negotiation of an extensive series of agreements complementary to the original JBNQA (Scott, forthcoming), dealing with matters of unresolved title and rights, mitigation, and compensation for development impacts; revenue sharing from resource-extractive activities; comanagement of territorial resources; and developing local and regional governance structures. Within this overall trajectory, a Cree-defined protected areas network and territory-wide conservation planning have occupied growing attention over the past fifteen years.

A role for anthropologists has been to advance interpretive frames and institutional means for enlarging the scope of Cree knowledge and decision making across a range of functions already alluded to: wildlife and habitat comanagement, environmental impact assessment, environmental rehabilitation, general conservation planning, evidence in land and resource rights litigation, health and social services, education, community development, and so forth. In these roles, anthropologists have been witnesses, participants, and coordinators in intellectual exchange between holders of Cree knowledge and various scientific, legal, and policy disciplines. We have participated in community-based innovations for the elaboration and intergenerational transmission of Cree knowledge, while responding to Cree requests for perspectives from scholarly theory and research. While open to, and increasingly fluent with, scientific information and perspectives, our Cree partners uphold the importance of Indigenous knowledge for addressing contemporary challenges. They seek to ensure its relevance for new generations of Cree youth, for whom cultural identity hinges on both old and new ways of connecting to, asserting rights over, and being responsible for, homelands and waters, while participating in new forms of "development" on their territory.

Enduring social relations of knowledge coproduction between local knowledge holders and academic researchers are fundamental. A moment's reflection tells us that knowledge production, whether in Indigenous or academic milieus, depends on long-term communication and collaboration—on generating shared questions for further inquiry, directed toward shared projects and the resolution of shared problems. Yet even in the context of resource comanagement institutions, true dialogue has been rare (Nadasdy 1999, 2005; Mulrennan and Scott 2005), because of the habitual authority of science in bureaucracy, the fact that the most knowledgeable Indigenous experts are seldom found at boardroom tables, and the often merely advisory role of Indigenous representatives in "co"-management.

Indigenous ontologies, epistemologies, and institutions of land and sea tenure retain, in variable measure, their capacity to shape social ecological relations. The autonomy of such orders, however, is an autonomy in relationship. The movement into Cree lives, lands, and waters of southern economic interests, of mass media, of politically intrusive administrations—not to mention Crees' own lively curiosity about what can be learned from others and usefully adapted to local purposes and social practices—ensures that Crees continually and perpetually negotiate their relationality, mental and material, with actors in "mainstream" and "global" arenas. The entanglements of Indigenous with scientific knowledge are iterative and not necessarily to be lamented; their separation would be untenable and illusory, for some of the reasons stated by Arun Agrawal (1995). But when the scope for locally determined choices is narrowed through domination, such entanglement may be associated with social dislocation and cultural loss. Conversely, when social orders and cultural understandings are reinvented in relational contexts of mutual respect, autonomy, and consent, actors can employ Indigenous knowledge to shape emergent realities, and in turn reconfigure their knowledge in relation to those realities, in a freer movement between cultural convention and invention (Wagner 1981).

Entanglement and hybridity, however, do not and should not occlude the possibility and the value of radical difference. Socioenvironmental relations of Cree hunting rest on ontological, epistemological, and ethical premises that can differ markedly, for example, from those of the management sciences often invoked by state authorities to legitimize regulatory interventions on Indigenous territory. Politically, ontological differences, with their epistemological and axiological corollaries, constitute not a universe but a pluriverse, "the partially connected unfolding of worlds" (Blaser 2014, 55), in which collective life projects must negotiate the conditions of their respective worlds, conditions not independent of one another. When knowledges compete and negotiate, it is a politics of "reality-making" (55) in which transcollective realignments result.

Partnership involves epistemological choice and imagination to open our research questions and procedures to the material, institutional, and knowledge world of Crees, no less than Crees experiment with bureaucratic resource management and the scientific idioms accompanying it. Implicit in this move are also ethical choice and imagination, since the conditions of existence of one world, let's say that of a mining or a hydro engineer, may conflict with the conditions of another, such as a Cree hunter's responsibility for life on a family territory. In this respect, at least, worlds intersect in a world that holds us in common. Where does this world in common begin and end? Does it consist merely of "bare material facts"—the incompatibility, say, between altered water quality in an engineered waterway and the ability of yellow sturgeon to reproduce? Or are more comprehensive relationships mutually discernible and hence shared? What do our imaginative leaps as academic researchers into the ontologies of others enable? Might we go so far as to rethink scientific paradigms in terms of Cree notions of relationship and respect, responsibility and consent, as embracing not just human relations, but other-than-human beings? Might engineers be "converted" to such premises? Might whole secular institutional and technological orders reinvent themselves accordingly? Between Indigenous "societies of nature" (Descola [1986] 1996) and secular humanist worlds of scientific rationality and authority, research partnerships invite shared journeys through networks of action, experience, and knowledge formation that, beyond dissolving modernist illusions of a society-nature divide (Latour 1993, 2004), might catalyze and propel new life projects into enlarged zones of ontological consensus.

Under what conditions are knowledge dialogues capable of circumventing or subverting the historical subordination of Indigenous knowledges and relationalities? Answers to this question rely on arenas of actual engagement, as defined by the ontologies, social relationships, and collective life projects of Indigenous people. The first challenge for academic researchers is to nurture relations of knowledge coproduction that are intelligible and useful from the perspective of Indigenous relationalities and life projects. Reciprocally, the life projects of researchers come to intersect with, if not be transformed by, those of Indigenous partners. Intersecting and allied projects foster knowledge coproduction capable of building shared views and community in ways that might possibly collapse the usual hegemonies.

Before returning to consider these processes in practical and everyday arenas, however, allow me to propose, however tentatively, some general contours of knowledge that seem to create conditions for the possibility of a "meeting of minds" beyond bare material facts.

Contours of Shared Knowledge

First, several motivations for knowledge suggest themselves to me as shared in some general way, even if expressed in diverse forms, as I reflect on research agendas shared with Cree partners. These motivations include a desire for true comprehension of the world; for how this comprehension informs right and good actions in the world; for the sharing and enactment of purpose and meaning in community; and for empowered agency in collectivity. I am ill prepared to argue the universality of these motivations, but more modestly, I report these general desires as present and intelligible across ontological contexts that I have experienced, suggesting to me that the confluence of motivation in research partnership might draw on something fundamental in the relational worlds of humans and our connections to other-than-humans.

Yet these generalities are accompanied by characteristics of knowledge or meaning from which ontological diversity might stem. One is the simultaneous necessity and insufficiency of signs: in cosmology, the irreducible tension between the vision and the void; in human purpose, the ever-shifting, never finished juxtaposition and concatenation of acts both shaping forward action and begging completion through sheer improvisation and invention; in the discursive play of subjugation and agency, ambivalence at the fulcrum of the hegemonic and the counter-hegemonic—the hair's-breadth tipping of one into the other, the anxious argument over what counts as political improvement; in science, the fallibility of systemic knowledge, which yet does not negate the need for logic and evidence in sustaining coherence and direction; in ethics, the need to justify our outlooks and actions with reference to the right and the good, even as our conceptions of these are challenged.

In brief, there is vast scope for contingency and heterogeneity, between and within social orders. The life worlds of elder Crees, their children and grandchildren—hunters, workers, and entrepreneurs—and the life worlds of researchers, seasoned and apprentice, from the multiple epistemological traditions of academe, might be thought to share no necessary congruence or complementarity. On the other hand, however, knowledge is responsive to social projects, including those in which diverse actors collaborate. The more sustained the collaboration, the stronger the tendency for collaborating social actors and holders/makers of knowledge to scrutinize the congruities and incongruities of their respective knowledges, to put the orders and practices of those knowledges into dialogue with one another. Such dialogue is comprehensive, if exploratory. A zone of emergent understandings develops between what is meaningful and motivating to an environmentally engaged university researcher, and what is meaningful and purposeful to a Cree hunter, as they consider the status and future of a living community in which both participate.

What is worth knowing about the world, what is or can be known, and what can and should be done about it are necessary questions for all parties to a collective project. All aspects and conditions of knowledge are simultaneously in play. The dialogue has no final conclusion, any more than any process of knowledge is ever complete. But some consensus is feasible, if not likely, as perspectives are considered in light of one another, about shared courses of action. Heterogeneous knowledges that appeared at the outset to be impossibly foreign to one another might, through mutual attention, yield translatability and mutually enhanced meaning; or areas of incommensurability may at least be acknowledged and functionally accommodated in pursuing a project of agreed importance.

Or, the premises of one might destabilize the premises of another. The impulse to translation, to render the other intelligible, is at the same time an exposure of the self to conversion by the other. Decolonization demands such openness to Indigenous knowledges subordinated in the colonial process. And the question will arise—what coproduced knowledge is better, more effective, more right, more true? If cultural relativism is an initial move beyond ethnocentrism to a starting position of openness and empathy, still the recruitment of a diverse collectivity to purposeful action calls for truths more than relative and arbitrary; truths must inspire consensus.

Conservation in Eeyou Istchee

Between 2003 and 2017, I served as a principal investigator and codirector (with Rodney Mark, former chief of the Cree Nation of Wemindji, and former deputy grand chief of the Grand Council of the Crees of Eeyou Istchee) of transdisciplinary research in partnership with Cree knowledge experts and land users, to advance the development of community-based protected areas (Mulrennan, Mark, and Scott, 2012; Mulrennan, Scott, and Scott, forthcoming; Scott and Brown, under review).[2] Concurrently, I have performed complementary research roles as a consultant with local and regional Cree governments and community-based organizations on land and sea conservation policy and planning, as well as Indigenous title and rights actions. Some two dozen senior researchers and graduate students, from multiple academic disciplines, and a similar number of undergraduate student researchers for briefer periods, have participated in this work. Our partnered knowledge dialogues in Eeyou Istchee are measured, for many participants, in years—for some, in decades—while all of us inherit a multigenerational legacy of Cree ontology, knowledge, and normative politics in collaboration with activist academics. Our project has been made possible by a convergence of commitments by all partners—whatever our diverse cultural, ontological, and epistemological origins—to the autonomy and flourishing of diverse forms of life in community, human and other-than-human. Ecology is the trope and paradigm attracting the allegiance of practitioners from the several fields of academe, while *pimaatisiiun*, the wellspring of life, the "continuous birthing of the world" (Scott 1996), is a no less compelling trope for Cree partners. It is anchored in a paradigm of trans-species relationality, of respect and reciprocity, that challenges us in the "Western" cultural mainstream to examine not only our understandings of objects and causality in the "natural" world, but the political relations in which these understandings are embedded and the foundational values to which they ultimately respond. There is no overhaul of Western knowledge without an overhaul of ethics; and both go back to radical meaning and purpose, to a vision true to life, and a project worth living.

Our project has engaged Cree hunters, leaders, and community members, together with university researchers, in work on multiple dimensions of the Eeyou Istchee environment and land-oriented lifeways and livelihoods, with a goal of enhancing the long-term prospects of both. We aim to do so in a manner that builds on Cree knowledge and practice as frontline institutions for environmental stewardship. At the same time, we grapple with models of development, externally imposed as well as homegrown, and their implications for Eeyou Istchee as a community of life. We seek to employ certain mechanisms of the state, in particular protected areas of various kinds, to buttress spaces for Cree lifeways and livelihoods, on terms that enhance rather than erode Cree autonomy.

Such strategies have risks and rewards. The jiujitsu of hegemony/counter-hegemony is, simply, an inescapable condition of life. It is a game that cannot be opted out of, only played through. We bear witness to proliferating resource-extractive pressures on Eeyou Istchee—hydroelectric megaprojects, broad-scale industrial forestry, mining, recreational hunting and fishing—and seek exemption for large areas deemed sacred by a people who occupy, use, and love these places and who are themselves, at the same time, significantly engaged in relations of capitalism and the state. The Crees of Eeyou Istchee are certainly among the more affluent and politically powerful Indigenous nations in Canada. Thanks to a successful history of regional nation building, including the human and financial resources to engage the state, the media, and domestic as well as international publics using a diverse repertoire of political and legal tools, the Crees have maneuvered themselves into the position where their consent is required for state governments or corporate industry to undertake activity on Cree territory (Scott 2008). This position has yielded multibillion-dollar treaty agreements (GCC-EI and Québec 2002; GCC-EI and Canada 2008), together with enhanced self-governance and cogovernance systems throughout their territory (GCC-EI and Québec 2012; GCC-EI and Canada 2017), that have attracted the attention of several neighboring Indigenous groups.

The question then becomes, how is this power used by Crees in enhancing and elaborating a "territory of difference" (Escobar 2008) for themselves? What goals for environmental protection and development gain traction from among competing perspectives and priorities internal to the Cree polity? There are those who are content in their relations with capitalism and the state, so long as "economic justice" in the form of equitable revenue sharing from industrial resource extraction is politically achievable. This perspective, however, fails to come to grips with the conundrum realized by other Crees: that the hunger for jobs and entrepreneurial opportunities of a growing population—if it is to be satisfied through ever-escalating resource extraction—could progressively undermine the ecological integrity of their homeland and waters. Hence, a politically sustainable vision and policy for Eeyou Istchee as a conserved territory is deemed urgent by many Crees. As researchers, activists, and environmentalists, non-Crees, too, must make our choices with which projects to align.

In certain respects, then, Eeyou Istchee is a microcosm both like and unlike the larger capitalist society. It has become involved in a similar triage between areas targeted or already surrendered for development and areas to be protected from the harsher consequences of industrial resource extraction. But Cree communities are also firmly engaged in land-based livelihoods that are critical to their economy, food security, health, and identity. The logic of relationships, and the social knowledge that emanates from this engagement with the land, conditions the Crees' terms of engagement with capitalism and with the state. The Crees of Eeyou Istchee have had success in gaining a measure of economic justice and a share of sovereign authority for their communities and their territory, through creative and sustained assertion of aboriginal and treaty rights. They occupy a space of both hegemonic accommodation and counter-hegemonic alternatives.

A collective life project on these terms, emerging in an Indigenous territory both of, and not of, the order of capital and state, may be transformative in ways that ramify and proliferate into adjacent and similar microcosms—and these are many across Indigenous territories in Canada and globally.[3] Our project is fundamentally local in its territorial objectives, but its fulfillment obliges work at the centers of growth economics and state power, and may entail interruptions of systems and routines at those centers, with consequences that reverberate globally. In any event, the Crees of Eeyou Istchee are at a point in their history when they have assembled the political and legal position and sufficient institutional strength to significantly shape the terms on which both development and environmental protection will proceed throughout their territories.

Cree ecological knowledge is a central matter for a project concerned with the protection of environment and land-based lifeways. For our Cree partners, there is no inherent separation of empirical and practical knowledge of the land from the ethical conduct of relations on the land—all participate in a paradigm of reciprocity, wherein respect is the anchoring value of positive reciprocity and consensual relationship building, while the negative reciprocity of force, greed, and subordination is its antithesis. Whether Cree knowledge's object is "environment" or "development," then, it addresses the status and quality of relationship, human to human, and human to other-than-human.

From the cultural perspective of Cree hunting, each of roughly three hundred family hunting territories that make up Eeyou Istchee is a conserved territory. Each development project that changes or degrades a portion of the ecology is directly and personally felt by someone. From this perspective, an excision of land and/or water for "development" purposes may be accepted by the community or the nation, but the duty of care of the extended family and the senior hunting territory steward on behalf of that family with respect to their customary territory does not end. If an area has not been "protected" in a strict sense, it nevertheless is subject to conservation measures. It is not merely abandoned to development; on the contrary, redoubled efforts to minimize damage and to rehabilitate habitat should ensue, as a matter of responsibility of the customary owners and stewards. This, of course, translates into demands on local and regional Cree institutions to maintain legal and political pressure on external industries and governments to pay for habitat restoration, to regulate operations, to control expansion, and so forth.

If state governments and resource-extractive industries see protected areas as local excisions from a landscape otherwise open for development, Cree hunters' perspective is on the continuous landscape as a community of life to be cared for, with local excisions for "development." This is an improvement on the mindset of many in state government, industry, and mainstream citizenries, for whom setting aside "protected areas" implies that everywhere else (understood to be the majority of the land/seascape) is "open for business." This discrepancy with Cree values and institutional practices notwithstanding, designating parts of their territories as "parks" or "protected areas" in forms congruent with state policies has strategic value for Crees, simply because these designations provide guarantees reinforced by the power of the state. This strategy, however, is accompanied by a more comprehensive regional conservation planning process (Cree Nation Government 2014) for the territory as a whole. Furthermore, the Cree Nations of Eeyou Istchee (2011) have signaled that they want a larger percentage of their territory protected than the now familiar targets of 10 percent of marine areas and 17 percent of terrestrial areas by 2020, adopted internationally (Convention on Biological Diversity 2010). The Cree Nations of Eeyou Istchee (2011) have also declared an expectation that cumulative development impacts on their territory be taken into account when the government of Quebec implements percentage area targets for protection. No management regime for a park or a protected area is likely to gain Cree consent unless it simultaneously enhances Cree governance of such areas—through both the authority of customary institutions of land management and that of the more recent electoral-bureaucratic institutions of regional Cree governance.

Conclusion

The negotiation of relationships in Cree territory unfolds in a Cree mode of politics, which seeks the inclusion of others, non-Cree no less than Cree, in normative relationships that assume, ontologically, the ubiquity of the law of reciprocity—preferably positive because if not, inevitably negative—in the world at large. This assumption is not quaint or isolated; it finds common ground with a political ecology that associates the negative reciprocity of environmental exploitation with rampant capitalist growth. As researchers, we inhabit and elaborate this common ground, and we are led to ask, how much of our scientific tradition, modernist outlook, and institutional life more broadly may be rethought through such a paradigm?

Readers might conclude that the Eeyou Istchee Cree case is somewhat exceptional, and certainly these Crees have generated an unusually well-organized and powerfully sustained national project within their territory. These qualities relate to several factors that are beyond the scope of the present chapter to address but include the unique legal and historical position of the Crees when hydroelectric megadevelopment came calling in the early 1970s; their capacity not to become locked into any once-and-for-all disposal of their rights by the state; their refusal on the whole to succumb to divide-and-conquer tactics from without, or to factional and centrifugal forces from within; and their sustained ability as a growing regional society to build politically and economically on their material, legal, and organizational resources and opportunities. A collaboration of knowledges, Cree and Euro-Canadian, has been fundamental to the trajectory of Cree society not only in the past half-century, but well back into earlier decades of fur-trade-era economy and society.

The case of the Crees is not without comparison, however, elsewhere in Canada and globally, where numerous Indigenous peoples have managed the regional solidarity, alliance building, and political imagination to significantly govern and defend their territories. In the shared knowledge projects of diverse allies, what counts in every case is respect and support for Indigenous life projects, an openness to the ontological and epistemological outlooks and practices of Indigenous allies, and above all a commitment to cultivating long-term relationships of politically engaged knowledge coproduction. These relationships must create the conditions for their own success, for there can be no doubt that Indigenous partners must accumulate power, if their knowledges, practices, values, and institutions are not to be subordinated to those of settler states and interstate orders.

All of us as humans reach for understandings of the world that inevitably exceed our grasp. Yet to abandon the quest for shared truths across our differences would subvert the inquiry of minds in community, would undermine allegiance to collective life projects, and would hinder consensus about the nature and importance of our relations with other life. It may be appropriate to conclude by acknowledging a possibility inherent in the "open-ended" quality of all cultural construction: we need not construe ontologies only as radically distinctive, incommensurable cultural visions in the plural; rather, dialogues of difference may converge on mutually recognizable truths about our being and relationship in the world, specifically laws of respect and reciprocity that, in the perspective of many of our Cree partners, bind us universally.

Notes

1. Eeyou Istchee today lies principally in northern Quebec, with portions extending into the James Bay and southeastern Hudson Bay areas of Nunavut, and into northeastern Ontario.
2. This work has been supported by the Social Sciences and Humanities Research Council of Canada (SSHRC), Northern Research Development Program; the SSHRC Community-University Research Alliances Program; the Fonds de Recherche du Québec sur la Société et la Culture (FRQSC), Soutien aux équipes de recherche programme; the FRQSC Regroupements stratégiques programme; the Quebec Centre for Biodiversity Science; and the McGill University Vice-Principal Research and International Relations Fund.
3. To encourage such proliferation, and cross-fertilization of knowledge and experience across Indigenous contexts, several of us have initiated the Indigenous Stewardship of Environment and Alternative Development (INSTEAD) trans-Americas research program, http://www.instead.ca, and the Centre for Indigenous Conservation and Development Alternatives (CICADA), http://www.cicada.world.

References

Adelson, Naomi. 2000. *"Being Alive Well": Health and the Politics of Cree Well-Being*. Toronto: University of Toronto Press.

Agrawal, Arun. 1995. "Dismantling the Divide Between Indigenous and Scientific Knowledge." *Development and Change* 26:413–39.

Blaser, Mario. 2014. "Ontology and Indigeneity: On the Political Ontology of Heterogeneous Assemblages." *Cultural Geographies* 21 (1): 49–58.

Blaser, Mario, Harvey A. Feit, and Glenn McRae, eds. 2004. *In the Way of Development: Indigenous Peoples, Life Projects, and Globalization*. London: Zed Books.

Bosum, Abel. 2001. "Community Dispersal and Organization: The Case of Oujé-Bougouou." In *Aboriginal Autonomy and Development in Northern Quebec and Labrador*, edited by Colin Scott, 277–88. Vancouver: UBC Press.

Chance, Norman, ed. 1968. *Conflict in Culture: Problems of Developmental Change Among the Cree*. Ottawa: Canadian Research Centre for Anthropology, Saint-Paul University.

Chance, Norman. 1970. *Developmental Change Among the Cree Indians of Quebec*. McGill University Cree Project. Ottawa: Department of Regional Economic Expansion.

Convention on Biological Diversity. 2010. *Strategic Plan for Biodiversity 2011–2020, Including Aichi Biodiversity Targets*. Nagoya, Aichi Prefecture, Japan. https://www.cbd.int/sp/default.shtml.

Coon Come, Matthew. 1994. "The Status and Rights of the James Bay Crees in the Context of Québec Secession from Canada." Address to the Center for Strategic and International Studies, Washington, DC, September 19, 1994.

Craik, Brian. 2004. "The Importance of Working Together: Exclusions, Conflicts and Participation in James Bay, Quebec." In *In the Way of Development: Indigenous Peoples, Life Projects, and Globalization*, edited by Mario Blaser, Harvey A. Feit, and Glenn McRae, 166–86. London: Zed Books.

Cree Nation Government. 2014. *Cree Regional Conservation Strategy*. Nemaska, QC: Cree Nation Government.

Cree Nations of Eeyou Istchee. 2011. *Cree Vision of Plan Nord*. Nemaska, QC: Cree Nations of Eeyou Istchee.

Descola, Philippe. (1986) 1996. *In the Society of Nature: A Native Ecology in Amazonia*. Cambridge: Cambridge University Press.

Diamond, Billy. 1985. "Aboriginal Rights: The James Bay Experience." In *The Quest for Justice: Aboriginal Peoples and Aboriginal Rights*, edited by M. Boldt, J. A. Long and L. Little Bear, 265–85. Toronto: University of Toronto Press.

Escobar, A. 2008. *Territories of Difference: Place, Movements, Life, Redes*. Durham, NC: Duke University Press.

Feit, Harvey A. 1986. "Hunting and the Quest for Power: The James Bay Cree and Whitemen in the Twentieth Century." In *Native Peoples: The Canadian Experience*, edited by R. B. Morrison and C. R. Wilson, 171–207. Toronto: McClelland and Stewart.

Feit, Harvey A. 1991. "The Construction of Algonquian Hunting Territories: Private Property as Moral Lesson, Policy Advocacy and Ethnographic Error." In *Colonial Situations: Essays on the Contextualization of Ethnographic Knowledge*, edited by G. W. Stocking, 109–34. Madison: University of Wisconsin Press.

Feit, Harvey A. 2004. "James Bay Crees' Life Projects and Politics: Histories of Place, Animal Partners, and Enduring Relationships." In *In the Way of Development: Indigenous Peoples, Life Projects, and Globalization*, edited by Mario Blaser, Harvey A. Feit, and Glenn McRae, 92–110. London: Zed Books.

Feit, Harvey A., and Robert Beaulieu. 2001. "Voices from a Disappearing Forest: Government, Corporate, and Cree Participatory Forestry Management Practices." In *Aboriginal Autonomy and Development in Northern Quebec and Labrador*, edited by Colin Scott, 119–48. Vancouver: UBC Press.

Grand Council of the Crees (GCC). 1995. *Sovereign Injustice: Forcible Inclusion of the James Bay Crees and the Cree Territory into a Sovereign Quebec*. Nemaska, QC: GCC.

Grand Council of the Crees (GCC) and le Gouvernement du Québec. 1976. *The James Bay and Northern Quebec Agreement*. Quebec City: Ministere des Communications, Editeur officiel du Québec.

Grand Council of the Crees (Eeyou Istchee) (GCC-EI) and le Gouvernement du Québec. 2002. *Agreement Concerning a New Relationship Between le Gouvernement du Québec and the Crees of Québec*. Quebec City: Secrétariat aux affaires autochtones.

Grand Council of the Crees (Eeyou Istchee) (GCC-EI) and le Gouvernement du Québec. 2012. *Agreement on Governance in the Eeyou Istchee James Bay Territory Between the Crees of Eeyou Istchee and the Gouvernement du Québec*. Nemaska, QC: GCC-EI and le Gouvernement du Québec.

Grand Council of the Crees (Eeyou Istchee) (GCC-EI) and the Government of Canada. 2008. *Agreement Concerning a New Relationship Between the Government of Canada and the Cree of Eeyou Istchee*. Ottawa: Indian and Northern Affairs Canada.

Grand Council of the Crees (Eeyou Istchee) (GCC-EI) and the Government of Canada. 2017. *Agreement on Cree Nation Governance Between the Crees of Eeyou Istchee and the Government of Canada*. Ottawa: Indigenous and Northern Affairs Canada.

Jacobs, Susan. 2001. "Building a Community in the Town of Chisasibi." In *Aboriginal Autonomy and Development in Northern Quebec and Labrador*, edited by Colin Scott, 304–15. Vancouver: UBC Press.

Kovach, Margaret. 2009. *Indigenous Methodologies: Characteristics, Conversations and Contexts*. Toronto: University of Toronto Press.

Latour, Bruno. 1993. *We Have Never Been Modern*. Cambridge, MA: Harvard University Press.

Latour, Bruno. 2004. *Politics of Nature*. Cambridge, MA: Harvard University Press.

Mejido Costoya, Manuel. 2013. "Latin American Post-Neoliberal Development Thinking: The Bolivian 'Turn' toward Suma Qamaña." *European Journal of Development Research* 25 (2): 213–29.

Morantz, Toby. 2002. *The White Man's Gonna Getcha: The Colonial Challenge to the Crees in Quebec*. Montreal: McGill-Queen's University Press.

Mulrennan, Monica, and Colin Scott. 2001. "Aboriginal Rights and Interests in Canadian Northern Seas." In *Aboriginal Autonomy and Development in Northern Quebec and Labrador*, edited by Colin Scott, 78–97. Vancouver: UBC Press.

Mulrennan, Monica, and Colin Scott. 2005. "Co-management—An Attainable Partnership? Two Cases from James Bay, Quebec, and Torres Strait, Queensland." *Anthropologica* 47 (2): 197–213.

Mulrennan, Monica, Rodney Mark, and Colin Scott. 2012. "Revamping Community-Based Conservation Through Participatory Research." *Canadian Geographer* 56 (2): 243–59.

Mulrennan, Monica, Colin Scott, and Katherine Scott, eds. Forthcoming. *Partnerships, Politics and Perspectives: Protected Area Creation in Wemindji Cree Territory*.

Nadasdy, Paul. 1999. "The Politics of TEK: Power and the 'Integration' of Knowledge." *Arctic Anthropology* 36 (1–2): 1–18.

Nadasdy, Paul. 2005. "The Anti-Politics of TEK: The Institutionalization of Comanagement Discourse and Practice." *Anthropologica* 47 (2): 215–32.

Nasr, Wren, and Colin Scott. Forthcoming. "The Politics of Traditional Ecological Knowledge in Environmental Development and Protection." In *Partnerships, Politics and Perspectives: Protected Area Creation in Wemindji Cree Territory*, edited by M. Mulrennan, K. Scott, and C. Scott. Vancouver: UBC Press.

Niezen, Ronald. (1998) 2009. *Defending the Land: Sovereignty and Forest Life in James Bay Cree Society*. Upper Saddle River, NJ: Pearson/Prentice Hall.

Patrick, Donna, and Peter Armitage. 2001. "Media Contestation of the James Bay and Northern Québec Agreement: The Social Construction of the 'Cree Problem.'" In

Aboriginal Autonomy and Development in Northern Quebec and Labrador, edited by Colin Scott, 206–32. Vancouver: UBC Press.

Preston, Richard. 1982. "The Politics of Community Relocation: An Eastern Cree Example." *Culture* 11 (3): 37–49.

Salisbury, Richard. 1986. *A Homeland for the Cree: Regional Development in James Bay, 1971–1981*. Montreal: McGill-Queen's University Press.

Scott, Colin. 1984. "Between 'Original Affluence' and Consumer Affluence: Domestic Production and Guaranteed Income for James Bay Cree Hunters." In *Affluence and Cultural Survival: 1981 Proceedings of the American Ethnological Society*, edited by Richard Salisbury and Elisabeth Tooker, 74–86. Washington, DC: American Ethnological Society.

Scott, Colin. 1988. "Property, Practice and Aboriginal Rights among Quebec Cree Hunters." In *Hunters and Gatherers—Property, Power and Ideology*, vol. 2, edited by James Woodburn, Tim Ingold, and David Riches, 35–51. London: Berg.

Scott, Colin. 1989. "Ideology of Reciprocity Between the James Bay Cree and the Whiteman State." In *Outwitting the State*, edited by Peter Skalnik, 81–108. New Brunswick, NJ: Transaction.

Scott, Colin. 1996. "Science for the West, Myth for the Rest? The Case of James Bay Cree Knowledge Construction." In *Naked Science: Anthropological Inquiries into Boundaries, Power and Knowledge*, edited by Laura Nader, 69–86. London: Routledge.

Scott, Colin. 2005. "Co-management and the Politics of Aboriginal Consent to Resource Development: The *Agreement Concerning a New Relationship between Le Gouvernement du Québec and the Crees of Quebec*." In *Canada: The State of the Federation, 2003—Re-Configuring Aboriginal-State Relations*, edited by Michael Murphy, 133–63. Montreal: McGill-Queen's University Press.

Scott, Colin. 2006. "Spirit and Practical Knowledge in the Person of the Bear Among Wemindji Cree Hunters." *Ethnos* 71 (1): 51–66.

Scott, Colin. 2008. "James Bay Cree." In *Handbook of North American Indians*, vol. 2, *Indians in Contemporary Society*, edited by Garrick Bailey, 252–60. Washington, DC: Smithsonian Institution.

Scott, Colin. 2013. "Ontology and Ethics in Cree Hunting: Animism, Totemism and Practical Knowledge." In *The Handbook of Contemporary Animism*, edited by Graham Harvey, 159–66. Durham, UK: Acumen.

Scott, Colin. 2017. "The Endurance of Relational Ontology: Encounters Between Eeyouch and Sport Hunters." In *Entangled Territorialities: Negotiating Indigenous Lands in Australia and Canada*, edited by Françoise Dussart and Sylvie Poirier, 51–69. Toronto: University of Toronto Press.

Scott, Colin. 2018. "Family Territories, Community Territories: Balancing Rights and Responsibilities Through Time." In "Who Shares the Land?: Algonquian Territoriality and Land Governance," edited by M. Chaplier, J. Habib, and C. Scott, special issue, *Anthropologica* 60 (1): 90–105.

Scott, Colin. Forthcoming. "On Nation-to-Nation Partnership and the Never-Ending Business of Treaty-Making: Reflections on the Experience of the Crees of Eeyou

Istchee (Eastern James Bay)." In "Living Together with the Land: Reaching and Honouring Treaties with Indigenous Peoples," edited by Sylvie Poirier and Clinton Westman, special issue, *Anthropologica*.

Scott, Colin, and Peter Brown, eds. Under review. "Dialoguing Knowledges: Finding our Way to Respect and Relationship."

Scott, Colin, and Harvey A. Feit. 1992. *The Income Security Program for Cree Hunters: Ecological, Social and Economic Effects*. PAD Monograph Series. Montreal: Programme in the Anthropology of Development, McGill University.

Scott, Colin, and Murray Humphries. Under review. "Metaphors, Models, and Ecological Relations: Intersections of Cree Knowledge and Scientific Ecology." In "Dialoguing Knowledges: Finding Our Way to Respect and Relationship," edited by C. H. Scott and P. G. Brown.

Scott, Colin, and Rodney Mark. Under review. "Responding to Environmental Decline in Eastern James Bay: Collaborative Approaches in Indigenous Knowledge and Trans-disciplinary Research." In "Indigenous Stewardship of Environment and Alternative Development," edited by C. Scott, E. Silva-Rivera, and K. Sinclair.

Scott, Colin, and James Morrison. 2004. "Frontières et territoires: Mode de tenure des terres des Cris de l'Est dans la région frontalière Québec/Ontario—I, Crise et effondrement." In "Propriété, territorialité et identité politique," edited by C. Scott, special issue, *Recherches Amérindiennes au Québec* 34 (3): 23–43.

Scott, Colin, and James Morrison. 2005. "Frontières et territoires: Mode de tenure des terres des Cris de l'Est dans la région frontalière Québec/Ontario—II, Reconstruction et renouveau." *Recherches Amérindiennes au Québec* 35 (1): 41–56.

Scott, Colin, and Jeremy Webber. 2001. "Conflicts Between Cree Hunting and Sport Hunting: Co-management Decision-Making at James Bay." In *Aboriginal Autonomy and Development in Northern Quebec and Labrador*, edited by Colin Scott, 149–74. Vancouver: UBC Press.

Smith, Linda Tuhiwai. 2012. *Decolonizing Methodologies: Research and Indigenous Peoples*. 2nd ed. London: Zed Books.

Tanner, Adrian. 1999. "Culture, Social Change, and Cree Opposition to the James Bay Hydroelectric Development." In *Social and Environmental Impacts of the James Bay Hydroelectric Project*, edited by James Hornig, 121–40. Montreal: McGill-Queen's University Press.

Wagner, Roy. 1981. *The Invention of Culture*. Chicago: University of Chicago Press.

Walsh, Catherine. 2010. "Development as *Buen Vivir*: Institutional Arrangements and (De)colonial Entanglements." *Development* 53 (1): 15–21.

Wilson, Shawn. 2008. *Research Is Ceremony: Indigenous Research Methods*. Halifax, NS: Fernwood.

PART II
MEXICO

FOUR

Legal Activism and Prison Workshops

The Paradoxes of Feminist Legal Anthropology and Cultural Work in Penitentiary Spaces

R. AÍDA HERNÁNDEZ CASTILLO

In this chapter, I reflect on the possibilities and limitations of a feminist legal anthropology based on an experience elaborating anthropological expert witness reports in defense of imprisoned Indigenous women, in particular through my participation in the case of Commander Nestora Salgado García, a member of the Regional Coordination of Communal Authorities (CRAC) of Guerrero, unjustly imprisoned for her participation in an Indigenous justice system.

This experience fit in what some authors have called legal activism through collaborative research, which implies the use of anthropological research for the coproduction of knowledges that can be used in the legal defense of Indigenous men and women. This methodological and epistemic option has faced strong criticism from those who, based on a positivist standpoint, defend the "neutrality" of anthropological science and disqualify any form of action research as "social work" or as mere "political activism." From other critical theoretical standpoints, judicial activism has also been questioned, with critics arguing that the practices of legal defense reproduce the language of power of the law, which contributes to construct subordinated subjectivities, or what Michel Foucault has called the power effect of legal discourse (Foucault 1977). In this chapter, I respond to these two questionings, asserting the epistemological wealth implied in producing knowledge in dialogue with the social actors with whom we work.

At the same time, based on my experiences elaborating anthropological expert witness reports, I argue that it is possible to analyze critically these systems of knowledge/power and their productive capacity while attempting to use rights discourses and legal spaces as emancipatory tools.

As a legal anthropologist and a feminist, I have faced the epistemic and political tension of always maintaining a critical outlook on positive law, as both a practice and a discourse, and on human rights as universalizing and globalized discourses, while participating in initiatives that support political struggles for the recognition of Indigenous peoples' rights both nationally and internationally. Some authors have suggested that these are irreconcilable options: either you engage in a critical analysis of the law and the juridization of political struggles, or you elect to reify the hegemonic perspectives of law and rights, supporting judicial activism. From these perspectives, the struggles for recognition of cultural rights tend to reproduce hegemonic definitions of culture and Indigenous peoples, and end up limiting political imaginaries around justice (Brown and Halley 2002).

Disagreeing with these perspectives, I have attempted throughout my academic career to maintain a permanent critical reflection on the law and rights, while participating in initiatives that support struggles for justice for Indigenous peoples and organizations, appropriating and resignifying national and international legislations. In recent years, I have participated in the elaboration of anthropological expert witness reports in support of the defense of Indigenous women in national and international legal actions.[1] The collective dialogues that have informed these reports have allowed me to contribute to a critical reflection on the Mexican state's justice system; therefore, the elaboration process has been as important as the report presented to the legal authorities.

For feminist anthropology, the relationship between the production of knowledge and a political commitment to social transformation has been, since its beginnings, a pivotal axis for its theoretical and methodological proposals (see Moore 1996). For that same reason, feminists have made important contributions to the critique of power networks that legitimize and reproduce scientific positivism, contributions that have often been overlooked by contemporary critical anthropology and postmodern theoreticians.[2] Latin American feminist anthropologists have developed these critiques not only in the theoretical and academic realms, but also in political and methodological practices that have taken the debates to the spaces of political struggle, popular education workshops, and collective organization, in which many feminist scholars participate.

In the development of a critical feminist legal anthropology in the Mexican context, the contributions from Indigenous women intellectuals have been vital. Working in the academic world and in political activism, they are developing their own theorizations in relation to the collective rights of their peoples and the rights of women. Their perspectives have been central for the development of a nonessentialist perspective of culture and Indigenous law. The academic production of authors such as Aura Estela Cumes (2007, 2009), Cristina Cucurí (Cervone and Cucurí 2017), Emma Delfina Chirix García (2003, 2013), Georgina Méndez Torres (2013), Millaray Painemal (2005), Martha Sánchez Néstor (2005), Irma Alicia Velásquez Nimatuj (2003), and Liliana Vianey Vargas Vásquez (2011, 2012), among others, have been fundamental in confronting essentialist perspectives of Indigenous cultures and in responding to the representations and victimizations of Indigenous women in the academic world and in public policies. It is impossible to continue to practice anthropology without addressing these new voices and representations; their theorizations are central for the decolonization of feminist anthropology.

The work of these scholars has inspired my development of a critical feminist perspective to frame this chapter. As a feminist scholar associated with a public research and graduate studies center, I have been simultaneously collaborating with and participating in various collective efforts toward the construction of a fairer life for women in alliance with Indigenous women's organizations (see Hernández Castillo 2016). Critical analyses of citizenship, the prison system, spaces for justice, public policies on gender—to mention some of the topics I have elaborated in my work—have represented not only problems for academic research, but also concerns that I have shared with my colleagues in organizations and other women with whom I have established epistemic and political dialogues.

Toward a Feminist Legal Anthropology

The history of legal anthropology, and of social anthropology more broadly, is closely related to the history of colonialism. The need to understand the political and legal systems of colonized peoples to better control and rule over them led colonial authorities to create alliances with those anthropologists whom we now recognize as the "forefathers" of our discipline. The history of this shameful alliance has been amply documented by anthropologists themselves (see Asad

1991; Leclerc 1973; Stocking 1991). While other disciplines, such as psychology, law, and sociology, have also been put at the service of domination, it must be acknowledged that the self-critical nature of anthropologists has had an influence on the production of a vast bibliography exploring this "dark history."

There is, however, a very limited record of how our discipline has contributed to denounce, disarticulate, or transform power and domination networks that affect the lives of the social actors with whom we work. And yet we know, especially through our "oral tradition," that many anthropologists have devoted their lives to defending the rights of Indigenous peoples, women, peasants, workers, migrants, and marginalized urban youths, without, however, much being written about the relationship between anthropology and emancipation or social justice.

The origins of Mexican legal anthropology are closely related to the alliances established between critical anthropologists and Indigenous organizations that struggled for recognition of their cultural and political rights. Although some of the ethnographic production of *indigenist anthropology* analyzed Indigenous forms of government and justice systems (see Aguirre Beltrán [1953] 1981), after August 1987, in response to a call by Rodolfo Stavenhagen, a work group was established to research Indigenous customary law, and a current of critical thought and analysis of interlegality started to develop, now internationally recognized as critical Mexican legal anthropology.[3]

These spaces of collective reflection arose in dialogue with a dynamic continental Indigenous movement that denounced the actuality of internal colonialism, rejected the monocultural nature of Latin American nation-states, and demanded recognition of Indigenous territorial and political rights. Echoing those demands, a group of Mexican anthropologists gave themselves to the task of critically analyzing national legal frames and further exploring the local spaces of justice administration. One result of these dialogues was the collective book *Entre la ley y la costumbre* (1990), edited by Rodolfo Stavenhagen and Diego Iturralde, a text that has become a classic of legal anthropological studies in Latin America.

One element that has characterized Mexican legal anthropology since that time is its questioning of functionalist understandings of *law and custom*, which prevailed in Anglo-Saxon legal anthropological studies of the time and which continue to conceive the legal space as an independent sphere that can be analyzed in isolation of other economic and social processes. Advocates of normative system analysis, heirs of Alfred R. Radcliffe-Brown's (1952) methodological tradition, and those who advocated legal process analysis, following Bronislaw

Malinowski ([1926] 1982), ignored how the systems or processes analyzed were inscribed in colonial or postcolonial relationships of domination. This silence concealed anthropologists' complicity with colonial enterprises.

In Mexico, the influence of Marxism and political economy in anthropology contributed to questioning these theoretical paradigms, giving rise to a critical legal anthropology that linked the analysis of power to the analysis of culture. For example, María Teresa Sierra analyzed the processes of dispute among Nahuas from Puebla and set them in the context of relations of domination with the nation-state. From an articulationist perspective, this critical legal anthropology analyzed the relationships between dominant and dominated normative systems, articulated through strategies developed by Indigenous peoples when resorting to one or the other (see Sierra 1993; Chenaut and Sierra 1995).

But the critical reflection of this legal anthropology was not limited to analyzing the contexts of domination of so-called legal pluralism, but, based on these reflections, political alliances were proposed to confront strategies of domination in contexts of internal colonialism. For example, the chapter by Magda Gómez, entitled "La defensoría jurídica de presos indígenas" (Legal advocacy for Indigenous prisoners), in the classic book by Stavenhagen and Iturralde (1990), denounces the institutional racism of the Mexican justice system and lays the foundations for the program to liberate Indigenous prisoners that Gómez promoted in the National Indigenist Institute. This theoretical, political perspective also oriented the work of Rodolfo Stavenhagen as UN special rapporteur on the situation of human rights and fundamental freedoms of Indigenous people from 2001 to 2008, a period during which he documented and denounced violations of the rights of Indigenous peoples internationally, maintaining a permanent dialogue with Indigenous organizations on five continents.

Other anthropologists chose to devote themselves full time to the defense of the rights of Indigenous peoples, as was the case with Abel Barrera with the creation of the Center for Human Rights of the Mountain of Tlachinollan, founded in 1993 in Tlapa de Comonfort, in the middle of one of the Indigenous regions hardest hit by government repression.[4] For more than two decades, the center has documented, denounced, and litigated thousands of violations of the human rights of Indigenous peoples. Using anthropological expert witness reports as a tool for defense in international courts, Tlachinollan's lawyers, with the support of legal anthropologists, have taken the Mexican state to the defendant's seat in the Inter-American Court of Human Rights, obtaining guilty sentences that have set precedents. In the cases of two Me'phaa Indigenous women,

Valentina Rosendo Cantú and Inés Fernández Ortega, a precedent was set in international justice by obtaining recognition of the collective grievance implied in sexual assault, recognition of military institutional violence committed by the Mexican state, and elimination of military jurisdiction in cases of human rights violations of civilians by members of the army (see Hernández Castillo 2016).

This critical legal anthropology has established dialogues with feminist activism, in which many of us, women anthropologists, have participated for several decades. As part of the epistemic and methodological pursuits that have arisen in these spaces, and in direct dialogue with the social actors with whom we have worked, we have developed a gender perspective that has questioned idealized notions of Indigenous law. These pursuits have implied taking the debates of legal anthropology to gender studies, and the debates of feminist anthropology to normative system studies.

In parallel, the Indigenous women's movement that arose under the influence of Zapatismo has produced its own theorizations and practices, including their specific rights as women in Indigenous justice systems. These Indigenous women's theorizations are reframing demands for recognition of the multicultural character of the nation, in the context of a broadened definition of culture that does not stop at its hegemonic representations and voices, but instead reveals the diversity within and the contradictory processes that give meaning to the life of a human collectivity. Instead of rejecting cultural diversity because it might give rise to practices that oppress and exclude them, Indigenous women decided to engage in a struggle over the very meaning of difference (see Speed, Hernández Castillo, and Stephen 2006; Hernández Castillo 2016; Méndez Torres et al. 2013). Their aim is to give it an emancipatory and nonexclusionary charge. Their demands for recognition of a culture that itself is in a process of change thus converge with the ideas put forward by some critical feminists regarding a politics of difference that does not mean exclusionary alterity or opposition but rather specificity and heterogeneity, where differences between groups are conceived in relational terms instead of defined by essential categories or attributes.

The Indigenous women´s perspectives on culture and gender justice have been important in the development of an activist legal anthropology in Mexico. Some of us arrived at the intersection of critical analysis of gender and legal anthropology based on concrete experiences in organizations with mestizo and Indigenous women that work on the legal defense of women who have been victims of sexual and domestic violence. One such organization, the Women's Group of San Cristóbal de Las Casas, was a support center for women and minors in an area where a large percentage of users were Indigenous women. In 1996, the search for more effective legal tools for the defense of women in contexts of cultural diversity and legal pluralism led me, with the Women's Group, to develop the coparticipatory research project "Positive Law and Customary Law in the Face of Sexual and Domestic Violence: An Exploratory Research Study in Search of Legal Alternatives in the Defense of Indigenous Women," which I coordinated; this was a pioneering project in the sense that it questioned the gender inequalities that mark both national and Indigenous law (see Hernández Castillo 2002).

This feminist legal anthropology has confronted idealized representations of Indigenous law promoted by some scholars in their defense of Indigenous rights, who, with their acritical perspectives, have silenced the voices and critiques of women in the communities themselves. These representations have been used by the power groups of those collectives to legitimize their privileges. The other end of this perspective has been that of those who, because of their colonial origin, disqualify all institutions and practices of Indigenous peoples, stereotyping their cultures and employing "selective labeling."[5]

I have participated politically in this debate, since for decades I was one of the voices critical of the essentialism of the Indigenous movement, which refused to deal with the issues of gender exclusions and domestic violence in Indigenous communities. My double identity as a scholar and an activist in a feminist organization working against sexual and domestic violence led me to the need to confront both the idealizing discourses regarding Indigenous culture by an important sector of Mexican anthropology and the ethnocentrism of an important sector of liberal feminism. In a polarized context where women's rights have been presented as incompatible with the collective rights of the peoples, it has been difficult to advocate for more nuanced perspectives on Indigenous cultures that recognize the power dialogues that constitute them, while also vindicating Indigenous peoples' right to their own culture and self-determination.

This polarization of feminist and Indianist standpoints deepened in the last two decades, after the Zapatista movement raised the need for constitutional reform that recognized the autonomous rights of Indigenous peoples (see Speed, Hernández Castillo, and Stephen 2006). In this context, an important sector of Mexican liberal feminism made alliances with antiautonomy liberal sectors, warning of the dangers that recognition of the collective rights of their peoples would presumably imply for Indigenous women. All of a sudden, several scholars who had never written a single line in favor of Indigenous women started to "worry" about their rights and even to cite, out of context, the work of some feminist scholars who had written about violence in Indigenous regions. This situation changed the context of our academic work, raising the need to contextualize our reflections about domestic violence beyond cultural analyses, including an analysis of state violence, highlighting the importance of the structural context in which this violence took place.

At this political crossroads, organized Indigenous women have given us clues on how to rethink Indigenous demands from a nonessentialist perspective. Their theorizations regarding culture, tradition, and gender equity have been set forth in political documents, memoirs of encounters, and public discourses. Indigenous women never requested such "protection" from liberal intellectuals or the state to limit the autonomy of their peoples. On the contrary, they have demanded the right to self-determination and their own culture, while struggling within the Indigenous movement to redefine the terms on which tradition and custom are understood and to participate actively in the construction of autonomous projects.

These theorizations have been fundamental in the development of a feminist legal anthropology that, reincorporating the analysis of interlegality by pioneering studies, has included the intersectional perspective to demonstrate how the multiple exclusions of gender, race, class, and generation mark Indigenous and peasant women's relations with national and communal justice systems (see Sierra 2004a; and Sierra, Hernández Castillo, and Sieder 2013). Many of these studies have been accomplished through relationships of collaboration and alliances with Indigenous organizations, such as the CRAC of Guerrero (see Arteaga Böhrt 2013; Sierra 2009, 2013, 2014), the Zapatista autonomous regions (Mora 2008, 2013, 2014), the Indigenous Women's Home in Cuetzalan (Mejía 2008, 2010; Mejía, Cruz Martín, and Rodríguez 2006; Terven 2005, 2009; Terven and Chávez 2013), and the Organization of Me'phaa Indigenous Peoples (Hernández Castillo 2017b), to mention only a few examples.

Personally, the issues posed by Indigenous women in the context of our political dialogues have led me to focus my legal anthropological work not only on an analysis of the limitations of communal justice, but also on a study of the structural racism that permeates penal justice, as well as the possibilities of Indigenous law when Indigenous women's active participation is achieved in the spaces of Indigenous administration of justice, as is the case in the Zapatista autonomous regions in Chiapas and in the CRAC in Guerrero.

In the following sections, I discuss, through the lens of feminist legal anthropology, two experiences of activist research in which I have participated in recent years.

The Sisters of the Shadow Publishing Collective and Prison Workshops

Throughout the last decade, the CIESAS legal anthropology research team, of which I am a part, has been studying the effects of multicultural constitutional reforms on the spaces of Indigenous justice.[6] Our research work has joined the voices of those who have pointed out the limitations of the so-called multicultural reforms, denouncing how these have been used by neoliberal governments as a new strategy for control and regulation (see Hale 2002, 2005; Hernández Castillo, Paz, and Sierra 2004). After at first celebrating the long overdue recognition of Indigenous peoples' rights in Latin American constitutions, we realized that, by leaving responsibilities that were formerly the state's in the hands of Indigenous peoples and communities, multicultural reforms responded to neoliberal agendas' need for decentralization and a more participatory civil society, contributing to the construction of what has been defined as neoliberal citizenship regimes (Yashar 2005).

Yet, this context seems to have changed substantially in the last decade. The discourse of multiculturalism is being replaced by a new discourse, which addresses Indigenous people as poor people who must be incorporated into development or as destabilizing agents who threaten national security. In Mexico, a new legislative reform—the Constitutional Reform on Penal Justice and Public Security, approved in June 2008—signaled the change from a neoliberal multiculturalism to an authoritarian conservatism that, in the name of the struggle against drug trafficking, has increased the vulnerability of Indigenous peoples in the penal justice system, militarized their communities, and criminalized social movements.[7]

In this context, as part of the CIESAS legal anthropology team, I decided to work on Indigenous women's experience with penal justice. The limited information available from the censuses indicated a 122 percent increase in the number of incarcerated Indigenous people (Hernández Castillo 2013). The most recent census information we have regarding Indigenous men and women in prison is from 2017, when the National Commission of Security from the

Ministry of Interior reported that 8,412 inmates were identified by the prison institutions as "Indigenous" from a total of 247,000. Of these inmates, 286 were women, and 8,126 were men. This same source offers a breakdown according to speakers of Indigenous languages: 1,849 Nahuatl speakers, 639 Zapotecos, 527 Mixtecos, 499 Tsotsil, 491 Tseltal, 412 Otomí, 403 Maya, 361 Mazateco, 356 Totonaca, 334 Tarahumara, 219 Chol, 216 Tepehuano, 212 Chinanteco, 196 Cora, 179 Huasteco, 173 Mixe, 172 Mayo, 158 Tlapaneco, 152 Mazahua, and 116 Huichol (CNDH 2017). Nonetheless, in my ten years of experience working in Morelos prisons and visiting and giving workshops in the states of Chiapas, Puebla, Yucatán, and Oaxaca, as well as Mexico City, I can confirm that much of the population originally from Indigenous communities tends to be considered exclusively as a poor population of peasant origins, thus erasing their ethnic ascription from the penitentiary census. The "nonidentification" is even more frequent when it is about the population that has lost their Indigenous mother language, a consequence of violent campaigns of acculturation, which have been promoted in Indigenous regions by public education institutions.

The main reason for imprisonment was their participation in cultivating natural drugs or small-scale drug dealing, characterized as "crimes against health." This tendency was being reproduced among incarcerated Indigenous women—57 percent of Indigenous women in prison had been jailed for that crime. This reality led me to want to review the criminal records of Indigenous women in prison, to analyze how the multiple exclusions of gender, race, and class had influenced their penal proceedings.[8] The Mexican penal system's lack of openness and transparency, however, made it impossible to gain access to those documents.

While seeking access to the legal records of Indigenous women in prison, I contacted the feminist poet Elena de Hoyos, who led a creative writing workshop in the Women's Area of the CERESO state prison in Morelos, locally known as the Female CERESO of Atlacholoaya. This was the beginning of a collective project on which I have worked since 2008, accompanying the processes of reflection and self-representation of a group of Indigenous and peasant women in prison, who, in dialogue with other mestizo prisoners, have created a prison publishing project, of which I am a member—the Colectiva Editorial Hermanas en la Sombra (Sisters of the Shadow Publishing Collective; see the works by Elena de Hoyos and Mariana Ruíz in Hernández Castillo 2017b).

Giving continuity to the creative writing workshop Woman, Writing Changes Your Life, led by Elena de Hoyos, in mid-2008 I started the Life Histories Workshop, in which ten female writers participated along with ten bilingual Indigenous women sharing their life histories, all of them imprisoned in the CERESO of Atlacholoaya. The formal objective of this workshop was "to train the participants in the technique of elaborating life histories as a literary resource and a means to reflect on gender inequalities."[9] Through the workshop, which has taken place weekly since October 2008 to the date of this writing (November 2018), each participant has worked on her own project, elaborating the life history of an Indigenous colleague in prison. Once a month, the women whose histories are being systematized attend the workshop to listen to the progress and comment on or question the representations of their lives made by the workshop's members.

This experience has allowed me to witness the importance of oral history as a tool for feminist reflection and as a strategy to destabilize colonial racist and sexist discourses. While feminist theoreticians have written much about the importance of recuperating the history of everyday life and of understanding women's experiences through oral history (see Wolf 1996; Reinharz 1992; Fonow and Cook 1991), I could not have imagined how the collective reconstruction of individual histories could build sorority among different women while writing a counter-history that made evident how the coloniality of power hinders access to justice for Indigenous and peasant women.

In this context, oral history is no longer a "methodological tool for the researcher," becoming instead a means for collective reflection demonstrating how ethnic and class hierarchies marked the various trajectories of women in prison's exclusion and lack of access to justice. Comparing the experiences of Indigenous and non-Indigenous women, peasants, workers, and professionals, homosexuals and heterosexuals, by sharing and reflecting on their life histories, has unveiled the hierarchies that characterize the justice system in Mexico and in society as a whole.

This was the beginning of a space for dialogue and collective construction of knowledge that has implied new challenges for me as a scholar and an activist. What began as a writing workshop became the Sisters of the Shadow Publishing Collective, which has already published fifteen books and multiple articles for cultural and prison magazines, and whose denunciations and histories have helped revise legal records and liberate several women who were unjustly incarcerated.[10] In 2015, several of the collective's members already out of prison launched the radio series *Songs from the Guamúchil: Life Histories of Indigenous and Peasant Women*, which is broadcast by the local radio station in Morelos and through digital radio by the International Work Group for Indigenous Affairs.[11]

The appropriation of creative writing for self-representation has confronted the long tradition of ventriloquism in anthropology. The anthropologist does not have the power to represent Indigenous women's life histories, but the Sisters of the Shadow members, through their editorial project, are using poetry, short stories, and autobiography to denounce the multiple violences that marked their path to prison.

Their voices and reflections have challenged ethnocentric viewpoints on what constitutes life with dignity, by questioning the notions of "backwardness" and "development" that tend to characterize the difference between the lives of Indigenous and urban mestizo women. By sharing their histories, we realized that in most cases, the national justice system did not represent "progress" relative to forms of communal justice:

> Since our detention, most of us suffered beatings, mistreatment, insults from law enforcement officers. And, in some cases, extortions that are not subject to trial. Magically, on the way from the Attorney's Office to the prison, the medical reports and testimonies of such aggressions disappear. Instead, a few lines appear saying that the defendant, now presumably responsible for the crime, showed up under no coercion whatsoever to declare. The *costalazos* [beatings] leave no marks, but they do leave an injured body like mine. (Fragment of *Los costalazos*, by Águila del Mar, in Colectiva Editorial Hermanas en la Sombra 2013, 32)

By sharing their life histories, Indigenous and non-Indigenous women realized that sexual and domestic violence assume different forms and are privatized in urban spaces, but they do not disappear. By comparing their histories, reflecting on them, and setting them down in a collective text, they were able not only to denounce racism, sexism, and classism in the penal system, but also to build new subjectivities by denaturalizing violence. In the spaces of collective reflection created to read the life histories, the participants started to express the need to strengthen themselves internally to confront it and, especially, to teach their daughters who are out of prison not to reproduce the types of relationships they had lived. In an exercise developed in the context of the workshop, the participants wrote letters addressed to women who were psychologically and physically mistreated:

> Break away from the chain of being submitted because of your low self-esteem. Find yourselves again and understand your surroundings. Life does not have to

be the way it was for our mothers, we must develop our own way of thinking and communicating with our spouses, to keep from repeating our families' forms of life. To have our own way of living, to know how to express our feelings, and to teach our children to express their own feelings both with the people around them and their spouses. To know how to say no to violence. (Exercise by Guadalupe Salgado in the Life Histories Workshop at the Female CERESO of Atlacholoaya, May 17, 2009)

Woman, if you dare to break the silence, perhaps you can stop the pattern of violence that surrounds you and that you probably reproduce. It is understandable that, if we live in a violent household, sooner or later we will reproduce that violence . . . but today I invite you to rebel against that which humiliates you and tramples on your dignity. Listen, you are invaluable, do not keep silent, scream, fight for your rights because, after all, you are a woman. (Exercise by Susuki Lee in the Life Histories Workshop at the Female CERESO of Atlacholoaya, May 17, 2009)

My experience with the inmates from Atlacholoaya is not unique; literary workshops have been a doorway for many scholars into prison spaces, and several analysts have pointed out the complicities that can be established between "instructors" and prison authorities when the workshops respond to the prison system's needs for control and domestication. The way in which the contents of literary workshops respond to the cultural context of the inmates and enable, or not, a critical reflection is decisive in the hegemonic or counter-hegemonic role that these spaces can assume.[12]

At the same time, the life histories written by the inmates provided a unique testimonial material that allowed me to give sustenance to my academic analysis of penal justice and institutional racism (see Hernández Castillo 2013, 2017a). This academic work also helped develop the script of the documentary video *Bajo la sombra del Guamúchil: Historias de vida de mujeres indígenas y campesinas en prisión* (Under the shade of the Guamúchil: Life histories of imprisoned Indigenous and peasant women), edited by Meztli Rodríguez, with the participation of the inmates who make up the collective.

I do not intend to idealize the intercultural dialogues that have taken place in the context of this activist research project; Marina Ruiz (2017), a poet and editor on our team, reflects on the challenges and limitations we have faced throughout these ten years. Despite our position as allies of the women in prison, in our role as coordinators of the workshops and members of the Sisters of the Shadow Publishing Collective, our dialogues with them have been marked by our ethnic and class differences. Nonetheless, by maintaining a permanent dialogue on the "why" of the life histories and testimonies, we have been able to somewhat compensate for these structural inequalities by turning these textual strategies into collective forms of knowledge production, as part of larger processes of struggle for self-representation. Transforming the old role of writers and anthropologists as "narrators of the life histories of other women" into that of partners in processes to systematize Indigenous women's own histories, and even in the creation of their own publishing projects, has been a part of our efforts to build and consolidate spaces for a collective construction of knowledge.

Cultural Expert Witness Reports and Access to Justice

Another area where legal activism by anthropologists has started to develop is the elaboration of cultural expert witness reports, or anthropological affidavits, for cases of litigation in the national justice system or in international courts. The multicultural reforms of the last decade have brought about changes in the criminal procedure codes that allow the use of cultural evidence presented by expert witnesses. These anthropological affidavits are reports elaborated by specialists that contribute to recognizing the cultural context of the defendant or the plaintiff. The main objective of these reports is to provide information to the judges on the importance of cultural differences in understanding a specific case. For many anthropologists who advocate the use of cultural expert witness reports, their use represents an improvement in Indigenous people's possibilities to access justice. Laura Valladares, a member of the board of directors of Colegio de Etnólogos y Antropólogos de México (Mexican Association of Ethnologists and Anthropologists)—one of the professional associations that certifies expert witnesses—says in this respect:

> Cultural expert work plays a relevant role in the sense that it contributes to the construction of processes of procurement of justice in conditions of greater equity for indigenous peoples and their members, while also contributing to create scenarios of legal pluralism.... [I]t is a tool that allows the establishment of a dialogic relationship between positive law and indigenous normative systems, as well as the construction of a society that respects cultural diversity. (Valladares 2012, 11–13)

The amendment to Article 2 of the Constitution in August 2001, known as the Law of Indigenous Rights and Culture, brought about changes in Mexico's Federal Code of Criminal Procedure, recognizing the right to a translator when the plaintiff or the defendant does not speak Spanish well and the possibility of presenting expert reports on the cultural factors that influenced the events being judged.[13] Prior to these reforms, lawyers representing Indigenous defendants, some of them pro bono defense lawyers from the National Indigenist Institute, attempted to diminish a sentence or liberate an Indigenous prisoner by resorted to the now revoked Article 49 of the Federal Code of Criminal Procedures, which considered sentence reductions for people considered to be in conditions of "extreme cultural backwardness"; in other words, they resorted to an article that reproduced the racism of Mexican society. Despite the multicultural reforms, this argument continues to be used by many lawyers who, despite their "good intentions," reify and reproduce racist viewpoints of Indigenous peoples in their defense (see Escalante Betancourt 2015).

While the use of expert witness reports can seem an improvement in access to justice, compared with the racist standpoints that invoked "cultural backwardness," they are a legal tool that presents new ethical and epistemic dilemmas for us anthropologists who defend legal activism. On one hand, expert witness reports reproduce the hierarchies of knowledge, legitimizing the anthropologist's cultural knowledge as superior to that of the Indigenous peoples themselves. We, the anthropologists, hold the legitimate cultural knowledge recognizable by the administrators of justice, and as such, we have the last word regarding what is a "true Indigenous cultural practice" or "true Indigenous law."

The anthropologist's role as a "cultural translator" before the state's administrators of justice is further complicated by having to accept the rules of legal discourse, where the complex and contextual perspectives of anthropological analysis are often considered out of place. In Australia, where anthropologists have traveled a long road in elaborating cultural expert witness reports to support Aborigines' struggle for recognition of their territorial rights, David Trigger describes the contradictions they face in accepting the "rules of the game" of state justice as "a tension here between the necessity for a researcher to fit investigations into this legal context, yet maintain professional independence such that one's own disciplinary standards and practices are not swamped by the force of the legal process" (2004, 31–32). The legal process, for example, needs "positive truths" regarding Indigenous peoples' cultures, which oftentimes implies reproducing essentialist representations of their cultures, where the internal diversity of the communities, the various perspectives regarding culture and tradition existing among genders and generations, are rendered invisible by homogenizing cultural descriptions.

How do we resolve these dilemmas? By staying away from legal spaces and allowing the "technologies of truth" used in legal systems to keep representing Indigenous peoples as "culturally backward"? My option has been to seek more participatory and dialogic ways of elaborating the reports, so that the process of developing the report can contribute to a collective reflection on the discourses of power that underlie the discourses and practices of the law.

Anthropological Expert Witness Work for the Defense of Nestora Salgado

The space of the Medical Tower of Tepepan, a hospital exclusively for patients serving sentences in Mexico City prisons, is very different from the prison of Atlacholoaya, where I had been doing collaborative research work with imprisoned Indigenous and peasant women. I could have been in any hospital room in the country were it not for the various strongly guarded security gates I had to go through. It was there that I first met Nestora Salgado García, commander of the CRAC of Guerrero, who since August 21, 2013, had been detained, undergoing three legal processes plagued with contradictions. Nestora was transferred to Tepepan from a high-security prison in Tepic, Nayarit, on May 28, 2015, after a hunger strike that almost ended her life.

I arrived at this prison space to work with her on her life history, but in a different context than the writing workshops of the Sisters of the Shadow Collective. Nestora was isolated, and there was no way to create a collective space of reflection such as we have in Atlacholoaya. The idea was to reconstruct, through in-depth interviews, her trajectory working on communal justice and her personal history, to elaborate an anthropological expert witness report requested by her defense attorneys. The purpose of this report was to argue that the crimes attributed to her, such as kidnapping and illegal detention, were actually legal detentions performed in the context of an Indigenous communal justice system recognized by various state, national, and international legislation.

The expert report required working for several months with Nestora, reconstructing her life trajectory and the political context that led her to participate in an organization formed by the inhabitants of Olinalá, to join the CRAC. At the same time, my colleague Héctor Ortiz Elizondo and I worked with several sectors of CRAC-Olinalá in focus groups.

The elaboration of the expert witness report involved translating into an academic language, accessible to the administrators of justice, processes that had already been described by Nestora in her depositions. Contextualizing the actions of the Olinalá police within the framework of broader processes of communal justice reconstruction, and locating the exercise of autonomous justice within legal and international frames, also required systematizing the collective memory of the members of the CRAC, a task that the CIESAS legal anthropology team had been undertaking for several years (see Arteaga Böhrt 2013; Sandoval 2005; Sierra 2004b, 2009, 2014). These studies have revealed the challenges and achievements of an Indigenous justice system created in 1998, called Communal Security, Administration of Justice, and Reeducation System, represented by the Regional Coordination of Communal Authorities Community Police (CRAC-PC). It is not an "ancestral justice" system of a single Indigenous people but a network of cooperation among communities and peoples with different traditions, worldviews, and languages, who had their own strategies for conflict resolution and who got together to create a common system of self-protection and administration of justice. This system of security and justice is based on an authority structure headed by a regional assembly, based in turn on community assemblies, which guarantee transparency and a democratic exercise.

Our research team had analyzed the processes of reconstituting Indigenous law and the importance of the "communal" in the conception of justice; women's role in reconceptualizing the so-called *usos y costumbres* (traditions and customs); and the impact of the multicultural reforms in these spaces of legal pluralism (see Arteaga Böhrt 2013; Sierra 2004b, 2009, 2014). The expert witness work required revisiting part of the road traveled in this research to contextualize the work of the CRAC-Olinalá within the broader framework of processes to reconstitute Indigenous justice. In the report, we needed to demonstrate that the citizen police force commanded by Nestora Salgado belonged to the Indigenous security and justice system known as the CRAC-PC, and that, therefore, its acts in the administration of justice were backed by Article 37 of Law 701, Recognition, Rights and Culture of the Indigenous Peoples and Communities of the State of Guerrero.

Through individual and collective interviews, we recuperated the historical memory regarding communal justice of the people from Olinalá and the most recent process whereby the decision was made to join the regional Indigenous justice system. We documented how, faced with the violence and impunity that reigned in the municipality, with a strong presence of organized crime, the inhabitants of Olinalá invited the regional coordinators of the San Luis Acatlán CRAC to share with them their experiences building a justice system based on Indigenous law. In December 2012, two months after the community police of Olinalá was created, a training workshop on Indigenous justice and the operational principles of the CRAC was held. In this workshop, about four hundred community police members participated, including women and elderly men of "knowledge," some of whom had participated in the Community Peasant Rounds (Rondas Comunitarias Campesinas) of the early twentieth century and were thus versed in the principles of Indigenous justice.

This workshop and a process of public consultations in neighborhood assemblies and home-to-home visits met the requirements set by the CRAC. A community's commitment to CRAC implied adopting the internal bylaws of the Communal Security, Justice, and Reeducation System of the Mountain and Costa Chica Regions of Guerrero as norms and the House of Justice of El Paraíso as the location where the processes to reeducate citizens who commit crimes are carried out.

The forty-three people "kidnapped," whose "illegal" detention Nestora Salgado was accused of, were citizens undergoing processes of reeducation at the House of Justice of El Paraíso, in the municipality of Ayutla de los Libres, Guerrero, and who were liberated by members of the Mexican army in a regional operation in August 2013. These people had been detained by the various community police forces of the region. None of the people liberated mentioned Nestora Salgado in their depositions, nor have they showed up for cross-examination to corroborate their denunciations.

Through interviews with some of the detainees, we were able to document the activities carried out in the process of reeducation, which consisted of performing community work according to each detainee's skills and abilities, as well as periodic talks with elders and CRAC authorities about the importance of changing the attitudes and behaviors that led to their detention. I do not intend to describe in detail what the expert reports elaborated, each of them related to a different legal process, but I do wish to point out the challenges that this type of legal activism implies, not only because of the context of violence in which the research takes place, but also because of the hierarchies that our reports reify.[14]

Nestora had already described all these processes in her deposition; our work consisted of systematizing, contextualizing, and describing analytically the principles and the operation of Indigenous justice in the region. Once again, we faced the ethical and political challenge of reproducing epistemic hierarchies that placed our specialized knowledge above the local knowledges of CRAC members. Given this dilemma, we decided to give a central role in our work to the oral histories of the CRAC members—not only the members of the community police of Olinalá, but also those who shared the experience of imprisonment, such as Gonzalo Molina, coordinator of the House of Justice of El Paraíso, imprisoned in Chilpancingo since November 2013 because of his participation in several mobilizations demanding Nestora Salgado's freedom.

Answering the question "May the experts explain the social and cultural circumstances that led the defendant to participate in the CRAC's system of justice and security" required reconstructing, in dialogue with Nestora, her life history and her trajectories of exclusion. Because of the strict rules of Mexico's penal system, we were not authorized to introduce recorders; therefore, the interviews were performed with the support of historian Nancy López Salais, who took notes of our dialogues and later transcribed them. This same material was reviewed in the following session by Nestora, and it deepened the reflection on the context of state violence, racism, and criminalization of Indigenous justice in which her detention took place. The transition from Nestora's oral testimony to Nancy's written words often implied changing the textual style in which things were said and the metaphors used, which were often left out of the transcription because of time limitations. Nestora carefully reviewed the written text, and if she recognized in it a voice that was not hers, she patiently corrected our version of her story, explaining the importance of the details we had overlooked. This almost archaeological work of reconstructing memory stimulated many emotions in her and in us, and we often ended up weeping together because of the impotence we felt in the face of impunity. The neutral and distant ethnographer, whose sole task is to describe a reality to be later analyzed, was never present in these dialogues among women, where we shared the same concern to give form and meaning to a version of reality that was silenced by legal discourse. The life history narrated by Nestora contrasted with what we found in her criminal record, where her voice had been transformed into a deposition transcribed and summarized by a secretary whose language was marked by legal discourse.

During our long conversations, which always began by sharing the details of her everyday life in prison, she told us about her childhood, what it meant for her to grow up in a militarized region, where her father, Fernando Salgado, a man of knowledge, a traditional healer renowned in the whole region, was continuously harassed by the army. Not without a tinge of humor, she described how the military would arrive at her house to search it, looking for any clue that could link her father to Lucio Cabaña's guerrillas, who were then active in the region. The only thing they found were his medicinal plants, his healing syrups, and sometimes a seriously ill patient he was sheltering. Don Fernando's home, like the home of his daughter Nestora decades later, was a space for encounter, where he not only saw patients, but also supported those who had problems. These were the values of solidarity that Nestora inherited from her parents.

Like many women from the region, Nestora married very young, and at the age of fifteen, she had already given birth to the first of her three daughters. Years later, she migrated to the United States with all her family in search of a better life. As an undocumented migrant, she suffered, among other vulnerabilities, domestic violence. It was this experience of violence that made her seek self-help groups, where she began to reflect on patriarchal violence and to help other migrant women who faced the same problems. The progressive laws of the city of Seattle, which protect women victims of violence, awarded her U.S. citizenship, which allowed her to return to Mexico after a thirteen-year absence.

On her return, she faced another type of patriarchal violence—the violence of organized crime, which had laid siege to Olinalá, charging *derecho de piso* (use rights) acting with total freedom, murdering and kidnapping those who refused to accept their demands.[15] Her experience supporting women victims of violence, her communal commitment, and her courage to denounce corruption contributed to developing her leadership and to her appointment as commander of the community police when the inhabitants of Olinalá decided to organize themselves to put a stop to violence and impunity. Nestora and the community police of Olinalá joined the Indigenous justice system of the CRAC, recognized by Law 701 of the state of Guerrero, Article 2 of the Mexican Constitution, and ILO Convention 169. CRAC was recognized by the state government, which provided it with communication equipment and transportation, but when the community police went beyond resolving minor local problems and started to confront organized crime networks that were colluding with local governments, CRAC's actions were declared illegal. Testimonies by CRAC-Olinalá members and even by people who had gone through the system of reeducation made it evident that her gender had influenced the virulence with which her leadership in the community police had been criminalized. For a woman to dare denounce the corruption of the narco-state and to refuse to sell out for any price was taken as a personal affront by those who hold local power.

Elaborating the expert witness report entailed not only demonstrating how CRAC's Indigenous justice system works today and the importance of the reeducation processes based on a conception of justice that breaks away from the punitive perspective of positive law, but also documenting the multiple exclusions that had marked Nestora Salgado's life and that continued to characterize her experience before the Mexican state's criminal justice system.

The almost one hundred pages of her life history were reduced to three fifteen-page reports, which left out all the metaphors, anecdotes, and experiences of pain and impotence that characterized her narration. Despite our concern for being as faithful as possible to her version of the story, the report required an extension and a format that once again required imposing the language of legality. The transcribed material, however, was used years later by Nestora and me, to write and publish her life story (Salgado and Hernández Castillo 2018). These are some of the main challenges that we confront as expert witnesses, when we accept having to speak the language of law. The richness of testimony is lost when we have to translate oral history in a legal document, although we can use other, parallel textual strategies to coproduce knowledge in alliance with the Indigenous people with whom we work, as we have done in this case.

The three reports were presented in November 2015, at the First Lower Court for Criminal Matters of the Judicial District of Morelos, in the city of Tlapa de Comonfort, Guerrero. On April 18, 2016, five months after the expert witness reports were presented in court, Nestora Salgado was set free. Her liberation was the result of a struggle that articulated the efforts of her lawyers in Mexico, Sandino Rivero and Leonel Rivero, and her international legal representative, Alejandra Gonza, with national and international solidarity and political pressure from the UN Working Group on Arbitrary Detention. Our reports were one of many elements in a larger political and legal strategy. Nestora's detention had political origins, and political pressure from different sectors in Mexico as well as international solidarity were crucial for her release.

Nestora's liberation and the organized struggle around her case demonstrated the legitimacy of Indigenous systems of justice in Mexico. It was a successful example of what can be achieved through political alliances in the struggle against the criminalization of Indigenous women.

Her life history, narrated by her and written collaboratively, has been essential to creating other informational products that have contributed to the international campaign for her freedom, such as the radio program created by the Sisters of the Shadow Collective in solidarity with Nestora as part of the series *Songs from the Guamúchil*, broadcast by the Morelos radio station and by the International Work Group for Indigenous Affairs through Internet radio; a TV program broadcast by HispanTV on the criminalization of Indigenous justice; and a series of articles in national newspapers.[16] Throughout the elaboration of the reports, we never lost sight of the fact that counter-hegemonic use of the law only makes sense if it is accompanied by other collective political efforts that allow diversifying the discourses and experiences that speak in the name of justice and legality.

Finally, in 2018 Nestora requested the notes of the long interviews we did during her incarceration, and she wrote her own testimony, in which she denounces the patriarchal violence and racism of the Mexican justice system (Salgado García and Hernández Castillo 2018). Today, Nestora Salgado is the first Indigenous woman elected senator in the Mexican Congress. After leading an international struggle for the liberation of Mexican political prisoners and in favor of Mexican immigrants in the United States, she accepted the invitation of the National Regeneration Movement (center-left political party) to run as a senatorial candidate. She ran for Congress after a public commitment with the CRAC authorities to defend Indigenous people's rights in the Senate and to struggle against Indigenous criminalization and dispossession of Indigenous lands.

Final Reflections

In this chapter, I try to demonstrate that legal activism does not have to be at odds with a critical reflection on rights discourses and state justice. The possibility of establishing intercultural dialogues around rights and justice not only questions the state's regulatory discourses but is also an opportunity to destabilize our certainties and broaden our emancipatory horizons. As a feminist, collaborative legal anthropology done in conjunction with Indigenous women has helped me rethink my own notions of gender rights and has led me to question my own complicities in the processes of "erasure" of other conceptions and expectations of justice for women.

The voices and experiences of the incarcerated women who participated in the Life Histories Workshop and Nestora Salgado's testimony are sources of theorization that speak of other ways to understand women's rights and their relationship to the collective rights of peoples. The theorizations that resulted from these collective spaces, and others that are being created in different regions of Latin America, reveal the new utopian horizons that organized Indigenous women are building based on a recovery of the historical memory of their peoples.

Creating knowledge through dialogues of knowledges necessarily implies changing how we understand theory, methodology, and, in a broader sense, our own function as anthropologists in a world that is increasingly characterized by inequality, violence, and impunity.

Notes

1. In other publications, I have analyzed my participation in expert witness reports for the Inter-American Court of Human Rights in the cases of Inés Fernández Ortega and Valentina Rosendo Cantú, two Me'phaa Indigenous women raped by members of the Mexican army (see Hernández Castillo, 2017a). The complete report for *Inés Fernández v. the Mexican State* can be seen at Hernández Castillo and Ortiz Elizondo (2012).
2. For an analysis of action research from the perspective of feminist scholarship, see Lykes and Coquillon (2007).
3. The term *indigenist* (*indigenista* in Spanish) is the term used to refer to a current of Mexican anthropology that was oriented to public policy making toward Indigenous peoples, as well as the usually promoted integration and acculturation.
4. See Tlachinollan: Centro de Derechos Humanos de la Montaña, last updated September 24, 2018, http://www.tlachinollan.org.
5. I borrow the term "selective labeling" from the work of Uma Narayan (1997) to refer to how certain features are selected (over others) as representative of a culture or as constitutive of an identity, asserting that a historical contextualization of so-called cultural traditions allows us to unveil the power networks hidden behind the representation of difference. A historical perspective of Indigenous identities allows us to perceive how certain features of a culture change without anyone believing that this puts cultural integrity at risk (for example, by incorporating cars, agricultural technology, media, etc.), while selectively deciding that other changes do constitute a cultural loss (inheritance of land by women, the rejection of fixed marriages, etc.).
6. CIESAS refers to the Centro de Investigación y Estudios Superiores en Antropología Social. The legal anthropology research team is made up of María Teresa Sierra, Rachel Sieder, Mariana Mora, and, more recently, Carolina Robledo and Dolores Figueroa. A generation of legal anthropologists has come out of our graduate program, including Yuri Escalante, Adriana Terven, Claudia Chávez, Ivette Vallejo, Juan Carlos Martínez, Ana Cecilia Arteaga, and Morna Macleod, among others.

7. Amendments were made to Articles 16–22; fractions 21 and 23 of Article 73; fraction 7 of Article 115; and fraction 13 of section B in Article 123, all in the Political Constitution of the United Mexican States.
8. I use the concept of *race* to refer to how political imaginaries on the difference between Indigenous and non-Indigenous people have been biologized in the Mexican context, constructing racial hierarchies that reproduce colonial structures. The concept of ethnicity, which is hegemonic in penal studies, does not account for this power relation, which enables us to speak of the actuality of internal colonialism and of what some authors call the coloniality of power (see Quijano 2000).
9. Program of the Life Histories Workshop, coordinated by Aída Hernández and registered in the Secretariat of Social Rehabilitation of the state of Morelos.
10. With the support of IWGIA and CIESAS, the publishing collective published the book and video *Bajo la sombra del Guamúchil: Historias de vida de mujeres indígenas y campesinas presas* (Under the shade of the Guamúchil: Life histories of Indigenous and peasant women in prison; 2010), the handcrafted books *Fragmentos de mujer* (Fragments of a woman; 2011) and *Mareas cautivas: Navegando las letras de las mujeres en prisión* (Captive tides: Navigating the letters of women in prison; 2012), and, with a grant from the National Institute of Fine Arts, the three-book collection *Revelaciones intramuros* (Intramural revelations).
11. See Colectiva Editorial Hermanas en la Sombra, "Cantos desde el Guamúchil: Literatura nacida en la cárcel," Radio Encuentros, streaming audio, 16:10 min., November 2015, https://soundcloud.com/radio-encuentros/cantos-desde-el-gua muchil-literatura-nacida-en-la-carcel.
12. In this regard, Ben Olguín (2009) compares the experience of Jean Trounstine (2001) in her literary workshop project *Shakespeare Behind Bars*, where the writer taught prisoners, mostly women of color, sixteenth-century English theater, spurning the writings of the inmates themselves, with the work of James B. Waldram (1997), who, following Paulo Freire's pedagogy, recuperated in the workshops the spirituality and traditional knowledges of the native population imprisoned in Canada. Sara Makowski argues that the Literary Workshop held at the Eastern Female Detention Center in Mexico City, where she did her research, was a space for counterpower: "In the Literary Workshop they speak of what in no other part of the prison can be even mentioned. There, afflictions are socialized and awareness is raised, in a group, of the ways to transform complaints and pain into critical judgment" (1994, 180).
13. In the Federal District, these changes to the Code of Criminal Procedures recognizing the right to a translator and to expert witness reports had been implemented more than a decade earlier, in January 1991, thus constituting pioneering legislation in terms of cultural reforms in the administration of justice.
14. The three expert witness reports that ethnologist Héctor Ortiz Elizondo and I elaborated refer to Penal Cause 05/2014 for the Crime of Aggravated Kidnapping, related to the detention of two minors with the written authorization of their

mothers to rescue them from organized crime networks; Penal Cause 196/2013-IP for Illegal Detention of the forty-three people detained at the House of Justice of El Paraíso; and Penal Cause 48/2014 for Illegal Detention of five people involved in a case of cattle rustling.

15. The expression *derecho de piso* has its origins in a contribution that farm workers had to pay to the land owner for the right to build their houses on the land. In modern usage, the expression describes organized crime's extortion of small business owners and citizens in return for respecting their lives.

16. See Colectiva Editorial Hermanas en la Sombra, "Criminalización de la justicia indígena: El caso de Nestora Salgado en México," Radio Encuentros, streaming audio, 14:59 min., January 12, 2016, https://soundcloud.com/radio-encuentros/criminalizacion-de-la-justicia-indigena-el-caso-de-nestora-salgado-en-mexico; Rosalva Aída Hernández, "Biodata," http://www.rosalvaaidahernandez.com/#!multimedia/c4nd; Rosalva Aída Hernández Castillo, "Nestora, el narcoestado y la violencia patriarcal," *La Jornada*, August 24, 2015, http://www.jornada.unam.mx/2015/08/24/opinion/022a2pol; Rosalva Aída Hernández Castillo, "El racismo judicial y las policías comunitarias en Guerrero," *La Jornada*, August 2, 2015, http://www.jornada.unam.mx/2015/08/03/opinion/019a1pol.

References

Aguirre Beltrán, Gonzalo. (1953) 1981. *Formas de gobierno indígena*. Mexico City: National Indigenist Institute.

Arteaga Böhrt, Ana Cecilia. 2013. "Todas somos la semilla: Ser mujer en la Policía Comunitaria de Guerrero—Ideologías de género, participación política y seguridad." Master's thesis, CIESAS, Mexico City.

Asad, Talal. 1991. "Afterword: From the History of Colonial Anthropology to the Anthropology of Western Hegemony." In *Colonial Situations: Essays on the Contextualization of Ethnographic Knowledge*, edited by George W. Stocking, 314–34. Madison: University of Wisconsin Press.

Brown, Wendy, and Janet Halley, eds. 2002. *Left Legalism/Left Critique*. Durham, NC: Duke University Press.

Cervone, Emma, and Cristina Cucurí. 2017. "Gender Inequality, Indigenous Justice and the Intercultural State: The Case of Chimborazo Ecuador." In *Demanding Justice and Security: Indigenous Women and Legal Pluralities in Latin America*, edited by Rachel Sieder, 120–49. New Brunswick, NJ: Rutgers University Press.

Chenaut, Victoria, and María Teresa Sierra. 1995. *Pueblos indígenas ante el derecho*. Mexico City: CIESAS.

Chirix García, Emma Delfina. 2003. *Alas y raíces: Afectividad de las mujeres mayas—Rik'in ruxik' y ruxe'il: Ronojel kajowab'al ri mayab' taq ixoqi'*. Guatemala: Grupo de Mujeres Mayas Kaqla.

Chirix García, Emma Delfina. 2013. *Cuerpos, poderes y políticas: Mujeres mayas en un internado católico*. Guatemala: Ediciones Maya' Na'oj.

Colectiva Editorial Hermanas en la Sombra. 2013. *Mareas cautivas: Navegando las letras de las mujeres en prisión*. Cuernavaca: Astrolabio Editorial.

Comisión Nacional de Derechos Humanos (CNDH). 2017. "Personas Indígenas en Reclusión." In *Informe Anual de Actividades 2017 de la Comisión Nacional de Derechos Humano*. Mexico City: CNDH.

Cumes, Aura Estela. 2007. "Las mujeres son 'mas indias': Género, multiculturalismo y mayanización. ¿Esquivando o retando opresiones?" Unpublished manuscript.

Cumes, Aura Estela. 2009. "Mujeres indígenas, poder y justicia: De guardianas a autoridades en la construcción de culturas y cosmovisiones." In *Mujeres indígenas y justicia ancestral*, edited by Miriam Lang and Anna Kucia, 33–50. Quito, Ecuador: UNIFEM Región Andina.

Escalante Betancourt, Yuri. 2015. *El racismo judicial en México: Análisis de sentencias y representación de la diversidad*. Mexico City: Juan Pablos Editor.

Fonow, Mary Margaret, and Judith Cook. 1991. *Beyond Methodology: Feminist Scholarship as Lived Research*. Bloomington: Indiana University Press.

Foucault, Michel. 1977. *Discipline and Punish: The Birth of the Prison*. New York: Pantheon Books.

Hale, Charles. 2002. "Does Multiculturalism Menace? Governance, Cultural Rights and the Politics of Identity in Guatemala." *Journal of Latin American Studies* 34 (2002): 485–524.

Hale, Charles. 2005. "Neoliberal Multiculturalism: The Remaking of Cultural Rights and Racial Dominance in Central America." *Political and Legal Anthropology Review* 28 (1): 10–28.

Hernández Castillo, Rosalva Aída. 2002. "National Law and Indigenous Customary Law: The Struggle for Justice of the Indigenous Women from Chiapas." In *Gender, Justice Development and Rights*, edited by Maxine Molyneux and Shahra Razavi, 384–413. Oxford: Oxford University Press.

Hernández Castillo, Rosalva Aída, ed. 2010. *Bajo la sombra del Guamúchil: Historias de vida de mujeres indígenas y campesinas en prisión*. With DVD, 41 min. Mexico City: IWGIA and Ore-media.

Hernández Castillo, Rosalva Aída. 2013. "¿Del estado multicultural al estado penal? Mujeres indígenas presas y criminalización de la pobreza en México." In *Justicias indígenas y estado: Violencias contemporáneas*, edited by María Teresa Sierra, R. Aída Hernández Castillo, and Rachel Sieder, 299–335. Mexico City: FLACSO-CIESAS.

Hernández Castillo, Rosalva Aída. 2016. *Multiple Injustices: Indigenous Women, Law, and Political Struggle*. Tucson: University of Arizona Press.

Hernández Castillo, Rosalva Aída. 2017a. "Between Community Justice and International Litigation: The Case of Inés Fernández before the Intre-American Court." In *Demanding Justice and Security: Indigenous Women and Legal Pluralities in Latin America*, edited by Rachel Sieder, 29–51. Mexico City: Rutgers University Press.

Hernández Castillo, Rosalva Aída, ed. 2017b. *Resistencias penitenciarias: Investigación activista en espacios de reclusión.* Mexico City: Juan Pablos Editores, IWGIA, Colectiva Editorial Hermanas en la Sombra, Libera Desarrollo Humano.

Hernández Castillo, Rosalva Aída, and Héctor Ortiz Elizondo. 2012. "Violación de una indígena Me'phaa por miembros del ejército Mexicano Presentado ante la Corte Interamericana de Derechos Humanos." *Boletín Colegio de Etnólogos y Antropólogos Sociales,* January–December 2012. http://media.wix.com/ugd/be8021_77d60becb 40b41ad80f062e61399bcb3.pdf.

Hernández Castillo, Rosalva Aída, Sarela Paz, and María Teresa Sierra, eds. 2004. *El estado y los indígenas en tiempos del PAN: Neoindigenismo, legalidad e identidad.* Mexico City: CIESAS-Porrúa.

Leclerc, Gerald. 1973. *Antropología y colonialismo.* Madrid: Editorial Comunicación Serie B.

Lykes, M., and M. Coquillon. 2007. "Participatory and Action Research and Feminisms: Towards Transformative Praxis." In *Handbook of Feminist Research: Theory and Praxis,* edited by Sharlene Nagy Hesse-Biber, 297–326. Thousand Oaks, CA: Sage.

Makowski, Sara. 1994. "Las flores del mal. Identidad y resistencia en cárceles de mujeres." Master's thesis, FLACSO, Mexico City.

Malinoswki, Bronislaw. (1926) 1982. *Crimen y costumbre en la sociedad salvaje.* Barcelona: Ariel.

Mejía, Susana. 2008. "Los derechos de las mujeres nahuas de Cuetzalan: La construcción de un feminismo indígena, desde la necesidad." In *Etnografía e historias de resistencia: Mujeres indígenas, procesos organizativos y nuevas identidades políticas,* edited by R. Aída Hernández Castillo, 453–502. Mexico City: CIESAS-PUEG-UNAM.

Mejía, Susana. 2010. "Resistencia y acción colectiva de las mujeres nahuas de Cuetzalan: ¿Construcción de un feminismo indígena?" PhD diss., UAM-Xochimilco, Mexico City.

Mejía, Susana, Celestina Cruz Martín, and Carlos Rodríguez. 2006. "Género y justicia en comunidades nahuas de Cuetzalan: La experiencia de la Casa de la Mujer Indígena." Paper presented at the 5th Congress of the Latin American Legal Anthropology Network (RELAJU), Oaxtepec, Mexico, November 2006.

Méndez Torres, Georgina. 2013. "Mujeres Mayas-Kichwas en la apuesta por la descolonización de los pensamientos y corazones." In *Senti-pensar el género: Perspectivas desde los pueblos originarios,* edited by Georgina Méndez Torres, Juan López Itzín, Sylvia Marcos, and Carmen Osorio Hernández, 27–63. Mexico City: Red de Feminismos Descoloniales.

Méndez Torres, Georgina, Juan López Itzín, Sylvia Marcos, and Carmen Osorio Hernández, eds. 2013. *Senti-pensar el género: Perspectivas desde los pueblos originarios.* Mexico City: Red de Feminismos Descoloniales.

Moore, Henrietta L. 1996. *Antropología y feminismo.* Colección Feminismo. Madrid: Cátedra.

Mora, Mariana. 2008. "Decolonizing Politics: Zapatista Indigenous Autonomy in an Era of Neoliberal Governance and Low Intensity Warfare." PhD diss., University of Texas at Austin.

Mora, Mariana. 2013. "La politización de la justicia zapatista frente a la guerra de baja intensidad." In *Justicias indígenas y estado: Violencias contemporáneas*, edited by María Teresa Sierra, Rosalva Aída Hernández Castillo, and Rachel Sieder, 195–224. Mexico City: FLACSO/CIESAS

Mora, Mariana. 2014. "Repensando la política y la descolonización en minúscula: Reflexiones sobre la praxis feminista desde el zapatismo." In *Más allá del feminismo: Caminos para andar*, edited by Márgara Millán, 155–82. Mexico City: Pez en el Agua/Red de Feminismos Descoloniales

Narayan, Uma. 1997. *Dislocating Cultures: Identities, Traditions, and Third World Feminism* New York: Routledge Press

Olguín, Ben. 2009. *La pinta: Chicana/o Prisoner Literature, Culture, and Politics*. Austin: University of Texas Press.

Painemal, Millaray. 2005. "La experiencia de las organizaciones de mujeres mapuche: Resistencias y desafíos ante una doble discriminación." In *La doble mirada: Voces e historias de mujeres indígenas de latinoamericanas*, edited by Martha Sánchez Néstor, 77–87. Mexico City: UNIFEM/ILSB.

Quijano, Anibal. 2000. "Coloniality of Power, Eurocentrism, and Latin America." In *Nepantla: Views from the South* 1 (3): 533–80.

Radcliffe-Brown, Alfred R. 1952. *Structure and Function in Primitive Society*. Glencoe, IL: Free Press.

Reinharz, Shulamit. 1992. *Feminist Methods in Social Research*. New York: Oxford University Press.

Ruíz, Mariana. 2017. "Flores en el Desierto: Ensayo sobre las Relaciones entre mujeres de adentro y de afuera del Cereso Morelos en el marco de un proyecto artístico-literario." In *Resistencias Penitenciarias. Investigación Activista en Espacios de Reclusión*, edited by R. Aída Hernández Castillo, 223–37, Mexico City: IWGIA–Juan Pablos Editores.

Salgado García, Nestora, and R. Aída Hernández Castillo. 2018. "Nestora Salgado García: Un testimonio de resistencias ante la violencia patriarcal y la criminalización de los pueblos indígenas." *Desacatos*, no. 57, 168–79.

Sánchez Néstor, Martha, ed. 2005. *La doble mirada: Voces e historias de mujeres indígenas latinoamericanas*. Mexico City: UNIFEM/ILSB.

Sandoval, Abigail. 2005. "No es lo mismo la teoría que la práctica: El ejercicio de la justicia comunitaria desde la cotidianeidad de los mixtecos de Buena Vista, municipio de San Luis Acatlán." Master's thesis, CIESAS, Mexico City.

Sierra, María Teresa. 1993. "Usos y desusos del derecho consuetudinario indígena." *Nueva Antropología*, México, 44 (agosto), 12–26.

Sierra, María Teresa, ed. 2004a. *Haciendo justicia: Interlegalidad, derecho y género en regiones indígenas*. Mexico City: CIESAS-Porrúa.

Sierra, María Teresa. 2004b. "Diálogos y prácticas interculturales. Derechos humanos, derechos de las mujeres y políticas de identidad." *Desacatos*, no. 15–16, 126–48.

Sierra, María Teresa. 2009. "Las mujeres indígenas ante la justicia comunitaria: Perspectivas desde la interculturalidad y los derechos." *Desacatos*, no. 31, 73–88.

Sierra, María Teresa. 2013. "Indigenous Women Fight for Justice: Gender Rights and Legal Pluralism in Mexico." In *Gender Justice and Legal Pluralities: Latin American and African Perspectives*, edited by Rachel Sieder and John-Andrew McNeish, 56–81. New York: Routledge.

Sierra, María Teresa. 2014. "Pueblos indígenas y usos contra-hegemónicos de la ley en la disputa por la justicia: La Policía Comunitaria de Guerrero." *Journal of Latin American and Caribbean Anthropology* 20 (1): 133–55.

Sierra, María Teresa, R. Aída Hernández Castillo, and Rachel Sieder. 2013. *Justicias indígenas y estado: Violencias contemporáneas*. Mexico City: FLACSO-CIESAS.

Speed, Shannon, R. Aída Hernández Castillo, and Lynn M. Stephen. 2006. *Dissident Women: Gender and Cultural Politics in Chiapas*. Austin: University of Texas Press.

Stavenhagen, Rodolfo, and Diego A. Iturralde, eds. 1990. *Entre la ley y la costumbre: El derecho consuetudinario indígena en América Latina*. Mexico City: Instituto Indigenista Interamericano, Instituto Interamericano de Derechos Humanos.

Stocking, George, Jr., ed. 1991. *Colonial Situations: Essays on the Contextualization of Ethnographic Knowledge*. History of Anthropology, vol. 7. Madison: University of Wisconsin Press.

Terven, Adriana. 2005. "Revitalización de la costumbre jurídica en el juzgado indígena de Cuetzalan: Retos desde el estado." Master's thesis, CIESAS, Mexico City.

Terven, Adriana. 2009. "Justicia indígena en tiempos multiculturales: Hacía la conformación de un proyecto colectivo propio—La experiencia organizativa de Cuetzalan." PhD diss., CIESAS, Mexico City.

Terven, Adriana, and Claudia Chávez. 2013. "Las prácticas de justicia indígena bajo el reconocimiento del estado: El caso poblano desde la experiencia organizativa de Cuetzalan." In *Justicias indígenas y estado: Violencias contemporáneas*, edited by María Teresa Sierra, Rosalva Aída Hernández Castillo, and Rachel Sieder, n.p. Mexico City: CIESAS/FLACSO.

Trigger, David. 2004. "Anthropology in Native Title Cases: Mere Pleading, Expert Opinions or Hearsay?" In *Crossing Boundaries: Cultural, Legal, Historical and Practice Issues in Native Title*, edited by Sandy Toussaint, 24–33. Carlton, VIC: Melbourne University Press.

Trounstine, Jean. 2001. *Shakespeare Behind Bars: The Power of Drama in a Women's Prison*. New York: St. Martin's.

Valladares, Laura. 2012. "La importancia del peritaje cultural: Avances, retos y acciones del Colegio de Etnólogos y Antropólogos Sociales AC (CEAS) para la certificación de perito." In *Peritaje antropológico en México: Reflexiones teórico metodológicas y experiencias*, 11–21. Mexico City: Boletín Colegio de Etnólogos y Antropólogos Sociales.

Vargas Vásquez, Liliana Vianey. 2011. *Las mujeres de Tlahuitoltepec Mixe, Oaxaca, frente a la impartición de la justicia local y el uso del derecho internacional (2000–2008)*. Mexico City: Instituto Nacional de las Mujeres.

Vargas Vásquez, Liliana Vianey. 2012. "Las mujeres de Tlahuitoltepec Mixe Frente a la impartición de la justicia local y el uso del derecho internacional (2000–2008)." In *Género, complementariedades y exclusiones en Mesoamérica y los Andes*, edited by R. Aída

Hernández Castillo and Andrew Canessa, 302–18. Quito, Ecuador: Abya Yala Press and IWGIA.

Velásquez Nimatuj, Irma Alicia. 2003. *La pequeña burguesía indígena comercial de Guatemala: Desigualdades de clase, raza y género*. Guatemala: SERJUS y CEDPA.

Waldram, James B. 1997. *Way of the Pipe: Aboriginal Spirituality and Symbolic Healing in Canadian Prisons*. Toronto: Broadview.

Wolf, Diane. 1996. *Feminist Dilemmas in Fieldwork*. Boulder, CO: Westview Press.

Yashar, Deborah. 2005. *Contesting Citizenship in Latin America: The Rise of Indigenous Movements and the Postliberal Challenge*. New York: Cambridge University Press.

FIVE

Decolonizing Anthropologists from Below and to the Left

XOCHITL LEYVA SOLANO

The editors of this book have invited us to reflect critically and from a situated knowledge position on our moral and political commitments with Indigenous peoples who work for their self-determination in the face of institutional and systemic forces (Hernández and Hutchings 2015).[1] To do this, I refer to key moments in my/our paths from 1994 to the present (2018). In the first part of this chapter, I relate how and why I/we were positioning ourselves "below and to the left." This happened because we agreed with the demands and political practices of the Zapatistas in the middle of a violent counterinsurgency war that the Mexican state had unleashed at the same time its functionaries were participating in roundtable dialogues to sign a peace accord. It was then that, with many others, I embarked on a continuing but complicated and painful process of decolonization and depatriarchalization. To talk about these personal-collective processes, I go back, in the second section of this chapter, to some of these experiences that I was part of on a double front. Simultaneously, I was a pro-Zapatista activist and a teacher of social anthropology. For more than twenty-four years now, I have received graduate and postgraduate students arriving in Chiapas attracted by Zapatismo. I also refer to some creative experiences with Maya members of the Chiapas Network of Artists, Community Communicators and Anthropologists, which we founded, inspired by the Zapatista struggle.[2] This was still amid a prolonged war of attrition, which is by now overlapping with another war against drug trafficking, as well as the global offensive of heteropatriarchal neoliberalism. I focus on how all this led us to experience firsthand the effects of anthropology's colonial legacy, and to begin to identify its systemic and heteropatriarchal logic. In the third part of this chapter, I tie in our experiences with three debates that make sense within both the academy and this book: (1) the long road of decolonizing anthropology; (2) the embodied and incardinated theory of various feminisms; and (3) the rise of other epistemologies, ontologies, and practices.

Decolonizing Our Anthropological Practices During Counterinsurgency

On January 1, 1994, as the North American Free Trade Agreement (NAFTA) between Mexico, the United States, and Canada became effective, the Zapatista Army of National Liberation (EZLN) rose up in arms and read the First Declaration of the Lacandon Forest:

> TO THE PEOPLE OF MEXICO: We, free and honest men and women, are aware that the war that we have declared is our last resort, but it is also a just one. The dictators have been waging an undeclared genocidal war against our people for many years. We therefore ask for your resolute participation in support of this plan of the Mexican people who struggle for *work, land, housing, food, health, education, independence, freedom, democracy, justice* and *peace*. We declare that we will not cease fighting until these basic demands of our people are met through the creation of a free and democratic government for our country. (General Command of the EZLN 1993, n.p., italics mine)

The Mexican government immediately mobilized under the logic of the DN-II (National Defense) Plan "with which the army combats an internal enemy that threatens national sovereignty and security" (Hidalgo Domínguez 2006, 165). Political analysts agree that the war in Chiapas has gone through various moments, stages, and modalities. I mention only some of them to give an idea of what we have lived through. I also want to show how and why under these circumstances neutrality and objectivity were losing importance, and how war, scholarly work, and activism started to blend together, at least for some of us.

The first twelve days of January 1994 were characterized by direct confrontation between the two armies, with losses on both sides, but also by the rape of

Indigenous women at military checkpoints and summary executions of Zapatistas from several municipalities at the hands of the army.[3] Mobilized civil society's repudiation of the war forced the Mexican president to declare a unilateral ceasefire and to offer amnesty to the rebels. This rejection of the war by civil society, together with its support of the Zapatistas' political demands, led to the establishment of the Cathedral Dialogues, the dialogue and negotiation tables, and finally the signing of peace accords in February 1996.

But the government's military strategy not only ran parallel to its political strategy, it was also highly counterinsurgent. The National Secretariat of the Defense (SEDENA) had drafted the "Plan de Campaña Chiapas 94" (Chiapas 94 campaign plan)—which we became aware of in 1998 because it was leaked to the press—with the declared objective of "achieving and maintaining peace." To that end, the plan's strategic and operational objective was "to destroy the EZLN's will to combat by isolating it from the civilian population and to obtain the latter's support for the operations," while its tactical objective was "to destroy and/or disorganize the EZLN's political and military structure." To accomplish these war objectives, operations were planned in the following areas: logistical, tactical, intelligence, psychological, and civilian, which according to the plan "includes an emergency aid plan for the population and its resources." The plan also included "advising," which in appendix H—not included in the leaked document—is described as "activities of the army to train and support self-defense forces or other paramilitary organizations, which can be the fundamental principle for mobilization of military and development operations." It also included "applying censorship to the various mass media outlets" and "elaborating a development plan to be submitted for consideration to the President of the Republic. . . . The Campaign Plan and the Development Plan will be directed," they stated, "to the lawbreakers and to the population" (SEDENA 1994, n.p.).

All these plans were decisive for what happened on the ground, not only to the Zapatistas but to all who supported their political demands, including us, that is, local and (inter)national scholars and students of the social sciences. Despite these plans, on December 19, 1994, the EZLN broke the military siege and announced the creation of thirty-eight autonomous municipalities in a state of rebellion, amid various actions that sought to besiege and destroy them: persecuting and issuing arrest warrants for presumed Zapatista leaders; ordering the construction of a large military complex at the heart of the Lacandon Forest; setting up military and police checkpoints throughout the state, but especially in the "conflict zone"; sending special forces to Chiapas; launching a persecution and media campaign that made Subcomandante Marcos's identity public; promoting and providing military training to local groups that ended up acting with impunity as paramilitary groups; fostering divisions among the local population to create confrontations and thus support the existence of "intercommunity conflicts," which were later used to cover up state crimes, such as the Acteal Massacre, committed on December 22, 1997, against nineteen women, fourteen girls, four boys, eight men, and four unborn babies from Las Abejas (the Bees Civil Society Organization).

But as we know, the intervention and solidarity of local, national, and international civil society has also played a key role in this war (see Leyva Solano 1998). Since the early days of 1994, sympathizers, supporters, and the merely curious arrived in Chiapas, some attracted by the Zapatistas' political demands, others by their revolutionary struggle of resistance and autonomy. From 1994 to the time of this writing (2018), we have seen an impressive number of young people from practically every continent coming to Chiapas. I personally have done political and academic work with more than one hundred of them. We have not only shared political positions, but also inhabited a rather tense space generated by the encounter of academia and antisystemic and alternative activism.

The students that came showed a deep, enduring practical commitment to the Zapatista communities in resistance. Many of them came only as activists in solidarity with Zapatismo. One of them explains: "I was not a sociologist when I arrived in Chiapas. My only experience is being close to them [Indigenous people], building homes and latrines, making bricks, making tortillas, milling maize, and splitting firewood. This has given me and many others an experience in collectivity and respect toward others, as well as a sense of the need for empathy as a necessary condition to transform the political, social, and economic spheres of our country" (Martínez López 2006, 1). But in many other cases, these young people arrived to do activist work as part of an interstitial experience whereby they intertwined academia, politics, and feminism:

> Of course I didn't come to Chiapas by chance, but rather, like many other people from my country, out of an interest in the Zapatista movement and in solidarity with it. . . . In our own country [Switzerland], we were in the midst of mobilizations against the World Trade Organization (WTO) and other bodies of world governance. Being in Chiapas, observing and learning, was part of our practice in

our own context. . . . [There] I was immersed in women's movements and feminist reflections that led us to want to transform everyday life, the functioning of organizations, and at the same time to relate to women with other histories and cultures. (Masson et al. 2008, 17)

These connections, reflections, and actions had to be undertaken in conditions of war, paramilitarization, and counterinsurgency, since we were then, as we are now, in the context of an unresolved political and military conflict, in an integral war of attrition.[4] All this implied many practical, theoretical, methodological, ethical, and epistemic challenges, both for the local scholars and the young students, as well as the EZLN itself. It seems, then, that we did all learn in the same process.

The first thing that several of us felt in that second half of the 1990s was that we did not have the adequate tools to undertake research work in contexts of war and counterinsurgent or paramilitary violence. We soon realized that many of our anthropological research methods would not be of much use. This was pointed out by several of the young people who asked us to host them as guest students between late 2003 and mid-2004—a period for which they obtained permission from the Zapatistas to do their thesis or dissertation work in rebel territory. The students describe their difficulties: "[Given] the conditions of low-intensity warfare in which we carried out our research, we found it impossible to record information with either modern devices or older methods, since not even notebooks were allowed, with the exception of a couple of cases that aroused strong suspicions" (Menchú Rivera 2005, 11). Others note, "The level of fear of repression and the organization's semi-clandestine nature made formal interviews with members of Zapatista communities entirely inappropriate. . . . Recorded interviews or video footage that could fall in the hands of the army at any of their checkpoints in the forest . . . could have potentially dangerous consequences for those interviewed" (Vergara Camus 2007, 42). In this new context, classical ethnography—anthropology's method par excellence—was openly questioned by others and by us, since it became a double-edged sword; highly detailed descriptions of the region and the movement's members could be used by their political enemies to more effectively attack them psychologically, politically, or militarily.

The war situation led many of us to ask ourselves basic questions, such as, Where do our anthropological methodologies come from? To what kind of academia do these methodologies belong to? To which interests are we responding?

We then asked ourselves, What makes us exclude basic questions, such as "research for what" and "for whom," from our work agendas? We arrived at these ethical reflections not through enlightenment or in a classroom exercise, but because out there the Acteal Massacre was being committed, paramilitary groups were on the rise, and Zapatista autonomous municipalities were being violently dismantled at the orders of the federal and state governments. These events left an indelible mark on many people in the communities, but also on several of our personal and academic trajectories and on us as people.

It was in this context of war that we asked ourselves how we were building knowledge outside and inside academia, outside and inside the movement and the networks we were then building and within which we think and act politically and academically. All this happened before work in "networks" became fashionable in academia and before "social networks"—which we use today— became part of our naturalized mode of communication and political action.

Decolonizing Anthropologists Under the Light of Zapatista Autonomous Practices

Undoubtedly, the way the EZLN treated research in its autonomous municipalities accelerated and reaffirmed our incipient personal and collective efforts at decolonization, depatriarchalization, and emancipation. One of the young activists who did her dissertation work with the Zapatistas says the following:

> In August 2003, Subcomandante [Marcos] published a series of communiqués announcing the creation of Zapatista regional centers, the Caracoles [Snails], and their Good Government Councils . . . as part of the reorganization of work in Zapatista territory. This intended to change social relations with NGOs, social organizations, and all political actors that were external to the communities, including researchers.
>
> In this new stage of autonomy, [the Zapatistas] declared that research would be welcome as long as it was at the service of the people and "benefited the communities." . . . With this declaration, the EZLN and its grassroots bases of support made it clear that knowledge production is a fundamental element in the construction of autonomy. If autonomy is intended to transform social relations between women and men in Indigenous communities, with the state, and between Indigenous and *mestizo* peoples . . . then research itself becomes a

contested terrain with the potential for social transformation and political debate. (Mora 2008, 3)

The institutional procedures of academic research, accustomed to defining topics, objectives, time frames, rhythms, and forms, suffered several dislocations with the practices that derived from what I have termed, in a political/academic grammar, the "Zapatista epistemic ¡*Ya Basta*! [Enough!]" (Leyva Solano [2011] 2014). As I have explained in another text, this Enough! was expressed in many ways. For example, when you wanted to do research in Zapatista autonomous territory, you were required to request permission from the Good Government Council and wait for the case to be analyzed before receiving an answer. The reply could be positive, negative, or "not for now" if there were other pressing political priorities or a period of red alert.

One of the young adherents to the Sixth Declaration of the Lacandon Forest, who was at the time writing her undergraduate thesis, obtained permission from the Good Government Council after having worked a significant amount of time in the communities performing practical activities in solidarity. She says:

> The first step consisted of a period of time to draw close to the Zapatistas and to negotiate with them. This was not well received by my field advisor from the university, who pointed out that my project had a specific time line that was approved by the Academic Council. She didn't like that it was rejected by the "subjects of study." The complete lack of control over the research work was unacceptable according to her evaluation criteria.
>
> In the second stage I faced two irreconcilable tensions. The first was between the time frame required by the university (five weeks) and the time that the *compañeros* took to meet and reach an agreement regarding when and under which circumstances I could work with them. Considering the fact that this is only one of many decisions that the Good Government Council has to take regarding problems that are undoubtedly more important or urgent, the time allotted was spent mainly in the process to gain entry to the community where the Reserve was located—Ocotal Section II in Huitepec.
>
> This is not hard to understand when you are in constant contact with the communities; the people who work with them are aware of this difference in times. However, arriving at the university and saying that my first period of fieldwork was spent only in "obtaining entry" into the community where I would be working, sounded like I had done absolutely nothing. Explaining to them that the time

frame they allotted for fieldwork made no sense when I presented it to the Good Government Council, put me in a very difficult situation.

The second tension was due to an understandable distance and somewhat reticent attitude generated by this stage among our "subjects of study." This tension arose not only as part of a "normal process of the encounter with otherness," for which they prepared us in some of our anthropology classes. It was also due to the strategy of low-intensity warfare that put a heavy strain on the Zapatistas. This situation is not "a minor obstacle," it is the context that permeates and that—together with other factors—shapes work relationships with the *compañeros*. (Fajardo Camacho 2011, 26–28)

Although in university classrooms students and scholars had read about self-criticism within the social sciences, the post-1994 political practices led us to rethink ourselves to the sad tune of the successive wars that were crushing us. Albeit in very different ways, we were all stuck in the middle of a battlefield, where the killing was done both with metal bullets and with ink and paper. The Zapatistas said so on many occasions without us fully understanding what they meant. We heard them, but we did not listen. We arrogantly assumed that we understood, while in reality we were unable to perceive all the implications of what they were saying, writing, and doing.

The political demands of the Zapatistas were expressed in terms of rights—Indigenous, women's, autonomic, and political rights—and they found an echo in many parts of the planet. As we were embarking on our own struggle for those rights, we moved away from the neutrality and objectivity in which we were trained in our academic disciplines, toward a place that the Zapatistas called "at the bottom and to the left": a geopolitical space that challenges representative democracy with its coordinates of "the right" and "the left" and its priority on who takes power. Strengthening their own path of autonomy, the Zapatistas offered a radical critique of this model and the practice of representative democracy, a critique with which important sectors of both Mexican and global society agreed.

The Sixth Declaration of the Lacandon Forest in particular strongly emphasized the need to organize ourselves "from below and to the left" in order to develop a different way of doing politics, that is, to construct the national plan for struggle and to develop a new constitution. The Zapatistas' spokesperson wrote in February 2005, in a letter published in a highly contentious pre-electoral context:

I therefore speak of the left that is found down below, the left that is marginalized by the "left" from above that the right is so fond of. . . . I mean political organizations that are not part of the political class nor of civil society. I mean those who are not driven by fashions, but by commitments. . . . Any initiative for a real transformation of our society must have them on board. . . .

[D]own below a book is written that does not know the word "end." Each person adds letters, words, pages, even entire chapters, such as the revolution that began in 1910 and the events of 1968. This book moves slowly, that's true, but its feet are those of the people for whom struggle is a way of life. . . . And continuing with the theme of the clock, let me tell you that, after the sixth hour, time ticks below and to the left. . . . I only remind you that according to our experience, we can see further when we take a look from below and to the left. (SCI Marcos 2005, n.p.)

The challenge the Zapatistas set up for us in that sixth political initiative was a great one, and several of us committed ourselves to this new summons based on what we had at our disposal: our bodies, our knowledge, our lives. By 2006 we were openly living the tensions between academia and activism. I was still a researcher and lecturer at a higher education center, but I was also a member of several activist collectives and networks that we had founded as part of the neo-Zapatista and alternative world/anticapitalist networks. Indeed, at the height of my activism, I belonged to nine different collective spaces. What I narrate now was happening within the realm of political activism but had repercussions in anthropology and academia for several reasons, the most general being, in the words of Haitian anthropologist Michel-Rolph Trouillot, "Anthropology is what anthropologists do."

Working "Outside" Academia with Maya Community Communicators and Artivists

In this context of war and violation of human rights, thirteen people including me got together at a cultural center that had been built in convergence with the Zapatista communities in resistance and was, at the time, the most important hub of neo-Zapatista activities in San Cristóbal de Las Casas. We thus held our first meeting at the heart of this colonial city, founded in 1528 under the name of Villa Real by the Spanish conqueror Diego de Mazariegos, in which the free transit of Indigenous people had been forbidden for centuries. It was not a meeting of scholarly colleagues but a political meeting where seven young Maya and three not-so-young non-Maya gathered. All of us shared a broader struggle for Indigenous peoples' rights and, especially, for the rights of Indigenous women and young people. The following paragraphs are an extract of our collective self-definition in a co-authored book and multimedia product that was one of the creative results of this process.[5]

> Beyond labels and going against the grain of the dehumanization suffered by humanity, we emphatically state that we are human beings, *bats'i ants viniketik* (true women and men) with different roots. . . . Seven of us have Mayan roots, one of us Mixteca roots, another one German roots, and another one Japanese roots. In addition to Spanish, those of us with Mayan roots speak: four, the Tsotsil language, two, the Tseltal language, and one, the Tojolabal language.
>
> Of the ten of us, eight are men and two are women. Two of us are painters, two are musicians, one is a photographer, three are community communicators and video makers, and the last two are anthropologists.[6]
>
> Seen from another angle, [we and] our book are the product of different intersections, for instance, the encounter with young people who are part of what we could call a new artistic/linguistic/cultural movement, including young members of a once legendary independent peasant movement of Indigenous peoples.
>
> Within this latter movement, some of us are working towards self-representation by appropriating and controlling audiovisual media [technology], in particular Indigenous video. Thus we have managed to strengthen our organizations' struggles and demands. And these organizations are, in particular, the Committee for the Defense of Indigenous Liberation (CDLI-Xi'nich), The Bees (Las Abejas) Civil Society Organization, and the Organization of Indigenous Medics and Midwives of the State of Chiapas (OMIECH). . . .[7]
>
> Now, what we call a new artistic/linguistic/cultural movement of the Indigenous peoples of Chiapas has taken many forms: theater, poetry, written narrative in Mayan languages, plastic arts and painting with Mayan roots, rock music in the Tsotsil language, or the demand to standardize writing in Mayan languages. (RACCACH 2012, n.p.; see also Köhler et al. 2010)

The way we started to work in this space of political convergence was different from "academic methodologies" since it was not an "academic research project"; rather, it followed the working methods of community assemblies and those of the grassroots political organizations to which some of the members had belonged since the early 1990s. These assembly working methods and the search for consensus also inspired our active membership in urban collectives that some of us had founded. But Zapatista autonomy in practice and without anyone's permission, a daily process, undoubtedly kindled our will to go beyond "normal" ways of doing things in our political organizations and in academia.

Here are some fragments that may help explain how we made the decision to work, organize, and create together a multimedia and multilanguage book using the written and the spoken word, photos, and painting reproductions, as well as three Mayan languages and Spanish. We baptized our creation with the Maya name *Sjalel kibeltik*, which can be translated as "weaving our roots" (Köhler et al. 2010).

> For thirteen months we held periodic plenary meetings [in the form of assemblies] and workshops; these served to give birth to the Chiapas Network of Artists, Community Communicators, and Anthropologists (RACCACH), its objectives and its short-, middle-, and long-term working plan. . . .
>
> Although [at these meetings] we all agreed that the focus of our work and our attention should be our communities, there were still many things to define: Whom do we address specifically in the community? What topics should we develop? . . .
>
> In the brainstorming session that took place during the meeting on February 9, 2008, we made a list of nine addressees. [But it was the work itself that set our agenda and led us to realize whom we were addressing], mainly Mayan youths from the communities and the cities. Young people like us: video makers, painters, photographers, musicians, anthropologists, or sociologists. Young people with roots, members of Indigenous peoples. Young people who could be in search of their roots, denying them, or making them flourish through their work, ideas, and struggles. . . .
>
> Writing on the chalkboard the ideas that each of us brought to the meeting, supporting or challenging what was said by the person sitting next to us, we collectively started to develop the main topics that guided us . . . and that were set down on the chalkboard as follows:
>
> Where do I come from? Where and what are my roots?
> Who am I, as an individual, as a Mayan/Indigenous person, as a member
>   of a peasant/Indigenous organization or a cultural/artistic group, as a
>   human being?

How did I start doing what I do? In which personal and political situation did I begin with it?

What role does video, painting, photography, and music, play in my community, in my organization, and for the Indigenous people that I belong to?

How has our (artistic, communication, academic) work contributed to the development of Indigenous peoples and humanity?

Where am I headed with my work, with my community, with my organization?

Where are the Indigenous people I belong to headed? (RACCACH 2012, n.p.)

The whole work took twenty-one months, during which the ten people involved embarked on an intrapersonal reflection, in one-to-one dialogues and plenary assemblies, connected in and through our network. It was an autonomous effort whose engine was our own human energy and that of the Zapatista anticapitalist political struggle that inspired us. With no external funding, we operated as political movements do: with each person contributing their own time, knowledge, and creativity to the collective cause. Through its mere existence, our way of working together challenged the logic of the academic projects in which I had formerly participated. Projects that usually only exist if one person conceives and elaborates them and manages to get funding for them; if this person (called the person "responsible" for the project) a priori defines each and every one of the steps of the project, as well as the time frames and the results to be obtained from it. Many of these academic projects are mainly circumscribed to the disciplinary field and are expressed in a scholarly language to be consumed by a small group of fellow academics.

Sjalel kibeltik and Decolonizing Academia

What did *Sjalel kibeltik* have to do with decolonizing academia? Why not just think of the project as part of a collective political action? Among the ten members of our network, one was a peasant video maker from a grassroots organization; another was a community communicator and member of a grassroots organization made up of survivors of the Acteal Massacre, relatives of the victims, and people displaced by it. Another was a youngster from San Juan Chamula, who had dropped out of high school to learn how to paint by himself and to found, with other young people, an autonomous creative space. Independent of their own personal stories, the other seven members had one thing in common: they had all been to college at some stage of their lives. Of those seven, four were Maya, all of them born in Indigenous communities of Chiapas, but they constantly went back and forth between their community and the city. Of those seven, three had been to art school, where two received academic training as musicians and the other as a painter. Of the remaining four, three had studied anthropology, and the fourth, sociology. Two of us were scholars at a research center, and three were current or former university students. For this reason, the role of the scientific or artistic knowledge we had acquired in the academy cannot be overlooked. But since this was not what brought us together, I believe that we were able to subordinate these specialized knowledges to the political and creative goals that drove us and that we at RACCACH agreed on collectively:

> 1) To nurture the seed of appreciating and respecting different knowledge, skills, abilities, and forms of communication, and to create a positive awareness of diversity; 2) To strengthen our ethnic identities; 3) To benefit the communities; 4) To encourage the struggle for our art, our organizations, and our communities; 5) To create the means to transmit our experiences and let them be known in the communities; 6) To unite for combating discrimination against Indigenous peoples; 7) To help each other giving shape to a body of personal and collective knowledge that can be transformed into a tool for change; 8) To work together in artistic activities and community communication; 9) To foster an appreciation for the creative potential of Indigenous youth; 10) To contribute to transform the consciousness of children and youth in the communities, to keep them from taking the easy road out (for example, by using alcohol and drugs, or committing suicide); 11) To provide learning opportunities in arts and culture; 12) To broaden the philosophic outlook of Mayan artists; 13) To foster the creation of youth committees in the communities to defend our objectives in life based on our own knowledge. (RACCACH 2012, n.p.)

In this particular context, participant observation, interviews, ethnography, and fieldwork made no sense; on the contrary, in the heat of a brainstorming session, we formed what we called *creative couples*, which in practice challenged the conventional academic hierarchies that reduce our interlocutors to "the other" and an "object of study." In fact, the two anthropologists who participated in the RACCACH had sought a Zapatismo-influenced path to decolonization. For that reason, we accepted the proposal by another member of our network, the leader of the musical group Sak Tzevul, to write our own chapters so that, as he said, we could "all uncover ourselves equally." Not a minor issue if we take into account that the Chiapas Highlands, where RACCACH, our network, was most active, had been the site of the first governmental agency of indigenism in the 1950s. The state policy of indigenism had been implemented after the Mexican Revolution as a nation-building device to integrate Indigenous people by converting them into mestizos. For decades also, Indigenous people of that region had been the "objects" of study for hundreds of foreign and Mexican anthropologists, subscribing to the indigenist ideology or working on a postindigenist agenda. After the 1994 Zapatista uprising, it was increasingly common to hear criticism, in the communities and in urban areas, blaming anthropologists for the objectification of Indigenous people and practicing academic ventriloquism. What was happening in the RACCACH must also be understood in this context of a growing weariness with academic research.

Certainly, the process of systematically recording everything we did stemmed from our disciplinary training in anthropology and sociology, but it did benefit the collective process. By recording twenty-five RACCACH plenary meetings and workshops and drawing up memoranda, a commission of us was able to weave together everyone's words to create an introductory text for our collective book. Once all the work was finished, we were able to obtain funds from two universities, a research center, and two international organizations. Thus we were able to publish a book with texts, photos, and audio content and put the results of our work on a website that has received more than three hundred thousand visits.

The common thread that connected us among ourselves and with the Zapatistas was the fight for Indigenous rights and the creation of autonomous spaces; that's how we explained it in our collective introduction. For you, dear reader, to get the gist, you would have to read the introduction and listen to the audio chapters on our website (see Köhler et al. 2010). That would allow you to get an idea of the effect that Zapatismo has had on all our lives. Half of our chapters mention Zapatismo explicitly as a foundational element of what we are: they refer to it as the creative inspiration for a rooted style of painting, making music, and doing photography or anthropology.

In the academic field, *Sjalel kibeltik* challenged many things, some of which I have already mentioned. I will add one more. It openly challenged the scholarly language of "knowledge production," a grammar that structures the jargon of *academic capitalism*.[8] This grammar still views knowledge as part of a production chain, whereby knowledge and skills are produced, distributed, and consumed, first to reproduce the academic apparatus, and then for the benefit of several industries, among them capitalist book production. In this mode of production, the engine is knowledge understood to be merchandise, whereas in the Zapatista mode, in that of *Sjalel kibeltik* and of many other groups, collectives, organizations, and movements, too numerous to all be mentioned here, the engine is human creativity and not productivity assessed according to the indicators of the knowledge market.

Decolonizing Anthropologists, Embodied and Incardinated Theory, and Other Epistemologies, Ontologies, and Practices

The road toward the decolonization of anthropology has been long and winding. What I have narrated so far can be understood as a small part of a bigger story. In fact, with the title of this chapter, I seek to allude to an abstract process involving an "academic discipline," but above all, I want to emphasize what happened amid insurgencies and counterinsurgencies, and in the flesh, to many women and young scholars across the social sciences.

The title also contains a double implication: for one, it alludes to how decolonization processes emerged in the new geopolitics "from below and to the left." At the same time, it emphasizes how precisely neo-Zapatista "below and to the left" was pushing, orienting, guiding, and urging us to decolonize. Seeing ourselves in the mirror of Zapatista women, and women from other Indigenous, black, or popular resistances, as well as lesbotransfeminists, we began to fight against machismo and homophobia. We also started to have the tools for understanding the logics of patriarchy—heteropatriarchy—in the intersection with other systems of oppression and domination. We began to reflect collectively on our own realities and experiences (Leyva Solano, forthcoming). Together we discovered *embodied and incardinated theory*, as it is called in feminist grammar (Leyva Solano 2018). All this provides another angle on my narrative. Let's take a closer look.

A declaration issued in 1977 by the African American lesbian-feminist Combahee River Collective, based in the United States, asserted that the most profound and radical policy is rooted in our own identity. Talking of racism and homophobia as the "real conditions of all our lives," African American lesbian feminist poet Audre Lorde quotes Simone de Beauvoir: "It is in the knowledge of the genuine conditions of our lives that we must draw our strength to live and our reasons for acting" (1983, 101).

And that is what I felt in each and every text of the thirty authors contributing to the collective production of *This Bridge Called My Back* (Moraga and Anzaldúa 1983). Being part of the movement of women of color in the United States, they introduce us to their roots, their injuries, and the concrete forms in which they suffered oppression in the flesh because of their race, class, and gender, sex, and sexuality. And they convinced us with a remarkably clear and simple, but also deep and creative, language. Their way of expressing themselves brings across an opposition to the universally rigid and cold theory of conventional and dominant social sciences, a way of theorizing that we may simply call *disembodied*, because it claims to be "neutral" and "objective" but has no "emotional, heartfelt grappling" (Moraga 1983, 29). It does not dare to fuse personal experiences and worldviews with the social reality we live in (Anzaldúa 1983, 170). And it prevents us from naming the enemy within because that "may mean giving up whatever privileges we have managed to squeeze out of this society by virtue of our gender, race, class, or sexuality," as Chicana poet, editor, playwright, and feminist Cherríe Moraga (1983, 29–30) reminds us.

Almost three decades lie between the publication of *This Bridge Called My Back* and that of *Sjalel kibeltik*, each the product of a particular moment in time and space. The authors of both books have created theory in an unconventional way, through collective practice, writing from outside the academy and challenging the academic grammar. They have indeed produced theory, and not only stories, narratives, testimonies, or a collection of texts and images. Their writings are not just "information" or raw material for a scientist to "explain," "interpret," or "analyze," only to be swallowed up by academic capitalism and the book industry. In both cases, collective thought-and-felt (*sentipensar*) practice produces *embodied theory*, a concept that the authors of *This Bridge Called My Back* developed very early on in clear opposition to the hegemonic and systemic idea that theory has to illuminate practice.

Both works have in common that their authors are participating in larger movements and, I argue, sharing perspectives that question the dominant notion and production of *disembodied theory*, itself the outcome of universal, rational, and masculine thought. And in their narratives we can appreciate another critical approach, one that questions the reduction of the thinking human subject to *abstract masculinity*, which constructs itself in opposition to others considered too corporeal and too feminine: women, ethnic others, children, nonhumans, and even matter itself. This important strand of criticism has been articulated in both political and academic grammars. In particular, it has been developed by multiple feminist theorists arguing for a new feminist materialism, but also by members of feminist poststructuralist materialism, feminist poets, as well as theorists of sexual difference, nomadic feminism, subaltern studies, postcolonial and decolonial feminism, and last but not least, barefoot feminists, from the bottom and to the left.[9]

In the intersection of feminism and academia, this debate has reopened discussions about old philosophical questions: What is theory? What does it mean to think? A discussion that is as old as those about the well-known dualisms of Western rationality, the polis, science, and academia. In some of these debates, the claim is that the terms of dialogue have changed and that now the question is rather, How does theory *matter*? in the double meaning that the word *matter* has in English: to have importance and to materialize. From the deep South, in Bolivia, urban feminists working in the Creative Women (Mujeres Creando) collective contend, "No decolonization without depatriarchalization." This motto encapsulates their conception of the depatriarchalization of the territory-body and the territory-land, without which any decolonization of formerly subjugated peoples is incoherent (cited in Vargas 2018). It has spread and has been echoed in feminist, Indigenous, and black movements across Latin America, the Caribbean, and in other countries.

There is a certain consensus that our present times, the early twenty-first century, can be characterized by a deep systemic and civilizational crisis, and that we are living at a point of history when the old has not finished dying while the new is still being born. It is impossible to go into all the details of these crises here, but I would like to address at least the crest of a wave of decolonizing and depatriarchalizing practices that are gaining in range and volume in many places, from Canada to Patagonia, from Guatemala and Chiapas to New Zealand and Lapland. Some American scholars highlight the existence of a "large-scale social movement of anticolonialist discourse" (López 1998, 226).[10] Others speak of a "methodologically contested present" (Denzin and Lincoln 2008, 4).[11] According to Chicana feminist communicator Chela Sandoval (2000), our time is characterized by the proliferation of Indigenous epistemologies and methodologies, and, we should add, black, popular, and feminist ones from the margins.

Within this context, in 2001, Susana Piñacué (2015), a Nasa member of the Bilingual and Intercultural Education Program of the Indigenous Regional Council of the Cauca (Colombia), who is also a university researcher, pointed out the importance of basic questions that Indigenous researchers should start out with: What is the approach you are using (in your research)? How are you writing it up? Where are you writing it up? What are you writing? Who are you writing it up for? Or, as our Cree colleague Margaret Kovach suggested in 2009, "We are now at a point where it is not only Indigenous knowledges themselves that require attention, but the processes by which Indigenous knowledges are generated" (2009, n.p.).

What seems to be happening over the last three and a half decades in Latin America and the Caribbean is the emergence of Indigenous and black researchers, analysts, and other professionals who are still very close to their communities of origin. They are going back and forth, revaluing and reconstructing their ontological-cultural-linguistic matrix in manifold ways. And from their professional positions, they question the epistemic racism, the academic extractivism, and the subalternization to which they (and their peoples) have historically been subjected through primary and secondary education, the university, the social sciences, and the academy. This is also occurring among Indigenous and black undergraduate and postgraduate students; in public and private educational institutions; in professional associations; and in those academic spaces created and managed by Indigenous and black peoples, as well as in the precarious neoliberal academy in general.

The insurrection of subjugated knowledges is part of the alternative globalization from below, which expresses itself in epistemic-ethical-ontological struggles that are part and parcel of resistance, autonomy by right, and the defense of life and territory. In this context, social research and knowledges are of not only strategic but also vital importance in opening up a new front in ongoing epistemic-ontological wars. On this front, Indigenous and black feminists, academics, university-trained professionals, community-based artivists, teachers, and community communicators play a central role as subjects of counter-power.[12]

This battleground stretches beyond academia, anthropology, and disciplinary borders. Indeed, more and more collective processes are under way in different trenches, with the aim of unlearning, relearning, unwiring, decolonizing, and depatriarchalizing not only the academy or the social sciences, but, in general, our bodies, minds, hearts, and lives. And this is happening in myriad different ways, and not only in social, political, or ethnopolitical movements. We are talking about people who are in plenty of ways asserting distinct but bountiful ways of inhabiting a territory, autonomy, and sovereignty, to name but a few of the fighting causes. In the academy or in politics, we usually conceptualize the protagonists as "actors" or "subjects," but first and foremost, they are human beings in interaction with other human and nonhuman beings, part of a cosmic, not only planetary, continuum.[13]

In this becoming, we experience disciplinary knowledge as a tool not only to know the world and transform it (in the key of abstract masculinity) but also to (re)make ourselves (in the key of embodied knowledge), to build those other possible worlds that are inspired by those already under construction: the autonomous Zapatista municipalities; the bottom-up alternative forms of organization of the peoples, tribes, and nations that make up the National Indigenous Congress in Mexico; and the many antisystemic collectives, networks, and movements on planet Earth.[14] That is the small big difference between before and now.

Notes

1. I would like to thank the writer Alejandro Reyes, the visual anthropologist Axel Köhler, and the economist Fionn O'Sullivan for the translation of this chapter into English as a way of connecting worlds, struggles, languages, and cultures.
2. Red de Artistas, Comunicadores Comunitarios y Antropólogos de Chiapas (RACCACH).
3. See the case of three Tseltal underage women raped in June 1994 at a checkpoint in the municipality of Altamirano, Chiapas (Press Release 2010). On the executions, see former U.S. attorney general Ramsey Clark (Global Exchange, CIEPAC, and CENCOS 2000, 125).
4. I resort to the concept "war of attrition," used by the Centro de Derechos Humanos Fray Bartolomé de Las Casas (2014), because it encompasses all the dimensions of this ongoing war.
5. Before you read this part, I suggest going to Köhler et al. (2010), at http://jkopkutik.org/sjalelkibeltik/, where the book and its multimedia content can be accessed.
6. The Maya photographer is also a sociologist, and one of the Maya video makers studied anthropology.
7. See Köhler et al. (2010); Las Abejas de Acteal, last updated October 2, 2018, http://acteal.blogspot.mx/; Association Mâ, accessed September 24, 2018, http://associationma.wixsite.com/website.
8. Several academic authors have used and debated this concept. For a good introduction to this debate, see Slaughter and Leslie (1999).

9. Krizia Nardini (2014) provides a good survey of several feminist theorists making contributions to this ongoing debate.
10. Gerardo R. López has studied the educational practices of Latinos and other migrants in the United States within a framework of critical race theory (1998, 226).
11. Norman K. Denzin and Yvonna S. Lincoln take as a starting point the contributions of African American, Chicanx, Latinx, Native American, African, Hawaiian, and Maori researchers and give the following overview: "In North America, qualitative research operates in a complex historical field that crosscuts at least eight historical moments. These moments overlap and simultaneously operate in the present. We define them as the *traditional* (1900–1950); the *modernist*, or golden, age (1950–1970); *blurred genres* (1970–1986); the *crisis of representation* (1986–1990); the *postmodern*, a period of experimental and new ethnographies (1990–1995); *postexperimental inquiry* (1995–2000); the *methodologically contested present* (2000–2008); and the *future* (2008–), which is now" (2008, 4).
12. It took us seven years to weave together the academic and political work of fifty-two Indigenous and non-Indigenous authors in a three-volume publication, in which we manage to delve into the copious other knowledge practices these authors have developed amid insurgencies, counterinsurgencies, uprisings, rebellions, and war (see Leyva Solano et al. 2015).
13. The Maya artists and communicators of RACCACH in *Sjalel kibeltik* coincided with what English sociologist Jenny Pearce (2015) emphasizes in her comparative research in the UK and in Latin America, that we are first human beings, before being anthropologists, actors, or subjects.
14. See more information at Enlace Zapatista, accessed September 22, 2018, http://enlacezapatista.ezln.org.mx/, and Congreso Nacional Indígena, last updated October 20, 2018, https://www.congresonacionalindigena.org/.

References

Anzaldúa, Gloria. 1983. "Speaking in Tongues: A Letter to Third World Women Writers." In *This Bridge Called My Back: Writings by Radical Women of Color*, edited by Cherríe Moraga and Gloria Anzaldúa, 165–74. New York: Women of Color Press.

Centro de Derechos Humanos Fray Bartolomé de Las Casas. 2014. "La contrainsurgencia sigue operando en Chiapas." Pronouncement, San Cristóbal de Las Casas, August 18, 2014.

Denzin, Norman K., and Yvonna S. Lincoln. 2008. "Introduction: Critical Methodologies and Indigenous Inquiry." In *Handbook of Critical and Indigenous Methodologies*, edited by Norman K. Denzin, Yvonna S. Lincoln, and Linda Tuhiwai Smith, 1–21. Thousand Oaks, CA: SAGE.

Fajardo Camacho, Andrea. 2011. "Las guerras por los 'recursos naturales' en el capitalismo neoliberal y la Reserva Autónoma Zapatista 'El Huitepec': Un estudio en camino a la decolonialidad." Bachelor's thesis, Universidad Veracruzana, Xalapa.

General Command of the EZLN. 1993. *Primera Declaración de la Selva Lacandona: Hoy decimos ¡Basta!* December 31, 1993. http://www.cedoz.org/site/content.php?doc=64.

Global Exchange, Centro de Investigaciones Económicas y Políticas de Acción Comunitaria (CIEPAC), and Centro Nacional de Comunicación Social (CENCOS). 2000. *Siempre cerca, siempre lejos: Las fuerzas armadas en México*. Mexico City: Global Exchange, CIEPAC, and CENCOS.

Hernández Castillo, Rosalva Aída, and Suzi Hutchings. 2015. "Alliances with, as Indigenous Peoples: The Obligations and Actions of Anthropologists in Mexico, Canada and Australia." Working paper.

Hidalgo Domínguez, Onésimo. 2006. *Tras los pasos de una guerra inconclusa (doce años de militarización en Chiapas)*. San Cristóbal de Las Casas: CIEPAC.

Köhler, Axel, Xochitl Leyva Solano, Xuno López Intzín, Damián Guadalupe Martínez, Rie Watanabe, Juan Chawuk, José Alfredo Jiménez Pérez, Floriano Enrique Hernández Cruz, Mariano Estrada Aguilar, and Pedro Agripino Icó Bautista. 2010. *Sjalel kibeltik / Sts'isjel ja kechtiki': Tejiendo nuestras raíces*. Mexico City: CIESAS, RACCACH. http://jkopkutik.org/sjalelkibeltik/.

Kovach, Margaret. 2009. *Indigenous Methodologies: Characteristics, Conversations and Contexts*. Toronto: University of Toronto Press.

Leyva Solano, Xochitl. 1998. "The New Zapatista Movement: Political Levels, Actors and Political Discourse in Contemporary Mexico." In *Encuentros antropológicos: Power, Identity and Mobility in Mexican Society*, edited by Valentina Napolitano and Xochitl Leyva Solano, 35–55. London: Institute of Latin American Studies.

Leyva Solano, Xochitl. (2011) 2014. "Akatemia versus aktivismi? Poliittis-teoreettisten käytäntöjen uudelleenajattelua." *Revista Kosmopolis* 44 (3–4): 9–25.

Leyva Solano, Xochitl. Forthcoming. "Guerras epistémicas, academia(s) y movimientos anti y alter: Desde el Sur profundo para el planeta Tierra." In *Conocimientos nacidos en las luchas: Construyendo las epistemologías del sur*, edited by Boaventura de Sousa Santos and María Paula Meneses. Barcelona: Akal.

Leyva Solano, Xochitl. 2018. "Undoing Colonial Patriarchies: Life and Struggle Pathways." In *Decolonization and Feminisms in Global Teaching and Learning*, edited by Sara de Jong, Rosalba Icaza, and Olivia Rutazibwa, 43–59. London: Routledge.

Leyva Solano, Xochitl, Jorge Alonso, R. Aída Hernández, Arturo Escobar, Axel Köhler, Aura Cumes, Rafael Sandoval, et al. 2015. *Prácticas otras de conocimiento(s): Entre crisis, entre guerras*. 3 vols. San Cristóbal de Las Casas: Cooperativa Editorial RETOS.

López, Gerardo R. 1998. "Reflections on Epistemology and Standpoint Theories: A Response to 'A Maori Approach to Creating Knowledge.'" *International Journal of Qualitative Studies in Education* 11 (2): 225–31.

Lorde, Audre. 1983. "The Master's Tools Will Never Dismantle the Master's House." In *This Bridge Called My Back: Writings by Radical Women of Color*, edited by Cherríe Moraga and Gloria Anzaldúa, 98–101. New York: Women of Color Press.

Martínez López, Gabriela. 2006. "Per a tothom, tot." Bachelor's thesis, University of Guadalajara.

Masson, Sabine, María Aguilar, Catalina Aguilar, Martha Aguilar, Juana Cruz, and Teresa Jiménez. 2008. *Tzome Ixuk: Una historia de mujeres tojolabales en lucha—Etnografía de una cooperativa en el marco de los movimientos sociales de Chiapas*. Mexico City: Plaza y Valdés.

Menchú Rivera, Rodrigo. 2005. "Los terrenos recuperados: Construcción identitaria de los zapatistas de la Cañada Patihuitz, Ocosingo, Chiapas—En torno al principio sociocultural del trabajo." Bachelor's thesis, ENAH, Mexico City.

Mora, Mariana. 2008. "La producción de conocimientos en el terreno de la autonomía: La investigación como tema de debate político." Lecture, Roundtable 1, Knowledge Production: For Whom, for What, How? First National Meeting of CIESAS Researchers, Querétaro, September 23, 2008.

Moraga, Cherríe. 1983. "La Güera." In *This Bridge Called My Back: Writings by Radical Women of Color*, edited by Cherríe Moraga and Gloria Anzaldúa, 27–34. New York: Women of Color Press.

Moraga, Cherríe, and Gloria Anzaldúa, eds. 1983. *This Bridge Called My Back: Writings by Radical Women of Color*. New York: Women of Color Press.

Nardini, Krizia. 2014. "Volverse otro: El pensamiento encarnado y la 'materia e importancia transformadora' de la teorización del (nuevo) materialismo feminista." *Revista Artnodes: Revista de arte, ciencia y tecnología* 14 (November): 18–25.

Pearce, Jenny. 2015. "'Avanzamos porque estamos perdidos': Reflexiones críticas sobre la co-producción de conocimiento." In *Prácticas otras de conocimiento(s): Entre crisis, entre guerras*, edited by Xochitl Leyva Solano, Jorge Alonso, R. Aída Hernández Castillo, Arturo Escobar, Axel Köhler, Aura Cumes, Rafael Sandoval, et al., 356–80. San Cristóbal de Las Casas: Cooperativa Editorial RETOS.

Piñacué, Susana. 2015. "Liderazgo y poder: Una cultura de la mujer nasa." In *Prácticas otras de conocimiento(s): Entre crisis, entre guerras*, edited by Xochitl Leyva Solano, Jorge Alonso, R. Aída Hernández Castillo, Arturo Escobar, Axel Köhler, Aura Cumes, Rafael Sandoval, et al., 313–22. San Cristóbal de Las Casas: Cooperativa Editorial RETOS.

Pérez, Ana González, Beatriz González Pérez, Celia González Pérez, and Delia Pérez de González. 2010. Press release. Ocosingo, Chiapas, October 20, 2010.

RACCACH. 2012. "Tejiendo nuestras raíces de cara a las múltiples crisis." In *Crisis y movimientos sociales en nuestra América: Cuerpos, territorios e imaginarios en disputa*, edited by Mar Daza, Raphael Hoetmer, and Virginia Vargas, n.p. Lima: Programa Democracia y Transformación Global, Coordinadora Interuniversitaria de Investigación sobre Movimientos Sociales y Cambios Político-Culturales.

Sandoval, Chela. 2000. *Methodology of the Oppressed: Theory Out of Bounds*. Minneapolis: University of Minnesota Press.

Secretaría de la Defensa Nacional (SEDENA). 1994. "Plan de Campaña Chiapas 94." Tuxtla Gutiérrez, Chiapas, VII Región Militar.

Subcomandante Insurgente (SCI) Marcos. 2005. "Abajo a la izquierda." *Enlace Zapatista*, February 28, 2005. http://enlacezapatista.ezln.org.mx/2005/02/28/abajo-a-la-izquierda/.

Slaughter, Sheila, and Larrie L. Leslie. 1999. *Academic Capitalism: Politics, Policies, and Entrepreneurial University*. Baltimore, MD: Johns Hopkins University Press.

Vargas, Virginia. 2018. "El cuerpo como categoría política y potencial de lucha desde la diversidad." In *Cuerpos racializados / cuerpos plurales en tiempos de muerte*, edited by Xochitl Leyva Solano and Rosalba Izaca, n.p. Buenos Aires: CLACSO, Cooperativa Editorial RETOS, ISS/EUR.

Vergara Camus, Leandro. 2007. "Neoliberal Globalization, Peasant Movements, Alternative Development and the State in Brazil and Mexico." PhD diss., York University, Toronto.

SIX

Maya Knowledges, Intercultural Dialogues, and Being a *Chan Laak'* in the Yucatán Peninsula

GENNER LLANES-ORTIZ

Years before I completed my first degree in social anthropology, my professional and personal trajectory as a self-identified Yucatec Maya scholar had already inspired me to search for alternative ways of practicing anthropology. My point of departure was involvement in different development initiatives led by Maya activists and non-Maya professionals in different parts of the Yucatán peninsula. A central element of these projects was the design of educational and training programs aimed to provide Indigenous community leaders with the necessary skills to negotiate increasingly hostile socioeconomic policies. We were deeply invested in designing the best strategies to develop culturally appropriate educational settings that made room for, and contributed to furthering, Indigenous knowledges. Another aim we all shared was the formation of Pan-Yucatec Maya networks through the study of regional history, Indigenous rights, and language revitalization. One of the main strategies in which we thought this could be achieved was by promoting *interculturality* as a transverse axis of nongovernmental organization (NGO) involvement with Maya actors and communities.

My personal involvement with alternative socioeconomic and political projects in the Yucatán peninsula began in 1994, when the Zapatista uprising took everybody in Mexico and the world by surprise. I joined a nascent network of NGOs from the three states of the peninsula: Quintana Roo, Campeche, and Yucatán.[1] Since then I have been a member of, worked for, accompanied, critiqued, and provided feedback to these and other local and regional groups, both of Maya and non-Maya people.

In this chapter, I discuss and explore the possibilities and limitations of an experimental collaboration with different social groups and actors in the peninsula as something that can be based on a practice rooted in Yucatec Maya pedagogies. At the same time, I offer an anthropological interpretation of the difficulties faced by Pan-Yucatec Maya individual and collective actors in defending their territorial, linguistic, and political rights. The governmental policies and political interests that have defined the first two decades of the twenty-first century in the region are prompting an interesting realignment of cultural representations, legal and social identities, intellectual practices, and organized mobilizations. In this context, a new form of engaged anthropological research is becoming even more necessary and urgent.

A Land of Ambiguous Identity Politics

The Yucatán peninsula and its society occupy a special place in Mexico's national imagination, a land that has been dubbed "a world apart" by intellectuals and scholars (Moseley and Terry 1980). The "godfather" of Mexican anthropology, Manuel Gamio, viewed the region as the only place were *mestizaje* (racial and cultural miscegenation) had been completely achieved (Gamio [1916] 1992, 13). Even in these times of renewed identity politics, Mexicans from other regions still find confusing that people in the Yucatán—who would be perceived as Indigenous somewhere else in Mexico—describe themselves as mestizos. Yucatecan mestizaje is one of the most established ideological discourses in the peninsula, in all three states: Campeche, Quintana Roo, and, perhaps most significantly, Yucatán. Mestizaje's powerful rhetoric and imagination create the illusion of terse relations between ethnic groups while reinscribing the basic differential status conferred to them by local elites. In the following text, I describe how this cultural imagery took hold of interethnic relations in the region.

Traditional historiography has always portrayed the colonization of the Yucatán in the sixteenth century as a process that brought under Spanish control several Native political units with a shared ethnic identity. Regional society has thus been painted as divided into two mutually exclusive ethnicities: the Maya and the Hispanic (also called creole, white, or simply non-Maya). This binomial characterization of regional society has lately come under heavy criticism by, among others, Peter Hervik (2001), Wolfgang Gabbert (2001), Matthew Restall (2004), and Quetzil E. Castañeda (2004). These scholars argue that a separate and unified ethnic identity cannot be simply inferred from the presence of one shared language (Yukatek Maya, or *maaya t'aan*) and core cultural traits. One piece of evidence often quoted is that speakers of *maaya t'aan* did not consistently identify themselves as Maya during the preconquest period (Restall 2004).

One could, on the other hand, respond that this basic dichotomy was enforced after the Spanish colonization. After Yucatán's (and Mexico's) independence in the early nineteenth century, however, things became much more complicated. In 1847, a peasant-led massive rebellion, known as the Caste War, erupted in the eastern peninsular region. After this conflict, the Yucatán peninsula was effectively divided in two areas (see Rugeley 2009). Rural towns in the western Hispanic-controlled area became a terrain where ethnic tensions were reinscribed through the ambiguous rhetoric of "pueblo mestizo" (Eiss 2008), which was offered as the "civilized" alternative to the rebel Maya world in the East. These Indigenous insurgents were varyingly labeled by Hispanic sources as "Indian savages," "barbarians," "aborigines," and "brave Orientals" (Rugeley 2009).

In the western peninsular region, *mestizo* became a common term used by Hispanic "white" elites to describe the Maya-speaking rural gentry of mixed heritage (Eiss 2008). In turn, these well-off mestizos would use the Maya term *máasewáal*, "common, Indigenous people," to refer to poor peasants and indentured plantation servants, effectively separating themselves from this "uncivilized" underclass. On the other hand, eastern Maya rebels would use *máasewáal*, although in a more political sense, to identify themselves. Throughout the dictatorship of Porfirio Díaz in Mexico (1876–1911), pueblo mestizo traditions crystallized in popular performances like *jaranas* and *vaquerías*. These were privileged spaces to represent the illusion of harmonious mestizaje, which so clearly fooled Mexico City's elites and our anthropological ancestors.

But it was not just the mestizo performances that confused Manuel Gamio, for even "white" elites in the peninsula's main cities (Mérida, Valladolid, and Campeche) had developed, after all, an intimate bond with Maya language and traditions. While they never stopped seeing Yucatecan "Indians" as an "inferior race," since the late nineteenth century, Hispanic "white" and mestizo intellectuals—like Catholic Bishop Crescencio Carrillo y Ancona—had been reclaiming aspects of Maya culture as a core element of Yucatecan regional identity. Unlike their peers in other parts of Mexico, Yucatán's "white" upper class spoke the Indigenous language daily, fluidly, and intimately.

Yucatecan Hispanic and mestizo appropriations of various elements of Indigenous material and intangible heritage in the early twentieth century have furthered the ambiguous cultural politics that prevails to this day. These appropriations have taken diverse forms: Indigenous-themed and Maya language literature (written by Yucatecan "whites" and mestizos; see Worley 2013), recreation of Maya architecture in public buildings (see Joseph 1988), reimaginations of Maya music for the regional songbook (see Martín Briceño 2011), state—and, increasingly, private—control of ancient Maya sites (see Breglia 2006), use of Maya symbols, "traditions" and "culture" as selling points for local and international tourism (see Magnoni, Arden, and Hutson 2007; Rogal 2012), among many others. All these operations work in tandem with Mexico's *indigenismo*, the central government's managed cultural assimilation of Indigenous peoples, a mixture of racism, romanticism, and developmentalism. Yet, because Maya cultural appropriations by the "white" and mestizo elites have been so crucial for their legitimization as privileged political and cultural brokers between the "Indigenous masses" and the post-Revolutionary state, indigenismo in the Yucatán has had ambivalent effects on regional identity politics.

Take, for example, the Yukatek Maya language. Until the mid-twentieth century, Maya was the peninsula's unofficial lingua franca. Even the Hispanic elites were proud of their intimate knowledge of the language. Lebanese, German, Cuban, and Catalonian immigrants, Korean plantation workers, and Indigenous Yaqui political prisoners, all had to learn Maya to do business, integrate, and survive. In the 1940s, however, indigenismo policies and the expansion of Spanish language education started to erode the prevalence of Maya. Overzealous rural teachers in the peninsula were crucial to this task. Spanish language was imposed (often through violent schooling practices) on Maya-speaking farmers all over the peninsula, and rural teachers were celebrated for their valuable "civilizing" services to the Mexican nation (see Fallaw 1997). At the same time, these teachers found in Maya language and oral literature a valuable source to support the mestizo nation-building project. They used them to re-create an "imagined community" to which all Maya-speaking peasants, both mestizo and *máasewáal*, belonged. In publications like *Yikal Maya Than* (The genius of Maya language), mestizo teachers published stories that portrayed Indigenous peasantry as the diminished heirs of the ancient Maya's "glorious" civilization (Mossbrucker, Pfeiler, and Maas Collí 1994). Meanwhile, members of the "white" wealthy elite gradually lost influence and interest in nationalist cultural politics and distanced themselves from Maya culture and language.

Yucatecan mestizaje's hegemony did not, however, translate into the abatement of racism and ethnic divisions, as Quetzil E. Castañeda (1997), Christine Kray (2005), Eugenia Iturriaga Acevedo (2010, 2011), Ricardo López Santillán (2010), and Ronald Loewe (2010) have shown. For example, Loewe finds that although the term *mestizo* still applies to a wide range of social and ethnic types in western Yucatán, those defined as *ts'úulo'ob* (the rich, the non-Maya, sometimes the "white") are the only ones perceived as *mestizos legítimos* (legitimate mixed-race; a "regional oxymoron"). In late-nineteenth-century fashion, this rural gentry are still thought to embody the standard of Yucatecan regionalism (Loewe 2010, 61). Loewe describes a hierarchical order in which different mestizo identities index differential statuses: the Indigenous mestizos at the bottom, and the "white" or "legitimate" mestizos at the top.

In the 1970s, a critique of Indigenous assimilation policies gave birth to a certain form of participatory indigenismo (see Martínez-Novo 2004). It was clear in the Yucatán, as well as in other parts of Mexico, that Indigenous identities, languages, and communities could not be easily integrated into the mestizo nation. This time, new Maya-Spanish bilingual agents from Indigenous communities were invited to act as political and cultural intermediaries. Many did so in the fields of Indigenous education and culture, while others joined the indigenista development institutions (Rosales González and Llanes-Ortiz 2003). The hegemonic status of pueblo mestizo representations, however, made it difficult for many of these new agents to identify themselves as Indigenous, despite their rural *máasewáal* origin. Recent work by Cornejo and Bellon (2009) and Iturriaga Acevedo (2010, 2011) has increased our knowledge of the powerful web of racist representations that, after centuries of cultural assimilation policies, unequivocally associate Indigenous Maya language, culture, and identities with poverty, ugliness, backwardness, and inferiority.

Pan-Yucatec Maya Activism and Its Critics

Today an intricate and deeply hierarchical repertoire of social classifiers is deployed in different parts of the Yucatán peninsula. These include categories like mestizo, *mayero* (Maya speaker), *máasewáal* (Indigenous), *ootsil* (poor), *ts'úul* (rich), white, *wach* (term applied to Mexican "foreigners" or people from central Mexico), *gente de pueblo* (small-town folk), *gente de ciudad* (city folk), among many others. This situation leads many social scientists to reject the idea of a single Maya ethnic identity. Some accept, however, the possible existence of an "implied ethnicity," in which "terms of self-identification imply membership in a loosely-defined ethnic group within the context of broader social and ethnoracial structures" (Restall 2004, 75). Others, like Christine Kray, propose to understand sociocultural identities in the Yucatán as "ethnic classes." These are social classifiers that represent "an overlap between economic standing, language, shared history, and other aspects of lifestyle" (2005, 339), and in which ideas of "race" become key ordering principles, too.

Given this context, many anthropologists tend to dismiss efforts to promote a Pan-Yucatec Maya identity. For example, Wolfgang Gabbert tells us that this "is a project advanced mainly by members of the ethnicized middle class, institutions such as INI [National Indigenist Institute] and, *last but not least*, Mexican and foreign intellectuals" (2001, 480; my emphasis). Maya political mobilization in the Yucatán also compares unfavorably with other Indigenous movements that have shown more strength and achieved greater success in both Mexico—in regions like Oaxaca and Chiapas—and Guatemala (Mattiace 2009; Loewe 2010, 146–47). Even some Maya scholars, like Juan Castillo Cocom, state that "the term 'indigenous movements' . . . —though it might apply to the Maya people of Guatemala—has no relevance when applied to Yucatán" (2005, 146).

My position in this debate is that an emphasis in solving the conundrum of Maya ethnicity when discussing Pan-Yucatec Maya cultural activism is wrongly placed. As the Guatemalan case shows, it is necessary to move away from "the irresolvable paradox of strategic essentialism" and to attend to "the multiplicity of agents, epistemologies, erasures, and transnational forces implicated in the construction of collective identities" (French 2008, 123). Working on the cultural politics of the Yucatán peninsula, I acknowledge that social labels and the identities they imply are contextually, relationally, and messily assigned. This is—as I hope to have shown before—the consequence of a "heritage of ambiguity," as Fernando Armstrong-Fumero (2009) calls it. Nevertheless, social actors create their own hybrid forms of classification and representation, which eventually become dominant, thus obscuring forms of self-adscription that in other historical circumstances might prove crucial in the mobilization of cultural or political identities. This is the regional background against which Pan-Yucatec Maya activism emerged in the 1980s, through a series of operations that, just like pueblo mestizo representations, responded to different cultural and political logics. These are to be found, not in a community-based, preexisting ethnicity, but in the dynamic interplay of national, regional, and subregional cultural politics.

Pan-Yucatec Maya activism is a heterogeneous cultural and political field that has laboriously and gradually taken shape in the peninsula in the last three decades. Although it is primarily led by Maya-speaking actors, it does not exclude the participation of non-Maya and even non-Yucatecan supporters. It involves cultural promoters, art practitioners, community groups, and regional networks, with strong ties to the Pan-Maya movement in Guatemala, and the Indian theology and the Zapatista movements in Chiapas. The particularities of Yucatecan cultural politics determine specific ways for these Pan-Maya identities (yes, in plural) to be negotiated. This is why I deem it necessary to stress the Yucatec character of the Pan-Maya approach, to differentiate it from the Chiapanecan and Guatemalan contexts.

The last quarter of the twentieth century gave way to new forms of imagining linguistic, class, and ethnic differences in the Yucatán peninsula. Some of them were promoted by Mexican revisionist indigenismo, others by leftist, developmentalist, and religious groups (Rosales González and Llanes-Ortiz 2003). Since then, several attempts have been (and are still) made to reconfigure supralocal and interclass relationships within the Maya-speaking population. These Pan-Yucatec Maya identity projects aspire to infuse a sense of common ancestry, political convergence, and economic solidarity among the descendants of the postclassic Maya in the region. I joined some of these efforts as a young anthropology student in the mid-1990s. In the following section, I reflect on the experience of working at this intersection between anthropology and activism.

Collaborative Research as Intercultural Dialogue

After several years of NGO activism in the peninsula, I returned to academia in the first decade of this century. Back then, I worked as a research assistant in a nationwide project led by the National Institute of Anthropology and History (INAH). This provided me with an opportunity to investigate why Indigenous organizations in the Yucatán seemed to be "lagging behind" other Indigenous movements in Mexico and, especially, Guatemala (see Rosales González and Llanes-Ortiz 2003). Anthropological research at INAH was not particularly prone to collaborative and dialogical research with Indigenous partners. When I was awarded a Ford Foundation International Fellowships grant in 2002, however, I had already decided to put my development practitioner experiences to good use in an exploration of new ways to engage with the politics of knowledge and representation of Mexican anthropology.

In 2003, I obtained a master's in anthropology of development at the University of Sussex in the United Kingdom. After securing another scholarship, from Mexico's National Council for Science and Technology, I embarked on a long PhD journey at the same university in 2004. My research focused on the construction of interculturality in some of the educational projects that I had contributed to creating in the peninsula during my NGO activist years. In the Department of Anthropology at the University of Sussex, I found the academic support to conduct collaborative research on the work of the Networking Peasant and Indigenous University, or Universidad Campesina Indígena en Red (UCI-Red). At the end of this academic adventure (Llanes-Ortiz 2010), I had come to realize that creating a space for *intercultural dialogue* between Maya and non-Maya partners was—clearly—easier said than done. In this same process, I began to understand that collaborative researching demanded an intercultural methodology as well.

All this redefined my role as a *chan láak'* (roughly translated as "little, or younger brother") in different efforts to promote a Pan-Yucatec Maya movement in the region. Over the centuries, Indigenous peoples have become painfully aware that research—particularly social research—fundamentally serves the goals determined by society's dominant groups. Consequently, Indigenous community members and activists often show a deep mistrust toward any kind of research and researchers (see Smith 1999). Most research tends to respond to theoretical interests and debates that originate in concerns not shared by Indigenous communities or organizations. And even when anthropologists, however "native," decide to contribute to the goals pursued by Indigenous social movements, they try to do so by imparting their "enlightened knowledge" onto their Indigenous "partners" (Papadakis 1993).

Anthropology has always been a site for the production of intercultural knowledge. But this knowledge has usually been wrapped in the self-evident delusion of Eurocentric naïve empiricism, which has hampered anthropology's capacity for a fruitful interaction and communication with the "other" (Van Binsbergen 1999). The principle of objectivity in social research has demanded in the past a detachment from the political concerns of the social actors with whom one works and interacts (Latour 2005; Smith 1999). Although this position has long been criticized, the shift toward a more open collaboration between the anthropologist and other research participants has not occurred without difficulties (Mutua and Swadener 2004; Warren and Jackson 2002). While assuming the duty of reflexivity and critical realism in ethnography (Davis 1999; Van Binsbergen 1999), my own approach to research in this context aims to respond to the challenge of creating the conditions for intercultural dialogue.

This kind of dialogue is at the center of discussions about interculturality in Latin America, which several scholars have delineated in different ways. From a historical perspective, Gunther Dietz locates the origins of this notion in the "pedagogization of multiculturalism," which responds to demands for the recognition of cultural diversity in education (2003, 69). He characterizes and discusses different types of interculturality (reified, personalized, and rationalized), which he sees emerging out of the overlapping of disciplinary traditions, like psychology, linguistics, pedagogy, philosophy, and business management. Catherine Walsh sees interculturality as developing from within the epistemological challenges that Indigenous movements present to Westernized forms of knowledge, originating particularly in the context of Ecuadorian identity politics in the 1990s. The value that she sees in this form of interculturality resides in the promise of a *plural universalism*, which would solve the fragmentation produced by different forms of multiculturalism (Walsh 2002). Finally, in an effort to understand the heterogenous definitions of interculturality in higher education institutions, Daniel Mato characterizes the demand of intercultural dialogue as a key element of Indigenous struggles for democratization and against the historical and structural marginalization of Indigenous communities and individuals in the region (Mato 2008). In my own work, I do not understand this dialogue as a goal to be achieved but fundamentally as a method to be followed in the construction of both social justice and anthropological knowledge. In this enterprise, I have adopted some of the questions posed by intercultural philosophers, like Raúl Fornet-Betancourt. He addresses the challenge of intercultural dialogue in these terms: "[The] strict meaning of intercultural dialogue as a method for a better knowledge of the other as well as of oneself is misunderstood . . . if 'knowledge' is understood in the sense of a simple 'taking note' or 'making known.' Rather, it concerns a process of information in which we inform ourselves (communicate) and allow ourselves to be in-formed (in the sense of given form) by what [and who] we know" (Fornet-Betancourt 2000, 11).

Inspired by these ideas, I conceived my PhD research as a series of observational practices within a more complex form of "respectful conversation"—or *tsikbal* in Yukatek Maya. Since then, people involved in the projects I have collaborated on—like UCI-Red, the seed exchange festivals, and the Independent Maya Festival U Cha'anil Kaaj—have been invited to make contributions to my research design and, in some cases, have asked me to organize the collective analysis of their experience.

In my research with UCI-Red, the organizing committee asked me to structure my conversations with them and other participants in a way that would improve their (our) understanding of interculturality—a commitment that I was happy to make. UCI-Red in the Yucatán peninsula had brought together a fluid coalition of Maya and non-Maya (mostly Central Mexican) development practitioners whose work was located in several microregions of the Yucatán peninsula (northern and southern Yucatán, southern Quintana Roo, Los Chenes in Campeche, and Camino Real across Campeche and Yucatán). Its main goal was to provide Maya-speaking peasants (men and women whose ages ranged from eighteen to sixty-five) with technically and culturally appropriate education to improve their self-reliance against the challenges of rural Mexico's neoliberalization. This training was conceived as a series of intermittent sessions based on a pedagogy aimed at creating the conditions for a "dialogue of knowledges" (*diálogo de saberes*) between, fundamentally, non-Maya educators and Maya trainees (see also Llanes-Ortiz 2005).

While working with UCI-Red members, I used this training space to share and discuss my interpretations and critiques of their work. The full-time dedication I showed to reading and commenting on the project's materials and plans was in the end seen more in terms of the project dynamics than as research. In turn, I started to see myself more as another coordinator of UCI-Red than as an external observer. As I worked in and around this educational project, my view of the Pan-Yucatec Maya initiative also became more and more critical. It was not that I no longer agreed with the idea of promoting interclass and interethnic solidarity and intercultural dialogue between the non-Maya NGO workers and the Maya peasants within this project. Rather, I found that the desire to shape intercultural dialogues through practices of schooling tended to override any other way of teaching and learning within UCI-Red. For instance, a strong emphasis was generally set on the development of verbal and logical-mathematical knowledge—including public presentations, planning, analysis, and evaluation of development projects in the classroom—to compensate for the lack of formal education. Indigenous knowledge was for the most part only "talked about" and "written down" (through systematization tasks) in order to be included in the sessions. Maya people contributed to these dialogues with fragmented pieces of the traditional knowledge they had inherited and reconfigured while dealing with "modernity." They would, on the one hand, painstakingly detail and reflect on the economic and cultural logics of Maya agriculture (on the key importance of maize and biocultural diversity integration, cyclic ordering, family-based organization, and environmental and supernatural correspondences). On the other hand, they were explaining and trying to make sense of their local history through a government construction of modern infrastructure. Despite these complex reconfigurations offered by local participants, UCI-Red pedagogues would find themselves often at a loss for not having a single book that defined what Indigenous identity, culture, and knowledge were, and how to include them in an intercultural education project. Maya language teachers were invited to lead literacy workshops directed to Maya-speaking participants, but never to non-Maya NGO workers.

In fact, NGO personnel saw themselves mostly as intercultural trainers and not as potential intercultural trainees. Furthermore, emphasis on schooling went against common notions and practices of learning (*kaanbal*) and teaching (*ka'ansaj*) that are reproduced among Maya farmers, where psychometrical and cognitive development occur in communities of practice. These are organized in steps, or stages, in which the most skilled participant in the activity shows, or demonstrates (*e'esaj*), and thus transmits the knowledge acquired, generally with little or no verbal interaction. Sitting still for hours in a classroom, listening to "experts" who had never practiced what they wanted to impart, was the antithesis of Maya learning practices.

The role that my anthropological input played in shifting the pedagogical strategies of UCI-Red toward a less formal and more open-ended process of learning was deemed crucial in the final stages of the project. Based on my recommendations, the training that was before directed only to Maya peasant participants this time included non-Maya advisers, who suddenly found themselves in processes of learning in which they did not have all the control. But my contribution did not only consist of imparting my newly gained anthropological understanding of interculturality onto UCI-Red project members. I was also personally involved in coordinating and reimagining, with new diploma courses (contributing new questions, reflecting on local knowledge, animating exchanges, and organizing and devolving local participants in the results of their own research projects, among other tasks). This eventually led to a reconsideration of the strong emphasis on schooling within UCI-Red and opened up new processes of collaboration between Maya and non-Maya participants. Nonetheless, not everything worked out well for everybody in the end. Some members of UCI-Red were intellectually and institutionally invested in making this a successful intercultural schooling project, and when the emphasis shifted, they lost interest and left to join other initiatives.

As for my personal learning, this effort to incorporate Indigenous knowledge into structured training processes made clear that a social pedagogy existed in Maya communities that we had not paid attention to before. While looking into how "education" is talked about in the Yukatek Maya language, I realized that some of these notions could help me understand collaborative learning in a broader sense.

E'esaj: To Demonstrate Is a Form of Partnership

There is an expression in Yukatek Maya that I began to examine while comparing learning practices, first among Indigenous peasants in Yucatán, and then in UCI-Red's training sessions. It derives from the root *e'es*, which according to colonial Maya dictionaries is the contraction of the transitive form of the verb *et*: "to show, to exhibit." David Bolles's comparative Mayan dictionary (2001, n.p.) tells us that *et* or *éet* can alternatively mean "with, and"; "a particle that denotes similarity, company"; "to carry"; "in noun formation: partner, similar"; "in verb formation: jointly, in company of"; "sometimes, a particle denoting comparison"; and "varied, other, similar, alike, same."

From the multiple meanings associated with this term, it follows that the contemporary transitive form *e'esaj*, "to show, to signal, to demonstrate, to teach (something)," can also be interpreted as "to work with, to make somebody your partner, your equal." *Taalo'ob ku ye'esikto'on le meyajo'*, which literally means, "they came to show us, or to demonstrate the job to us," can also be interpreted as "they came to make us their partners in the job." In some ways, this means disclosing the inner workings of a certain job or task to other people, which is often how teaching tends to be understood among Maya-speaking farmers—a notion that became apparent in my conversations with participants in UCI-Red sessions. This is how people come to collaborate and work together in everyday life. When I began my PhD research, I placed a lot of emphasis on the Maya notion of *tsikbal* (respectful conversation) as the culturally appropriate way of engaging with other research subjects in the field. I came later to the conclusion that the best way to promote collaboration with Maya people (and in my work's case, with Pan-Yucatec Maya activists) was by exploring different forms of *e'es-ajil*: "the act of showing, signaling, demonstrating and/or teaching."

One way of *e'esaj*-ing (showing, demonstrating, partnering in) my research work was having an open agenda. Dialogue and collaboration with other research participants demanded their involvement in the layout and development of the research. This meant allowing research participants to have a decisive say in what needed to be investigated. It also meant that we had to unpack together some key concepts like *culture, knowledge, learning*, and *identity*, and to acknowledge that their definitions were as good (or as limited) as any other offered by anthropology. But this did not mean that I had to give up my critical analysis of their work. In this research, *e'esaj*-ing also meant disclosing these criticisms to them, that is, sharing the inner workings of anthropological analysis in an honest face-to-face interaction.

To a great extent, this was possible because the people involved in this project already saw me as part of their family. After all, I had grown up working with them and contributing to the same goals before I embarked on a PhD program on the other side of the world. In the Yukatek Maya language, members of the nuclear family are classified according to age. Older siblings are differentiated by gender. The elder brother is known as *suku'un*; the elder sister is called *kiik*. Calling somebody your *suku'un* or your *kiik* acknowledges the person's hierarchy and authority; it is a sign of deep respect. Younger siblings are generically called *íits'in*, regardless of gender. In my interactions with Maya members of the UCI-Red project, I was often called an *íits'in*, which reflected how I was perceived for being one of the youngest collaborators. Family terminology implies a level of trust that, later on, I have had to build with other Maya groups and activists in the peninsula. In the collaborations that followed my engagement with UCI-Red, however, I have strived to create a relationship that goes beyond this age and gender hierarchy. By continuing to be frank about my research objectives and open to including other people's research ideas in my own, some Maya activists have started to consider me not an *íits'in* or a *suku'un* but a *láak'*.

Láak' is the generic term that describes a relationship with somebody, without necessarily establishing a differential status. It primarily means "a similar other," but it also stands for "relative," "friend," "companion," "equal," "peer," or "fellow person." Since I started reflecting on this, I have felt more encouraged to undertake collaborative research, and to use this term to describe the kind of relationship that I seek to establish with my Maya peers. In the last six years, I have thus developed new collaborative relations that turned me into a *láak'* of Pan-Maya activists in Mexico, Belize, and Guatemala.

Being a *Chan Láak'* as a Collaborative Anthropology Practice

In 2011, I joined the multidisciplinary research project Indigeneity in the Contemporary World: Performance, Politics, Belonging, based in Royal Holloway University of London and led by Helen Gilbert, a well-known theater and dance scholar from Australia. As the name of the project suggests, it revolved fundamentally around two main themes. One was *indigeneity*, which was understood as a field of dynamic, culturally relevant, and politically strategic self-representations of Indigenous peoples. The other focus was on *performance*, which was conceived in its broader sense to include practices that ranged from theater, film, music, and dance to mixed-media and digital work, Olympic pageantry, festival events, political protests, and cultural displays within tourism ventures.[2] The Indigeneity project also had a strong emphasis on ethical protocols, which suited the kind of research that I had already begun in the Yucatán.

Within the Indigeneity project, I conducted a comparative study about performance practices involved in the work of Pan-Yucatec Maya activists and the Belizean Maya movement.[3] In the Yucatán, my research focused on a series of festivals for the exchange of maize seeds, which I have characterized as the *fiestas y ferias de semillas* movement (Llanes-Ortiz 2015b). I worked again with community-based groups of Maya peasants and their generally non-Maya NGO allies, but I followed a slightly different strategy from the one I employed with UCI-Red. This time I held several meetings to present, receive feedback, and adapt my original research proposal before developing it in full. Time constraints determined the level of involvement that I was able to sustain with these organizations. My interest was set on capturing how Maya forms of knowledge and artistic expression were creatively performed and reassembled in these festivals. The *fiestas y ferias de semillas* movement celebrates fourteen years of history in 2016. During this time, these gatherings have included rituals, storytelling, theatrical plays, poetry recitation, music performances, group conversations, academic talks, and political demonstrations, besides the actual trading of seeds of, among other crops, maize, beans, squash, and roots. In the process of safeguarding the agricultural legacy inherited from our Maya ancestors, *fiestas y ferias de semillas* facilitators have activated new ways of being Maya in the twenty-first century. I documented these practices in 2013 through video recordings, which I later used to produce two short ethnographic documentaries.[4] These short films became my main contribution to their efforts of recuperating and revitalizing Maya cultural knowledge. For example, an NGO that gives support and advice to one of the community-based Maya organization has used one of these shorts to promote their annual festival.[5] In this collaborative research, I have thus contributed to highlighting their new representations of Maya culture. These are not homogenous and tend to vary along clear ideological accentuations: some expressions focus mainly on the socioeconomic importance of maize and milpa agriculture for Maya identity, while others are more preoccupied with the religious symbols that support Mayaneity. My collaborative research has hinted at these complex negotiations inside the movement about whether some innovations (both economic and ritual) are necessary, who has the right to introduce them, and how this should be done (for more on this, see Llanes-Ortiz 2015b).

One crucial aspect I had to translate and negotiate with some research participants was the concept of performance itself. Some were strongly preoccupied with the idea that describing ceremonial practice in festivals as performance could be misrepresenting the practice as "theatrics" or mere "show." The conversations we had about how *performance* offered interesting analytical insights into how cultural pedagogies work in public celebrations, while the Anglo-Saxon scope of the concept was ill-fitting to Maya understandings of ceremony, participation, and spectacle, inspired me to write a short bilingual Maya-Spanish piece about the translatability of academic categories (Llanes-Ortiz 2015a).

My research has stressed the significance of the *fiestas y ferias* movement as an articulate response to neoliberal government policies, which have greatly affected the capacity of Maya communities to cope with severe cuts in agricultural subsidies and the liberalization of food markets. The movement celebrates the sophisticated plant-breeding knowledge and biodiversity management skills of Maya peasants, and thus challenges the central role that technical expertise has in the "neoliberal corn regime" (see Fitting 2011). The latest festivals have vocally expressed their rejection of introducing GMO crops in Maya territories, which is promoted by agribusiness corporations with the active endorsement of the Mexican agriculture ministry, among other national agencies. This resistance has aligned Indigenous peasant concerns with renewed views of self-determination, identity, territoriality and sustainability in some of the poorest corners of the peninsula (among them, again, southern Yucatán, Los Chenes in Campeche, and southern Quintana Roo). My research has aimed to show that far from being the result of a knee-jerk reaction from traditionalist Indigenous communities, the anti-GMO movement in the Yucatán is part of a global conversation about fair trade, food sovereignty, healthy consumption, and local knowledges.

Resistance to the commoditization of Maya culture also characterizes another Pan-Yucatec Maya movement with which I have developed a collaborative relationship in recent years. My interest in the "festivalization of culture" (Bennett, Taylor, and Woodward 2014) and my close association with many Pan-Yucatec Maya activists got me involved in the organization of the Independent Maya Festival U Cha'anil Kaaj.[6] I was still living and working in the United Kingdom when this movement burst onto the public scene as a firm response to the exclusionary decisions that characterize the International Festival of Mayan Culture (FICMaya). This government-funded festival was the brainchild of the political boss of regional arts, Yucatecan mestizo playwright Jorge Esma. It was conceived as an opportunity to attract national and international tourism to the state of Yucatán, by taking advantage of the global interest in the region that the "end of the Maya calendar" produced in 2012. Nonetheless, and despite of the festival's name, FICMaya's organizing committee did not include a single representative of Maya artistic communities or their organizations. In the first year of the FICMaya, the participation of Maya artists and intellectuals was marginal, if nonexistent. Most of the "Maya" artistic performances consisted of staging pueblo mestizo traditions, like jaranas, vaquerías, and regional music. Still, nobody in the Pan-Yucatec Maya activism circles protested or said anything.

The second FICMaya, in 2013, featured talks by Deepak Chopra; concerts by Yanni, Filippa Giordano, Joan Manuel Serrat, and Joaquín Sabina; and performances by Chinese and Russian classic ballets, among its principal (and most expensive) artistic events. The "Mayan Culture" component was covered by academic conferences of Mexican and international scholars (who spoke mainly about historical Maya culture) and by the tokenistic presence of Guatemalan Maya Nobel Prize–winner Rigoberta Menchú. This time a group of Pan-Yucatec Maya activists used social media to vent their frustration at having, again, been completely ignored by the organizers of FICMaya. From this outburst, a counter-festival organization emerged, of which I was a distant participant and witness. On October 18, 2013, a protest letter was published on the AVAAZ.org public petitions website. In this letter, the people who joined in the organization of the Independent Maya Festival U Cha'anil Kaaj expressed their views about FICMaya and asked Rigoberta Menchú, Joaquín Sabina, and Joan Manuel Serrat to decline their participation in the governmental event. The letter denounced that "in the organization and decision-making of this festival [FICMaya], the Yucatec Maya people's intellectuals, artists and members were first excluded and then ignored. This festival is paid with millions of pesos and has all the resources that money can buy, but it lacks something very important because the legitimate presence of the Maya people of the Yucatán peninsula is absent."[7] This statement also pointed out that when the government had realized that a protest movement was on the rise, state agents had tried to co-opt and bribe some of the Independent Maya Festival organizers and supporters to stop their participation. It also made clear that the FICMaya boss had ordered some media outlets to build a wall of silence around the activities of U Cha'anil Kaaj. I was one of first signatories of this letter, which galvanized the support of more than 1,300 people online.

U Cha'anil Kaaj 2013 included a wide range of activities, which began with a long cultural caravan march from Maya rebel territory to "mestizo" urban spaces, followed by Maya-speaking radio programs, theatrical plays, poetry recitals, and music concerts; public commemorations of forgotten Maya historical figures; Maya book, comics, and film presentations; workshops on ancient Maya writing; conferences and talks on different topics by Maya experts; and even a special vaquería event in San Francisco, California (where a significant number of Yucatec Maya live). The festival program reads like a who's who of Pan-Yucatec Maya activism in Campeche, Quintana Roo, Yucatán, Guatemala, and even the United States, a program in which the most salient feature is that all its events were selected, organized, and led by Maya activists and not by the Yucatecan mestizo cultural bureaucracy.[8] The spontaneous organization and wide reach of U Cha'anil Kaaj foregrounded the existence of a Pan-Yucatec Maya community with the potential to challenge Mexican state definitions of what Maya culture is and how it must be "celebrated." The festival allowed activists to show their diverse, sometimes even competing, ideas of Mayaneity. Some cultural expressions were reexplorations of "traditional" storytelling and cultural knowledge in comic books, theater, or film; others harked back to the ancient past, as in the Maya epigraphy workshops; and some were more politicized, reflecting on human rights abuses and racism, or on neo-Zapatista politics.

In 2014, I participated more directly in the second edition of the Independent Maya Festival as a collaborator and researcher. I followed and video recorded as many events of U Cha'anil Kaaj as I could and talked informally to the main organizers as well as to spontaneous supporters. This year, the FIC-Maya director recruited a Mexico City–based Maya writer, Jorge Cocom Pech, to organize a Meeting of Maya Language Writers, with a handsome budget that allowed him to invite prominent authors from Guatemala, Chiapas, and Oaxaca, among other places. U Cha'anil Kaaj and its supporters made an open call to lesser known community writers to have their work digitally printed on plastic canvases for a public exhibition in the main square of Mérida, the capital of Yucatán. As I followed the activities of U Cha'anil Kaaj, I could not shake the feeling of being part of a turf war between the independent festival and FICMaya, one in which the latter had all the resources of the state and private businesses at its disposal, while the other struggled to find time, money, and support to organize even the most modest of events. I still need to publish a full account and analysis of my collaborative engagement with U Cha'anil Kaaj in 2014; however, by the end of my fieldwork, I asked some of the main organizers to get together to share with them my first thoughts. I named this activity U Suutul Kaanbal, or the Devolving of Learnings (following an idea advanced by a young Maya scholar, Yazmin Novelo). I offered them my general impression of the festival, with the help of a PowerPoint presentation, describing what I thought were its best practices and its most evident weaknesses. They, in turn, recorded what I said in the hope that they could discuss it further with other participants who could not be with us that night.[9] The effort to understand an event through a reflexive conversation with its main actors was taken in good spirit by members of U Cha'anil Kaaj. This was the culmination of a long series of conversations that I'd had over those two or three weeks with several of its promoters on the road, while arranging chairs, fixing microphones, or receiving and transporting speakers to different venues. It prompted a collective reckoning (mine as well as theirs) of what had happened with the festival that year; the energy invested, the numbers reached, the absences, the ebbs and flows of participation, and the meaning and direction of the activities developed. For many of the younger activists, the Independent Maya Festival's essence resided in its proximity to nonactivist Maya people and not so much in the numbers of non-Maya spectators they attracted. This last meeting of U Cha'anil Kaaj was for me the beginning of a much bigger conversation with this younger generation of Pan-Yucatec Maya activists, whose enthusiasm and quests I have continued to share. The festival has since changed and found new forms of organizing. In 2015, instead of a central event, U Cha'anil Kaaj worked as an umbrella for a series of local festivals that took place in Kinil, Cholul, and Ticul, among other localities, which shows the aperture and willingness of this Pan-Yucatec Maya activism network to change and adapt.

In a Manner of Conclusion

What is collaborative anthropology, and how can it be done from the position of a self-ascribed Maya scholar in Yucatán? In this chapter, I examine my personal attempts to make sense of this question based on the practice that I have led as a "Native" anthropologist working in collaboration with Pan-Yucatec Maya initiatives. The practice of Native researchers demands of them an effort to develop new "forms of motivated and stylized dislocation," by becoming self-styled "foreigners" (Gupta and Ferguson 1997, 37) in their own communities. Having learned this trade studying anthropology in college, and in my quest for alternative ways to practice the discipline, I have explored different forms of "returning" some of this knowledge to all of my communities: Pan-Yucatec Maya activism networks and Indigenous and non-Indigenous academic circles.

Collaborative research has demanded that I, as a Maya scholar, undergo a process of negotiation with Maya and non-Maya research participants to close the gap between external and internal participants. But it has also required that I make an effort to understand, explain, and theorize my practice using a language that makes sense anthropologically as well as in Yukatek Maya—as I had to do with the concept of performance. This is where the notion of *e'esaj* as a form of sharing, demonstrating, and partnering in the learning process has emerged. In all these collaborative endeavors, *e'esaj*-ing my research to and with both older and younger Maya activists has entailed translating and unpacking old-fashioned and problematic anthropological notions that became common jargon in the 1990s, like *culture* and *identity* (Wright 1998). A big challenge has been to work in and around the strategic essentialism that often pervades reformulations and representations of "Maya culture," not just among Pan-Yucatec Maya activists but also in the spheres of governmental politics, heritage management, and global tourism. This has led me to acknowledge that anthropological (and historical) knowledge is as fluid and constructed as indigeneity, or in this case, as Maya culture. Therefore, deconstructing Pan-Yucatec Maya strategic essentialism also requires dismantling pueblo mestizo's hegemonic, ambiguous, and still racist cultural politics in the peninsula.

In this task, my viewpoints as a *chan láak'*, a "younger peer," have to be expressed with tact, intelligence, and affect. I have to be respectful and appreciative of the experiences of previous and new generations of activists, and recognize that I have never had to endure the racism and violence that they have sometimes suffered. This principle has also made me realize that "being Maya" in the twenty-first century means different things to different people. And that we need to allow this "hetero-Mayaneity" reach its full potential to fight racism, marginalization, and authoritarianism, not just from the national state but among us, Pan-Yucatec Maya activists, too. This work is not easy, and it is still unfolding, but I believe that a collaborative anthropology based on frank dialogue from an assumed Maya position has great potential, not just to defend Maya knowledges but to increase their scope, too.

Collaborative endeavors are forms of intercultural dialogue, a dialogue that implies negotiation and change, the shifting of research agendas and the acceptance of criticism and diversity. While the lessons learned from this experience are still to be absorbed in their entirety, I hope to have shown in this chapter some that I have gained so far.

Notes

1. While I am fully aware that another such region exists in the northern part of the country (Baja California), in this chapter, I use "the peninsula" exclusively to refer to Mexico's southeastern region.
2. See the Indigeneity in the Contemporary World website, accessed April 1, 2016, http://indigeneity.net.
3. The research I conducted in Belize was also based on a collaborative methodology, but I do not talk about this particular engagement with Belizean Maya organizations in this chapter as I feel that it would upset the focus of the discussion I am leading here, which relates to my own community in the Yucatán. I hope to find another opportunity in the future to reflect on collaborations across the Pan-Maya region, as my work with Chiapanecan, Belizean, and Guatemalan Maya organizations has proved highly inspirational.
4. These two short documentaries can be watched at Vimeo: *Fiesta of Maize in Yucatán*, uploaded by Genner Llanes-Ortiz, May 2, 2013, http://vimeo.com/65300894; and *Feria of Native Seeds in Quintana Roo*, uploaded by Genner Llanes-Ortiz, uploaded May 22, 2013, http://vimeo.com/66728193.
5. See "Sobre la Feria de las Semillas 2013," *Educe*, March 8, 2015, http://educe.org.mx/?p=151.
6. *U cha'anil kaaj* is an expression that in the Yucatecan context refers to the annual patron saint's festival, which takes place in every town in the peninsula. In the

context of the Independent Maya Festival, however, this expression is intended to mean also "the Maya people's festival."

7. "En la organización y toma de decisiones de ese festival los intelectuales, artistas y miembros del pueblo maya yucateco fuimos primero excluidos y luego ignorados. Ese festival se hace con sumas millonarias y con todos los recursos que el dinero puede comprar, pero carece de lo más importante: en ese festival está ausente la presencia legítima del pueblo maya de la península de Yucatán"; A favor del respeto al pueblo y la cultura Maya petition, AVAAZ.org, Peticiones de la comunidad, October 18, 2013, http://secure.avaaz.org/es/petition/A_favor _del_respeto_al _pueblo_y_la _cultura _maya/.

8. The complete program of U Cha'anil Kaaj, October 2013, is available on Issuu, uploaded by Cha'anil Kaaj on September 27, 2013, https://issuu.com/chaanilkaaj /docs/cha___anil_kaaj.

9. One of the organizers later published my recorded voice in their SoundCloud page online ("Palabras Genner," audio, Axólotl Studio, SoundCloud, accessed April 1, 2016, http://soundcloud.com/axolotlstudio-1/palabras-genner). I do not know if the recording has motivated any other reactions than the ones I received in person that day.

References

Armstrong-Fumero, Fernando. 2009. "A Heritage of Ambiguity: The Historical Substrate of Vernacular Multiculturalism in Yucatán, México." *American Ethnologist* 36 (2): 300–316.

Bennett, Andy, Jodie Taylor, and Ian Woodward. 2014. *The Festivalization of Culture*. Burlington, VT: Ashgate.

Bolles, David. 2001. *Combined Dictionary–Concordance of the Yucatecan Mayan Language*. FAMSI. http://www.famsi.org/reports/96072/index.html.

Breglia, Lisa C. 2006. *Monumental Ambivalence: The Politics of Heritage*. Austin: University of Texas Press.

Castañeda, Quetzil E. 1997. "On the Correct Training of 'Indios' in the Handicraft Market at Chichen Itzá: Tactics and Tactility of Gender, Class, Race and State." *Journal of Latin American Anthropology* 2 (2): 106–43.

Castañeda, Quetzil E. 2004. "'We Are Not Indigenous!'; An Introduction to the Maya Identity of Yucatan." *Journal of Latin American Anthropology* 9 (1): 36–63.

Castillo Cocom, Juan. 2005. "'It Was Simply Their Word': Yucatec Maya PRInces in YucaPAN and the Politics of Respect." *Critique of Anthropology* 25 (2): 131–55.

Cornejo, I., and E. Bellon. 2009. "Cuando alguien habla maya, se nota que son pobres." *Revista Paz y Conflictos* 3:6–22.

Davis, Charlotte Aull. 1999. *Reflexive Ethnography: A Guide to Researching Selves and Others*. London: Routledge.

Dietz, Gunther. 2003. *Multiculturalismo, interculturalidad y educación: Una aproximación antropológica*. Granada: Editorial Universidad de Granada.

Eiss, Paul K. 2008. "El Pueblo Mestizo: Modernity, Tradition, and Statecraft in Yucatan, 1870–1907." *Ethnohistory* 55 (4): 525–52.

Fallaw, Ben W. 1997. "Cárdenas and the Caste War that Wasn't: State Power and Indigenismo in Post-Revolutionary Yucatán." *Americas* 53 (4): 551–77.

Fitting, Elizabeth. 2011. *The Struggle for Maize; Campesinos, Workers, and Transgenic Corn in the Mexican Countryside*. Durham, NC: Duke University Press.

Fornet-Betancourt, Raúl. 2000. "Philosophical Presuppositions of Intercultural Dialogue." *Polylog: Forum for Intercultural Philosophy* 1:1–60.

French, Brigittine M. 2008. "Guatemala: Essentialisms and Cultural Politics." In *A Companion to Latin American Anthropology*, edited by Deborah Poole, 109–27. Malden, MA: Blackwell.

Gabbert, Wolfgang. 2001. "Social Categories, Ethnicity and the State in Yucatan, Mexico." *Journal of Latin American Studies* 33 (3): 459–84.

Gamio, Manuel. (1916) 1992. *Forjando patria*. 4th ed. Mexico City: Editorial Porrúa.

Gupta, Akhil, and James Ferguson. 1997. "Discipline and Practice: 'The Field' as Site, Method, and Location in Anthropology." In *Anthropological Locations: Boundaries and Grounds of a Field Science*, edited by Akhil Gupta and James Ferguson, 1–46. Berkeley: University of California Press.

Hervik, Peter. 2001. "Narrations of Shifting Maya Identities." *Bulletin of Latin American Research* 20 (3): 342–59.

Iturriaga Acevedo, Eugenia. 2010. "Racismo y representaciones: 'Lo Yucateco' en la televisión local." In *Representaciones culturales: Imágenes e imaginación de lo yucateco*, edited by Igor Ayora Díaz and Gabriela Vargas Cetina, 137–65. Mérida: Ediciones de la Universidad Autónoma de Yucatán.

Iturriaga Acevedo, Eugenia. 2011. "Las élites de la ciudad blanca: Racismo, prácticas y discriminación étnica en Mérida, Yucatán." PhD diss., Instituto de Investigaciones Antropológicas, UNAM, Mexico City.

Joseph, Gilbert M. 1988. *Revolution from Without: Yucatan, Mexico, and the United States, 1880–1924*. 2nd ed. Durham, NC: Duke University Press.

Kray, Christine. 2005. "The Sense of Tranquility: Bodily Practice and Ethnic Classes in Yucatán." *Ethnology* 44 (4): 337–55.

Latour, Bruno. 2005. *Reassembling the Social: An Introduction to Actor-Network-Theory*. Oxford: Oxford University Press.

Llanes-Ortiz, Genner. 2005. "Construyendo el diálogo de saberes desde la base: Universidades indígenas en América Latina: reflexiones y experiencias sobre la 'interculturalidad.'" In *Etnicidad en Latinoamérica: Movimientos sociales, cuestión indígena y diásporas migratorias*, edited by Joan J. Pujadas and Gunther Dietz, 193–209. Sevilla: FAAEE, Fundación El Monte, Asana.

Llanes-Ortiz, Genner. 2010. "Indigenous Universities and the Construction of Interculturality: The Case of the Peasant and Indigenous University Network in Yucatan, Mexico." PhD diss., University of Sussex, Brighton, United Kingdom.

Llanes-Ortiz, Genner. 2014. "Everyday work as spectacle: celebrating Maya embodied culture in Belize." In *Recasting Commodity and Spectacle in the Indigenous Americas*,

edited by Gilbert, Helen and Charlotte Gleghorn, 151–166. London: School of Advanced Study, University of London.
Llanes-Ortiz, Genner. 2015a. "Yaan Muuk' Ich Cha'anil / El potencial de Cha'anil: Un concepto maya para la revitalización lingüística." *Ichan Tecolotl / La Casa del Tecolote* 26 (301): 28–30.
Llanes-Ortiz, Genner. 2015b. "Seeds of Maya Development: The 'Fiestas y Ferias de Semillas' Movement in Yucatan." *Alternautas: (Re)searching Development, the Abya Yala Chapter* 2 (2): 10–20.
Loewe, Ronald. 2010. *Maya or Mestizo? Nationalism, Modernity, and Its Discontents*. Toronto: University of Toronto Press.
López Santillán, Ricardo. 2010. *Etnicidad y clase media: Los profesionistas mayas en Mérida*. Mexico City: UNAM, ICY-CONACULTA, CEPHCIS.
Magnoni, Aline, Traci Arden, and Scott Hutson. 2007. "Tourism in the Mundo Maya: Inventions and (Mis)Representations of Maya Identities and Heritage." *Archaeologies: Journal of the World Archaeological Congress* 3 (3): 353–83.
Martín Briceño, Enrique. 2011. "Los cantos mayas que procreó la Revolución." In *Las músicas que nos dieron patria: Músicas regionales en las luchas de Independencia y Revolución, México*, edited by DGCP-CONACULTA, 189–211. Mexico City: Programa de Desarrollo Cultural Regional–Tierra Caliente.
Martínez-Novo, Carmen. 2004. "'We Are Against the Government, Although We Are the Government': State Institutions and Indigenous Migrants in Baja California, Mexico, in the 1990s." *Journal of Latin American and Caribbean Anthropology* 9 (2): 352–81.
Mato, Daniel. 2008. "Diversidad cultural e interculturalidad en educación superior: Problemas, retos, oportunidades y experiencias en América Latina." In *Diversidad cultural e interculturalidad en educación superior: Experiencias en América Latina*, edited by Daniel Mato, 23–79. Caracas: IESALC-UNESCO, ASCUN.
Mattiace, Shannan L. 2009. "Ethnic Mobilization Among the Maya of Yucatán." *Latin American and Caribbean Ethnic Studies* 4 (2): 137–69.
Moseley, Edward H., and Edward D. Terry, eds. 1980. *Yucatan: A World Apart*. Tuscaloosa: University of Alabama Press.
Mossbrucker, Harald, Barbara Pfeiler, and Hilaria Maas Collí. 1994. "La identidad cultural o étnica en la revista literaria 'Yikal Maya Than.'" *Boletín de Antropología Americana* 29:153–62.
Mutua, Kagendo, and Beth Blue Swadener. 2004. Introduction to *Decolonizing Research in Cross-Cultural Contexts: Critical Personal Narratives*, edited by Kagendo Mutua and Beth Blue Swadener, 1–23. Albany: State University of New York Press.
Papadakis, Elim. 1993. "Intervention in New Social Movements." In *Social Research: Philosophy, Politics and Practice*, edited by M. Hammersley, 83–104. London: Sage.
Restall, Matthew. 2004. "Maya Ethnogenesis." *Journal of Latin American Anthropology* 9:64–89.
Rogal, María. 2012. "Identity and Representation: The (Yucatec) Maya in the Visual Culture of Tourism." *Latin American and Caribbean Ethnic Studies* 7 (1): 49–69.

Rosales González, Margarita, and Genner Llanes-Ortiz. 2003. "La defensa y la transformación de un legado: Organizaciones indígenas en la Península de Yucatán." In *Los Investigadores de la Cultura Maya*, vol. 11, book 2, 548–63. Campeche, Mexico: Universidad Autónoma de Campeche.

Rugeley, Terry. 2009. *Rebellion Now and Forever: Mayas, Hispanics, and Caste War Violence in Yucatán, 1800–1880*. Stanford, CA: Stanford University Press.

Smith, Linda Tuhiwai. 1999. *Decolonizing Methodologies: Research and Indigenous Peoples*. London: Zed Books.

Van Binsbergen, Wim. 1999. "'Cultures Do Not Exist': Exploding Self-Evidences in the Investigation of Interculturality." *Quest: An African Journal of Philosophy* 13 (1–2): 37–114.

Walsh, Catherine. 2002. "(De) construir la interculturalidad: Consideraciones críticas desde la política, la colonialidad y los movimientos indígenas y negros en el Ecuador." In *Interculturalidad y política: Desafíos y posibilidades*, edited by Norma Fuller, 115–42. Lima: Red para el Desarrollo de las Ciencias Sociales.

Warren, Kay B., and Jean E. Jackson. 2002. "Introduction: Studying Indigenous Activism in Latin America." In *Indigenous Movements, Self-Representation, and the State in Latin America*, edited by Kay B. Warren and Jean E. Jackson, 1–46. Austin: University of Texas Press.

Worley, Paul M. 2013. *Telling and Being Told: Storytelling and Cultural Control in Contemporary Yucatec Maya Literatures*. Tucson: University of Arizona Press.

Wright, Susan. 1998. "The Politicization of 'Culture.'" *Anthropology Today* 14 (1): 7–15.

PART III
AUSTRALIA

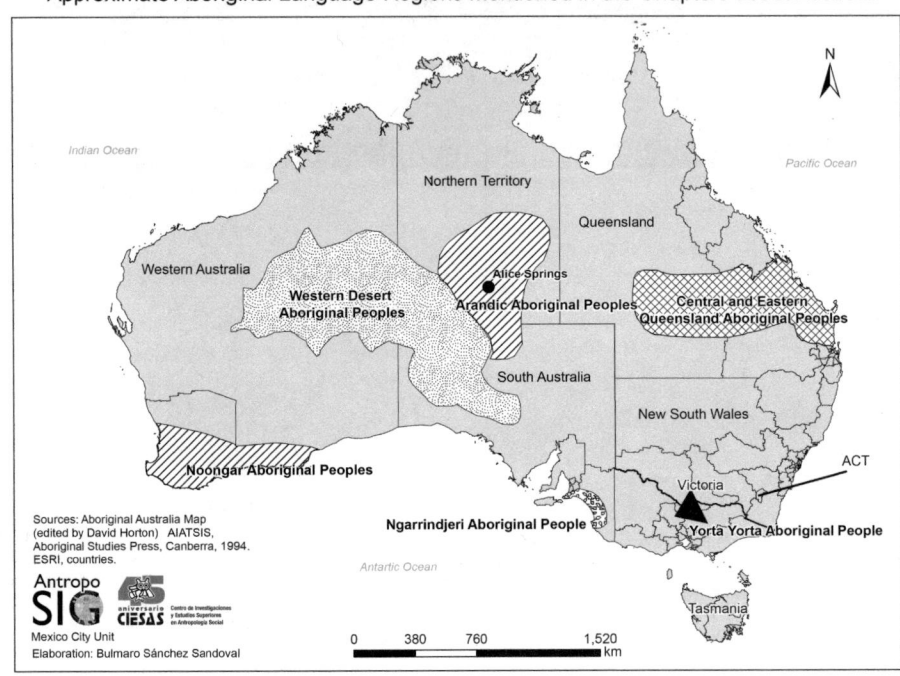

SEVEN

Indigenous Anthropologists Caught in the Middle

The Fragmentation of Indigenous Knowledge in Native Title Anthropology, Law, and Policy in Urban and Rural Australia

SUZI HUTCHINGS

In this chapter I focus on some implications of emerging trends in how the Australian state develops new kinds of settlements with Indigenous Australians, in contemporary manifestations of an ongoing colonial project. In particular, I examine some of the consequences for the development of rights through Indigenous responses. I deliberately couch this chapter within the time frame of the *native title* era, a period that extends more than twenty-five years from today, with 2017 marking the twenty-fifth anniversary of the recognition of native title in Australia. This chapter covers three broad themes that affect Indigenous relations with the Australian state:

Recognition, decolonization, and sovereignty
Native title and land rights
Indigeneity, identity, and authenticity

Ultimately I ask, can Indigenous resistance in modern Australia be included in a more global Indigenous movement toward decolonization? Or will Indigenous Australians be forever caught within the reconciliation gap of mere recognition by the state?

I undertake this discussion from the liminal position of an Indigenous professional by exploring some of the cultural and ethical issues that derive from my work as a native title anthropologist and as an Indigenous woman anthropologist. I also raise issues concerning the disjuncture in meanings of identity, relationships to country, kinship, and authenticity for some of the main players—Indigenous claimants, lawyers, judges, and anthropologists—in the native title process. I particularly question the position in this process for Indigenous anthropologists who are engaged as consultants.

My mother's family is Central Arrernte, whose country is in the Alice Springs region of Central Australia. As I explain further below, my Aboriginal identity can be described as a *double-edged sword* or as *being stuck in the middle*. Professionally, I am a social anthropologist, and I have worked as a native title consultant for more than seventeen years. I have also been engaged by the Federal Magistrates Court of Australia and courts in South Australia to provide expert reports on Indigenous cultural matters. As an expert witness, I have worked almost exclusively with Aboriginal families and communities in rural and urban Australia. Recently, I have worked in central Queensland and coastal Western Australia.[1] In this chapter, I draw on cases from this work.

The number of qualified Indigenous anthropologists working in native title in Australia can be counted on one hand. I chose to train as an anthropologist specifically to assist Aboriginal people, to develop a conduit for recognition of their Indigenous knowledges within the colonial legal and welfare systems, which they have relied on for survival. My role as an Indigenous anthropologist is therefore pivotal to the issues I raise in this chapter. Specifically, I discuss three matters:

> The imposition of the burden of proof for native title on Aboriginal communities who have historically suffered removals from land and tradition as a result of colonization.
>
> How native title has failed to reempower certain disenfranchised urban and regional Aboriginal communities and to reinstate and redefine their cultural traditions.
>
> The invidious position of anthropologists who are also Indigenous working on native title claims and other land-based consultancies involving rural and urban Indigenous communities.[2]

I raise these questions: What is the role for Indigenous anthropologists in Australia when they invariably occupy an interstitial position between anthropological and Indigenous cultural knowledge spaces? And what are the contradictions, confusions, and erasures that operate between colonial, anthropological, and Indigenous knowledges and interpretations in this space? By exploring different forms of cultural interpretation of the conduct of ethnography for native title, I tease out and consider some of the implications of such processes on the construction of a contemporary Aboriginal authenticity.

This chapter emanates from presentations I have given at Australian and international conferences over nineteen years, discussing recurring issues I have faced as an Indigenous anthropologist working in Australia. The long time frame, from 1999 to the present, highlights an unshifting and fundamental location of the Indigenous at the center of anthropological observation as "subject," as well as on the margins as qualified working professionals in the discipline of anthropology. This complex and contradictory positioning of Indigenous anthropologists in Australia is intrinsically linked to the criteria for legitimate Indigenous identity as determined by Aboriginal people, on the one hand, and by non-Aboriginal anthropologists and other professionals on the other. A core theme in commentaries and analyses by Aboriginal people, about Aboriginal people, which challenge settler understandings, is whether they can be recognized through their traditionality (see Carlson 2016; Grant 2016; Watson 2015; Heiss 2014). That is, can Aboriginal people prove their links to Aboriginal ancestors? Furthermore, can they demonstrate that their Indigenous identity is different from imposed colonial-settler stereotypes of what an Indigenous person, and specifically an Aboriginal person, should look like?

In 1999 I presented my first conference paper on these themes at Melbourne University. This paper, entitled "Centring on the Periphery: An Indigenous Reading of the Location of Spencer and Gillen's Colonial Imagery in Contemporary Australian Anthropology" (Hutchings 1999), provides an Indigenous scrutiny and critique of contemporary anthropological and historical analyses of the ethnographic works Sir Baldwin Spencer and Francis James Gillen wrote about the Aboriginal peoples of Central Australia in the late 1800s (Spencer and Gillen 1938). It has been argued that Spencer and Gillen "played a leading role in the development of a recognisably modern anthropology" (Mulvaney, Morphy, and Petch 1997, 41; see Petch 2000). Diane J. Austin-Broos (1999) has highlighted, however, that Spencer and Gillen were integral to the social Darwinism prevalent at that time, and this, by implication, infiltrated so-called modern Australian anthropology, which is based on a colonial construction of the authentic Indigenous.

In 2014 and in 2017, I presented workshops with my colleague Deanne Hanchant-Nichols to the World Indigenous Peoples Conference on Education in Honolulu and Toronto (Hutchings and Hanchant-Nichols 2014, 2017).[3] These workshops looked specifically at how certain forms of Aboriginal identity are imposed on Indigenous people. We explored the construction of Indigenous identities by individuals, communities, and outsiders. In asking the question "Does color matter?" the workshops presented and investigated Indigenous challenges to institutional creations of what it means to be a contemporary Indigenous person.

This chapter also draws on two presentations at international anthropological conferences. I gave one presentation in December 2014 to the American Anthropological Association Conference in Washington, DC, in a panel session from which this book is derived (Hutchings 2014). The panel was made up of Indigenous and non-Indigenous anthropologists who have since contributed to this volume along with guest authors from Canada, Mexico, and Australia. As detailed in the introduction to this book, the conference theme, Producing Anthropology, called for anthropologists to examine the truths they encounter, produce, and communicate through anthropological theories and methods. The other presentation is my keynote address to the Australian Anthropological Association in December 2017 (Hutchings 2017). That paper was the culmination of my rethinking of ideas that I had been examining since 1999 on Indigenous identity and the positioning of the Indigenous anthropologist in the frame of native title as a colonial construct. This chapter is therefore an amalgamation and a reexamination of these earlier analyses, with the intention to contribute to an emerging Australian Indigenous position within the current global Indigenous dialogues on recognition, decolonization, and sovereignty.

Recognition, Decolonization, and Sovereignty

I align myself with several Indigenous theorists in naming colonization as *ongoing* rather than postcolonial, because despite the 2007 *United Nations Declaration on the Rights of Indigenous Peoples*, recognizing, considering, and affirming the rights of Indigenous peoples, the logic of colonization remains embedded in Australia within the artifice of providing substantive rights through these processes. As legal scholar Irene Watson comments, for instance, "The illusion of recognition works its power so as to conceal the ongoing character and intent of the colonial project—that is, to maintain hegemony and do nothing about returning balance and power to the colonised" (2015, 2). And further, "Recognition only falls to First Nations at the moment we become dispossessed, by way of transferring our sovereignty to the colonising powers" (2–3). This contemporary reality for Indigenous Australians was demonstrated most profoundly in the recent outright rejection by the then prime minister of Australia, Malcolm Turnbull, of the requests outlined in the "Uluru Statement from the Heart," a rejection that Aboriginal lawyer and activist Noel Pearson in 2017 called a betrayal of past acknowledgments by the prime minister that the government would seriously consider establishing an Indigenous voice in the Australian Parliament (Referendum Council 2017; Pearson 2017).

The Uluru statement was devised at the First Nations National Constitutional Convention, convened in May 2017 with bipartisan political support. A Referendum Council had been appointed by the prime minister and the leader of the opposition party to discuss and agree on an approach to constitutional reform enabling *recognition* of Aboriginal and Torres Strait Islander peoples in the Australian constitution. The convention, held at Uluru, in Central Australia, was the culmination of consultations between Aboriginal and Torres Strait Islander peoples and the Referendum Council over the previous twelve months.

The Uluru statement outlines the nature of constitutional reform desired by Indigenous Australians without proposing detail on how this reform should occur. Most importantly, it asserts and affirms the sovereignty of Aboriginal and Torres Strait Islander peoples, which was never ceded to the British colonial government at the time of settlement. It also affirms the continuing connection of Indigenous Australians with the land on which modern Australia is built. To outline the social realities of Indigenous peoples living in contemporary Australia, the statement includes a pronouncement about high incarceration rates and alienation from family resulting from state-sanctioned Indigenous child removals. Significantly, it counters the position taken by the Recognise campaign, that Indigenous Australians should be *symbolically* recognized in the Australian constitution.[4] Rather, the statement calls for more than mere recognition. It calls for substantive reform to federal governance, with the establishment of an Indigenous body to represent Australian Indigenous people in Parliament.

Importantly, the statement does not provide the details of how this body should be constructed, leaving this to be defined by Parliament, thus acknowledging the legitimacy of the Australian parliamentary system and not seeking to question its power over such important issues for the entire nation. It also calls for the establishment of a Makarrata Commission—a treaty commission that would supervise this process and be a mechanism for truth telling about the joint history of Indigenous and settler peoples in Australia.[5] Thus, "We seek constitutional reforms to empower our people and take a rightful place in our own country. When we have power over our destiny our children will flourish. They will walk in two worlds and their culture will be a gift to their country." (Referendum Council 2017, 1)

Since the Howard government era, between 1996 and 2007, Indigenous people in Australia have become used to profound dismissals of our collective requests for greater representation in federal Indigenous affairs. Infamously, on Sorry Day in 1998, then prime minister John Howard refused to apologize to the "stolen generation," people who had suffered removals and generational trauma instigated under a history of institutionalization.[6] In 2005, Parliament abolished the Aboriginal and Torres Strait Islander Commission (ATSIC), which had been established under the ATSIC Act in 1989 to formally involve Aboriginal and Torres Strait Islanders in the process of government on Indigenous issues.

Within the context of such an overwhelming history of government control of Indigenous people, and concomitant dismissal of Indigenous cultural initiatives around self-determination, the Uluru statement is no doubt modest and, some may argue, simplistic. Yet, it *is* a considered document formulated by key Indigenous political and social thinkers from across Australia, and from a range of community backgrounds, over a sustained period. Therefore, I ask, Does the Uluru statement contain an inherent genius? If, as suggested, an Indigenous body is enshrined in the constitution, future governments would be unable to dismantle a representative body such as ATSIC.

But the Uluru statement is more than this. It is a proposal put forward to the sovereign Australian state by sovereign Indigenous people as an offer of recognition on Indigenous terms, and as a blueprint for negotiation to find new ways to relate that are meaningful and will positively improve Indigenous lives, making a better country for all.

Attempts by Indigenous peoples in Australia to negotiate from the position of a sovereign people to challenge the right of the colonizers to occupy Aboriginal land and legitimize state control is by no means new. The 1971 Gove land rights case saw Justice Richard Blackburn's ratification of the legality of terra nullius (land belonging to no one). This legal position was ultimately overturned twenty-one years later with the decision in *Mabo v. Queensland* (No. 2) ([1992] HCA 23 (3 June 1992)). The maturity in how the Uluru statement was devised, however, mirrors statesmanship, the coming together of independent

Indigenous nations to discuss national issues of relevance to a successful Australian future. The genius therefore lies in the challenge to what Elizabeth A. Povinelli has identified as the "cunning of recognition" (1999); that is, to negotiate with Indigenous peoples, the state must recognize us as similar, as more than just "good" or "bad" Aborigines or children who need discipline and control, but as sovereign equals coming together to discuss issues of major importance to the future of the Australian nation.

Nevertheless, the federal government's response to Indigenous sovereignty has explicitly highlighted the flaw in this proposition. As Indigenous scholar Glen Sean Coulthard argues, in his seminal work *Red Skins, White Masks* (2014), on Indigenous relations between the Canadian state and First Nations people, a "settler-colonial relationship is one characterised by a particular form of domination which cements structures of power" (Coulthard 2014, 6–7). This cementing has occurred in Canada, notwithstanding Indigenous protests during the 1970s, which generated a new politics of recognition. The new politics may now *recognize* and *accommodate* the Indigenous, but "despite this modification [the Indigenous-state relationship] has remained *colonial* to its foundation" (Coulthard 2014, 6); it has just shifted in its disguise.

In Australia, this desire to approach the settler state from a sovereign Indigenous position to negotiate over shared resources, particularly land, is happening in local contexts, and a precedent is developing. In 2010, the Yorta Yorta entered into a traditional owner land management agreement with the Victorian state government. This occurred outside the native title process. The Yorta Yorta are renowned as the first Australian Indigenous claimants to have submitted a native title claim in the state of Victoria after the enactment of the Native Title Act (1993), a claim that was just as famously dismissed by the federal court in 1998. This decision was later ratified in 2002 by the High Court of Australia on appeal.

Significantly, both Yorta Yorta and the Victorian state government allege that the Yorta Yorta came directly to the government to negotiate a land settlement agreement after the dramatic failure of their native title claim in the courts. But in presenting themselves as a sovereign people, willing to negotiate with the state on new terms to secure a determination over their home country, the Yorta Yorta have also had to relinquish their legal rights to claim under the native title legislative process in any future proceedings.

Conversely, in taking ownership of the meaning and direction of Indigenous affairs, the Victorian state government defined itself as progressive in providing a policy-driven avenue for successful negotiations with Indigenous peoples in its jurisdiction. Indeed, the Victorian government is building on this reputation as enlightened toward Indigenous people through its current negotiations to establish a treaty or treaties with Indigenous peoples in the state (see Marks 2018). Whatever the underlying pitfalls for the success of these negotiations, particularly whether a change in state government will see the negotiations through and the treaty outcome honored, the current Victorian government's position on negotiating with Indigenous peoples stands in stark contrast to that of the federal government in its dismissal of Indigenous sovereignty by refusing to entertain the requests outlined in the Uluru statement.[7]

Indigenous Identity—Fluidity and Rigidity

This disparity between current Victorian and federal government positions echoes the disparity and incommensurability of parallel streams of knowledge generated within processes of negotiation between Indigenous peoples and the state through legislative frameworks, including native title. These streams of knowledge run through history and present Aboriginal social life from particular historical positions, which either exclude the lived reality of Aboriginal people or operate within the bounds of Aboriginal reality in specific ways.

By rejecting the Uluru statement, the Australian federal government is refusing to recognize Aboriginal sovereignty. This echoes the refusal to recognize that certain categories of Aboriginal people have native title rights and interests in land, including Aboriginal people on the margins of traditionality who, at the same time, resemble in targeted ways the very settlers who have colonized them. I further develop these arguments by exploring my position as an Indigenous anthropologist working in the context of native title with Indigenous claimants. I may resemble a settler to some, having fair skin and living in the city, but I nevertheless retain an Indigenous identity through traditionality, genealogy, and history.

The invidious position of anthropologists involved in court cases on Aboriginal issues has been previously discussed by anthropologists such as Rod Lucas (1996) and Elizabeth Povinelli (1999). Lucas, for instance, wrote about the enmity between anthropologists and other stakeholders when the anthropologists were tasked with interpreting different Aboriginal knowledges in relation to the validity of women's business in the Hindmarsh Island Bridge case in

South Australia.⁸ Povinelli has written about the transformation of Aboriginal knowledge as anthropologists reinterpret such knowledge to meet the requirements of land title legal processes. Aboriginal people are validated against the legal interpretation of proof, and this new legally and anthropologically constructed knowledge becomes an artifact, or "thing," as Povinelli puts it, that sits outside its origins and is thus reconstituted as traditional Aboriginal knowledge.

What I bring to the debate is the unique position of Aboriginal anthropologists. In an emerging pan-Aboriginal convention, not necessarily defined by a specific Aboriginal culture, the construction of new interpretations of knowledge from materials housed in the dominant society's museums and archives becomes part of a process normalizing Aboriginal interaction with native title law. In these contexts, where Aboriginal claimants conduct their own research, orality becomes redefined by historical ethnographic literature and documentation, including photographs and material culture. Recognition of kinship to immediate and distant relatives for many Aboriginal people relies not only on the genealogical connection between members in terms of named relationships, such as father's father's father or mother's sister's son and so forth, but on physical characteristics that can be matched to people's memories of an ancestor.

So what does an Indigenous anthropologist offer in these contexts? Indigenous anthropologists are anointed with an authentic cultural identity and are sought out by Aboriginal claimants to aid in finding documentation to support claims of authenticity. This is a privileged position, carrying very different expectations than those of non-Aboriginal anthropologists. It is also a contested position and performance. It is "authentic" because of the anthropologist's aboriginality, and it is privileged because the Indigenous anthropologist is allowed to access and use family information provided by claimants. Informants have different expectations of Aboriginal anthropologists because they expect them to "get it," and there is pressure to be the claimant's advocate using the evidence they have constructed from various sources as proof of their native title rights and interests, to know that these are some of the ways in which Aboriginal people "see" relatedness and identify family where a relationship is uncertain. The relationship between claimant and Indigenous anthropologist is therefore intense with an expectation to understand instantly the cultural performance and information claimants divulge.

Indigenous anthropologists therefore wear three hats—and find themselves in positions that are often incompatible and difficult to manage:

1. As an expert witness whose duty is to the court
2. As an Aboriginal person who is expected to act in a culturally appropriate way as kin and who is connected to claimants by ethnicity/aboriginality.
3. As an anthropologist

I am certainly not the first Indigenous anthropologist to pose these questions, or to investigate the dilemmas of being an Indigenous anthropologist investigating "the Native" from within. Beatrice Medicine articulates the tricky position of the "Native" anthropologist as being both insider and outsider in her selected writings, *Learning to Be an Anthropologist and Remaining "Native"* (2001). She comments on insider status as a privileged social position whereby access to knowledge is gained after passing various social tests and demonstrating a commitment to Native cultural understandings: "Native populations are wary of others' interpretations of their behavior, even when they are dealing with 'one of their own.' An added Native concern is that areas of living will be presented that they do not want revealed" (2001, 5).

Medicine's writing in this area has come on the back of a legacy of Native critiques of the role anthropologists and other professional observers play as handmaidens to the colonial process, in providing evidence of Native customs to governments, churches, and other authorities insidiously intent on controlling Indigenous populations. Indeed, Vine Deloria Jr. argues that the views of such non-Indigenous "experts" becomes authoritative at the expense of Indigenous peoples' intrinsic and lived understandings of their own culture. "When realities of Indian belief and existence have become so misunderstood and distorted at this point that when a real Indian stands up and speaks the truth at any given moment he or she is not only unlikely to be believed, but will probably be publicly contradicted and 'corrected' by the citation of some non-Indian and totally inaccurate 'expert'" (Deloria quoted in Churchill 1994, 219; see Deloria, Scinta, and Foehner 1999).[9]

Contemporary Indigenous anthropologists also confront this legacy in the everyday practice of their profession. Furthermore, within this historical fabric, Indigenous people judge their own members who have taken on the role of anthropologist. Given this, and the fact that few Indigenous anthropologists are working in Australia, not many insider critiques of the anthropological enterprise have been written by Australian Indigenous anthropologists.[10] An important exception are the recent writings of anthropologist Marcia Langton. Langton highlights a different problem than that identified by Vine Deloria Jr., arguing that contemporary writers, including anthropologists, who comment on the deteriorating state of Aboriginal communities face criticism if they are not Indigenous, because they are not insiders and therefore cannot be taken seriously. Langton further argues that this form of essentializing Aboriginal people and culture assists in perpetuating racism and the disregard of individual Indigenous Australians' rights to economic security:

> The present human rights debate about indigenous people in Australia, conducted in the shadow of a long history of human rights abuses and vilification, especially of men, has led to the situation in which it is almost impossible to raise the rights of indigenous women and children and the public health policy settings that would improve their lives. To do so, as I have learnt, is to encounter aggressive and selfserving arguments about indigenous rights that privilege indigenous men and their dignity over the rights of others. (Langton 2011, 19)

With the exception of Langton, the major critiques of anthropology and anthropologists are from those who work in other fields. Watson, coming from a legal background, examines the court evidence and findings in the Hindmarsh Island Bridge Royal Commission and demonstrates how certain Ngarrindjeri people are constructed as inauthentic Aborigines who fabricate evidence when this evidence is held up under the scrutiny of the Australian legal system. She poses the question of how such evidence might have been evaluated if it had been examined under Aboriginal law, known as *ruwe* in this region of Australia, instead of by a royal commission founded under the South Australian state government and subject to the Australian legal system.[11]

Aileen Moreton-Robinson has discussed how the "logics of white possession and the disavowal of Indigenous sovereignty are materially and discursively linked" (2015, xiii). She highlights Indigenous people as living within and outside the discourses to which we are subject. Thus, while disciplines such as anthropology within the academy "insist on producing cultural difference in order to manage the existence and claims of Indigenous people," they fail to take into account our "density," including the complexities of kinship relations as we live them as insiders and therefore cannot escape (Moreton-Robinson 2015, xv, xvii; see Langton 1981).

In the 1980s and 1990s, in the wake of Indigenous criticism from Vine Deloria Jr. and other earlier commentators and philosophers (Fanon 1967, 1968; Said 1993) about the destructive impact of the colonial project on those colonized, the discipline of anthropology started to self-reflect on its role in this colonial project. These analyses offered an understanding of the differing engagements Indigenous people had with colonizers, which were in turn dependent on the various historical trajectories of their political and economic engagement with the agents of these dominant colonial regimes (e.g., Comaroff and Comaroff 1997).

James Clifford and George E. Marcus (1986) famously generated a movement for anthropologists to critique ethnographies and anthropological texts as texts. In so doing, anthropologists examined anthropology's changing relations with the societies it investigates (Clifford and Marcus 1986). David F. Martin (2015), referencing Marshall David Sahlins in his discussion on Native entitlement under native title in Australia, notes that Indigenous people do not resist modernization and new technologies in fashioning their own understandings or texts. Rather, they create their own cultural space—what Sahlins calls the "indigenization of modernity" (Sahlins 1999, 409; Martin 2015, 120), which is simultaneously the "modernization of indigeneity" (Hannerz 2002, 53, as quoted in Martin 2015, 120).

But how far have we come in the development of anthropological critique that takes into account the Indigenous space and cultural mindset of the insider since Deloria's appraisal? The authenticity of indigeneity is under constant scrutiny from outside, even if we are trained as anthropologists. For the past twenty years, a well-known senior anthropologist working as a native title expert has questioned my aboriginality to others in the discipline. It has been reported to me that this person regularly asks other Aboriginal people if they have heard of me and know of my family connections. As this male anthropologist is a member of the dominant settler society in Australia, he apparently takes it as his unquestioned right to challenge my authenticity on behalf of the authorities who determine who can claim aboriginality. This is despite readily available genealogical evidence of my Central Arrernte kin connections, housed in the Strehlow Research Centre in Alice Springs and in the ethnography of Frederick G. G. Rose (1962), combined with reinforcement of my socially enacted everyday kin relations within extended Aboriginal family.[12]

I raise this personal example because for many Indigenous native title claimants who do not fit a stereotype of the authentic or "traditional" Aborigine, the process of gathering evidence for a native title claim in Australia is fraught with such issues of identity. As a fair-skinned Aboriginal person, I do not fit the colonial stereotype of a dark brown- or black-skinned "Aborigine." And a great many native title claimants do not fit this stereotype either. As Watson saliently points out, however, this does not deny them Aboriginal identity or traditionality: "One can be as black as black encased in the skin colour white, or white as white encased in the skin colour black. The colour black connotes not just a perceived physical reality; it encompasses other dimensions—for example, culture, law, obligation, land and relationships to kin. Being black in a white skin can be a matter of the colour of one's heart or one's love for the land or one's kin and the source of that feeling comes with the spirit and one's connection to Kaldowinyeri and our black history" (2015, 84).[13]

I suggest that the link between Indigenous and academic knowledge is embodied at its most powerful in the personal—a self that can never be truly known by academics working from the outside. Nonetheless, the amount and quality of traditional knowledge handed down to descendants, combined with judgments on how closely these people may resemble a "traditional aborigine," are also heavily scrutinized by agents of the state for native title claimants. Indigenous anthropologists can bring a unique reading to these complex situations, given that we are of both worlds of knowledge—Indigenous (other) and anthropologist (representative of colonial knowledge). This may also be a dangerous position according to the anthropological discipline, however, because "going native" is considered unacceptable. So what happens when we are already Native—already there? Or partly there, of Aboriginal descent but not traditional, or black, or "really" Indigenous—only part Indigenous? This intervening space, which incorporates different knowledge positions of the dominant and the other, is potentially problematic because it leads both claimants and state representatives to be suspicious about whose side we are really on.

Native Title—A Landmark Decision

According to the National Native Title Tribunal in Australia, as of May 2018, 297 native title applications were pending. As of the same date, a total of 422 native title determinations (by consent, by litigation, or unopposed) had been made by a court or other recognized body across Australia.[14] The comments and arguments I put forward in this chapter do not imply that native title claims are not successful—but those that are take many years to come to fruition, and often the issues I outline below are relevant for these successful claims before they are legally settled. For the purposes of this chapter, I restrict my analysis to claims prepared for litigation.

In 2011 former Australian prime minister Paul Keating, during his compelling speech at the Lowitja O'Donoghue Oration at the University of Adelaide, revisited the history of native title law and the passing of the Native Title Act in Australia, under his leadership, by the federal Labor government in 1993.[15] The most telling message in his speech was the change in intent of the act as it has been executed during the intervening nineteen years.

In 1992, the landmark Australian High Court decision in *Mabo v. Queensland* (No 2), overturned the doctrine of terra nullius with the common-law recognition of Aboriginal title. The federal Labor government subsequently passed the Native Title Act in 1993. This act has been amended in the intervening twenty-five years. Most significantly, in 1996 the Liberal coalition government introduced changes in what became known as the Ten Point Plan. Based on the Ten Point Plan, the Native Title Amendment Act was passed in 1998, after much parliamentary debate, media interest, and public discussion. These debates, I argue, solidified a widespread perception that native title was not a preexisting title recognized under the common law of Australia (despite this being established law in the Mabo decision), but that Aboriginal prior occupation had to be *proved* by Aboriginal people claiming native title. The Native Title Amendment Act was designed to give effect to the conservative Liberal government's desire to control existing native title rights for Indigenous peoples through government management of the native title process. This amendment established a more rigorous registration test for native title applicants, a new scheme for Indigenous land-use agreements, and a reworking of the type of land-use grants and state government provisions that could extinguish native title.

I argue, therefore, that the colonial project continues under the guise of native title, as preexisting land title for Aboriginal people in Australia becomes reconstructed as a gift given to Aboriginal Australians by a magnanimous federal government. This "gift" is conditional on Aboriginal people being able to prove that they are worthy with evidence of their remnant traditionality. This view is consistent with the observation by anthropologist Patrick Wolfe that the Native Title Act, rather than enabling an historical rupture sufficient to allow reconstitution of the relationship between Aboriginal and settler societies, does not, at a fundamental level, constitute a break with the past (Wolfe 1994). The elementary logic of Australian colonialism remains intact. This logic includes the insistence that Aboriginal people prove their rights and interests through demonstrated cultural and spiritual connections to country claimed. Inevitably, this creates divisions among Aboriginal people according to who can verify their links at the expense of others whose cultural capital is more tenuous because of a historically uneven enactment of colonial dispossession.

Thus, despite native title being an existing title recognized by the common law of Australia, the burden of proof is now firmly the responsibility of Aboriginal people. Aboriginal communities whose traditional country is now located in rural or urban regions have suffered more than two hundred years of government and church removals of knowledgeable members. This variously disrupts a lineage of laws and customs needed to show a continuous connection to the lands they once occupied. As I point out above, the burden of proof imposition was ratified in the High Court decision in the Yorta Yorta case in 2002, which upheld the previous federal court determination that the "tide of history" had washed away, and thereby extinguished, Yorta Yorta native title rights. Significantly, this case involved Aboriginal people whose traditional lands occupied a highly settled rural region in the state of Victoria. The bar for the burden of proof was considerably higher than it might have been if the Yorta Yorta had been from remote Australia, and if their traditions had not been substantially disrupted by colonial invasion and settlement.

Since the Yorta Yorta ruling, the requirements of proof under the Native Title Act have been relaxed as a result of legal reviews, analysis, and commentary. The persistence of Chief Justice Robert French of the High Court of Australia has been influential in instigating the Australian Law Reform Commission investigations of, among other things, whether connection requirements should include "a presumption of continuity of acknowledgement and observance of traditional laws and customs and connection" (ALRC 2015, 13). It is no longer essential that *all* applicants can prove a continuous connection to traditional country, but the apical ancestors of the claim group must be shown to have had a traditional connection to the land being claimed. Given this, the claimants must prove a genealogical connection to these apical ancestors, and at least some members must retain a demonstrated knowledge and practice of traditional laws and customs.

On the surface these changes to the native title process may appear to have improved how native title is legally determined for Aboriginal people. Yet, I argue, a new imbalance in the scale of tradition versus proof of authenticity for Aboriginal people has been introduced. For those who now live away from their traditional lands in an urban or rural environment, the level of proof of prior occupation required to obtain native title rights and interests is almost insurmountable. For instance, it is also mandatory for those applying for native title to show that certain of their laws and customs have been substantially maintained and that their native title society has continued to exist since sovereignty. Martin has argued, "From this perspective, native title claims can be seen as constituting a state-resourced and mandated project of 'traditionalism'—understood as the reconstruction of an idealised representation of the relevant *Indigenous people as they supposedly are, in terms of how they supposedly were in the pre-colonial past*" (Martin 2015, 115, citations omitted; emphasis added).

Aside from the changes to the native title process, therefore, the social and intellectual spaces that the burden of proof has generated have led to many claimants and community members reinterpreting and combining the piecemeal knowledge they have learned from their elders into an Indigenous knowledge that they believe does meet the requirements of proof.

In doing this, these Indigenous claimants, in a struggle for self-determination through the native title process, are instinctively decolonizing a system imposed on them by introducing an alternate type of knowledge, a knowledge that Indigenous scholar Linda Tuhiwai Smith has identified as "rewriting our position in history." As she sets in sharp relief, "It is not simply about giving an oral account or a genealogical naming of the land and the events which raged over it, but a very powerful need to give testimony to and restore a spirit, to bring back into existence a world fragmented and dying" (2012, 29–30).

Such information produced by Indigenous claimants, however, rarely reaches the bar of traditional knowledge required under the Native Title Act or, by implication, the expectations of anthropologists as they investigate the existence of Aboriginal laws and customs providing evidence of a society. While gathering family information is an obvious part of the native title process and research, it is not necessarily given the same weight by practitioners of the process as a comparable form of knowledge to, or with the same level of authenticity as, that of the very legal system that insists on it. As Watson states, "For it is in anthropology's naming of us that anthropologists determine authenticity or otherwise, as they are empowered and mandated by colonialism" (2015, 72–73).

This is especially the case for those claimants with tenuous knowledge of their traditional laws and customs, their genealogies, and their claimed country. In rural and urban Queensland and Western Australia, this is the situation for many claimants. The question is, Can claimants prove a genealogical connection to apical ancestors who had a traditional connection to claimed land, making them the "right people for country"? Invariably this leads to the formation of political splits and alliances, as descendants vie for legal recognition as "genuine" descendants.

For many native title applicants and claimants, knowledge of their genealogies is fragmented as a result of forced government removals, in the late nineteenth and early twentieth centuries, off traditional country to missions and reserves like Cherbourg and Woorabinda in Queensland. This fragmentation persisted later when families moved into towns for work. In the contemporary native title context, applicants to a claim remember pieces of information heard as children about their grandparents' and great-grandparents' generations. Inevitably, they rely on this information as proof of a family connection with a named apical ancestor. In my experience, to give weight to such information when depth of oral tradition is lacking, applicants search out archival material, such as government records, to fill the gaps in stories of family connections.

Ironically, Aboriginal people in Queensland are fortunate in this regard. The government gaze has been long and relentless as part of the colonial project to keep Aboriginal people under surveillance and control. Many archives hold information on families that were removed. What are generally missing are details of traditional connections to country, and here claimants rely on the early ethnographies and notebooks of anthropologists and government protectors.

Even though the Native Title Act provides for compensation for people who may not be in a position to claim as a result of dispossession, many Aboriginal families continue to pursue a native title outcome because of the perceived symbolic and monetary gain native title rights and interests provide. From my experience working on claims in Queensland, the right to "walk the line" to clear land of Aboriginal sites of significance, the right to speak for country in a national park, and the right to negotiate over mining and other land developments provide important income for the community. Thus, these activities attract money for community groups, and those applicants whose claimed traditional country lies in areas of intense rural and urban colonization often view native title as a form of exclusive "property rights over land," rather than the right to negotiate with other parties with an interest in the land. With these cases, anthropologists most often find themselves intensely "caught in the middle."

Given the pressure under native title processes to demonstrate a traditional authenticity, many native title claimants in my experience will rely on old photographs from archives to indicate proof of connection between generations, by comparing these with more recent snapshots of contemporary family members. Often claimants will point out an apparent physical likeness between a person in a sepia or black-and-white photograph from an earlier era and people portrayed in modern times. For instance, "proof" of connection will be insisted on because the character from the present has the "same nose" or stands in a similar pose and so forth to the image of an alleged ancestor.

In two separate claims in central and far west Queensland, for example, claimants showed me photographs they had sourced from archives to illustrate how a living member of the group "must be related" to an ancestor because of the perceived similarities in physical characteristics between the photograph and the person whose identity as a claimant is in question. In other instances, claimants, in describing how a member of the claimant group walks or another idiosyncratic mannerism, would instantly associate them with an ancestor who had a similar gait or physical trait. Or, they may identify the claimant whose authenticity is being questioned with an ancestral being such as a kangaroo or an emu-like creature, because the claimant possesses particular physical mannerisms instantly identifiable as belonging to these animals. To these claimants, such "evidence" is indisputable proof, based on their understanding of what is required by the native title process, according to their traditional knowledge, of the veracity of their right to a native title claim.

The situation, from my experience working with Aboriginal groups claiming native title, is especially intense in overlapping claims, where the "right traditional owners for the country" are in dispute. For example, claimants might relate how their uncle would always know when drought or other disaster was inevitable because emus were absent from the country. In such cases, birds and animals are named as a significant ancestor or a claimant's totem. When the nephews visit the country, perhaps for the first time, the presence of emus reinforces their "claim" and becomes the "evidence" of their connection to country and to their uncle. It provides the cultural justification to their native title claim, which they relate to the anthropologist. Martin has identified the irony here in the need for Aboriginal claimants to appear traditional by providing evidence of connection to an Aboriginal past while being denied this reality in the production of identities that are actually dependent on the modern world through photography and archival records housed in libraries and institutions. "Even in the most remote of locales, Indigenous people's systems of connections, meanings, values, and practices—and thus identities—are variously produced and reproduced, transmitted and transformed through processes involving engagement with forms whose origins lie in the wider society, and ultimately globally" (2015, 118).

Thus, even though driven by native title processes, the need to authenticate is firmly attached to understandings of the enactment and display of kinship in Aboriginal groups, which are believed to be authentic. Anthropologists know about these constructions of kinship as a cultural process, but because such information is not relevant to the type of evidence collected for native title, it can be subject to ridicule and dismissed as inauthentic out of earshot of claimants or during social gatherings of professionals. In other cases, claimants will gather information from archives on language and ceremony, combine this with memories of words, phrases, and ceremonial practices, such as dances taught by their elders, and reincorporate these into their contemporary cultural practices—often reenacted on the country being claimed. Over time and if performed regularly, and preferably in front of an audience of lawyers, anthropologists, and the judge, these performances become the physical proof of the continuation of cultural practices handed down to them by their elders.

While these Aboriginal claimants may, by their own admissions, have gathered information from archives, museums, and other state collections, they view this process as authentically Indigenous in a modern world. This is a world that enshrined their cultural practices and kinship as frozen in timeless authenticity and where representatives of the dominant society require documentation of the "truth" of Indigenous claims. I argue that these processes of reinterpretation of knowledge by dispossessed Aboriginal people actually form an Indigenous knowledge that these claimants believe meets the requirements of the burden of proof. This is because the knowledge is couched within accepted Indigenous cultural practices of knowing what constitutes aboriginality, kinship, and family. Aboriginal claimants mimic the behavior of the dominant society in native title contexts in order to reiterate and reinforce their otherness and to solidify the "fantasy of 'ancient law'" as inviolate (Povinelli 1999, 45).

Eric Hobsbawm (1983) shows that the reconstruction or invention of tradition is not exclusive to Australian Aboriginal people. Nevertheless, within the native title environment, such reconstructions of tradition take on particular meanings that operate to define Aboriginal people as authentic or not. Regardless, the recreation of "authentic" traditional practices by Aboriginal people is reinforced by professions that demand a level of purity in an Aboriginal cultural tradition. Despite allowance in native title for adaptation to tradition since colonization, claimants are still expected to operate within a traditional Aboriginal cultural paradigm that is uncorrupted from its ancient past. Povinelli argues this point in her description of how lawyers, anthropologists, and claimants micromanage the fantasy of "ancient law" to reinforce examples of cultural practice as the right way to do kinship in land rights cases (1999, 44).

Although Aboriginal people have become adept at describing their kin relationships in ways that take into account a history of oppression and removals from traditional country, in the native title context, this invariably becomes evidence of a loss of tradition and of "not really knowing." Many face accusations by other Aboriginal claimants, some anthropologists, and legal professionals that they are inauthentic, having fabricated evidence to suit a political position at the expense of their more traditionally genuine relatives, who are the "real" traditional owners. The stakes are high in the native title game if Indigenous claimants in Australia are to prove cultural recognition as traditional owners with rights and interests in land. Those claimants who are most affected by the history of colonialism in Australia inevitably face skepticism from lawyers, judges, and anthropologists, who suspect that their knowledge is inauthentic and likely fabricated to suit their inclusion in the native title process in order to gain monetary benefits from "walking the line" for mining and development companies. A redefining of Indigenous knowledge based within innovative blends of traditional memory and archival retrieval may be considered culturally legitimate by many Indigenous claimants but may also be the very "thing" that cements a label of inauthentic under native title law.

Conclusion

I contend that we are at a critical juncture in how indigeneity and Indigenous identity are understood and recognized in modern Australia. In the native title context, this is played out in particular ways that have implications for certain categories of Indigenous Australians, affecting their success in native title processes. A core theme is whether Aboriginal people can be recognized through their traditionality; that is, do Aboriginal people have the ability to prove that they have links to Aboriginal ancestors. Importantly, establishing an Aboriginal identity that is based in genealogy and tradition indicative of a normative system of rights and interests in land is essential for the successful recognition of native title. For numerous individuals, families, and even whole communities, however, this standard of recognition is not possible because of the effects of colonization on these people, and native title is either denied to them or not even pursued.

In the context of native title, indigeneity should be based not on skin color but on heritage and personal identity. Wolfe (1994) has illustrated that the legitimacy of a claimed Aboriginal identity is inextricably related to control of land and the need to maintain this control by the settler society. In stark juxtaposition to state control of Aboriginal identities, Emma Kowal and Yin Paradies (2017) convincingly argue that many contemporary white-skinned Indigenous Australians refuse to identify as white and, in so doing, refuse whiteness by *demanding* state recognition as Aboriginal people. For light-skinned Aboriginal people, to identify as white is to run the risk of being mistaken as enjoying white privilege. Moreton-Robinson argues that the possessive logic of white privilege "is compelled to deny and refuse what it cannot own—the sovereignty of the Indigenous other" (2011, 647). I argue that many light-skinned Aboriginal people demonstrate their sovereignty by the very act of identifying as Indigenous, and many of these people in turn are actively engaged in native title claims for their communities.

I would further add that in taking up individual Indigenous identity as a sovereign position, Aboriginal people have developed a "multiplex of Aboriginal identities," which Kowal and Paradies refer to, to live within the modern world of the nation-state *as Indigenous people*, regardless of the tone of their complexion.[16] In the Australian setting, many Aboriginal people are expressing their Indigenous sovereignty as individuals and demanding to be recognized by the nation-state as Indigenous *because* they are light skinned, and they also have a demonstrable connection to Aboriginal family, community, and land. In so doing, these people unwaveringly believe they meet the three-point definition of aboriginality as

> a person who has Aboriginal and/or Torres Strait Islander descent, who also
> identifies as an Aboriginal and/or Torres Strait Islander person and
> is accepted as such by the Aboriginal and/or Torres Strait Islander community
>   in which they live (or come from).

This definition was adopted by the federal government and has also been enshrined in the native title process through its acceptance by Justice Gerard Brennan in the *Mabo v. Queensland* (No. 2) judgment.

Importantly, as Patrick Wolfe makes clear, the real basis for settler hostility is the fear of prior entitlement, "of being there at the beginning" as aborigine, as inherently connected to, and of, the land so prized by the nation-state (1994,

114). Thus, the logic of eliminating color, which pervades colonization from invasion through the policy era of assimilation, with the removal of Aboriginal children from their families and their land, ensured that the bulk of the Aboriginal population was excluded from the benefits of native title (Wolfe 1994, 123). At the same time, the further removed these people are from the "mythic authenticity" of aboriginality (Wolfe 1994, 117), the greater ideological threat they pose to settler society, and the greater the need to control them. The threat is miscegenation and the development of a "multiplex, heterogeneous and, above all, *historical* set of Aboriginalities which refuse to be contained within the ideal polarity [of black and white] that the logic of elimination requires" (Wolfe 1994, 118). Irene Watson further underscores this point by addressing dispossession from an Indigenous position, arguing that sovereignty among Indigenous Australians was never ceded despite the imposition of the legal fiction of terra nullius. Nevertheless, the relentless project to eliminate remnant physical aboriginality and to assimilate Aboriginal people into the dominant culture means that "Imposed colonial views of aboriginality have worked toward death, invisibility, and our final absorption into a clothed whiteness of being" (Watson 2015, 84).

From the point of view of the settler state, the position of connection with our black history remains a threat, and this is particularly so for those Indigenous Australians who seek native title recognition but remain outside state-sanctioned understandings of traditionality. Rather, to control an Indigenous other, it would seem important that white Aborigines remain a viable component of the Indigenous population for the very reason that they are recognizable to the dominant society in a memetic contract to save them.

Here I explicitly borrow from Michael Taussig's (1993) analysis of amateur ethnologist Richard O. Marsh's search for the white Indians of Darien. Taussig analyzes the phenomena by which the Cuna Indians invited European and U.S. anthropologists to study their whiteness, their culture, and the surrounding ecosystem as a way for the Cuna to gain autonomy from the "black" Panamanian state. Importantly, Taussig notes that this interaction was successful because of a "mimetic contract" of "unconscious complicities" between the whites from outside and the Indians they are studying and saving by recording their culture for institutions such as the Smithsonian. The Indians to be saved are recognizable because they are white like the people who are studying them. This is the case even though these people are not afforded *authenticity* as really Indian. In the Australian instance, white Aborigines are familiar to the state as they resemble members of the dominant society and, in this image, can be engaged with as the "good savages" (Taussig 1993, 142) whose connections to land are constructed as tenuous or nonexistent, especially within the legal framework of native title, and therefore they are apparently less threatening to the colonial project of land acquisition and control.

So, how far have we come in the development of anthropological critique that takes into account the Indigenous space and the cultural mindset of the insider? As I argue throughout this chapter, the authenticity of indigeneity is under constant scrutiny from outside, even if we are trained as anthropologists and work on the "inside." But notwithstanding Indigenous anthropologists being restrained by this invidious "insider/outsider" position we find ourselves in, is there in fact something even more powerful going on within the Indigenous/colonial space that disrupts the mimetic contract of recognition between Indigenous and settler, and that cannot be contained within the ongoing colonial project?

In the apparent simplicity of the Uluru statement, Australia is witness to a declaration of Indigenous sovereignty over lands never ceded and a formula for decolonization through a Makarrata. For Aboriginal people who disrupt the norm of state definitions of aboriginality, but who, in contemporary Australia, challenge this norm by taking up a sovereign position as Indigenous through their very being, is this where decolonization begins and continues?

Notes

1. My work in Queensland includes anthropological work with Maiawali Karuwali people; Karingbal people and Wadja people. Regarding Western Australia, for many years I was engaged as an anthropologist on the Esperance Nyungar Native Title Claim (WAD6097/1998). This claim was successfully determined in the Federal Court of Australia in 2014. The Esperance Nyungar people are part of a larger language group also known as Noongar Aboriginal peoples, as depicted on the map of Australia in this book.
2. Other land-based consultancies include Aboriginal cultural heritage surveys to determine whether a site of cultural significance may be damaged or destroyed by development or mining.
3. Deanne Hanchant-Nichols is a Tanganekald/Barkindji Aboriginal woman. She is employed at the University of South Australia as a consultant on Aboriginal and Torres Strait Islander employment and development, people, talent, and culture.
4. See the Recognise campaign page, Reconciliation Australia, accessed September 28, 2018, http://www.recognise.org.au/index.html.
5. Proposals for a Makarrata or a treaty of commitment between the Commonwealth of Australia and Aboriginal people was first considered by the Aboriginal

Treaty Committee in 1983. This committee was established as a result of the Senate Standing Committee on Constitutional and Legal Affairs in a report entitled *Two Hundred Years Later* (1983). Makarrata is a complex Yolngu term that describes processes for conflict resolution, making peace, and instigating truth and justice. The Yolngu are people of northeast Arnhem Land in the far north of Australia. The cultural importance of the customary practice of Makarrata among Aboriginal people of northeast Arnhem Land as a form of treaty or resolution between disputing parties was highlighted in the Australian Law Reform Commission report on Aborginal Customary Laws in 1986 (ALRC 1986, paragraphs 67, 500, 710, 891 and 1018).

6. John Winston Howard was Australia's twenty-fifth prime minister, from 1996 to 2007, and leader of the Australian Liberal Party. Sorry Day has been celebrated on May 26 each year in Australia since 1998. The day commemorates the release of the *Bringing Them Home Report* in 1997 by the Australian Human Rights Commission. This document reported on the effects of the separation of Indigenous children from their families under successive Australian government agencies and church missions. Sorry Day now also celebrates the anniversary of the Stolen Generations Apology by former prime minister Kevin Rudd in 2008. Rudd was prime minister of Australia from December 2007 to June 2010 and in 2013 from June to September. He was leader of the Australian Labor Party during this time.

7. It is entirely possible that treaty negotiations will be suspended in Victoria upon a change to a conservative government, as happened in South Australia after the March 2018 elections, where the recently elected conservative Liberal government halted treaty discussions with Indigenous groups in the state.

8. The Hindmarsh Island Bridge Royal Commission was established by the South Australian state government in 1995 to investigate the veracity of Ngarrindjeri women's cultural knowledge where a bridge from Goolwa, on the mainland, to Hindmarsh Island was to be built. The royal commission found that the "secret women's business" was fabricated. The federal Liberal coalition government passed the Hindmarsh Island Bridge Act in 1997, allowing construction of the bridge to proceed.

9. From a statement made by Vine Deloria Jr in 1982 to the Western Social Science Association Conference.

10. There are signs that this will change in the near future, as a growing number of Indigenous students are studying anthropology at Australian universities.

11. Watson, a Tangankald and Meintangk woman, describes ruwe as "an extension of ourselves; to take the land from us, and to develop and damage the ruwe is also to damage our relationship to country" (2015, 20).

12. The Strehlow Research Centre in Alice Springs, in the Northern Territory of Australia, manages the collection of fieldwork, writings, and other recordings of T. G. H. Strehlow on the Aranda (Arrernte) of Central Australia.

13. Watson describes Kaldowinyeri as "a concept, which is difficult to translate, but in part it means 'a long time ago, the beginning of time itself.' It is a word from

the languages of the First Nations Peoples of the Lakes and Coorong region in southeast South Australia" (2015, 11).
14. See the National Native Title Tribunal website, accessed May 15, 2018, http://www.nntt.gov.au/Pages/Home-Page.aspx.
15. Lowitja O'Donoghue is one of Australia's most famous Aboriginal leaders and public administrators.
16. In contrast, Audra Simpson (2014) describes how the Mohawk refuse state recognition and the gifts it may bestow, such as citizenship, in defiant assertion of Indigenous sovereignty and physical and ideological separation from the nation-state.

References

Austin-Broos, Diane J. 1999. "Bringing Spencer and Gillen Home." *Oceania* 69 (3): 209–16.
Australian Law Reform Commission (ALRC). 1986. *The Recognition of Aboriginal Customary Laws*. ALRC Report 31. Canberra: Australian Government Publishing Service.
Australian Law Reform Commission (ALRC). 2015. *Connection to Country: Review of the Native Title Act 1993 (Cth)*. ALRC Report 126. Sydney: ALRC.
Carlson, B. 2016. *The Politics of Identity: Who Counts as Aboriginal Today?* Canberra: Aboriginal Studies Press.
Churchill, W. 1994. *Indians Are Us? Culture and Genocide in Native North America*. Monroe, ME: Common Courage Press.
Clifford, James, and George E. Marcus. 1986. *Writing Culture: The Poetics and Politics of Ethnography*. Berkeley: University of California Press.
Comaroff, J., and J. L. Comaroff. 1997. "Postcolonial Politics and Discourses of Democracy in Southern Africa: An Anthropological Reflection on African Political Modernities." *Journal of Anthropological Research* 53 (2): 123–46.
Coulthard, Glen Sean. 2014. *Red Skin, White Masks: Rejecting the Colonial Politics of Recognition*. Minneapolis: University of Minnesota Press.
Deloria, Vine, S. Scinta, and K. Foehner. 1999. *Spirit and Reason: The Vine Deloria Jr. Reader*. New York: Fulcrum.
Fanon, F. 1967. *The Wretched of the Earth*. Preface by Jean-Paul Sartre. Translated by Constance Farrington. Harmondsworth: Penguin.
Fanon, F. 1968. *Black Skin, White Masks*. New York: Grove Press.
Grant, S. 2016. *Talking to My Country*. Sydney: HarperCollins Australia.
Hannerz, U. 2002. *Transnational Connections: Culture, People, Places*. London: Routledge.
Heiss, A. 2014. *Am I Black Enough for You?* Honolulu: University of Hawai'i Press.
Hobsbawm, Eric. 1983. "Introduction: Inventing Traditions." In *The Invention of Tradition*, edited by Eric Hobsbawm and Terence Ranger, 1–14. New York: Cambridge University Press.
Hutchings, Suzi. 1999. "Centring on the Periphery: Indigenous Women's Knowledge and the Academic Legacy of Spencer and Gillian's Colonial Imagery." Paper presented at

"A Century at the Centre: Spencer, Gillen and *The Native Tribes of Central Australia*," University of Melbourne, October 2–3, 1999.

Hutchings, Suzi. 2014. "Caught in the Middle: The Fragmentation of Indigenous Knowledge Through the Native Title Process in Urban and Rural Australia." Paper presented at the American Anthropological Association Conference, Washington DC, December 2–7, 2014.

Hutchings, Suzi. 2017. "Inside Out: Indigeneity in the Era of Native Title in Australia." Keynote address, "Shifting States," the Australian Anthropological Society Annual Conference, University of Adelaide, December 11–15, 2017.

Hutchings, Suzi, and Deanne Hanchant-Nichols. 2014. "Who Defines Indigenous Identity?" Paper presented at the World Indigenous People's Conference on Education, Honolulu, Hawaii, May 19–24, 2014.

Hutchings, Suzi, and Deanne Hanchant-Nichols. 2017. "Defining Indigenous Identity—Who Calls the Shots?" Paper presented at the World Indigenous People's Conference on Education, Toronto, Ontario, July 24–28, 2017.

Kowal, Emma, and Yin Paradies. 2017. "Indigeneity and the Refusal of Whiteness." *Postcolonial Studies* 20 (1): 101–17.

Langton, Marcia. 1981. "Urbanizing Aborigines: The Social Scientists' Great Deception." *Social Alternatives* 2 (2): 16–22.

Langton, Marcia. 2011. "Anthropology, Politics and the Changing World of Aboriginal Australians." *Anthropological Forum* 21 (1): 1–22.

Lucas, Rod. 1996. "The Failure of Anthropology." *Journal of Australian Studies* 20 (48): 40–51.

Marks, Kathy. 2018. "Trick or Treaty: Will States Redress a Founding Flaw?" *Griffith Law Review* 60:157–79.

Martin, David F. 2015. "Does Native Title Merely Provide an Entitlement to Be Native? Indigenes, Identities, and Applied Anthropological Practice." *Australian Journal of Anthropology* 26 (1): 112–27.

Medicine, Beatrice. 2001. *Learning to Be an Anthropologist and Remaining "Native": Selected Writings*. Edited by Sue-Ellen Jacobs. Urbana: University of Illinois Press.

Moreton-Robinson, Aileen. 2011. "Virtuous Racial States: The Possessive Logic of Patriarchal White Sovereignty and the United Nations Declaration on the Rights of Indigenous Peoples." *Griffith Law Review* 20 (3): 641–58.

Moreton-Robinson, Aileen. 2015. *The White Possessive: Property, Power, and Indigenous Sovereignty*. Minneapolis: University of Minnesota Press.

Mulvaney, J., H. Morphy, and A. Petch. 1997. *My Dear Spencer: The Letters of F. J. Gillen to Baldwin Spencer*. Melbourne: Hyland House.

Pearson, Noel. 2017. "Betrayal: The Turnbull Government Has Burned the Bridge of Bipartisanship." *Monthly*, December 2016–January 2017. https://www.themonthly.com.au/issue/2017/december/1512046800/noel-pearson/betrayal.

Petch, Alison. 2000. "Spencer and Gillen's Collaborative Fieldwork in Central Australia and Its Legacy." *Journal of the Anthropological Society of Oxford* 31 (3): 309–28.

Povinelli, Elizabeth A. 1999. "Settler Modernity and the Quest for an Indigenous Tradition." *Public Culture* 11 (1): 19–48.

Referendum Council. 2017. "Uluru Statement from the Heart." Referendum Council website, May 26, 2017. https://www.referendumcouncil.org.au/sites/default/files/2017-05/Uluru_Statement_From_The_Heart_0.PDF.

Rose, Frederick G. G. 1962. *The Wind of Change in Central Australia: The Aborigines at Angas Downs*. Berlin: Akademie-Verlag.

Sahlins, Marshall David. 1999. "Two or Three Things that I Know About Culture." *Journal of the Royal Anthropological Institute* 5 (3): 399–421.

Said, E. W. 1993. *Culture and Imperialism*. London: Chatto and Windus.

Senate Standing Committee on Constitutional and Legal Affairs. 1983. *Two Hundred Years On*. Canberra: Australian Government Publishing Service.

Simpson, Audra. 2014. *Mohawk Interruptus: Political Life Across the Borders of Settler States*. Durham, NC: Duke University Press.

Smith, Linda Tuhiwai. 2012. *Decolonizing Methodologies: Research and Indigenous Peoples*. 2nd ed. London: Zed Books.

Spencer, Baldwin, and Francis James Gillen. 1938. *The Native Tribes of Central Australia*. 1st ed., reprinted with preface. London: Macmillan.

Taussig, Michael. 1993. *Mimesis and Alterity: A Particular History of the Senses*. London: Routledge.

United Nations General Assembly. 2007. *United Nations Declaration on the Rights of Indigenous Peoples*. New York: United Nations. http://www.un.org/esa/socdev/unpfii/documents/DRIPS_en.pdf.

Watson, Irene. 2015. *Aboriginal Peoples, Colonialism and International Law: Raw Law*. London: Routledge.

Wolfe, Patrick. 1994. "Nation and MiscegeNation: Discursive Continuity in the Post-Mabo Era." *Social Analysis: The International Journal of Social and Cultural Practice*, no. 36, 93–152.

EIGHT

Eclipsing Rights

Property Rights as Indigenous Human Rights in Australia

SARAH HOLCOMBE

This chapter focuses on Australianist anthropology since the 1970s, a period in which arguably the most powerful formative element has been research on rights to land, beginning with the 1971 Justice Blackburn decision, culminating in the Northern Territory's Aboriginal Land Rights Act in 1976. Indeed, anthropologists were strong advocates for recognizing Indigenous property rights and were instrumental in developing the categories at law that now define Indigenous Australian land tenure in these legally discursive contexts. With the recognition of native title following the Mabo decision in 1992, even more anthropologists became involved in writing claims for native title recognition or assisting with heritage clearances to facilitate land-use agreements.[1] The comfort of this historical fit, however, has since been called into question, principally from within the discipline. While I concur with some aspects of this disenchantment, my argument articulates a broader set of political and moral frameworks than has typically been used. I argue that land rights have eclipsed an ethnographic focus on other aspects of Indigenous human rights. An exception to this has been Jon Altman's focus on customary economic rights leveraging off these property rights (Altman 1987; Altman and Kerins 2012). In this chapter, I argue that this tendency to focus on such a narrow form of cultural rights—expressed as land rights—has decoupled the anthropological project from the broader set of human rights concerns, such as substantive civil and political rights. This has created a legacy that is difficult to shift yet is also reflective of the broader Australian political milieu.

Land Rights Research and Policy Critique: Overdetermining Australian Anthropology?

The political landscape in Australia has changed radically since 1983, more than thirty years ago now, when Nicolas Peterson and Marcia Langton co-edited *Aborigines, Land and Land Rights* in a tone of optimism. At that time, they were reinvigorating an overdue scholarly engagement with Aboriginal land tenure systems and beginning the discussion on the legal processes that formally recognized them as property rights. Since the Aboriginal Land Rights Act of 1976 was legislated for the Northern Territory, approximately half of the land in that jurisdiction is now inalienable freehold title held by Aboriginal land trusts and managed by four Aboriginal land councils. Today there are a range of other forms of Indigenous title across Australia, in each state and territory, plus the 1993 Native Title Act, which is Australia wide. Of note, most of this land is in remote areas—such as the Northern Territory, Western Australia, and South Australia, where there has been little non-Indigenous settlement and where most residents are Aboriginal and still speak their own languages. Social anthropologists have been, and still are, instrumental in these legal processes, providing evidence of "primary spiritual responsibility"—under the Aboriginal Land Rights Act—and of "continuity of connection" under the Native Title Act.[2]

While I concur with Peterson and Langton that land rights have encompassed "regaining some fraction of the personal and group autonomy which existed prior to colonisation" (1983, 3), the focus on the "performance of cultural continuity" required for the recognition of rights to land has had contradictory effects, as Elizabeth A. Povinelli articulated as the *Cunning of Recognition* (2002). For my purposes, one of these effects is that land rights essentially became a moniker for Indigenous human rights and, thus, as *the* right worthy of anthropological attention. I count myself as complicit here, as I worked in my early career for the two major Northern Territory land councils for almost ten years, focusing on research for land claims. Many Australianist anthropologists seem to have been so preoccupied with the applied research to gain back this land that the dissonance between these ideal codified social structures—the local descent groups and kinship structures; the ceremonial performances tying these groups to land, and so on—and the more challenging daily social vulnerabilities for many people living on this land has been neglected as a field of activist or advocacy research. An early exception to this trend was the research of feminist anthropologist Diane Bell, who first raised the issue of intraracial rape, employing the language of human rights and social justice in a remote Aboriginal context. With her key Aboriginal colleague, senior community leader Topsy Nelson, Diane Bell co-authored an article, "Speaking About Rape Is Everyone's Business" (1989). Though several other social anthropologists have been working in this field of Indigenous social vulnerabilities, notably on substance abuse in remote and rural communities (e.g., Brady 1992; McKnight 2002), Bell has been the exception in explicitly drawing on the language of rights to highlight issues of social exclusion and moral exceptionalism.[3]

Nonetheless, at that time, this research was an outlier in the academy and, in different ways, marginalized by the anthropological mainstream. This was notably the case for Bell's research on intraracial rape, which Indigenous and non-Indigenous female academics strongly opposed (see Huggins et al. 1991; Bell 1991). Indigenous academic Jackie Huggins responded, "We dispute the central proposition that rape is 'everyone's business.' . . . What this reflects is white imperialism of others' cultures which are theirs to appropriate, criticise and castigate" (Huggins et al. 1991, 506; Moreton-Robinson 2000). The relations of power between Indigenous and non-Indigenous women were deeply unequal (though Bell and Nelson were, respectively, non-Indigenous and Indigenous). The Indigenous female politic at that time was "We are women and men together who have suffered grave injustices by the white invaders. We have all suffered" (Huggins et al. 1991, 506). And so the rights of the "Indigenous collective" were prioritized over the rights of the individuals within that collective.

The field of Indigenous women's decolonizing scholarship in Australia has since expanded significantly, however, and for some shifted to one of accommodation. As Aileen Moreton-Robinson states: "Indigenous and feminist scholars share an understanding that their respective production of knowledge is a site of constant struggle against normative patriarchal conceptual frameworks" (2013, 331). Likewise, Canadian Cree-Métis feminist scholar Verna St. Denis stated that she also once maintained that feminism was not relevant to Aboriginal people, that to be feminist one had to choose between gender and culture or nation. Now, however, she argues, "The diversity of perspectives among Aboriginal peoples in our strategies and perspectives for change cannot be used as a justification for maintaining the status quo of inequality and marginalisation. Increasingly more Aboriginal women are beginning to identify as feminists or at least with some of the goals of feminism, such as ending violence against women and children" (2007, 37).

This has also been the case for Australian Indigenous female academics working and researching in this area of Indigenous women's rights, where there appears to be a consensus that "Indigenous feminism differs to white feminisms" (Davis 2007, 20). As Indigenous legal scholar Megan Davis argues, "The problems concerning Indigenous women were overshadowed by the problems facing Indigenous people, which in reality equated to problems facing Indigenous men" (2012, 4). This historical invisibility of Indigenous women's issues in Australia has ongoing implications, and Davis and others (including Moreton-Robinson 2013; Langton 2007, 2008, 2010) have begun to claim some ground in feminizing the debate. With the exception of the work of Indigenous anthropologist Marcia Langton (see especially 2010) there has, however, been little dialogue within the academy between Indigenous and non-Indigenous academics and activists researching and working in this field.[4] While this is primarily the result of different methodological approaches—the ethnographic method of anthropology versus the Indigenous standpoint theory of a decolonizing approach—the outcome has been, perhaps, a siloing of perspectives. Although this is shifting with an increasing trend toward interdisciplinarity, it is fair to say that this type of dialogue is nascent in Australia.

For the anthropological academy, only relatively recently has the raft of social issues—family and gender violence, chronic unemployment, poor health, low life expectancy, low formal education outcomes, and substance abuse—gained widespread prominence. It was notably catalyzed by Peter Sutton, who, tellingly, is one of the most renowned Australian anthropologists for his breadth of research on land claims under the Aboriginal Land Rights Act and the Native Title Act. His provocative and polemical text *The Politics of Suffering* (2001, 2009) is a reference to the moralization of politics as he explores why, after three decades (post–land rights) of liberal policy, "the suffering and grief" of many remote Aboriginal communities has worsened. Perhaps unsurprisingly, he was deeply dismissive of the "rights agenda," referring to it as "an abstract notion constrained by a liberal consensus" (2009, 127).

Sutton draws a direct correlation between the "liberal progressive" policies of this period and "the seriously dysfunctional state" of many remote communities (2009, 55). In doing so, he sets up a dichotomy between the "glamour" of the rights, justice, and self-determination agenda and the work of those on the frontline in the caring business, those "who dress the wounds of battered women in remote area clinics" (2009, 11). Yet, Sutton's appeal to individualism in the prevention of one individual's suffering at a time through state intervention has since become the (neo-)liberal rights consensus. He has simply been selective in which ideological frame of the rights apparatus he has chosen to champion (see also Whyte 2012; Holcombe 2015). The dichotomy Sutton sets up between the "progressive rights" (as he terms them) of collective self-determination and postcolonial justice and the "vital human right of freedom from abuse," the right to adequate nutrition, medical care, and so on (2009, 12), is ultimately a false one. The work of this dichotomous approach to the application of a rights agenda, however, can also be seen in current policy approach. There seems to have been a failure in the anthropological imagination to explore what a rapprochement between these apparently disparate rights agendas might look like.

Sutton's text is claimed by some to have provided the intellectual capital for federal government intervention in the Northern Territory in 2007. This unprecedented set of policy interventions, referred to as the Northern Territory Emergency Response (NTER), was triggered by widespread allegations of child sexual abuse as cataloged in the report of the Northern Territory Board of Inquiry into the Protection of Aboriginal Children from Sexual Abuse: *Ampe Akelyerenmane Meke Mekarle, "Little Children are Sacred"* (2007). This raft of policy interventions, far broader than the protection of children and infringing on many fundamental rights, both galvanized and polarized politico-moral anthropological and broader debate (Altman and Hinkson 2007). In particular, the diverse essays in *Culture Crisis: Anthropology and Politics in Aboriginal Australia* (Altman and Hinkson 2010) and Dianne Austin-Broos's *A Different Inequality* (2011) provide insight into what developed as a deeply divisive public anthropology (see also Hage 2012).

This reflective turn cannot be adequately summarized here, though I draw inspiration from Hinkson's question: "Was our work over-determined by the policy approach of self-determination?" (Hinkson 2010, 3). The introduction of this policy of self-determination by the progressive Whitlam Labor government in 1972 signaled the era of land rights, and, as a radical shift from the long-running policy of assimilation, its immediate effect was a rejection of the deeply paternalistic language and policies of the past. It also mirrored the emerging Indigenous rights discourse that was developing at the United Nations (Niezen 2003; De Costa 2006) and the civil rights movement in the

United States (Attwood 2003). It seems to me that our advocacy work—as it focused on land claims—was indeed overdetermined by the political ideal of self-determination. In many ways, this was and is laudable, as this focus was ethically appropriate at that time. The land rights movement was driven by Aboriginal people seeking to regain control over their customary land, which had been alienated from them by non-Indigenous colonial interests. A 1975 photo of then prime minister Gough Whitlam pouring red soil into the hand of Vincent Lingiari became a powerful and poignant image of a proud Gurindji leader reclaiming what was rightfully his, as he led the land rights movement to regain his people's land from pastoral interests, at the same time revealing deeply exploitative labor conditions (see Wright 1998; Attwood 2003, 257–307). Such rights are quintessentially "Indigenous."

Yet, the signature byline, "Our Land, Our Life," of *Land Rights News*, published by the two major Northern Territory land councils, which manage these vast swathes of now Aboriginal land, has lost much of its political and sentimental potency. Indeed, it is "under attack" according to these same newspapers. The current conservative governments of the Northern Territory and the Commonwealth (federal) are pushing for land reform (and not for the first time) in order, they argue, to promote economic development, home ownership, and employment; they contend that the collective form of land tenure of inalienable Aboriginal freehold title has held back "development" (see Hughes 2007; Johns 2011).

Sutton's observation about the close relationship between statistical "disadvantage," remoteness, and the practice of "culture" (2009) is relevant to consider here. For those who work in these remote areas, myself included, this interplay has led to a morally relativist anthropology. As Melinda Hinkson has observed, "The relationships we develop over time orient us, in most cases in moral alignment with and obligation to the community of people among who we work, rather than in a position from which criticism and negative judgement might easily follow" (Hinkson 2010, 7). While this relativist approach is now widely acknowledged as problematic, I nevertheless suggest that respect for cultural relativism—the hallmark of the discipline—has underpinned the lack of engagement with the ethnographic treatment of human rights in Australian anthropology. And here I have in mind a memory from my own PhD field research in Central Australia, in the mid-1990s, of teenagers with cans held to their noses sniffing petrol, walking around the community zombie-like. At that time in this place, there were no formal programs that families and users could access, and community leaders were doing the best they could to curb this substance abuse. Large meetings were held, and the sniffers were publicly chastised and shamed by senior men and women. The situation was largely understood as Aboriginal business to be dealt with at a local family level, and non-Indigenous people, including me, were not invited to intervene. And while I also felt powerless to act, the language and resources for such action were not then available, either to me or to Anangu.[5] Furthermore, as an outside researcher, I was actively managed by the Anangu I lived and worked with; they channeled my research interests to testify to their local and traditional authenticity as a deeply political statement of continuity (see, in particular, Holcombe 2004). While this local management of me must also be understood as an assertion of self-determination, the relativist stance that I also nonetheless practiced was, at that time, standard fieldwork method. What is now remembered in hindsight as a petrol-sniffing crisis—with both high mortality rates and major long-term health issues for a generation of youth (Brady 1992, 37–68)—was barely a footnote in my research. This brief outline of the complex set of factors at play in how topics for anthropological research are chosen could perhaps be the case in any colonized state; the usually non-Indigenous researchers are deeply conscious of their "white [man's] burden" (Easterly 2007).

Limited Legitimacy: Australian Human Rights

One of the key issues that makes human rights research in the Australian context unique is Australia's anomalous status as the only liberal democratic state without a national bill or charter of rights (Byrnes, Charlesworth, and McKinnon 2009). As Australianist anthropologists have shied away from directly engaging with this rights discourse as a field of ethnographic research, we are also reflecting the wider societal norm. To quote constitutional legal scholar George Williams, "In the absence of a charter of rights, human rights ideas can lack legitimacy in the parliament and in the community" (2010).[6] I briefly explore this hiatus in anthropological rights research as it also sheds some light on the challenges of this field of inquiry as part of a national anthropology.

In Australianist anthropology's critical analysis of Indigenous contemporary social welfare issues and government interventions, the language used has been the language of policy. Where elements of Indigenous rights discourse have crept in, they have done so via critique of policy rhetoric such as *self-determination* and *inequality*. As the policy debate has tended to frame the critique, it has also led to political and ideological factions—as Sutton's text and the "culture crisis" debate highlighted. I humbly suggest that a reason for this divide is the play into this more specific set of political constructions, so that the often passionate ethnographic critiques, though critically engaged, are reactive and thus limited by the existing toolkit that the state offers up in its discourse.[7] As such, the "failure" of self-determination can be the only outcome (see also Hage 2012). This anthropological relationship with government has been described as a "complex symbiotic dependency" (Hinkson 2010, 5). Goodale's statement that "ethnography of human rights practices [are a] fertile source of new ideas about the complex relationships between normativity, agency and social and political intentionality" (2012, 468) is useful here. New ideas are needed to reframe and reexamine the seemingly intractable issues and long-standing debates that remote Indigenous inequality poses to a contemporary social ethic. Not only does the language and discourse of human rights offer this potential, but many of the foundational elements of this discourse can be found in the operations of government policy. Yet, they are rarely explicitly articulated.

Perhaps yet another reason that Australianist anthropologists have been tardy or dismissive of applying this rights discourse within the Australian context is because of the "co-nationals" status of our "subjects," as Jeremy Beckett (2010) has referred to the settler colony politic. For my purposes, this national anthropology identified by Beckett has had the instrumental effect of eliding the value of this rights discourse. Regardless of our ideological perspectives on the values of neoliberalism and formal rights *or* the welfare state and substantive rights, Indigenous Australians as cocitizens surely don't require the same recourse to human rights instruments as, say, those in war-torn or corrupt states in Africa or South America. As part of a stated multicultural Australia, the policy rhetoric of equality in Indigenous-focused policies such as "Closing the Gap" surely doesn't require recourse to human rights by activist anthropologists. And even as the state rejects Indigenous self-determination in favor of "mainstreaming" and plays an increasingly paternalistic and directive role within Aboriginal people's lives (such as through the NTER), surely they still have the capacity to be agents in resisting or reinventing this engagement at a local level. Indeed, this creative resistance as a "society against the state" has been a focus of much of my previous research (Holcombe 2004, 2005), as it has been the focus of others (see Hinkson and Smith 2005, in particular the Merlan and Batty articles).

Human Rights as a Tacit Discourse

In a 2009 seminar that specifically focused on the UN *Declaration on the Rights of Indigenous Peoples*, which had been recently endorsed by the Australian government, I stated that, "The *Declaration on the Rights of Indigenous Peoples* is potentially a powerful instrument.... However, there is no point having rights unless they can be exercised and, likewise, unless those who need to have them recognised and activated are aware that such rights exist."

When I wrote this, I hadn't begun the research on the potential of a multicultural human rights in central Australia and the critical translation work of the human rights language into the local language of Pintupi Luritja. So when I returned to this piece of writing, it seemed on reflection very naïve, as though the "exercise" of rights was simply a matter of being aware of them. Yet, I have since grown to realize that while this is not the whole picture, it is a significant element of it.[8] The people I work with who refer to themselves as Anangu, with a few notable exceptions, heard these words "universal human rights" and the core principles they embody for the first time from discussions with me. Of course, they are familiar with their own rights and responsibilities toward their land and families and their rights as articulated in the process of land claims. Citizenship rights in the state and in relationships with one another are different kinds of rights.

Though this general lack of awareness may be understood as at the extreme end of the spectrum—a remote context in central Australia on Aboriginal land in the Northern Territory—it is no way exceptional. A 2009 Australia-wide Human Rights Consultation Committee on public awareness and concern for human rights and the possibilities for developing a national bill or charter of rights confirmed that "the clearest finding from our work is that Australians know little about their human rights—what they are, where they come from and how they are protected" (Brennan 2009, v).[9] So while this lack of rights awareness may be part of a broader trend in Australia, it is exacerbated in remote areas where inhabitants also confront a raft of structural inequalities, including the geopolitics of remoteness from the centers of policy development and the centers of political power.

Ironically, in early 2014, as I was realizing how invisible the rights language was during one of my visits to Papunya (one of the two remote communities I work in), I received an email notification from the Australian government's Attorney Generals Department stating that they had ceased funding human rights education. Education about human rights had been a key plank in the previous Labor government's commitment to the Human Rights Framework, which was to operate instead of a national bill of rights.[10] And while this education had not (yet) reached this remote area, the Human Rights Framework has also quietly dropped off the new conservative government's policy agenda, though as I write this, one can still find the document on government web pages. The lack of exposure to human rights discourse seems to be another form of disadvantage and exclusion that Aboriginal people in remote areas face. While most adults are familiar with land rights, the interconnection between the rights to land and human rights is not readily drawn.

Perhaps not surprisingly, the focus of the last two conservative governments has been on private property rights. Mal Brough, the minister for Aboriginal affairs responsible for introducing the NTER set of policies, stated to the media during the hectic introduction of the legislation in 2007 that land rights had "locked" people into collective tenure. As he explained, "We need to actually recognise that communism didn't work, collectivism didn't work. It doesn't work to say that a collective owns it and you will never have anything."[11] Brough makes the link between private ownership and economic opportunity. Yet it is useful to revisit his selective reading of property rights as fundamentally private. This is a narrow and inaccurate interpretation of property rights as outlined in Article 17 of the *Universal Declaration of Human Rights*, which addresses both private and collective land ownership: "Everyone has the right to own property alone or *in association* with others" (italics mine). Note also the second part of this article: "No one shall be arbitrarily deprived of his property."[12] The point of reminding ourselves of these universal human rights is not only to contest the legitimacy of the dominant interpretation but also to reframe the issue on a larger, less parochial, scale. The right to private property was one of the founding civil rights, and liberal conservatives hold it very dear indeed. If we, and those Aboriginal land owners most affected, are reminded that the state is attempting to enforce only a partial reading, then we are more readily able to challenge partisan policy. Visibility can be politically powerful. In an early translation of Article 17 of *Universal Declaration of Human Rights* into Pintupi-Luritja, by Papunya-based translators Lance Macdonald and Sheila Joyce Dixon, amid much dialogue, rendered the (final) free translation as

> This word stands for us all that you can buy your own block of land with money if you want to live in your own house in the middle of the city, in the town or in the bush. The country of Aboriginal people does not belong to one person or one

family member. Aboriginal people's country is for all the family. If one person wants to build a house or something on this land then they have to ask correctly.[13]

An earlier draft included the phrase "Aboriginal land is different" to emphasize the values inherent in this collective estate. An Aboriginal redefinition of this human right might be "The land owns us. We don't own the land." The ethnography dwells on the ways in which land use is closely bound with a deeply interdependent set of human-environment relationships that are not amenable to individualistic notions of ownership (Myers 1986, 1988). Wendy Brown, drawing on a Marxist approach, observed that this right can be seen in light of the paradox that "the right to private property is a vehicle for the accumulation of wealth through the production of another's poverty" (2000, 232). Revealing aspects of the contested work of this human right in this remote context begins a dialogue across difference, but even within the dominant frame of property rights, the work of rights is often tacit, as the state cherrypicks which rights it chooses to engage and indeed enforce, even from within the one article.

While there is little effective relationship of human rights to law in Australia, these normative concepts operate on multiple levels: as tacit elements of contemporary mainstream "culture"; as discursive political tools (as evidenced in the early land rights struggles); as a set of principles to which various governing bodies abide (such as corporations); as merely rhetoric; and as a moniker for modernity and globalization (see Holcombe 2014). It is telling that this diverse work of rights is often hidden in euphemism, the most common of which is "good (corporate) governance." This governmentality is expressed in the responsibilization discourses of accountability and representation. It can be found in the policies of "shared responsibility agreements," and variations thereof, that operate in remote communities as a form of discretionary tied aid (Sullivan 2011; Hage and Eckersley 2012). These are the regulatory dimensions of rights, as the entailments of citizenship. If the standards of these regulatory dimensions are not met, then a raft of punitive measures are applied in relation to servicing the social security (unemployment) contract, children's school attendance, and so forth—the list of finable offences is extensive. The question Sally E. Merry poses, "Instead of asking if human rights are a good idea . . . explore what difference they make," is a useful one (2006b, 39). In remote Australia, the assimilatory functions of rights are the focus of government policy. For an activist anthropologist, elements of this diverse work of human rights reveals sites of state power. For social justice movements, the rights discourse is a generative source for a modern moral imagination, with its core principles of equality, nondiscrimination, and dignity. And for my purposes, exploring Aboriginal people's discursive capacity to challenge existing power relations within the Aboriginal polity and between Aboriginal people and the state is a fundamental element of the emancipatory potential of rights discourse.

Ethnographic research among minority and Indigenous peoples in many other countries, including the work of my Mexican and Canadian colleagues in the other chapters in this volume, indicate that a lack of local awareness is not a global phenomenon and that local engagements with the emancipatory discourse of human rights can be a powerful political tool (see Speed 2006; Pitarch, Speed, and Solano 2008). Likewise, translations of the *Universal Declaration of Human Rights* (*UDHR*) into local languages, for instance, are increasingly common. Indeed, according to the UN, the *UDHR* is the most translated document globally, into more than 465 languages.[14] Earlier, at 370 translations, it made a Guinness World Record for the most translated document in the world.[15] To the best of my knowledge the translation of the *UDHR* that I undertook in 2015, with two local translators and a linguist, into the language of Pintupi-Luritja is the first time it had been translated into an Indigenous Australian language (Holcombe 2015).

Why does this lack of exposure to the language of human rights matter in these remote places? Is it merely another aspect of discrimination, of Aboriginal marginalization? More importantly, perhaps: Can other rights principles, such as Article 3, "the right to life, liberty and security of person," or in plain English, "the right to be free from violence," also gain the same political and practical momentum as rights to land did in the late 1960s and 1970s?

I ask this question as the issue of gender violence—often expressed in this remote context in terms of family and domestic violence—is, arguably, one of the more pressing human rights issues in the Northern Territory. Spousal or intimate partner violence compels an extensive range of interactions with formal rights via the legal system, at the same time revealing, often in contradistinction, Aboriginal responsibilities in customary terms. Such responsibilities do not sit readily with the "victim" tag that the legal system applies to these women. Rather, for Aboriginal women the contradictions and tensions between the formal legal system as it operates on and for them as individual "victims" contrasts with their sociocentric subject position among family and community, with their collective rights.

Drawing inspiration from Sally Merry's question, I ask, How do women take up a position in one discourse rather than another? In Central Australia, because of the mandatory sentencing and domestic-violence-reporting regimes, there is some fluidity between these discourses of (civil, legal) human rights and customary entailments. It is not often a clearly demarcated dichotomy, because these legal regimes circumscribe women's choices or discretion in taking up a position. Instead, they are compelled to do so through the "protective" legal system. Yet, how they manage within and beyond this system, in actively calling the police themselves, seeking a domestic violence order, or separating from their violent spouse, *are* indicators of taking up a rights-holder position.

The statistical facts of gender violence reveal startling figures in the Northern Territory. Almost three thousand Aboriginal women experienced violence from their spouse in 2011–2012, compared to approximately three hundred non-Aboriginal women in the same period. Considering the Aboriginal population of the Northern Territory is 30 percent of the total, this proportion is pretty staggering. Or to contextualize it another way, while Aboriginal women in the Northern Territory make up only 0.3 percent of the broader Australian population, they account for 14 percent of female hospitalizations for assault in the entire country (Sharp 2014). These extremely high figures are correlated with equally disproportionate imprisonment rates for Aboriginal men, the most recent of which are found in the Australian Bureau of Statistics prison data. The proportion of adult prisoners in the Northern Territory who identified as Aboriginal or Torres Strait Islander is 84 percent (1,349 prisoners) according to 2017 data. This was the largest proportion of Aboriginal and Torres Strait Islander prisoners of any state or territory, with a national average of 27 percent in 2017. Acts intended to cause injury are the most common offense for the Indigenous population, at 35 percent of offenses according to the most recent figures (ABS 2017).

The Northern Territory is the disproportionately high bar in figure 1 (facing page). This figure has not necessarily increased since 1989, when anthropologist Diane Bell first raised the issue of Aboriginal women's human rights in relation to intraracial rape in remote Central Australia, but the legal system has changed to now criminalize domestic and family violence. This includes mandated prosecution via mandatory sentencing regimes, thus taking away magistrate discretion. The reporting of domestic and family violence is also now mandatory and highly visible, as these imprisonment data indicate.

As the Northern Territory is "governed through crime," to borrow Loïc Wacquant's phrase (2010), these imprisonment data tell us as much about the criminalizing of the Indigenous population as they do about the actual crimes, because freedom from violence is mandated. The phrase "Women go to the clinic, and men go to jail" speaks to this cycle, as the clinic staff must now report these incidents to police. The work of the state in attempting to mandate this

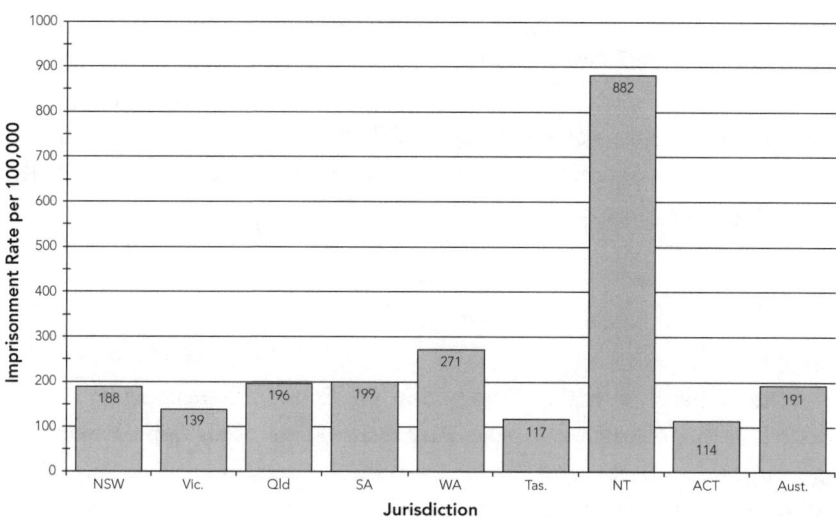

FIGURE 1 Estimated adult imprisonment rates by jurisdiction, 2014–15. *Source*: Northern Territory Department of Correctional Services Annual Statistics.

"freedom," however, is inevitably only temporary. Women, and men, need the support of their family to be free from violence, and this requires an active Aboriginal polity that refuses violence *as well as* a supportive state.

The concern of the state was not always so active, as it is now in mandatory terms. Indeed, it mirrored the wider society, in which domestic violence was commonly viewed as a private matter. This attitude calls to mind an incident from the early 1990s, when I was working at the Central Land Council (CLC) in the Central Australian town of Alice Springs, in my first professional job. At that stage, the CLC office backed onto the Charles Creek Aboriginal town camp, and there would often be traffic from the camp through the grounds of the office, and sometimes even inside, to use the ablution facilities. From the vantage point of my office window, I recall seeing a young Aboriginal woman obviously in distress; she looked bruised and teary. She was walking through the grounds and appeared to be heading for the pay phone at the service station across the road. I mentioned this to another colleague, who replied, "That's probably [so and so]; happens all the time." Although I recall being taken aback by this complacency, the fact that I am more shocked at this memory now than I was when it happened speaks strongly to the shift in public sentiment about such violence. I do explicitly recall thinking about how intrusive it might appear were I to somehow intervene; it did seem to be her business. Yet, today I wouldn't think twice about offering support, and I suspect that colleague wouldn't either. This shift in public consciousness is the work of realizing women's rights as human rights. As the non-Aboriginal public legitimates this discourse, so too does this "relational gaze," to borrow a concept from Gillian Cowlishaw (2004), begin to have positive, rather than negative, effects.

Conclusions

It seems to me that writing from within the frame of human rights cannot be done with a dispassionate gaze. Any such writing needs to be understood as a form of political action. As Ghassan Hage states, Indigenous Australian self-determination can't be reduced to only state politics or state policy. It also needs to be argued and understood as "an anti-colonial politics: a politics that is precisely directed at resisting encompassment" (2012, 410). Reimagining the framework of human rights as a multicultural and more porous one that encompasses self-determination can assist in reimagining an ethical politics that confronts the ongoing colonial project.

As Ayten Gundogdu states, "Human rights do not exist independently of human plurality. . . . [I]ntersubjective guarantees and mutual agreements are required" (2011, 18). Yet, in this intercultural sphere, the challenge of developing "mutual agreements" also entails making transparent the workings of the discourse of rights, the expectations contained in this contract of citizenship. Many central Australian Aboriginal people are simply not privy to this contract; the expectations contained within it are tacit. Only by having access to this global discourse can Aboriginal people be truly informed of the expectations of the state and so be enabled to engage on equal terms. In doing so, they might begin to challenge the contingency of human rights and indeed also articulate a contemporary argument for maintaining the inalienable rights to their land—if this is what they continue to seek.

Notes

1. The 1993 Native Title Act was a landmark case in the High Court of Australia, overturning the colonial doctrine of terra nullius bought to court by Torres Strait Islander Eddie Mabo. It recognizes Indigenous prior occupation, through recog-

nition via court proceedings to Native title rights. These rights are not exclusive, but if successful, they comprise a "bundle of rights"—which tends to include the "right to negotiate" with development interests. In the Northern Territory, land that is not already inalienable freehold Aboriginal land (under the Land Rights Act of 1976) is either recognized as Native title land or under a Native title claim.
2. In the Northern Territory, however, there has been a shift away from claiming land (before the 1993 sunset clause) and toward a focus on land management and stewardship.
3. Note, however, that they all took very different approaches to their subject matter.
4. One of the reasons for this lack of dialogue is that so few Indigenous Australian anthropologists work within the academy or as activist anthropologists; Marcia Langton is possibly the most recognized as both anthropologist and public intellectual.
5. The Central Australian Youth Link-Up Service (CAYLUS) began operation in 2002 with a specific focus on youth diversion from substance abuse—notably volatile substances. The group has been highly successful in stopping petrol sniffing with the widespread, but not total, introduction of low-aromatic opal fuel. CAYLUS is now focusing on other volatile and addictive substances. See "About CAYLUS," CAYLUS website, accessed January 11, 2016, http://caylus.org.au/about-caylus/#about.
6. Several states and territories, such as Victoria and Australian Capital Territory (ACT), have human rights acts. The ACT has the Human Rights Act (2004) and Victoria has the Charter of Human Rights and Responsibilities (2006). Yet, there is no Australia-wide bill of rights under Commonwealth legislation (see Byrnes, Charlesworth, and McKinnon 2009; Williams 2010). Note that a "bill of rights" is a list of rights encompassed in a legal act.
7. Nevertheless, several anthropologists have engaged in some explicit consideration of Indigenous rights discourse, such as Francesca Merlan in several articles and commentaries, including a brief article entitled "More than Rights" (2009), and Mary Edmunds, who wrote a paper for the Human Rights Council of Australia providing an anthropological perspective of the NTER in terms of human rights (2010). These works outline important conceptual signposts on the path to critically engaging with this discourse and the challenges of applying it in absolute terms in remote Aboriginal communities. When Gillian Cowlishaw was president of the Australian Anthropology Society (AAS) in 2007, she also wrote a strongly worded two-page response in the AAS newsletter (AAS 2007) to the Australian government's refusal to endorse the UN *Declaration on the Rights of Indigenous Peoples*. Yet, the ethnographic treatment of this rights discourse has not been favored in Australia.
8. I have further articulated many of the ideas in this chapter in *Remote Freedoms: Politics, Personhood, and Human Rights in Aboriginal Central Australia*, Studies in Human Rights (Stanford, CA: Stanford University Press, 2018) .

9. This consultation was the fourth effort since federation in 1901 by a Labor government to consider implementing a national human rights charter or bill.
10. See Commonwealth of Australia, *Australia's Human Rights Framework*, April 2010, https://www.ag.gov.au/Consultations/Documents/Publicsubmissionsonthedraft baselinestudy/AustraliasHumanRightsFramework.pdf.
11. See transcript of the Q&A with Mal Brough, *Age*, August 16, 2007, http://www.theage.com.au/news/national/question-and-answer-session/2007/08/15/1186857591353.html.
12. Perhaps a more anticipated reading of Indigenous property rights can be found in Article 26 of the *UN Declaration on the Rights of Indigenous Peoples*, which strongly endorses collective property rights.
13. See "Universal Declaration of Human Rights, Pintupi-Luritja," UN Human Rights Office of the High Commissioner, posted July 10, 2015, http://www.ohchr.org/EN/UDHR/Pages/Language.aspx?LangID=piu.
14. See "About the Universal Declaration of Human Rights Translation Project," UN Human Rights Office of the High Commissioner, accessed January 5, 2016, http://www.ohchr.org/EN/UDHR/Pages/Introduction.aspx.
15. "The Universal Declaration of Human Rights in 370 Languages," UN Human Rights Office of the High Commissioner, December 7, 2009, http://www.ohchr.org/EN/NewsEvents/Pages/UDHRin370languages.aspx.

References

Altman, Jon C. 1987. *Hunter-Gatherers Today: An Aboriginal Economy in Northern Australia*. Canberra: Australian Aboriginal Studies Press.

Altman, Jon C., and Melinda Hinkson, eds. 2007. *Coercive Reconciliation: Stabilise, Normalise and Exit Aboriginal Australia*. Melbourne: Arena.

Altman, Jon C., and Melinda Hinkson. 2010. *Culture Crisis: Anthropology and Politics in Aboriginal Australia*. Sydney: UNSW Press.

Altman, Jon C., and Sean Kerins. 2012. *People on Country: Vital Landscapes / Indigenous Futures*. Annandale, NSW: Federation Press.

Attwood, Bain. 2003. *Rights for Aborigines*. St. Leonards, NSW: Allen and Unwin.

Austin-Broos, Diane. 2011. *A Different Inequality: The Politics of Debate about Remote Aboriginal Australia*. Crows Nest, NSW: Allen and Unwin.

Australian Anthropological Society. 2007. "Indigenous Rights: AAS Statement." *Australian Anthropological Society Newsletter*, no. 108, 1. http://www.aas.membes2.com.au/public/36/files/The%20Q%20Archive/101–110/108%20AAS%20Newsletter%20Dec%202007.pdf.

Australian Bureau of Statistics (ABS). 2017. *4517.0. Prisoners in Australia, 2017*. http://www.abs.gov.au/ausstats/abs@.nsf/mf/4517.0.

Batty, P. 2005. "Private Politics, Public Strategies: White Advisors and Their Aboriginal Subjects." In "Figuring the Intercultural in Aboriginal Australia," edited by Melinda Hinkson and Benjamin Smith, special issue, *Oceania* 75 (3): 209–11.

Beckett, Jeremy. 2010. "National Anthropologies and Their Problems." In *Culture Crisis: Anthropology and Politics in Aboriginal Australia*, edited by Jon Altman and Melinda Hinkson, 32–44. Sydney: University of New South Wales Press.

Bell, Diane. 1991. "Intra-racial Rape Revisited: On Forging a Feminist Future Beyond Factions and Frightening Politics." *Women's Studies International Forum* 14 (5): 385–412.

Bell, Diane, and Topsy N. Nelson. 1989. "Speaking About Rape Is Everyone's Business." *Women's Studies International Forum* 12 (4): 403–16.

Brady, Maggie. 1992. *Heavy Metal: The Social Meaning of Petrol Sniffing in Australia*. Canberra: Aboriginal Studies Press.

Brennan, Frank. 2009. Foreword to the *National Human Rights Consultation: Report*, by Human Rights Consultation Committee, v–vi. Barton, ACT: Commonwealth of Australia.

Brown, Wendy. 2000. "Suffering Rights as Paradoxes." *Constellations* 7 (2): 230–41.

Byrnes, Andrew, Hilary Charlesworth, and Gabrielle McKinnon. 2009. *Bills of Rights in Australia: History, Politics and Law*. Sydney: UNSW Press.

Cowlishaw, Gillian. 2004. *Blackfellas, Whitefellas, and the Hidden Injuries of Race*. Malden, MA: Blackwell.

Davis, Megan. 2007. "Arguing over Indigenous Rights: Australia and the United Nations." In *Coercive Reconciliation: Stabilise, Normalise, Exit Aboriginal Australia*, edited by Jon Altman and Melinda Hinkson, 97–107. Melbourne: Arena.

Davis, Megan. 2012. "An Alternative Framework for Re-Imagining Self-Determination." The NAARM Oration, Melbourne University, November 2012. http://sheilas.org.au/2012/12/an-alternative-framework/.

De Costa, R. 2006. *A Higher Authority: Indigenous Transnationalism and Australia*. Sydney: UNSW Press.

Easterly, William. 2007. *White Man's Burden: Why the West's Effort to Aid the Rest Have Done So Much Ill and So Little Good*. New York: Oxford University Press.

Edmunds, Mary. 2010. "The Northern Territory Intervention and Human Rights: An Anthropological Perspective." Perspectives 3, Whitlam Institute, University of Western Sydney, November 30, 2010. https://jenna-beck-f8w5.squarespace.com/publications/the-northern-territory-intervention-and-human-rights?rq=Perspectives.

Goodale, Mark. 2012. "Human Rights." In *A Companion to Moral Anthropology*, edited by Didier Fassin, 468. Malden, MA: Wiley Blackwell.

Gundogdu, Ayten. 2011. "Perplexities on the Rights of Man: Arendt on the Aporias of Human Rights." *European Journal of Political Theory* 11 (1): 4–24.

Hage, Ghassan. 2012. "Truncating Anthropology's Political Imagination." *Australian Journal of Anthropology* 23:406–12.

Hage, Ghassan, and Robyn Eckersley. 2012. *Responsibility*. Carlton, VIC: Melbourne University Press.

Hinkson, Melinda. 2010. "Introduction: Anthropology and the Culture Wars." In *Culture Crisis: Anthropology and Politics in Aboriginal Australia*, edited by Jon C. Altman and Melinda Hinkson, 1–13. Sydney: UNSW Press.

Hinkson, Melinda, and Benjamin Smith, eds. 2005. "Figuring the Intercultural in Aboriginal Australia." Special issue, *Oceania* 75 (3).
Holcombe, Sarah. 2004. "The Politico-Historical Construction of the Pintupi-Luritja and the Concept of Tribe." *Oceania* 74 (4): 257–75.
Holcombe, Sarah. 2005. "Luritja Management of the State." In "Figuring the Intercultural in Aboriginal Australia," edited by Melinda Hinkson and Benjamin Smith, special issue, *Oceania* 75 (3): 222–33.
Holcombe, Sarah. 2014. "The Contingency of 'Rights': Locating a Transnational Discourse in Aboriginal Central Australia." *Australian Journal of Anthropology*. Published online ahead of print, August 19, 2014, http://onlinelibrary.wiley.com/doi/10.1111/taja.12100/pdf.
Holcombe, Sarah. 2015. "The Revealing Processes of Interpretation: Translating Human Rights Principles into Pintupi-Luritja." In "Anthropology and Morality," edited by I. Keen and B. Blakeman, special issue, *Australian Journal of Anthropology* 26 (3): 428–41.
Huggins, J., J. Willmott, I. Tarrago, K. Willetts, L. Bond, L. Holt, E. Bourke, M. Bin-Salik, P. Fowell, J. Schmider, V. Craigie, and L. Levi-McBride. 1991. Letters to the Editor. *Women's Studies International Forum* 14 (5): 506–13.
Hughes, H. 2007. *Lands of Shame: Aboriginal and Torres Strait Islander "Homelands" in Transition*. Sydney: Centre for Independent Studies.
Human Rights Consultation Committee. 2009. *National Human Rights Consultation: Report*. 2009. Barton, ACT: Commonwealth of Australia.
Johns, Gary. 2011. *Aboriginal Self-Determination: A White Man's Dream*. Ballan, VIC: Connorcourt.
Klein, Renate. 1991. Editorial. *Women's Studies International Forum* 14 (5): 505–6.
Langton, Marcia. 2007. "Trapped in the Aboriginal Reality Show." *Griffith Review*, no. 19, 143–59.
Langton, Marcia. 2008. "The End of Big Men Politics." *Griffith Review*, no. 22, 13–38.
Langton, Marcia. 2010. "The Shock of the New: The Post-colonial Dilemma for Australian Anthropology." In *Culture Crisis: Anthropology and Politics in Aboriginal Australia*, edited by Jon C. Altman and Melinda Hinkson, 91–115. Sydney: UNSW Press.
McKnight, David. 2002. *From Hunting to Drinking: The Devastating Effects of Alcohol on an Australian Aboriginal Community*. London: Routledge.
Merlan, Francesca. 2005. "Explorations Towards Intercultural Accounts of Socio-Cultural Reproduction and Change." In "Figuring the Intercultural in Aboriginal Australia," edited by Melinda Hinkson and Benjamin Smith, special issue, *Oceania* 75 (3): 167–82.
Merlan, Francesca. 2009. "More than Rights." *Inside Story*, March 11, 2009. https://insidestory.org.au/more-than-rights/.
Merry, Sally E. 2006a. *Human Rights and Gender Violence: Translating International Law into Local Justice*. Chicago: University of Chicago Press.
Merry, Sally E. 2006b. "Transnational Human Rights and Local Activism: Mapping the Middle." *American Anthropologist* 108 (1): 38–51.

Moreton-Robinson, Aileen. 2000. *Talkin' up to the White Woman: Indigenous Women and Feminism*. St. Lucia: University of Queensland Press.
Moreton-Robinson, Aileen. 2013. "Towards an Indigenous Women's Standpoint Theory." *Australian Feminist Studies* 28 (78): 331–47.
Myers, Fred R. 1986. *Pintupi Country, Pintupi Self: Sentiment, Place, and Politics Among Western Desert Aborigines*. Canberra: Australian Institute of Aboriginal Studies.
Myers, Fred R. 1988. "Burning the Truck and Holding the Country: Property, Time and the Negotiation of Identity Among Pintupi Aborigines." In *Hunters and Gatherers 2: Property, Power and Ideology*, edited by Tim Ingold, David Riches, and James Woodburn, 52–74. Oxford: Berg.
Niezen, Ronald. 2003. *The Origins of Indigenism: Human Rights and the Politics of Identity*. Berkeley: University of California Press.
Northern Territory Board of Inquiry into the Protection of Aboriginal Children from Sexual Abuse. 2007. *Ampe Akelyerenmane Meke Mekarle, "Little Children Are Sacred."* Darwin: Northern Territory Government of Australia.
Peterson, Nicolas, and Marcia Langton, eds. 1983. *Aborigines, Land and Land Rights*. Canberra: Australian Institute of Aboriginal Studies.
Pitarch, P., S. Speed, and X. L. Solano, eds. 2008. *Human Rights in the Maya Region*. Durham, NC: Duke University Press.
Povinelli, Elizabeth A. 2002. *The Cunning of Recognition: Indigenous Alterities and the Making of Australian Multiculturalism*. Durham, NC: Duke University Press.
Sharp, Jared. 2014. "Tackling Family Violence in the Northern Territory." Powerpoint presentation on behalf of the North Australian Aboriginal Justice Agency, at the Australian Institute of Criminology Crime Prevention and Communities Conference, Melbourne, June 10–11, 2014. http://www.aic.gov.au/media_library/conferences/2014-crimeprevention/presentations/tue-103-1600-Jared-Sharp.pdf.
Speed, S. 2006. "At the Crossroads of Human Rights and Anthropology: Toward a Critically Engaged Activist Research." *American Anthropologist* 108 (1): 66–76.
St. Denis, Verna. 2007. "Feminism Is for Everybody: Aboriginal Women, Feminism and Diversity." In *Making Space for Indigenous Feminism*, edited by Joyce A. Green, 33–52. Blackwood, NS: Fernwood.
Sullivan, P. 2011. *Belonging Together: Dealing with the Politics of Disenchantment in Australian Indigenous Policy*. Canberra: Aboriginal Studies Press.
Sutton, Peter. 2001. "The Politics of Suffering: Indigenous Policy in Australia Since the 1970s." *Anthropological Forum: A Journal of Social Anthropology and Comparative Sociology* 11 (2): 125–73.
Sutton, Peter. 2009. *The Politics of Suffering: Indigenous Australia and the End of the Liberal Consensus*. Carlton, VIC: Melbourne University Press.
Taylor, C. 1992. "The Politics of Recognition." In *Multiculturalism and the Politics of Recognition*, edited by A. Gutman, 25–73. Princeton, NJ: Princeton University Press.
Wacquant, Loïc. 2010. "Crafting the Neoliberal State: Workfare, Prisonfare and Social Insecurity." *Sociological Forum* 25 (2): 197–219.
Whyte, J. 2012. "On the Politics of Suffering." *Arena Magazine*, no. 118, 37–39.

Williams, G. 2010. "The Future of the Australian Bill of Rights Debate." Alice Tay Lecture on Law and Human Rights, Freilich Foundation, Australian National University, September 16, 2010. http://www.gtcentre.unsw.edu.au/sites/gtcentre.unsw.edu.au/files/mdocs/Alice_Tay_Lecture_2010.pdf.

Wright, A., ed. 1998. *Take Power Like This Old Man Here: An Anthology Celebrating Twenty Years of Land Rights in Central Australia.* Alice Springs, NT: Jukurrpa Books.

Epilogue

Grounded Allies: Acting-With, Regenerating Together

BRIAN NOBLE

Three Terrains of Action

In their introduction, my activist colleagues and fellow anthropologists R. Aída Hernández Castillo and Suzi Hutchings astutely lay forth the historical and contemporary milieus of the three nation-states in which our contributing authors are putting to work their expert support in the justice struggles of Indigenous peoples. In this epilogue, I draw from those contributions to detect the pragmatic and political consequences for decolonial action research. The allied research actions assembled here offer a highly flexible set of action-oriented research praxes for decolonial emancipation, as responses to the call for support from Indigenous peoples who continue to face oppression, dispossession, and injustice within these three colonially configured nation-states.

The abiding question for me, therefore, is, How might we begin to align the diversity of ways contributors take up the concerns and causes of Indigenous peoples in their struggles for freedom and self-determination? As my attempt to address this question, I lay out a series of critical *topoi*, or terrains of action, that coalesce in the assembled essays. These topoi are not single sites but instead comerging modes and distributed locales of action that organize or arise consistently across the cases presented here, and in which these actions in struggle play out.

The first topos is that of—*Antidotes from the Fourth World*—the common conviction to exercise curative actions against the forces of toxic coloniality met in all the milieus addressed. The Fourth World, a nascent worldwide Indigenous movement proposed by Secwepemc activist leader Chief George Manuel in the 1970s, is drawn on as a touchstone for thinking about the character and persistence of Indigenous peoples' efforts to enliven and press forward such decolonial antidotes in shared struggle.

The second topos—*Decolonial Acting-With / Methods of Intervention*—is more pointedly about practices, captured by the conjunction *acting-with*. These are specific decolonial techniques of intervening—I use the term *methods*, but these practices are something other, beyond, and more flexible than mere methods. They are the techniques of critically considered, deeply respectful action research conducted in the alliances of anthropological experts with Indigenous peoples, communities, and persons as witnessed in the contributing chapters

The third and culminating topos presented—*Regenerating, Regrounding Together*—gestures to the conjoining of polities—Indigenous to settler or non-Indigenous—along the lines of treaty relationality as discussed by Sherry Pictou in this volume, but apparent in varying degrees in the exposés of all the contributing authors. This move of allied researchers situates and activates each of us in our respective polities, mindful of the larger demand to supersede and cogenerate substantive ethical-political alternatives to capitalist nation-state hegemonies.

Before I move to discussing the antidotes topos, I wish to offer a few other overarching observations about the contributions. First, these accounts are all *grounded* in the land and lives of Indigenous peoples. They are relayed in stories, experiences, dialogues, and alliances of, by, and with peoples who have lived relational lives—often disrupted ones—in their respective territories prior to European arrival and subsequent dispossession. At the same time, all these Indigenous peoples are witnessing an active resurgence in efforts to sustain and intensify their relational ways of being in their lands, even while subjected to the often-brutal vagaries of colonial and state control. As such, all these accounts may be set against these Indigenous peoples' undying practices of freedom and self-determination on and with the lands, and with all the human and more-than-human beings who also occupy these lands. These echo the commitments to a praxis of *grounded normativity*, the overall contours of which have been posited by Yellowknives Déné scholar Glen Sean Coulthard and Michi Saagiig Nishnaabeg writer-activist Leanne Betasamosake Simpson, who write, "Our relationship to the land itself generates the processes, practices, and knowledges that inform our political systems, and through which we practice solidarity" (Coulthard and Simpson 2016, 254; see also Asch et al. 2018).

A second key dimension of this volume to foreground is that of women's action research praxes. This volume's strength is marked by Indigenous and non-Indigenous women's interventionist presence throughout: two of the three Indigenous contributors are women, and in total, six of the nine contributors to the volume are women. This points to another vital decolonizing move accelerating recently—both in the academy and in the renewed resurgence movements of Indigenous peoples—around the rise of women at the forefront of these decolonial actions.

My attention in considering all three topoi will be to foreground the intricate movements of thought and practice between and among the authors, both in their local nation-state context, and between those state contexts. Drawing out the words and ideas of the contributors helps then to highlight the rich borrowing, cross-fertilization, and mutuality of research action—and ethical-political commitment—resonating across these three milieus. To some extent, there will be some mirroring back to observations from my colleagues in their introductory chapter, but with a more particular aim to delineate operative conditions and praxes. Surfacing through all this is an elaborate ricochet of practices that are giving shape to a richly transformative moment of engaged research alliances coming from Indigenous peoples themselves, and emerging *between* action-committed anthropologists and the Indigenous peoples with whom we are in such close, vital, and supportive dialogues.

Antidotes from the Fourth World (First Topos)

ANTIDOTES

All the contributing scholars to this volume—including me—have been through the trials of being caught in the politics of the colonial encounter, caught between the possibility of emancipation and the continuing constraints of living in what contributors call variously the *neoliberal state*, the *settler state*, the *capitalist state*—Mexico, Canada, and Australia fit each of those bills in varying ways.

These chapters also share a certain commonality of sought-after effect. Each of the contributors, in their own way, seeks a cure, a remedy, a corrective to the complex sources of oppression inflicted on Indigenous peoples—they seek antidotes.

But antidotes to what? In a word: coloniality.

Echoing many of the senses developed by Latin American decolonial scholars, I have written elsewhere that *coloniality* is an insidious political praxis that works by way of asymmetrical power relations both in "oppositional encounters that are difficult to reconcile" and as an encompassing and controlling "apparatus or milieu imposing coordinates of potentially divisive thought upon us, thereby conditioning and often disrupting the possibility of our working together as peoples" (Noble 2015a, 413).[1] Coloniality frames and sustains the power relations of the colonizer and the colonized, as well as the middle position from which we seek to dissolve these inequalities.

All the contributors to this volume, in varying ways, are intimately engaging with the violence or oppressions from this colonial *between*. From there, all have come to understand particular conditions of the toxicity of neocolonial power relations, which exist in the "muddy middle ground" as Canadian L. Jane McMillan put it in her chapter, or when "caught in the middle," as Arrernte anthropologist Suzi Hutchings named it in titling hers. From there, they have also achieved clarity about the specific challenges of overcoming this toxicity of relations and the apparatuses of imposition—helping them to conceive and devise the right concoctions, the most effective antidotes to meet these challenges in their situated specificity.

Likewise, each of the authors brings detailed empirical knowledges of how and why the locally specific conditions of coloniality persist, shift, and get reproduced. Immersive ethnographic intimacy enables them to be responsive and effective in this regard. Consequently, each also identifies the emergent practices of freedom, or resistance, that Indigenous peoples enact and seek to cultivate.

Crucially, the action research approaches laid forth in each of the chapters consistently operate by a collaborative ethos—decolonial alliances between Indigenous persons and peoples and action-engaged anthropologists. Working as "allied anthropologists," to borrow McMillan's term, with Indigenous peoples creates a mutuality of immersion in action against the conditioning political project of multiple colonialities—finding solidarity further in sharing the burden of personal and professional cost to be paid for taking an activist stance. Our situated alliances bring us variant antidotes to variant colonialisms, and add to the curative potency of the decolonial, antidotal agents and procedures that each of the contributors discusses.

So much turns ultimately on connections to—or disconnections by colonial disruption from—the land. Recalling again my colleagues' opening remarks, the political histories of the encompassing states very much condition the modes of decolonial possibility in different ways, and in far more complexity than we are able to capture in this single limited volume. For Indigenous peoples, land relations, tenure, and authority become an unavoidable locus to think with. For instance, Canada's recognition politics (Coulthard 2014) are yet deeply colonial in character, still presuming the supreme authority of "the Crown" (i.e., now assumed by federal and provincial legislatures), while yielding no legitimate room to date on Indigenous peoples' jurisdiction over their territories—if allowing modest opening to *coadministration*, as in the case of the James Bay Crees discussed by Colin Scott (this volume). Indeed, some observers argue that Canada's approach on matters of Indigenous land recognition is little more than an intricate, liberal political rights termination process (Diabo 2018).

In regard to Australia and land rights, as Hutchings notes in her contribution, although *terra nullius* principles may have been set aside in the Mabo decision, native title declarations remain elusive and vexing to obtain for many Indigenous peoples, while, like Canada, such affirmations are substantively at the behest of cumbersome state decision processes and subordinate to state sovereign authority (see also Noble 2008, 476–78). In Mexico, the question of land tenure and related rights has been pushed so substantially to the margins by state privatization and other subordinating praxes such as dispossession by megaprojects (Bastian Duarte and Vasundhara 2018), that we see decolonial action far more often in the form of organized protest and conflict, solidarity among allied groups, cultural and new media interventions, and directed involvement in arenas of the legal and justice system—as intricately detailed in the contributions of Llanes-Ortiz, Leyva Solano, and Hernández Castillo.

The violence of state *misrecognition* both in law and politics could not be more blatantly stated than in Jane McMillan's remark on the case of Donald Marshall Jr.'s wrongful conviction as "a story so horrifying in its revelations of blatant and systemic racism, in policing specifically and more broadly in the justice system, that it shook the foundations of the courts and exposed the extensive unequal treatment of Indigenous peoples before the law." I call attention to these aspects of land relations and recognition politics, as they will resurface throughout my discussion, most notably in the second topos, acting-with, where I sample the specific modes of activist decolonial praxis within each of these state milieus.

FOURTH WORLD REDUX

The situation in Mexico, Canada, and Australia can still largely be characterized as colonialism, all the way down, with the hegemon of state power always looming over Indigenous lives, lands, and bodies. But while these colonialisms persist, cutting across them and bringing them into wider conversation is the activist work of Indigenous peoples themselves. Indeed, the interconnectedness facilitated over several decades of transnational Indigenous activism is perhaps the most potent source of decolonial antidotal action (Manuel and Derrickson 2017). I take up the Fourth World movement as a critical counter-milieu to the colonial state hegemonies faced by all in this volume.

The Fourth World movement, explained by Secwepemc leader George Manuel and Michael Posluns in their 1974 soon to be republished book *The Fourth World: An Indian Reality*, sought in its time to offer a new "middle ground," as Anthony Hall (2003, 238–45) has noted, and echoes conditions we have witnessed in this volume. Manuel actively sought "alternatives for coexistence that would take place in the Fourth World—an alternative to the new world, the old world, and the Third World," which he posited as "the place occupied by Indigenous nations within colonial nation-states."[2] Manuel took strong inspiration from Indigenous activists the world over—reaching from Africa, Norway, and Australia—and then further shared this activism in many countries, most notably during speaking tours in Latin America in the 1980s. At heart, his vision of coexistence, had room for progressive, engaged anthropologists—as are all the contributors in this volume—who came when asked to the aid of Indigenous peoples in their anticolonial struggles. He contrasted those, however, with the majority up to that point, who came only to study Indigenous peoples and gave nothing back, as Vine Deloria so famously noted (1969).[3]

Manuel wrote almost fifty years ago of the fact of resurgence in the face of coloniality, as if foreseeing the contemporary moment of transnational Indigenous activism we are witness to in 2019. With some notable adjustments to then-current concerns, his words presaged the very conditions considered in this volume:

> It is very much a mistake to identify the cultural and political renaissance that is going on among Indian societies today as a new Indian resistance. The fact of the matter is that there was never a time since the beginning of colonial conquest when Indian people were not resisting the four destructive forces besetting us: the state through the Indian agent; the church through the priests; the church and state through the schools; the state and industry through the traders.
>
> Today's renaissance can be seen in the resurgence of our languages, in the growth of political institutions both old and new, in the revival of Indian relation

in urban Indian centres as well as on the reserves, in the growing number of young people seeking out the wisdom of the grandfathers and finding ways to apply it in their own lives, however different their lives may appear from the old ways. These are the real signs of the renaissance; there is no separation between the cultural artifacts—the drums, totem poles, and moccasins anyone can collect—and the day to day life in which the culture is evident, through the work, or family life, words of friendship, and music.

The renaissance of today is the fruit of the accumulated labour of our grandfathers. (Manuel and Posluns 1974, 69–70)

Manuel's identification of this transnational "fourth space" of political action was revolutionary for the times and helped set in motion the wider development of transnational Indigenous activist movements. Consider the multiplicity of these movements: the National Indian Brotherhood, the forty-thousand-strong bicentenary Indigenous protests of 1988 in Sydney, the Zapatista Army of National Liberation (EZLN) in Chiapas. Today we witness many other pan-Indigenous local and transnational movements across the Fourth World; the women-inspired Idle No More movement in North America and the localized movements from Mexico described by Hernández Castillo, Leyva Solano, and Llanes-Ortiz are part of this potent counter-landscape to state colonial conditions, inspiring other decolonial possibilities.

Considered in these broader terms, a generative space for sourcing and trading in potential antidotes comes from the diasporic and transnational connections of these activist networks. With this Fourth World sourcing of antidotes, we can consider the contributions to this volume as bearing witness to a transformative and resurgent Fourth World ethos and milieu, one in which engaged anthropologists are modulating their own practices, from the shared *colonial between*, resulting in new relations of decolonial activism within the three state settings of Canada, Mexico, and Australia.

With these motivations and conditions posed as the working milieus of the contributors, I now move to my second topos, that of decolonial acting-with.

Decolonial Acting-With / Methods of Intervention (Second Topos)

These decolonial methods of intervention derive, in part at least, from two key potencies of anthropological engagement, first in being immersed in justice-seeking political dialogues with Indigenous peoples (whether we are Indigenous or newcomer-descendants in Indigenous lands); and second in responding, beyond the normative distancing constraints of academic documentation and critique, to specific emancipatory action moves.

The abiding ethos of all the Indigenous-allied anthropologists working from within this political-legal middle ground is a practice that I call *acting-with*. By that I mean something different from classic "collaboration," which might simply be thought of as two or more people working together toward a common goal. Rather, the crucial distinction in acting-with is the grounding of research action in a deep, reflexive orientation of *respect* for the thinking, struggles, political and legal situations, knowing, embodied experiences, and idioms of practice of Indigenous peoples with whom we are in dialogue (see Asch 2015; Noble 2008). Such an orientation is a requisite to acting-with. Correspondingly, in Joshua Smith's compelling intellectual history of the long-marginalized *action anthropology* associated with American anthropologist Sol Tax, he notes that this kind of engagement must "necessarily engage with or theorize the state's history and coloniality as a starting point" (Smith 2015, 453)—as do all in this volume. Gesturing to the political nuance of this move, Smith contends further that collaboration without such engagement risks reproducing "the very configurations of the liberal state's colonial power that Indigenous demands have sought to transcend" (Smith 453).

With this as my starting point, in what follows, I return to the texts of our contributors to identify and draw out examples of an array of decolonial acting-with methods that emerge repeatedly in their actions. The scholars captured in this volume engage the colonial and decolonial simultaneously; they are resilient in the face of colonial discomfort. They rethink normative praxes, they disrupt, they refuse. They are open to ontic politics. They mobilize alternative media and they use their own expertise to unsettle the status quo. Finally, they reoccupy elided spaces and practices as they work to generate a decolonized world. The elaboration on these themes that follows constitutes a contingent but emergent toolkit of allied and grounded decolonial research.

ENGAGING THE COLONIAL AND THE DECOLONIAL AT ONCE

> Intersections bound by neoliberal colonial capitalism raise a challenge for Indigenous researchers in evoking decolonizing approaches to research while maintaining a relational responsibility to our communities and to the academic institutions under which research is being pursued. (Pictou, this volume)

Sherry Pictou's comment makes resoundingly clear the dialogic research challenge of engaging the colonial in its current neoliberal and capitalist formulation. Even when pointing to the colonial, however, Pictou also invokes the decolonizing Fourth World resurgence ethos discussed previously, in her attunement to the "relational responsibility to our communities."

Aída Hernández Castillo's piece in this volume also demonstrates this double commitment for challenging the colonial setup but then responding with critical interventions She underscored her efforts to "maintain a permanent critical reflection on the law and rights, while participating in initiatives that support struggles for justice for indigenous peoples and organizations, appropriating and resignifying national and international legislation." The local colonial context sets the stage for the consequent actions of all our contributors, as each seeks decolonial tools and moves best suited to the job at hand.

RESILIENCE TO COLONIAL DISCOMFORT

Engaging colonial and decolonial milieus often takes a toll, generating uncertainty and discomfort. This is part of the terrain of action. Suzi Hutchings describes how the colonial setup too often sets the stage for failure, leading her to ask the unnerving question, "Will Indigenous Australians be forever caught within the reconciliation gap of mere recognition by the state?" The brutality of this discomfort becomes clearest when Indigenous anthropologists and Indigenous claimants themselves face extreme discomfort, as, for example, in native title adjudications and formal processes where "those claimants who are most affected by the history of colonialism in Australia inevitably face skepticism from lawyers, judges, and anthropologists, who suspect that their knowledge is inauthentic and likely fabricated to suit their inclusion in the native title process in order to gain monetary benefits from 'walking the line' for mining and development companies." Part of the extended toolkit, therefore, of engaging the colonial is a much needed resilience to deal with the prospect of deep discomfort when we are "tripped up" by the power asymmetries that structure the recognition apparatus's constitution (Noble 2015b). Sarah Holcombe is equally uncomfortable with the limitations of the land recognition engagement for anthropologists, but from a different angle. She shows how Australian anthropology since the 1970s has become increasingly narrow by specializing in the land "recognition space," and seeks to shake up this disciplinary positioning: "With the recognition of native title following the Mabo decision in 1992, even more anthropologists became involved in writing claims for native title recognition or assisting with heritage clearances to facilitate land-use agreements. The comfort of this historical fit, however, has since been called into question, principally from within the discipline." The particularities of discomfort are always linked to the particularities of inequalities in the encounter, as Aída Hernández Castillo identifies with reference to power differences in her prison work:

> Despite our position as allies of the women in prison, in our role as coordinators of the workshops and members of the Sisters of the Shadow Publishing Collective, our dialogues with them have been marked by our ethnic and class differences. Nonetheless, by maintaining a permanent dialogue on the "why" of the life histories and testimonies, we have been able to somewhat compensate for these structural inequalities by turning these textual strategies into collective forms of knowledge production.

In this, Hernández Castillo confronts the disjuncture and discomfort of difference and power with full reflexive consideration, joining with the imprisoned allies in strategies that move them together in a generative way.

RETHINKING NORMATIVE PRAXES

All this, in turn, frames a constitutive opposition to the normative praxes of anthropology, some of which I have alluded to already. Each of the contributors seeks room for maneuver within the milieus in which they ally, recognizing that modern practices of knowledge production themselves are part of the problem, and must be replaced or at least modulated to achieve decolonial effectiveness. Hernández Castillo's practical feminist legal interventions set normative praxes of anthropological, justice, and Indigenous gender orthodoxies into high relief, part of a commitment to hone more nuanced and responsive approaches to justice efforts.

Echoing this orientation, Mi'kmaw resurgence activist and scholar Sherry Pictou saw how the academy's normative limitations of discounting the colonial setup would not square with the everyday struggles of her community engagements when she asks, "If I was finding it difficult to situate my experience with L'sɨtkuk and our allies in the academy, how was I going to undertake research that proposed to do the same?" Once more, the conditions of colonial encounter and milieu reach into every setting of engagement, both among the author's own people and in the dominant settings of research praxis. The demands of acting-with shift considerably from locale to locale, situation to situation, and in a pervasive way. Genner Llanes-Ortiz's observations resonate with this in seeking allied research beyond normative collaboration and toward "a more complex form of 'respectful conversation'—or *tsikbal* in Yukatek Maya," in which kin-responsive relational modes of praxis trouble and displace knowledge production as usual.

DISRUPTING AND REFUSING

When taken up consciously, such moves against the normative orders of the hegemon can be understood as *methods* or *modes of disruption*. This applies equally whether aimed against state practice, coloniality, disciplinary convention, gendered and classed positionality, liberal and neoliberal accommodation, conscripted Indigenous lifeways, or modern modes of thought themselves. Such moves are also predicated, at least in modest dialogical terms, on what Audra Simpson (2007) refers to as "refusal," which many Indigenous peoples live out when their lives and ways are either attacked or conscripted, without their consent, by the state as means to subsume them within the state's assumed sovereignty. Such refusals are present in all three nation-state situations in which our authors conduct research.

Suzi Hutchings concludes her chapter with the injunction to disruption as the pragmatic modus operandus of decolonizing work: "For Aboriginal people who disrupt the norm of state definitions of aboriginality, but who, in contemporary Australia, challenge this norm by taking up a sovereign position as Indigenous through their very being, is this where decolonization begins and continues?" The question is rhetorical, and an explicit challenge to those (Indigenous and non-Indigenous) engaging in current debates on the value of reconciliation in Australia, pointing to a resounding *yes*. Echoing Sherry Pictou's concerns to reckon with the expansive hegemony of "neoliberal colonial capitalism," Xochitl Leyva Solano likewise adopts a refusalist stance within the contours of a more heterogeneous activist-political project. She calls for the "insurrection of subjugated knowledges [as] part of the alternative globalization from below, which expresses itself in epistemic-ethical-ontological struggles that are part and parcel of resistance, autonomy by right, and the defense of life and territory." Put simply, refusing and disrupting that which colonizes supports and amplifies that which decolonizes.

OPENING TO ONTIC POLITICS

Leyva Solano's eliciting of "epistemic-ethical-ontological struggles" moves us to yet another frame of anthropological, activist concern that has been accelerating throughout the past decade—that of *ontic politics* (Verran 2001), or as Mario Blaser (2014) and Marisol de la Cadena (2010) have focused, the concern of "political ontologies" (also see Viveiros de Castro 2004). This has been a point of direct dialogue among the engaged anthropologies of Latin America, Canada, and Australia (also see Clammer, Poirier, and Schwimmer 2004).

Colin Scott directly engages the demand to embrace alternative ontologies—beingness—not as matters of differing cultural beliefs, but as active force conditions in the constituting of "worlds." This move aligns with the depth of responsiveness engendered by the acting-with methodological orientation.

The concern with alternate or shifting ontologies—and their political consequences—arises especially in work with those Indigenous peoples who have been able to sustain strong relational praxes with the land. They invoke the many more-than-human beings in their territories—from agentful ancestors and animals, to unseen forces called forth and acting on us and the world in which our encounters unfold. To once again invoke the Zapatista slogan from the introduction, this is a transformative horizon in world anthropologies of late, enabling the collective, dialogical cogenerating of a "world where many worlds may fit."

MOBILIZING ALTERNATIVE MEDIA

Our contributors from Mexico, Genner Llanes-Ortiz and Xochitl Leyva Solano, exemplify the generative, interruptive potential of new and alternative media. Leyva Solano discusses her project "to work, organize, and create together a multimedia and multilanguage book using the written and the spoken word, photos and painting reproductions, as well as three Mayan languages and Spanish. We baptized our creation with the Maya name *Sjalel kibeltik*, which can be translated as 'weaving our roots.'"

New media is also taken up in the course of decolonial acting-with commitments, as a means for making relations that connect people, and so displacing disconnective ones. The deployment of creative projects, art and media, saw a successful rise in the 1990s, in the actions of the EZLN and Zapatismo (Khasnabish)—the hybrid continuation of which we witness in the strong collective, dialogical, and kin-making projects of the Mexico-based contributors to this volume.

UNSETTLING BY MEANS OF EXPERTISE

Of course, all who are engaged in these allied-anthropological engagements understand the power of the privilege and status accorded to expertise. Moreover, inhabiting the middle position pulls us closer to the people with whom we research. The result is a more genuine connection, an intensified empirical veracity—what feminist science studies scholar Sandra Harding (1993) has referred to as "strong objectivity," which emerges through engaging a multitude of assembled partial perspectives.

That said, in certain situations, as in the case of expert witnessing in juridical and quasi-juridical settings, classic modes of practiced expertise—documentary interviews, archival documentation, oral histories—are often the most effective knowledge forms. This is evident in Hernández Castillo's long involvements in "elaboration of anthropological expert witness reports in support of the defense of indigenous women in national and international legal actions" and in Hutchings's expert witnessing roles in native title claims cases. Similarly, Jane McMillan locates her activist research within well-proven methodological frameworks, writing, "Engaged and applied research methodologies work to counter the denial of the consequences of colonialism, cultural disruption, and oppression and focus on stemming the erosion of gender and generational logic through community-capacity rebuilding in customary legal enactments and institution building."

The shift or modulation from established praxis to decolonial praxis, however, is often subtle and gradual. New possibilities of modern colonial interruptions via methodological shifts arise from working in coloniality-sensitized partnership. As Hernández Castillo remarked on her collective's work, "Transforming the old role of writers and anthropologists as 'narrators of the life histories of other women' into that of partners in processes to systematize Indigenous women's own history, and even in the creation of their own publishing projects, has been a part of our efforts to build and consolidate spaces for a collective construction of knowledge." Colin Scott shows the reciprocal effect of partnering in unsettling usual modes of expertise, when "acknowledging a possibility inherent in the 'open-ended' quality of all cultural construction: we need not construe ontologies only as radically distinctive, incommensurable cultural visions in the plural; rather, dialogues of difference may converge on mutually recognizable truths about our being and relationship in the world, specifically laws of respect and reciprocity that, in the perspective of many of our Cree partners, bind us universally."

This productive susceptibility to have ourselves and our methods and practices changed by responsive acting-with is also clear in the contributions of McMillan and Llanes-Ortiz. McMillan points out how she strategically deploys or adjusts her practice in invoking "concepts of law and justice in the daily struggles of Indigenous peoples as they fight to rupture patterns of dependency, challenge inequality, and invest in or resist alliances and autonomy." Llanes-Ortiz notes how just sharing between two interlocutors as partners didn't necessarily capture the translational dynamics at play. This implies a need for adjusted methods: "I had come to realize that creating a space for *intercultural dialogue* between Maya and non-Maya partners was—clearly—easier said than done. In this same process, I began to understand that collaborative researching demanded an intercultural methodology as well." Our very performing in the acting-with ethos pushes us to make methodological adjustments responsively at every turn, thereby reconstituting the modes of expertise. Hernández Castillo also points to the integrative potency of dialogical interculturality beyond mere partnering, noting how the "possibility of establishing intercultural dialogues around rights and justice not only questions the state's regulatory discourses but is also an opportunity to destabilize our certainties and broaden our emancipatory horizons."

REOCCUPYING ELIDED SPACES AND PRACTICES

Across all the chapters is a strongly recurring discussion of "spaces" of action—or more precisely, spaces *and* practices elided or otherwise ignored by colonial and state impositions of law, property, knowledge, power, and the "spaces" they configure. These are highly potent locations for decolonization, further opportunities for interruptive research partnering, and indicators of a ricochet of politically and morally engaged decolonial praxes in the two continents and three countries represented.

Jane McMillan's work takes up the elision of Mi'kmaw nationhood and laws, and the displacement of Indigenous fishing lifeways, by the imposition of Crown laws. Sherry Pictou calls out how the highly colonized "treaty tables" elide the true spirit of treaty relations as exercised by Mi'kmaw people, and seeks to decolonize these by reactivating what she refers to as "small *t* treaty" relations, after the propositions of James Tully. Hernández Castillo challenges penitentiary spaces to support the struggle and emancipation of incarcerated Indigenous activist women. Colin Scott's allied research with Crees seeks to reinforce "spaces for Cree lifeways and livelihoods, on terms that enhance rather than erode Cree autonomy." Leyva Solano works dynamically and *insurgently* in and across multiple *collective*, *autonomous*, *academic*, and *privileged* spaces.

Hutchings and Holcombe are both challenged by and seek antidotes to the restrictiveness of the "recognition spaces" of native title claims processes in Australia. Indeed, Sarah Holcombe offers a critical cautionary note to all with her injunction to *avoid* falling into the trap of overfetishizing "territory" when encountered as state-conscripted rights processes. In Australia, she notes, Indigenous people and anthropological experts have been drawn into the territory/title recognition space despite it being situated within the colonial ethos and apparatus. She and Suzi Hutchings both call for a stronger and more reflexive nuance in this terrain of action. Hutchings understands and details this poignantly, from her stance as both Indigenous person and anthropological expert.

Holcombe also demonstrates how other practices and spaces—those associated with violence against Indigenous women in Australia, especially in remote out-of-the-way communities—are obscured in multiple ways. One widely discussed example is gendered sexual violence, which takes place often hidden from public view in domestic settings and is made all the more invisible by the lack of reporting that results from victims' fear and distrust of colonial and oppressive police and policing institutions. Adding to this is how little attention such violence receives from anthropology, de facto elided by the overfocus of practice in land adjudication processes. This stages Holcombe's powerful argument for anthropology to foreground and *reoccupy* the elided spaces of human rights action, ones that may be applied in support of Indigenous women, and seek recourse that will alter conditions of gendered silencing that enable and allow violence to go unchecked. She adds explicitly how violence is hidden when framed as a domestic concern, not as a rights concern, remarking, "The issue of gender violence—often expressed in this remote context in terms of family and domestic violence—is one of the more pressing human rights issues in the Northern Territory."

In short, elided spaces and practices become locations for new knowledge and critical work: correcting for, reanimating, and reoccupying that which has been dismissed, erased, denigrated, or overlooked. They are spaces for regenerating and regrounding, the focus of my third and final topos of decolonial action.

Regrounding, Regenerating Together (Third Topos)

To bring this full circle, the first move I offered in looking back at the collected exposés was to situate them as decolonizing *antidotes* to state-imposed colonialities, which emerge in the context of resurgent Indigenous Fourth World political movements. The next move was to draw out the techniques, methods, and conditions of decolonial acting-with praxes that move within and between the approaches offered by the authors.

Now, I turn to *consequences for practices of freedom* of and by Indigenous peoples, enhanced by the productive and interruptive alliances with anthropologists—who, in turn, find freedom in refusing the colonial conventions of their disciplines and of the hegemonic political milieus in which they are practiced.[4]

I draw out two entwined consequences, which are also modes of praxis: the *regrounding* of Indigenous lives and worlds by *regenerating* good relations, as persons and as peoples. I also offer comment on how these consequences move us toward meeting the challenge set by our colleagues from the Committee on World Anthropologies—to decolonize our shared and diversely distributed disciplinary formation, anthropology.

REGROUNDING AND REGENERATING

Recalling Coulthard and Simpson's commitment to a political normativity grounded in Indigenous place and land relations, a critical consequence of the work presented throughout this volume is *regrounding* Indigenous lives and relations. This applies not solely to places and lands, but also to bodies and lives—the latter most notable in legal and moral inequities inflicted personally on those who stand up for their rights (see the cases presented in McMillan and in Hutchings) and those so brutally abjected by gendered and political violence from accessing even the barest justice or rights recourse (see the cases presented by Holcombe and Hernández Castillo). Supporting the formal pursuit of legal, political, land, Indigenous-based, and human rights is a critical pathway to regrounding—strengthening Indigenous peoples' capacities and resolve for exercising their political freedoms within and beyond the Fourth World ethos spoken of by George Manuel.

Sherry Pictou's call for a "relationality grounded in Indigenous knowledge and experience" highlights a crucial aspect of regrounding: restoring the pluralities of Indigenous knowing, language, kinship, and ontic relations, as self-determining practices—especially in the face of state histories disrupting these basic cultural and political freedoms. Reconnecting to land, place, and relations is made all the more imperative when those relational responsibilities have been so forcibly disrupted by ongoing coloniality. In Colin Scott's experience with the Cree Nations of Eeyou Istchee, he saw the power of relational dialogues, once more, to effect and strengthen self-determination by reciprocal, mutual respect.

But while hope in regrounding relations has been politically thinkable in the shifting decolonial political milieu of Canada / northern Turtle Island, the contributors from Mexico and Australia are more subdued on such potential. The recalcitrance of neocolonial state legal frameworks and political practices in those two countries creates conditions in which the work of allied research necessarily concentrates on resistance to, and interruption of, state-driven processes. Suzi Hutchings posits "that the link between Indigenous and academic knowledge is embodied at its most powerful in the personal," where conjoined work gives more space for Indigenous peoples to understand and articulate themselves and their struggles on their terms, not on those of academics or of state actors. In other words, in Mexico and Australia, action for engaged allied research is mostly situated at the register of the interpersonal.

What this contrast marks, in my view, is that the array of projects and the ricochet of strategies for allied research remains highly diverse and dynamic but necessarily and deeply situated in locality, history, place, and territory, and in relation to state-constrained conditions of possibility. That particularity is further intensified by the specificity of individual relationships between anthropologists and those with whom they undertake acting-with research. From all that is presented in this volume, the mutual, allied commitment to decolonize together remains perhaps the strongest source for thinking of regenerating relations, including regenerating the relational practices of engaged anthropology.

ALLYING TOGETHER, AS PERSONS AND PEOPLES

The final consequence emerging from the research efforts presented in this volume is how the research partnerships themselves—through whatever discomforts are encountered—generate newly promising horizontal and reciprocal relations of their own. Here, the continuity between what we do interpersonally in our research relations may also make possible alternative interpolitical relations.

As we've seen, the practice of learning-with and acting-with, decolonially, demands a mutuality between partners that can be transformative for both. One of the most poignant commentaries on this is in Genner Llanes-Ortiz's chapter, discussing his coming into mutual recognition with Maya activists through the role of *chan láak'* (little brother). He explores how taking on this role and then "performing" the Mayan "notion of e'esaj as a form of sharing, demonstrating, and partnering in the learning process" identifies and tethers him and his allies to kin-like obligation and reciprocity. The trade here is mutual. In "all these collaborative endeavors," he writes, "*e'esaj*-ing my research to and with both older and younger Maya activists has entailed translating and unpacking old-fashioned and problematic anthropological notions." Through such moves, he argues, "a body of Indigenous collaborative scholarship can be developed in order to fight discrimination and disempowerment, as well as to open up fruitful conversations with and for Indigenous rights demands." This is an instance of what some have referred to as *coproduction* of knowledge, but which we may also see as *cogeneration* of knowledge relations between peoples.

The resonance between Llanes-Ortiz's thinking and Sherry Pictou's are striking. She writes, "The alliance of Indigenous and anthropological perspectives as a decolonizing practice further addresses our Mi'kmaw/Indigenous experience, rooted in Indigenous knowledge and land-based practices for food and lifeways, as a concept of treaty against extended forms of colonialism, . . . which seek to undermine the very knowledges and practices the treaties were founded on." Pictou takes up the concept of treaty relations in an interruptive and generative way, stressing the reciprocity of methods when anthropologists engage with Indigenous political struggles. This broader application of treaty relations, Pictou points out, aligns "Indigenous and anthropological understandings of treaties as renewing relations and the responsibilities for ensuring reciprocal obligations among all people" (see also Noble 2018).

What is so powerful from the thinking and practice of these two Indigenous scholars is how both—even in their far-flung, apparently disconnected state milieus—speak to practices of freedom and self-determination through mutuality of engagement. This also braces the principle of self-determination as a relational process of mutual recognition that applies *both* to individual persons and to political collectivities, that is, to peoples—the latter a tenet explicitly laid out in the *United Nations Declaration of the Rights of Indigenous Peoples* (*UNDRIP*).

It is impossible to say whether and how the specific efforts offered by the authors in this volume might contribute to the transformative set of political changes we all seek—the full-scale self-determination of Indigenous peoples as envisioned in *UNDRIP*. But Colin Scott expresses a grounded, speculative hope that the relational generativity of acting-with research offers a larger promise: "common ground with a political ecology that associates the negative reciprocity of environmental exploitation with rampant capitalist growth. As researchers, we inhabit and elaborate this common ground, and we are led to ask, how much of our scientific tradition, modernist outlook, and institutional life more broadly may be rethought through such a paradigm?"

Through all the ricochet action visible in the works collected here, new shifts, new coalescences, and new matters of hope emerge. All the contributions also provide a decisive rebuke to Talal Asad's famous, but now rather problematic, claim that anthropology has somehow become "professionally at peace" with colonialism (Asad 1973, 18).[5] To the contrary, much of the decolonial hope provided in this volume is located in the potential of grounded, mutual alliances—what Sherry Pictou refers to in her local Mi'kmaw territorial situation as "small *t* treaty" relations. Such relations are abundantly evident in the reflexive, decolonial acting-with "methods" we have witnessed in the contributions to this volume, methods that lead to the decisive action of regrounding and regenerating together. These are, in my view, the most promising moves for expanding, locally animated decolonial world anthropologies.

The intense engagements and interventions offered in this volume from Australia, Mexico, and Canada align and indicate a potent turn toward effective Indigenous-allied anthropologies that hold considerable promise, in at least three critical ways. The first promise lies in in our increasing capacity to aid the practices of freedom of Indigenous peoples, transcontinentally, across an increasingly resurgent decolonizing Fourth World. The second promise is in how these moves are also inspiring new locally distinct yet partially shared anthropological praxes that respond effectively to decolonizing imperatives arising in many locales and transforming the academy in diverse ways around the world today.

The third and perhaps most consequential promise lies in how acting-with Indigenous peoples in their situated, deeply grounded struggles also helps us as anthropologists to imagine, if not generate, alternative interpeople and land relations—what James Tully (2018) has called a "double reconciliation" enacted "here on Earth." Such relations undercut the brutal antirelations of ongoing coloniality in each of the states considered in this volume, while enhancing respectful, nonexploitative relations among peoples and with the living lands and waters on which—quite simply—we all rely for survival.

Notes

1. By "Latin American decolonial scholars," I refer to the work of Quijano and Ennis (2000); Mignolo (2012); Escobar (2004); and Moraña, Dussel, and Jáuregui (2008) on the "coloniality of power."
2. Texts from the description page for the new edition on the University of Minnesota Press website, accessed May 22, 2018, https://www.upress.umn.edu/book-division/books/the-fourth-world.

3. See also Michael Asch's incisive article "Anthropology, Colonialism and the Reflexive Turn: Finding a Place to Stand" (2015).
4. The phrase "practices of freedom" is used in the sense provided by political philosopher James Tully (2002), which comes down to an empowering of self-determining agency of persons and of peoples. He writes of the "permanent task of making sure that the multiplicity of practices of governance in which we act together do not become closed structures of domination under settled forms of justice, but are always open to practices of freedom by which those subject to them have a say and a hand over" (552).
5. See Asad (1973, 18). In this, the contributing authors also give full expression to a vital, reflexive anticolonial commitment in many currents of anthropology that is too often elided in historical sketches and critiques of anthropological praxis, a matter long argued by political anthropologist Michael Asch (2015).

References

Asad, Talal. 1973. *Anthropology and the Colonial Encounter*. London: Ithaca Press.

Asch, Michael. 2015. "Anthropology, Colonialism and the Reflexive Turn: Finding a Place to Stand." *Anthropologica* 57 (2): 481–89.

Asch, Michael, John Borrows, and James Tully, eds. 2018. *Resurgence and Reconciliation: Indigenous–Settler Relations and Earth Teachings*. Toronto: University of Toronto Press.

Bastian Duarte, Angela Ixkic, and Jairath Vasundhara. 2018. "Dispossession and Resistance in India and Mexico." Ritimo, May 14, 2018. https://www.ritimo.org/Dispossession-and-Resistance-in-India-and-Mexico.

Blaser, Mario 2014. "Ontology and Indigeneity: On the Political Ontology of Heterogeneous Assemblages." *Cultural Geographies* 21 (1): 49–58.

Clammer, John, Sylvie Poirier, and Eric Schwimmer, eds. 2004. *Figured Worlds: Ontological Obstacles in Intercultural Relations*. Toronto: University of Toronto Press.

Coulthard, Glen Sean. 2014. *Red Skin, White Masks: Rejecting the Colonial Politics of Recognition*. Minneapolis: University of Minnesota Press.

Coulthard, Glen Sean, and Leanne Betasomosoke Simpson. 2016. "Grounded Normativity / Place-Based Solidarity." *American Quarterly* 68 (2): 249–55.

de la Cadena, Marisol. 2010. "Indigenous Cosmopolitics in the Andes: Conceptual Reflections Beyond 'Politics.'" *Cultural Anthropology* 25 (2): 334–70.

Deloria, Vine. 1969. *Custer Died for Your Sins: An Indian Manifesto*. New York: Avon.

Diabo, Russ. 2018. "Our Right of Indigenous Self-Determination Is Being Hijacked by Trudeau: Recognition and Implementation of Rights Framework." *First Nations Strategic Bulletin* 16 (1–3): 1–15. http://mediacoop.ca/sites/mediacoop.ca/files2/mc/fnsb_jan_mar_18.pdf.

Escobar, Arturo. 2004. "Beyond the Third World: Imperial Globality, Global Coloniality and Anti-Globalization Social Movements." *Third World Quarterly* 25 (1): 207–30.

Hall, Anthony J. 2003. *The American Empire and the Fourth World*. Montreal: McGill-Queen's University Press.

Harding, Sandra. 1993. "Rethinking Standpoint Epistemology: 'What is Strong Objectivity?'" In *Feminist Epistemologies*, edited by L. Alcoff and E. Potter, 49–82. New York: Routledge.

Khasnabish, Alex. 2008. *Zapatismo Beyond Borders*. Toronto: University of Toronto Press.

Manuel, Arthur, and G. C. Ron Derrickson. 2017. *The Reconciliation Manifesto: Recovering the Land and Rebuilding the Economy*. Toronto: Lorimer.

Manuel, George, and Michael Posluns. 1974. *The Fourth World: An Indian Reality*. New York: Collier Macmillan Canada.

Mignolo, Walter. 2012. *Local Histories / Global Designs: Coloniality, Subaltern Knowledges, and Border Thinking*. Princeton, NJ: Princeton University Press.

Moraña, Mabel, Enrique D. Dussel, and Carlos A. Jáuregui, eds. 2008. *Coloniality at Large: Latin America and the Postcolonial Debate*. Durham, NC: Duke University Press.

Noble, Brian. 2008. "Owning as Belonging/Owning as Property: The Crisis of Power and Respect in First Nations Heritage Transactions with Canada." In *First Nations Cultural Heritage and Law: Case Studies, Voices, and Perspectives*, edited by Catherine Bell and Val Napoleon, 465–88. Vancouver: UBC Press.

———. 2015a. "Consent, Collaboration, Treaty: Toward Anti-Colonial Praxis in Indigenous-Settler Research Relations." *Anthropologica* 57 (2): 411–17.

———. 2015b. "Tripped up by Coloniality: Anthropologists as Instruments or Agents in Indigenous-Settler Political Relations?" *Anthropologica* 57 (2): 427–43.

———. 2018. "Treaty-Ecologies: With Persons, Peoples, Animals and the Land." In *Resurgence and Reconciliation: Indigenous-Settler Relations and Earth Teachings*, edited by Michael Asch, John Borrows, and James Tully, 315–42. Toronto: University of Toronto Press.

Quijano, Anibal, and Michael Ennis. 2000. *Coloniality of Power, Eurocentrism, and Latin America*. Durham, NC: Duke University Press.

Salmond, Amiria. 2014. "Transforming translations (part 2): Addressing Ontological Alterity." *HAU: Journal of Ethnographic Theory*. 4(1): 155–187.

Scott, Colin. 2017. "The Endurance of Relational Ontology: Encounters between Eeyouch and Sport Hunters." In *Entangled Territorialities: Negotiating Indigenous Lands in Australia and Canada*, edited by Françoise Dussart and Sylvie Poirier, 51–69. Toronto: University of Toronto Press.

Simpson, Audra. 2007. "On Ethnographic Refusal: Indigeneity, 'Voice' and Colonial Citizenship." *Junctures*, December 9, 2007, 67–80.

Smith, Joshua. 2015. "Standing with Sol: The Spirit and Intent of Action Anthropology." *Anthropologica* 57 (2): 445–56.

Tully, James. 2002. "Political Philosophy as a Critical Activity." *Political Theory* 30 (4): 533–55.

———. 2018. "Reconciliation Here on Earth." In *Resurgence and Reconciliation: Indigenous-Settler Relations and Earth Teachings*, edited by Michael Asch, John Borrows, and James Tully, 81–129. Toronto: University of Toronto Press.

Verran, Helen. 2001. *Science and an African Logic*. Chicago: University of Chicago Press.

Viveiros de Castro, Eduardo. 2004. "Exchanging Perspectives: The Transformation of Objects into Subjects in Amerindian Ontologies." *Common Knowledge* 10 (3): 463–84.

CONTRIBUTORS

Rosalva Aída Hernández Castillo was born in Ensenada, Baja California, and earned her doctorate in anthropology from Stanford University in 1996. She is professor and senior researcher at the Center for Research and Advanced Studies in Social Anthropology in Mexico City. She has done field work in Indigenous communities in the Mexican states of Chiapas, Sinaloa, Guerrero, and Morelos, and with Guatemalan refugees and with African immigrants in the South of Spain. She has published twenty-two books, and her academic work has been translated to English, French, Portuguese, and Japanese. Her more recent book, *Multiple Injustices: Indigenous Women, Law, and Political Struggle in Latin America*, was published by the University of Arizona Press. She is recipient of the Martin Diskin Oxfam Award for her activist research and of the Simon Bolivar Chair (2013–2014), granted by Cambridge University, for her academic work.

Sarah Holcombe is a social anthropologist with more than twenty years' experience working with Aboriginal peoples in Australia, within NGOs and at the Australian National University in several research centers, including the Centre for Aboriginal Economic Policy Research (where she was also the social science coordinator for the Desert Knowledge Cooperative Research Centre) and the National Centre for Indigenous Studies. She has published widely on a diverse range of issues, including human rights and intersectional challenges to implementation, extractive industries and sustainable development, social exclusion, marginality, postcoloniality, gender violence, Aboriginal community governance, service delivery in remote settlements, and the ethical governance of intellectual property and collaborative knowledges. Sarah's anthropological method unsettles the ground between anthropologist as advocate and change agent and anthropologist as practicing a discursive science. Sarah is currently a senior fellow at the University of Queensland, and her latest book is *Remote Freedoms: Politics, Personhood and Human Rights in Aboriginal Central Australia*.

Suzi Hutchings is a social anthropologist. She has worked with Indigenous peoples in Australia for more than twenty years in the fields of native title, social justice, and identity politics. She is a member of the Central Arrernte peoples of the Northern Territory. As an expert witness, Suzi has produced many government and court reports. She has also published on Aboriginal heritage and land matters, youth and criminal justice, and Indigenous youth music. She has been the recipient of prestigious research grants, including an Endeavour Research Fellowship for Indigenous Australians, with a placement at New York University to investigate the social messages and styles of minority hip-hop music, art, and performance. Suzi also produces the radio program *Crossing Tracks* for community radio in Australia. She is currently teaching at senior level in criminology and justice studies in the School of Global, Urban and Social Studies at RMIT University in Melbourne.

Xochitl Leyva Solano is a barefoot feminist, a member of antisystemic networks as well as those practicing collaborative and decolonizing research, a researcher and professor at the Center for Research and Advanced Studies in Social Anthropology located in San Cristóbal de Las Casas, Chiapas (Mexico). She has published in Mayan, Spanish, English, French, and Finnish on several continents. Over three decades, her work has been with Indigenous people (women and youth, mainly) from communities in resistance. Among other books, she has co-edited *Human Rights in the Mayan Region* and *Anthropological Encounters: Power, Identity and Mobility in Mexican Society*.

Genner Llanes-Ortiz is a Maya scholar from Yucatán, Mexico. He trained as a social anthropologist at the Universidad Autónoma de Yucatán and completed a DPhil in social anthropology in 2010 at the University of Sussex, in the United Kingdom. He was awarded an International Fellowships scholarship from the Ford Foundation in 2001 and has also been funded by the Mexican

Council for Science and Technology. His research has been focused on Indigenous movements, intercultural dialogue, subaltern epistemologies, and Indigenous performing arts. He has conducted collaborative research with NGOs and Indigenous organizations in the Yucatán peninsula, Ecuador, Belize, and Guatemala. His work has explored forms of representing Indigenous knowledge in intercultural education projects in Latin America. He has also worked on aspects of performatic expression in the cultural and political mobilization in the Maya region. More recently, he is focusing on various Indigenous artistic forms (like performance art, cinema, and music) and their relation to antiracism and language revitalization.

He was part of the Indigeneity in the Contemporary World project in Royal Holloway University of London (2011–2013) and has worked at the Center for Research and Advanced Studies in Social Anthropology in Mexico City (2014–2015). He is currently assistant professor of heritage of Indigenous peoples in the Faculty of Archaeology at the University of Leiden in the Netherlands.

L. Jane McMillan, PhD, is the former Canada Research Chair for Indigenous Peoples and Sustainable Communities (2006–2016) and current chair and associate professor of the Department of Anthropology at St. Francis Xavier University, Antigonish, Nova Scotia. As a former eel fisher and one of the original defendants with Donald Marshall Jr. in the SCC Marshall decision (1999), she follows with special interest the significant changes that have occurred in Mi'kma'ki since the court case. Jane is a sociocultural and legal anthropologist who has conducted applied research with Mi'kmaq communities in Atlantic Canada for more than twenty-five years, including ethnographic research, policy analyses, and advocating for the holistic implementation of Mi'kmaw legal principles and Indigenous treaty rights in all sectors from justice to health, education, economic development, and resource governance. She is the author of the legal ethnography *Truth and Conviction: Donald Marshall Jr. and the Mi'kmaq Quest for Justice*.

Brian Noble is an associate professor in Dalhousie's Department of Sociology and Social Anthropology. A settler Canadian, he has collaborated extensively with Canadian First Nations peoples and activists on practices of decolonization in settler state / Indigenous peoples' relations for the last two decades, addressing matters ranging from Indigenous knowledges and intellectual and cultural property rights to relations with the Canadian state and international regimes of law, treaty, and Indigenous peoples' territorial authority. His current anthropological research addresses issues of our present ethnoecological moment, and the sociopolitical conditions allowing for redress of political relations between First Nations and Canada within that milieu, the rise of Indigenous law, and the processes both animating and empowering Indigenous land, resource, and knowledge rights in rapidly shifting state and global arenas in response to worldwide environmental crises. He has worked with Piikani Blackfoot, Secwepemc, Kwakwka'awakw, Mi'kmaq, and Cree communities. He also works in the anthropology of science and techniques.

Sherry M. Pictou is a Mi'kmaw woman from L'sitkuk (water cuts through high rocks) known as Bear River First Nation, Nova Scotia, and is an assistant professor in the Women's Studies Department at Mount Saint Vincent University, Halifax, Nova Scotia, with a focus on Indigenous feminism. She is also a former chief for her community and the former cochair of the World Forum of Fisher Peoples. Currently she is a research fellow for the Yellowhead Institute at Ryerson University, providing critical policy perspectives on Indigenous issues (www.yellowheadinstitute.org). Her research interests are in decolonizing treaty relations, social justice for Indigenous women, Indigenous women's role in food and lifeways, and Indigenous knowledge and food systems.

Colin Scott is an anthropologist at McGill University in Montreal. His research has focused on Indigenous ecological knowledge, land and sea tenure, conservation governance, and the political and legal processes of Indigenous rights among hunting and fishing peoples in subarctic Canada as well as in Torres Strait in northern Australia. He directs the Centre for Indigenous Conservation and Development Alternatives (www.cicada.world) and the Indigenous Stewardship of Environment and Alternative Development (www.instead.ca) research program. Both are transnational partnerships for knowledge coproduction involving universities, Indigenous peoples, and nongovernmental organizations to improve conditions for the ecological integrity of Indigenous territories, associated land- and sea-based livelihoods, and self-determined futures.

INDEX

Aboriginal and Torres Strait Islander Commission, 28n8, 198
Aboriginal Land Rights (NT) Act, 11, 20, 21, 26, 28n10, 220, 221, 223
academic capitalism, 157–58
acting-with, 247, 248, 252, 253–54, 258–59
action research, 27, 113, 135n2, 243, 244, 248
activism, 143, 146, 148, 151, 172, 178, 181–85; legal, 113, 134
activist networks, 25, 98, 148, 151, 166, 172, 184, 247
activist research, 7, 22, 24, 25, 249–58
allied anthropologies and projects, 47–50, 88, 94, 98, 246–49
allied research, 4, 94–95, 98, 105, 257
Altman, Jon, 220, 224
American Anthropological Association (AAA), 3, 27n1, 196. *See* Committee on World Anthropologies
anthropology, 19, 56, 93, 95–96; anthropological practices, 144; engaged anthropological research, 167; feminist anthropology, 114, 115, 120; legal anthropology, 114, 115; world anthropologies, 3, 6, 256

antidotes, 74, 82–88, 150, 193, 194, 209, 242–44
Asch, Michael, 11, 49, 52, 243, 248, 260n3. *See* treaty practices
Atlacholoaya, 122, 123, 125
autonomous regions, 14, 145, 148
Australian Capital Territory, 235n6

Bell, Dianne, 222, 232
below and to the left, 143, 150, 151, 157
Blaser, Mario, 94
Bringing Them Home Report, 216n6

capitalism, 38, 39, 40, 49, 248–49, 251; academic capitalism, 157–58; neoliberal colonial capitalism, 39, 40, 47–49, 55, 57
Captain Cook, 10
Caste War, 168
chan láak', 166, 173, 178, 179, 185
Chiapas, 14, 25, 143–46, 152, 153, 155, 156, 159
Chiapas Network. *See* RACCACH
civil rights, 224, 229
civil society, 145, 146, 151, 152
coexistence, 77, 246

collective knowledge, 25, 155
colonial discomfort, 247–50
colonial genealogies, 7, 8
colonialism, 38–43, 49, 56, 100, 243, 244, 248
coloniality, 7, 123, 136n8, 242–44; apparatus of, 248, 253; as double-bind, 52
colonization, 67, 70, 72–73, 75, 100. *See also* decolonization
Committee on World Anthropologies (CWA) of American Anthropological Association, 3, 6, 256
conservation, 93–96, 100–101, 103–4
consultation, 66, 83
Coulthard, Glen, 40, 75, 242–43
counterinsurgency, 143, 144, 147
CRAC. *See* Regional Coordination of Communal Authorities of Guerrero (CRAC)
Crees of Eeyou Istchee, 94–96, 100–106
criminalization, 65, 73, 83
customary tenure, 94–95

decolonial alliances, 3, 5, 8, 11, 13, 16, 27, 66, 242–44, 259; and Mexican legal anthropology, 115–20; with Mi'kmaw Nation, 47–51, 56–58
decolonial ethos, 23, 27, 159, 248–49
decolonial method, 4, 48, 147, 242, 247–59; and anthropological methodology, 93–94; and Maya people, 152–53, 173–74; and Mi'kmaw Nation, 69, 70
decolonization, 3, 4, 6, 13, 15, 23–25, 56, 251, 254, 256; of anthropologists, 143, 148, 157, 256; and Australian Aboriginal people, 193, 196, 215; and Cree Nation, 94, 100; of feminist anthropology, 115; and Mi'kmaw Nation, 45; regrounding, 256–59; of scholarship, 222, 223, 243; understanding decolonization, 37, 39, 41; and Zapatista movement, 143, 148, 156, 157, 159. *See also* allied research
Deloria, Vine, 56, 202, 204, 246
dialogical engagement, 172, 254
double reconciliation, 259

e'esaj, 177–78, 184
elided spaces, 254–55
emancipatory human rights, 231, 248, 254
embodied and incardinated theory, 144, 157
engaged anthropological research, 167
epistemic dialogues, 15, 16, 98, 100–101
epistemologies, 144, 157, 159, 171, 265
Escobar, Arturo, 102
ethical-political commitment, 95, 99, 101
ethics, 95, 99, 101
expert witnesses, 19, 21, 23, 25, 253; reports from, 114, 117, 126
EZLN. *See* Zapatista movement

Feit, Harvey, 94
feminism, 144, 146, 159; feminist anthropology, 114, 115, 120; Indigenous, 222, 223
fishing. *See* hunting and fishing
Fourth World, 243, 246, 247

gender justice, 118, 134
gender violence, 124, 125, 223, 231, 255
Goodale, Mark, 227
Gove land rights case, 10, 11, 198
governance, 73, 74, 96, 102, 104
Gurindji, 10

heteropatriarchal neoliberalism, 144
Hindmarsh Island Bridge Royal Commission, 200, 203, 216n8
Hinkson, Melinda, 224, 225, 227
Howard, John, 28n8, 198, 216n6
human rights, 220, 221, 225, 227, 228
hunting and fishing, 42, 54, 93–95, 97, 102–3; food fishery, 54, 56; moose hunting, 47, 54, 56

Idle No More, 46, 247
Indian Residential Schools, 8, 12
Indigeneity, 179, 184, 193, 204, 212–13, 215
Indigenismo, 169, 170, 172
Indigenous feminism, 222, 223
Indigenous identity, 170, 173, 180, 184

Indigenous knowledges, 4, 98, 100, 160, 166, 195, 200, 265
Indigenous law, 118, 119, 129, 130
Indigenous methodologies, 69–70, 93
Indigenous rights, 93, 96, 101, 103, 105, 114, 121, 127, 166, 245, 254–56
Indigenous sovereignty, 66, 79, 83
Indigenous women, 41, 42, 115, 118, 120, 121, 145, 150, 152, 203, 222–23, 243
Indigenous worldviews, 47, 48, 49, 52, 55. *See* Ways of Being
insurrection of subjugated knowledges, 160, 251
intercultural dialogues, 25, 125, 134, 166, 172, 173, 174, 175, 185, 254, 265
interculturality, 166, 173, 174, 177, 185, 254
intersectional perspective, 120

justice; gender, 118, 134; state, 121, 123, 124

knowledge, 249–58; co-generation, 258; co-production, 93–95, 97–98, 105, 258; collective, 25, 155; Indigenous, 4, 98, 100, 160, 166, 195, 200, 265; production, 97; situated, 143; subjugated, 160, 251
Keating, Paul, 206

L'sɨtkuk, 37; Bear River First Nation, 43
Lacandon Forest, 144, 145, 149, 150
land claims, 44–46, 49
land relations, 40, 42, 245, 256, 259; among Australian Aboriginal people, 194, 209; among Cree people, 96, 101, 103; among Mi'kmaw people, 48–53
land rights, 6, 8–15, 245; and anthropologists, 93, 96; and Australian Aboriginal people, 26, 28n10, 193, 198, 212, 220–21, 223–25, 229–30; and Cree people, 101, 103; and legal activism, 19, 20–21
land-based practice, 258
Langton, Marcia, 21, 202, 203, 221, 223, 235n4
language revitalization, 166

Latour, Bruno, 98
legal activism, 19, 22–25, 113, 134
legal anthropology, 66, 69, 71–73, 114, 115
legal consciousness, 68, 72, 79
life histories, 122, 124, 133
life projects, 94, 97–98
livelihoods, 68, 74, 76, 85, 94–95, 101, 103
low-intensity warfare, 147, 150
Lucas, Rod, 200

máasewáal, 168–70
Mabo, 10, 20, 26, 198, 206, 213, 250
Makarrata, 197, 215–16n5
Manuel, George, 246–47, 256
Marcos, Subcomandante, 146, 148
Martin, David, 204, 208, 210
Marshall decision, 37–38, 41, 42–43, 47, 53, 55, 88n2; Donald Marshall Jr., 37, 67–68, 94
Maya, 15, 16, 18, 25, 143, 151–55, 252–58; Yucatec, 166, 167, 175
Maya knowledges, 166, 176, 177, 180, 185
Merry, Sally, 230, 231
Mestizos/Mestizaje, 167–68, 170–71, 184
methodologies, Indigenous, 69–70, 93
Mi'kmaw/Mi'kmaq, 37–38, 42, 44–51, 53, 57n1, 67, 72, 75
middle position, 3, 21, 24, 244, 248, 253
modes of disruption, 251
moose. *See* hunting and fishing
Moreton-Robinson, Eileen, 4, 5, 13, 203, 213, 222, 223
multiculturalism, 121, 126, 174; and human rights, 227–28, 234

National Native Title Tribunal (NNTT), 205, 217n14
native title, 15, 16; and anthropology, 193–96; in Australia, 9–11, 18, 20–21, 26, 199–201, 204–15; and decolonial possibility, 245, 255; rights to, 220, 221, 223, 234–35n1
Native Title Act, 10, 20, 21, 199, 206–9, 221, 234–35n1

Native Title Amendment Act, 206
New South Wales, 28n10,
neoliberalism, 19, 38–40, 227; heteropatriarchal, 144
Northern Territory, 9, 10, 11, 20, 21, 21, 216n12, 220, 221, 224, 225, 228, 231, 232, 233, 234–35n1, 235n2, 255, 264
netukulimk, 51, 55, 56, 77–78
Ngarrindjeri, 203, 216n8
normative limitations, 212, 222, 230, 248, 250

obligation, 49–57, 65, 83, 88, 257–58
Olinalá, 128, 129, 130, 132
ontology, ontologies, 17, 24, 81, 93, 98, 94–101, 105, 144; legal ontologies, 70; ontological responsibilities, 24, 66; ontological diversity, 99; ontological matrices, 160; ontological struggle, 251–52; ontic politics, 248. *See also* relational ontologies. *See also* ways of being
other possible worlds, 161

Pan-Yucatec Maya networks, 166–67, 170–72, 178–79, 181, 183–84
paramilitary groups, 145–48
Pearson, Noel, 197
Pintupi-Luritja, 228, 229, 231
Pitjantjatjara, 28n10,
plural universalism, 174
political ecology, 105
politics, 95, 97–99, 101–4; of recognition. *See* recognition politics
Povinelli, Elizabeth, 199, 200, 201, 211, 221
power differences, 244, 248–50
prison workshops, 123, 124, 125
property rights, 229, 230, 236n12
protected areas, 94, 96, 101–4

Queensland, 194, 198, 206, 208–10, 213, 215n1
Quijano, Anibal, 136n8, 259n1

RACCACH, 152–56, 161n2, 162n13
racism, 67, 73
reciprocity; among peoples and the natural world, 42, 48–49; obligation to, 51–52, 257–58; and political ecology, 103–6; and relationality, 97–98, 101; and research partnerships, 93–95
recognition politics, 7–10, 14–16, 245, 249, 257–60; and Australian Aboriginal people, 193, 194, 196–99, 201, 209, 212–15, 220–21; and legal activism, 19–21; and Mexican legal anthropology, 114, 116, 118, 119, 127, 129; and Mi'kmaw Nation, 82–83, 87, 89
recognition space, 249, 255
reconciliation, 65, 85, 87; double, 259
regenerating, 256–57
Regional Coordination of Communal Authorities of Guerrero (CRAC), 113, 120, 130, 131
regrounding, 256–59
relational ontologies, 94–95
relationality, 49, 52, 93–94, 97–99, 101, 242, 256; relational understandings, 54, 55–56; and research partnerships, 253–54
reoccupation, 254–55
research partnerships, 93–94, 98, 253–54
resistance, 68, 70
respect, 4, 248, 251, 253, 257, 261; and collectivity, 146, 155; and research partnerships, 93, 95, 97–98, 101, 103, 105–6; and treaty negotiations, 51, 52, 82, 83, 85, 87
resurgence, 7, 20, 47–49, 69, 81, 248–49
Rigney, Lester-Irabinna, 4
Royal Commission on Aboriginal Peoples (RCAP), 72

Salgado, Nestora, 113, 128, 130
self-determination, 224–27, 234, 258; elided spaces, 254–55; and land, 242–43
Simpson, Audra, 217n16, 251
Simpson, Leanne Betasamosake, 242–43

Sisters of the Shadow Publishing Collective, 120, 123–24, 126
situated knowledge, 143
Sjalel kibeltik, 153–54, 156–58, 162n13
Sorry Day, 198, 216n6
sovereignty; of Australian Aboriginal people, 193, 196–200, 203, 208, 213–15, 217n16, 245, 251; of Cree Nation, 96
South Australia, 10, 21, 28n10, 194, 201, 203, 215n3, 216n7, 217n8, 216–17n13, 221
state justice, 121, 123, 124
stewardship, 93, 101, 103–4
Stolen Generation, 11, 21, 198, 216n6
Subcomandante Marcos, 146, 148
Supreme Court of Canada, 65, 74, 76, 92
Sutton, Peter, 225, 227
systemic and civilizational crisis, 159
systemic discrimination, 66, 67, 70, 73

Taussig, Michael, 214–15
Tax, Sol, 248
Ten Point Plan, 206
termination, 41, 245
terra nullius, 8, 9, 10, 20, 245
terrains of action, 168, 242
topos, 168, 242
traditions and customs, 119, 120
translation, 84, 100, 228, 229, 231, 254
treaty practices, 40–42, 49–57, 258, 259; Michal Asch, and treaties, 51, 52; James Tully, and small 't' treaty, 53; treaty turn, 53
treaty rights, 9, 12–13, 19, 254, 258; and Cree Nation, 96, 102–3; and Mi'kmaw Nation, 38–42, 44–45, 49, 50, 65–66, 68–69, 83–88; negotiation of, 53; privatization of, 40, 44; and world anthropologies, 3, 6, 256

Truth and Reconciliation Commission (TRC), 41, 55, 57n2
Tully, James, 53, 259. *See* treaty practices

UCI-Red, 175–77
Uluru Statement from the Heart, 197–98, 200, 215
United Nations Declaration on the Rights of Indigenous Peoples (UNDRIP), 41, 258
universalism, plural, 174
usos y costumbres, 119, 120

Victorian state government, 199
Victoria (Australia), 199, 200, 207, 216n7, 235n6

Wacquant, Loic, 232
Watson, Irene, 4, 13, 15, 195, 196, 203, 204–5, 208, 214, 216n11, 216–17n13
warfare, low-intensity, 147, 150
Wave Hill,
ways of being, Indigenous, 215, 251; Maya, 180; relational, 17, 49, 53–54. See also *chan láak'*
Western Australia, 10, 21, 194, 208, 215n1, 221
Wilson, Shawn, 48, 93
Wolfe, Patrick, 206, 213, 214
world anthropologies, 3, 6, 256

Yorta Yorta, 192, 199, 207
Yucatec Maya, 166, 167, 175
Yucatecan regional identity, 168–69

Zapatista autonomous territory, 120, 148, 149
Zapatista movement, 14, 18, 25, 118–20, 143–51, 146, 156, 166, 172, 182, 252; pro-Zapatista activism, 143